The Popes at Avignon
1305–1378

The Popes at Avignon

1305–1378

G. MOLLAT

*Honorary Professor at the University
of Strasbourg
Membre de l'Institut*

TRANSLATED FROM
THE NINTH FRENCH EDITION
1949

Thomas Nelson and Sons Ltd

London Edinburgh Paris Melbourne Johannesburg
Toronto and New York

THOMAS NELSON AND SONS LTD
Parkside Works Edinburgh 9
36 Park Street London W1
117 Latrobe Street Melbourne C1

THOMAS NELSON AND SONS (AFRICA) (Pty) Ltd
P.O. Box 9881 Johannesburg

THOMAS NELSON AND SONS (CANADA) LTD
91–93 Wellington Street West Toronto 1

THOMAS NELSON AND SONS
81 East 41st Street New York 17

SOCIÉTÉ FRANÇAISE D'ÉDITIONS NELSON
97 rue Monge Paris 5

© Thomas Nelson & Sons 1963

Translated by Janet Love

Printed in Great Britain by
Thomas Nelson and Sons Ltd, Edinburgh

Contents

CONTENTS

Note to the Ninth French Edition

THE ninth edition of *The Popes at Avignon* differs considerably from earlier editions and is almost a new book. The preface and several passages of the original text have been rewritten, revised or expanded. Chapter I of Book Two has been almost entirely recast and much expanded. Greater light is thus thrown on the Holy See's policy in Italy. Chapters II and IV in the same Book, dealing respectively with the Church's relations with the Empire and with England, have undergone considerable change and development.

G. M.

PARIS, 19 *March* 1949

Select Bibliography

THE period of the Avignon papacy has been the subject of a large number of important studies of varying scope and size and also of many articles and reviews. A complete bibliography will be found in the French edition, *Les Papes d'Avignon*, Paris 1949. The following are among the more important of those of a relatively early date.

E. Déprez, *Les préliminaires de la guerre de Cent Ans. La papauté, la France et l'Angleterre*, Paris 1902

N. Valois, 'Jacques Duèse, pape sous le nom de Jean XXII,' in *Histoire littéraire de la France*, VOL. XXXIV, 1915, pp. 391–630

G. Lizerand, *Clément V et Philippe IV le Bel*, Paris 1910

R. Caggese, *Roberto d'Angiò e i suoi tempi*, Florence 1922

E. B. Graves, 'The Legal Significance of the Statutes of Praemunire of 1353,' in *Hastings Anniversary Essays*, Cambridge, Mass., 1929

E. Léonard, *Histoire de Jeanne Iʳᵉ, reine de Naples, comtesse de Provence (1343–1382)*, Paris 1932–7, 3 vols.

F. Filippini, *Il cardinale Egidio Albornoz*, Bologna 1933

E. Perroy, *L'Angleterre et le Grand Schisme d'Occident*, Paris 1933 (the first chapter deals with Gregory XI)

List of Abbreviations

Annuaire-Bulletin	*Annuaire-Bulletin de la Société de l'histoire de France*
Archiv	*Archiv für Literatur und Kirchengeschichte*
A.S.P.N.	*Archivio storico per le provincie napoletane*
A.S.R.S.P.	*Archivio della Società Romana di storia patria*
B.E.C.	*Bibliothèque de l'École des Chartes*
Bulletin historique	*Bulletin historique et philologique du comité des travaux historiques et scientifiques*
Coulon	*Lettres secrètes et curiales du pape Jean XXII relatives à la France*
Daumet	*Benoît XII. Lettres closes, patentes et curiales se rapportant à la France*
Déprez, *Clément VI*	*Clément VI. Lettres closes, patentes et curiales se rapportant à la France*
Déprez, *Innocent VI*	*Innocent VI. Lettres closes, patentes et curiales se rapportant à la France*
Lecacheux	*Urbain V. Lettres secrètes et curiales se rapportant à la France*
Mélanges	*Mélanges d'archéologie et d'histoire de l'École française de Rome*
Mittheilungen	*Mittheilungen des Instituts für österreichische Geschichtsforschung*
Mollat	*Jean XXII. Lettres communes*
Muratori	*Rerum Italicarum scriptores*
Not. et extr. des mss.	*Notices et extraits des manuscrits*
Pastor	*Geschichte der Päpste*
Quellen	*Quellen und Forschungen aus italienischen Archiven und Bibliotheken*
R.H.E.	*Revue d'histoire ecclésiastique*
Rinaldi	*Annales ecclesiastici*
Römische Quartalschrift	*Römische Quartalschrift für christliche Altertumskunde und Kirchengeschichte*
R.Q.H.	*Revue des questions historiques*
Soc. hist. Fr.	Société de l'histoire de France
Vidal	*Benoît XII. Lettres communes*
V.S.W.G.	*Vierteljahrschrift für Social- und Wirtschaftsgeschichte*
Z.S.S.R.G.Kan.	*Zeitschrift der Savigny-Stiftung für Rechtsgeschichte. Kanonistische Abteilung*

Preface

BETWEEN 1305 and 1378 seven popes succeeded one another on the throne of St Peter and lived, more or less continuously, in Avignon, on the banks of the Rhône.

Was it an unheard-of occurrence and in fact a 'scandal' in the annals of the Church for them to reside outside Rome? The majority of non-French writers, from Platina onwards, seem to suggest it. Yet, for all they were bishops of Rome, a large number of the popes were elected and crowned elsewhere than at Rome and governed the world from some place other than Rome. During the latter half of the thirteenth century their subjects' unrest made it impossible for the popes to reside in the Eternal City and they were obliged to emigrate, to such an extent that it became exceptional for them to live in Rome.

Nothing is more enlightening in this respect than the itinerary followed by the popes throughout the half-century preceding their installation at Avignon. After a stay of five months and a few days in Rome, where he suffered the greatest restriction of his liberty and had his authority impeded by the noble families, Benedict XI (1303–04) left for Perugia where he died. According to Ferreto Ferreti of Vicenza, he was thinking of making an indefinite stay in Lombardy.[1] His predecessor, Boniface VIII (1294–1303), was much less frequently to be found at the Lateran palace than at Anagni, Orvieto or Velletri. Celestine V (1294), the holy hermit, never saw Rome; elected at Perugia and crowned at Aquila, he proceeded to Sulmona, Capua and Naples, where he renounced his title. Nicholas IV (1288–92) was elected at Rome and sometimes resided at Santa Maria Maggiore; but he lived as a rule at Rieti and Orvieto. Honorius IV (1285–7), after his election at Perugia, liked to live at Santa Sabina; only in the extreme heat of summer did he retreat to Tivoli or Palombara. Martin IV (1281–5), a Frenchman, elected at Viterbo, *ubi tunc residebat Romana Curia*, never went outside Tuscany and Umbria. Also elected at Viterbo, Nicholas III (1277–80) was unusual in being crowned at Rome; he divided his time between that city, Sutri, Vetralla and Viterbo. John XXI (1276–7) never left Viterbo, where he had been elected and where he died and was buried beneath the walls of his own palace. Innocent V and Adrian V occupied the pontifical throne

---

[1] Muratori, VOL. IX, col. 1012.

for brief periods only, during the first six months of the year 1276. After two months' stay in Rome, Gregory X (1271–6) went to Orvieto and then to France, where he summoned the fourteenth œcumenical council at Lyons. His return journey to Italy was made in short stages, with many halts in 'the sweet land of Provence.' He went to Orange, Beaucaire and Valence and back to Vienne, in order to return to Italy by way of Switzerland and he died at Arezzo. The French Pope Clement IV (1265–8) did not issue a single document from Rome. He went to Perugia, Assisi, Orvieto, Montefiascone and Viterbo. Urban IV (1261–4), another Frenchman, had only three residences, Viterbo, Montefiascone and Orvieto; he died in his litter on the way from Orvieto to Perugia. Alexander IV (1254–61) was elected and crowned at Naples, and had a liking for Anagni and Viterbo; at the beginning and end of his pontificate, he spent a few months at the Lateran Palace, and died at Viterbo. Innocent IV (1243–54), who was elected and consecrated at Anagni, spent only a very short time at Rome; he was obliged to flee from Frederick II and to take refuge at Lyons from 1244 until 1251. When he returned to Italy, he settled in the peaceful country of Umbria and then went to Naples, where he died.[1]

To go still further back in history would be just as easy. Gregory IX (1227–41), who reigned for about fourteen years, spent more than eight of them away from Rome. It was in all probability the fickleness of the Romans that led Innocent III in 1209 to lay the foundations of an ecclesiastical state beyond the Alps. By virtue of a convention drawn up with Count Raymond VI of Toulouse, the Holy See received, as a pledge of his conversion, seven castles in Provence which were later handed over to Raymond VII in exchange for the Comtat-Venaissin. Between August 1099 and January 1198, the Roman pontiffs spent fifty-five years and a few months away from Rome and of these eight and a half years were spent in France. In short, it has been calculated that 'In the two hundred and four years from 1100 until 1304, the popes spent one hundred and twenty-two away from Rome and eighty-two in Rome: that is, forty years more away from Rome than in it.'[2]

The establishment of the papacy outside Rome in the fourteenth century, then, does not constitute an unheard-of revolution in history; it was brought about and prepared by a long series of circumstances and events. The really extraordinary and unprecedented

---

[1] Potthast, *Regesta pontificum Romanorum*, Berlin 1874–5, passim. See also registers of the popes of the thirteenth century published by the French School at Rome.
[2] L. Gayet, *Le Grand Schisme d'Occident*, Florence 1889, p. 3.

circumstance is the prolonged residence of the popes outside Italy. Moreover the Italians, once they were deprived of the considerable advantages provided by the presence of the papacy, did not fail to follow Petrarch [1] and St Catherine of Siena [2] in copious expressions of blame and complaint. Ughelli—to quote only one of the best known —goes so far as to assert that the transference of the Holy See to Avignon was a greater disaster for his country than the barbarian invasions.[3] German scholarship has echoed these sentiments. Gregorovius declares that the Avignon popes were the 'slaves' of the kings of France;[4] Hase refers to them as 'bishops of the French court';[5] Martens maintains that they would not have dared to exercise any sovereign authority without the approval of the French kings.[6] Pastor yields to the general opinion: he reproaches the papacy with having caused the Church to lose its universality by becoming French and thus arousing popular suspicion and feelings of hostility; he alleges that this move precipitated the decline of religious feeling.[7] Other writers, both in France and elsewhere, have bitterly denounced the excessive concern of the court at Avignon with finance, the looseness of its morals, its extravagant tastes, its nepotism and absolutism.[8] In a word, according to the majority of historians, the Avignon papacy was the source of the greatest evils for the Church and, in the last analysis, the chief cause of the great schism of the West. Whatever may have been claimed in its defence,[9] the judgment of history remains unfavourable towards it. Is this judgment confirmed or

[1] See especially *Epistolae sine titulo*, V, VIII, X, XII–XV, XVII–XIX; Books VII and IX of *Rerum senilium*; the Sonnets *La falsa Babilonia* and *Fontana di dolor*'; and the attacks on Avignon in his works, Basle edition, pp. 852, 1081. See also P. Piur, *Petrarcas Buch ohne Namen und die päpstliche Kurie*, Halle 1925. (Critical edition of *Epistolae sine titulo* preceded by a long introduction in which the author adopts Petrarch's pessimistic view of the court at Avignon.)

[2] *Lettere ridotte a migliore lezione e in ordine nuovo disposte*, ed. Tommaseo, Florence 1860.

[3] *Italia sacra*, VOL. I, Venice 1717, p. 71.

[4] *Storia della Città di Roma*, VOL. III, Rome 1901, pp. 203–04.

[5] *Kirchengeschichte*, 10th edn. 1877, p. 293.

[6] *Die Beziehungen der Überordnung, Nebenordnung und Unterordnung zwischen Kirche und Staat*, Stuttgart 1877, p. 130.

[7] Pastor, VOL. I, pp. 74 f.

[8] Fr. Tridichum, *Papsttum und Reformation im Mittelalter (1143–1517)*, Leipzig 1903; F. Rocquain, *La Cour de Rome et l'esprit de réforme avant Luther*, VOL. II, Paris 1895; J. Michelet, *Histoire de France*, VOL. VII, Paris 1876, pp. 349–50; J. Haller, *Papsttum und Kirchenreform. Vier Kapitel zur Geschichte des ausgehenden Mittelalters*, Berlin 1903; J.-F. André, *Histoire de la papauté d'Avignon*, Paris 1887.

[9] C. Hœfler, 'Die avignonesischen Päpste, ihre Machtfülle und ihr Untergang,' *Almanach der Kaiserlichen Akademie der Wissenschaften*, 21st year, Vienna 1871, pp. 231–85; Baluze, in the Preface of his *Vitae*; G.-Fr. Berthier, *Histoire de l'Église gallicane*, VOLS. XII–XIV, Paris 1745; *Discours sur le pontificat de Clément V*, VOL. XIII, pp. i–xxiv; J.-B. Christophe, *Histoire de la papauté pendant le XIVe siècle*, Paris 1853, especially the preface to VOL. III; P. Fournier, *Bulletin Critique*, 2nd Series, VOL. VII, 1901, pp. 162–7; VOL. VIII, 1902, pp. 84–9; P. Richard, 'La Captivité de Babylone à Avignon (1316–78),' *L'Université catholique*, VOL. LXVI, 1911, pp. 81–101.

invalidated by the publication of the Papal Registers and the studies that have appeared since the opening of the Vatican Archives? A statement of the facts will make a reply possible.

We shall endeavour, in the following pages, to study in detail and with reference to the texts of the Archives, the pontificates of Clement V, John XXII, Benedict XII, Clement VI, Innocent VI, Urban V and Gregory XI. These have usually been the victims of prejudice caused by a chauvinism which is not, on this occasion, French. We are not writing a defence, but an historical account, sketching biographies, clarifying policy and describing institutions without any preconceived notion save that of stating what the texts imply.

Introduction

The Establishment of the Holy See
at Avignon

THE chronicler Ptolemy of Lucca reports that as soon as Bertrand de Got was elected pope, 'he determined to fix his residence in the Comtat-Venaissin and never to cross the Alps.'[1] This is a misstatement. It is true that the cardinals' letters, giving notice of the election, were expressed in such a way as to deter Clement V from going to Italy. They depicted that country as given over to anarchy and the Papal States as devastated by war.[2] Nevertheless, the pope announced his intention of going to Italy as soon as peace was made between the kings of England and France, and the crusade organised. He chose the place for his coronation on imperial soil, at Vienne in Dauphiné, a town on the main road to Italy.[3] He invited only a limited number of cardinals to his coronation: two bishops, two priests and two deacons.[4]

Although Clement V subsequently changed his plans, he still had every intention of leaving France, where circumstances had detained him. In 1306 the ambassador of Aragon wrote to James II: 'The pope signified [to the cardinals] that it was his intention to stay here until the coming month of March. For then he will give leave to the court to cross the Alps and will meet with the king of France at Poitiers, that he may persuade him to receive the cross and ratify the peace between himself and the king of England. And from that time forward, without tarrying in any other place, my said lord the pope will go to Italy.'[5] According to the same ambassador, during the meeting at Poitiers in 1308, the supreme pontiff expressed his joy at encountering Philip the Fair, for it was his intention to go to Rome but to entertain the king before his departure.[6] On 11 April 1308, Clement was considering the restoration of the ciborium to the high altar of St John Lateran and said: 'By the grace of God we propose

---

[1] Baluze-Mollat, *Vitae paparum Avenionensium*, VOL. I, Paris 1916, p. 24.
[2] Mansi, *Conciliorum nova et amplissima collectio*, VOL. XXV, col. 127.
[3] C. Wenck, *Clemens V und Heinrich VII*, Halle 1882, p. 169.
[4] H. Finke, *Acta Aragonensia*, Münster 1908, pp. 199, 403.
[5] H. Finke, *Papsttum und Untergang des Templerordens*, VOL. II, Münster 1907, pp. 21–2.   [6] *Ibid.* p. 34.

to put back with our own hands the most famous wooden altar in the place where it formerly was.'[1] Moreover, in the next year he was promising that within the space of two years he would himself crown the Emperor Henry VII at Rome.[2] Why did Clement V not carry out these intentions that he had so often expressed?

The pope's object in choosing to hold his coronation at Vienne and not on Italian soil was to attract the kings of France and England to the ceremony and to take advantage of their presence to work for the conclusion of a lasting peace between them. In this he was carrying out a cherished plan of the late Boniface VIII, who had dreamt of going to France to settle the Anglo-French differences.[3] Like his predecessor, Clement V considered that the crusade would be impossible without the effective co-operation of France and England. Such co-operation could not properly be sought until the day when the two countries had signed the peace. Clement V worked untiringly to reconcile them. He arranged the marriage of Isabella of France with the future Edward II. Despite his efforts, final reconciliation was not achieved until 1312.[4]

On 28 November 1306, however, Clement V declared that peace negotiations, which by that date were well advanced, could have been completed by the intervention of nuncios alone.[5] But other causes hindered his departure for Rome. Chief among these was the pressure exercised by the French court. As early as July and August 1305, French ambassadors sought Clement V and reminded him that the action brought against the deceased Boniface VIII was not yet finished. The pope, anxious to avoid a renewal of this action, made a concession that was to have considerable consequences: he decreed that his coronation should now take place not at Vienne but at Lyons. On 14 November 1305 this ceremony was performed in that city in the presence of Philip the Fair. It was followed by very important negotiations. The king of France was insistent that the trial of Boniface VIII should be renewed. It was agreed that this should be discussed at a future meeting; with the result that Clement V was obliged to put off until a more favourable time his departure for Italy.

The pope made his way from Lyons to Mâcon and Cluny and then reached Languedoc by way of Nevers, Bourges, Limoges and Périgueux. An illness which almost proved fatal helped to keep him for nearly a year in the Bordeaux area (May 1306–March 1307) and

---

[1] *Regestum Clementis papae V*, no. 3592. [2] *Ibid.* no. 4302.
[3] C. Wenck, *op. cit.* p. 41.
[4] G. Lizerand, *Clément V et Philippe IV le Bel*, Paris 1910, pp. 61–4, 69.
[5] C. Wenck, *op. cit.* p. 43.

prevented the proposed meeting with Philip the Fair from taking place at Michaelmas 1306. After a partial recovery, Clement V once more set out on his journeyings and reached Poitiers in April 1307. Here he could come to no understanding with the king of France, who refused to agree to all the proposed compromises to end the law-suit against Boniface VIII, which was still hanging fire. They parted without coming to any decision. On 13 October 1307 a sensational event took place: the mass arrest of the Templars. A further inter-view with Philip the Fair became necessary. This, too, took place at Poitiers (May–July 1308). The king's demands on this occasion were such that Clement V resolved not to proceed with his enterprise. He could not contemplate going to Rome. It would have been madness to leave Philip the Fair master of the situation on the eve of the opening of the Council of Vienne, where decisions would be taken gravely affecting the interests of the Church, and where in particular the scandalous trial of the Templars would be debated. In complete agreement with the cardinals, Clement V decided to transfer the court to Avignon (August 1308).[1]

This city possessed valuable assets. Rapid and frequent com-munication with Italy was ensured by both land and water routes. It was near France but not dependent upon her. There was nothing to fear from the suzerains of Avignon, the Angevin princes of Naples; their energies were largely absorbed in defending the integrity of their kingdom of the Two Sicilies against the encroachments of the ambitious house of Aragon, and in the promotion of Guelph interests in the rest of the peninsula; moreover, were they not vassals of the Church? Lastly, the city of Avignon formed an enclave in the Comtat-Venaissin, a possession of the Holy See. No town could provide the papacy with a more peaceful refuge and more powerful guarantees of independence and security.

Once he had taken this decision, Clement V made his way by short stages across the south of France. In March 1309 he entered Avignon and so inaugurated the papacy's long exile which was to last for more than seventy years and which, through ill-justified comparison with the sojourn of the Chosen People in a strange land, has come to be known as 'the Babylonian captivity.'

The pope's establishment at Avignon still remained provisional in character. Clement V lived unpretentiously in the convent of the Dominicans.[2] He caused only the registers of letters of his two

[1] H. Finke, *Papsttum und Untergang des Templerordens*, VOL. II, p. 156.
[2] M. Faucon, 'Les Arts à la cour d'Avignon sous Clément V et Jean XXII,' *Mélanges*, VOL. II, 1882, p. 39.

predecessors to be brought from Italy, and left the greater part of the pontifical treasure at the church of St Francis of Assisi.[1] He stayed for only a very short time in Avignon itself, preferring the towns and castles of the Comtat-Venaissin.

The lawsuit brought against Boniface VIII caused the supreme pontiff the gravest anxiety between 1309 and 1311. Clement V was skilful enough to succeed in delaying the proceedings as much as possible and ultimately in silencing the worst accusers of the dead pope. As for the trial of the Templars, this was settled at the Council of Vienne (16 October 1311–6 May 1312). At the very moment when Clement might have gone to Italy, his health, never very robust, took a turn for the worse. According to the chronicler Ptolemy of Lucca, who had his information from the lips of the pope's confessor, it declined rapidly after the promulgation, at the Council of Vienne, of the Constitution *Exivi de Paradiso*.[2] The pope, feeling that his end was near, dictated his will on 9 June 1312.[3] His sickness grew worse in the course of the years 1313 and 1314 and finally overcame him on 20 April 1314.

Even if Clement V had enjoyed better health, he could not have crossed the Alps in 1312 or 1313. Henry VII's entry into Italy had set the whole country in revolt. From 7 May 1312, Rome served only as a battlefield where Guelphs and Ghibellines attacked each other brutally. Henry VII lost no time in treating the papacy as an enemy and in defying the threat of excommunication against anyone attacking the king of Naples. In such circumstances who can blame Clement V for staying in the Comtat-Venaissin? Where else could he have found so safe a refuge?

Under the successors of Clement V, Rome and Italy, despite their peoples' protestations and repeated appeals, remained inhospitable to the papacy. 'Ah! Italy, abode of sorrow,' wrote Dante, 'vessel without a helmsman amidst a dreadful storm, no longer art thou mistress of thy peoples, but a place of prostitution. Now, those who live in thy dominions wage implacable war amongst themselves; those protected by the same wall and the same ramparts rend each other. Search, unhappy country, around thy shores and see if in thy bosom a single one of thy provinces enjoys peace.' Italy was indeed incessantly laid waste by war in the reign of John XXII. In 1332 the

[1] *Regestum Clementis papae V*, Introduction, p. xxxi. F. Ehrle, *Historia bibliothecae pontificum Romanorum*, Rome 1890, pp. 11–12; 'Nachträge zur Geschichte der drei ältesten päpstlichen Biblioteken,' *Kirchengeschichtliche Festgaben Anton de Waal*, Freiburg-im-Breisgau 1913, pp. 337–69.
[2] Baluze-Mollat, *op. cit.* VOL. I, pp. 52–3.
[3] F. Ehrle, 'Der Nachlass Clemens V,' etc. *Archiv*, VOL. V, 1889, p. 26.

pope contemplated crossing the Alps, after Bertrand du Poujet's victories over the Ghibellines. He conceived the plan of pacifying Lombardy and Tuscany, and then proceeding to Rome. Bologna, which had yielded to the Church, was provisionally chosen as a place of residence. Preparations for the pope's reception were made: a citadel was built at the Galliera gate; an order even reached Rome itself for the pontifical dwellings to be restored and the gardens cultivated afresh.[1] The rebellion of Bologna and the completion of arrangements for the crusade put a speedy end to the pope's plans.[2] In 1333 the king of France was appointed captain-general of the Christian army. That year and the next negotiations were more active than ever between the courts of Paris and Avignon. The departure of the Holy See for Italy would have displeased Philip VI —who had been much angered by the intentions of John XXII— and would have hindered the preparations for the expedition which seemed definitely arranged; undoubtedly it would have gravely compromised the ultimate success of the crusade.[3]

At the beginning of his pontificate, Benedict XII listened to the grievances of the ambassadors sent him by the Romans. In a Consistory held in July 1335, he decided, with the unanimous consent of his cardinals, that the court would leave Avignon about the first of the following October and transfer provisionally to Bologna.[4] The cardinals changed their minds in a second Consistory. They considered it best to postpone the departure for Italy, for, in addition to the many difficulties of the journey itself, they thought that a move on the part of the Holy See would interfere with the plans for the crusade and the settling of urgent business.[5] Moreover, an investigation made on the spot gave ample evidence that sedition at Bologna was still causing too much unrest to justify the transfer of the Holy See within its walls.[6] The cardinals' foresight was justified. Bologna speedily revolted once more against the Church; elsewhere, in Romagna and in the Marches, the nobles were planning to become independent; while at Rome revolution reigned from 1347 until 1354.

Under Clement VI war became inevitable. It was to devastate Italy until the day when the fierce sword of Albornoz conquered the

[1] L. Ciaccio, *Il cardinale legato Bertrando del Poggetto*, Bologna 1906, pp. 144–52.
[2] *Not. et extr. des mss.*, VOL. XXXV, pt. 2, pp. 417–19; *Regesta Vaticana*, VOL. CXVI, f. 217ʳ, col. 1096–8; VOL. CXVII, f. 108ʳ, col. 534.
[3] N. Valois, 'Jacques Duèse, pape sous le nom de Jean XXII,' *Histoire littéraire de la France*, VOL. XXXIV, 1915, pp. 485–7, 498–511.
[4] J. M. Vidal, *Lettres closes et patentes de Benoît XII*, VOL. I, Paris 1919, no. 476.
[5] Daumet, nos. 112, 139, 141.
[6] A. Theiner, *Codex diplomaticus dominii temporalis Sanctae Sedis*, VOL. I, Rome 1861, doc. DCCLXVII and DCCLXIX.

various tyrants, great and small, who were disturbing the peace. Urban V thought this a favourable moment to re-establish the papacy in Rome. As is well known, the hostility of his own subjects forced him to return to Avignon.[1] The pope's fears were not illusory. Under Gregory XI the Roman factions were once more aroused. They plotted to massacre the foreigners who made up the papal court and the non-Italian cardinals, so as to compel the pope to settle forever in the Eternal City.[2] What is worse, a Roman cardinal, in order to seize the triple crown for himself,[3] is alleged to have had the dire thought of making an attempt on the life of Gregory XI. According to other contemporaries, if Gregory XI had left Italy again, as he had shown that he intended to do, the Romans would have created an antipope in opposition to him.[4] In any event, the precautions taken by the supreme pontiff on 19 March 1378 show clearly how much he feared serious trouble after his death.[5]

To sum up, the fact that for many years the popes did not live in Italy is explained by that country's persistent hostility. The popes of the fourteenth century were bound to have fresh in their minds the memory of the attempt on the life of Boniface VIII perpetrated at Anagni; this attack had only been made possible by the connivance of the Romans.

The continued residence of the popes on the banks of the Rhône is thus adequately explained and even justified by the need to put an end to the suit brought against Boniface VIII and to wind up the trial of the Templars, by the imminence of the crusade, by the attempts at conciliation between France and England, and above all by the unsettled state of Italy. To these primary causes must be added some secondary ones: the preponderance of French cardinals in the Sacred College and their marked distaste for Italian soil; the construction by Benedict XII of the Palace of the Popes, at once an admirable work of art and a fortress which for long guaranteed the most complete security; the purchase of Avignon from Joanna I, queen of Naples, in 1348; Clement VI's devotion to his country; the age and infirmity of Innocent VI;[6] the manœuvres and intrigues of the kings of France, who wished to keep the papal court within their sphere of influence; and the popes' anxiety to preserve friendly relations with the only genuine allies on whom they could count in the bitter conflict with Louis of Bavaria.

[1] See below, pp. 57–8.
[2] L. Gayet, *Le Grand Schisme d'Occident*, VOL. I, Paris 1889, p. 120 (documentary evidence).   [3] *Ibid.* VOL. II, p. 162.   [4] *Ibid.* VOL. I, pp. 119, 157.
[5] N. Valois, *La France et le Grand Schisme d'Occident*, VOL. I, Paris 1896, pp. 8–9.
[6] Martène and Durand, *Thesaurus novus anecdotorum,* VOL. II, Paris 1717, cols. 946–7.

Book One: The Popes

CHAPTER I

Clement V 1305–14

AT the beginning of the conclave at Perugia on 18 July 1304, the Sacred College was seriously divided. The larger party, almost entirely composed of Italians, demanded atonement for the outrage committed on the person of Boniface VIII by Nogaret at Anagni, and was out to thwart French policy; it was led by Matteo Rosso Orsini, and had as many as ten members. The French faction, under the leadership of the young Napoleone Orsini, sought the re-instatement of the two Cardinals Colonna, whom Boniface VIII had deprived of their honours, and the renewal, at any price, of the agreement with Philip the Fair; it could count on six votes.

The antagonism of the two opposing parties was too well defined for the election to be speedily concluded. If a pope were chosen from among the cardinals, it must eventually follow that Boniface VIII's conduct towards France was to be either approved or condemned. Moreover, Guillaume de Nogaret was venting his ill-will upon the followers of Boniface in truculent proclamations and memoranda. What could be more threatening than language such as this?—'If some Antichrist invade the Holy See, we must resist him; there is no offence to the Church in such resistance; if order cannot be restored without force, we must not waive our right; if, in the cause of right, violence is committed, we are not responsible.'[1]

The cardinals, aware of the danger of the situation, looked beyond the confines of the Sacred College. Some supporters of Boniface put forward the name of the archbishop of Bordeaux, Bertrand de Got; but the rest of their adherents, together with Napoleone Orsini, rejected it.

Napoleone Orsini soon regretted his refusal and, before attempting any action, investigated the intentions of the archbishop of Bordeaux and those of Philip the Fair.

Bertrand de Got was an influential figure at the king's court, with which he had maintained a friendly relationship for many years. His family was in favour with the prince, who in 1305 gave eloquent

---

[1] Lizerand, *Clément V et Philippe le Bel*, Paris 1910, p. 17.

3

expression to his feelings for him: 'Considering the good conduct, the great loyalty and the firm constancy that we have found in Arnaud-Garsias de Got and in Bertrand, son of the aforesaid knight, and in those of their lineage. . . .'[1] The archbishop's journey to Rome, in the thick of the armed conflict between Boniface and Philip the Fair, had not caused an estrangement with his sovereign. Shrewd statesman that he was, Bertrand de Got had thrown in his lot with the French bishops against the pope, and took advantage of attending the synod at Rome to work for the ending of hostilities. The king took so lenient a view of his journey that in April 1304 he took up Bertrand's defence against the officers of his kingdom. Orsini's overtures were well received. Philip who knew the true character of Bertrand de Got, had the most sanguine hopes of his elevation to the papacy.

Armed with this information, Napoleone Orsini gave vigorous support to the candidature of Bertrand de Got, which was also upheld by a French embassy which had come to Perugia early in 1305. He cleverly flattered Matteo Rosso Orsini in public and made a show of being reconciled with him, while secret emissaries were busy persuading certain of the supporters of Boniface of the defection and treachery of their leader. Napoleone Orsini himself brought Cardinal Pierre d'Espagne completely to his way of thinking; he in his turn brought with him two cardinals from his faction, Leonardo Patrassi and Francesco Caetani. This was enough to shift the majority and to unite ten votes in favour of Bertrand de Got. The minority, reduced to five votes, had no alternative but to declare that they acceded to the election (5 June 1305).[2]

Giovanni Villani has given a quite different account of the election at Perugia, which, despite the extraordinary reputation it has enjoyed, is entirely fanciful. According to Villani,[3] Cardinal Niccolò de Prato, one of the French party, persuaded the Boniface faction to agree to a compromise; Boniface's supporters nominated three candidates, and from these their opponents chose Bertrand de Got. Philip the Fair, warned by Nicolas de Prato, wished to make sure of Bertrand's intentions. A meeting took place in an abbey hidden deep in the woods near St Jean d'Angély. The archbishop of Bordeaux was assured of the papal crown provided that he made six promises: to reconcile the king unconditionally with the Church; to release him and his followers from the excommunication incurred at the time of his quarrels with Boniface VIII; to assign to him five tenths on all the benefices of the kingdom; to condemn the memory of Boniface; to rehabilitate the

[1] Lizerand, *Clément V et Philippe le Bel,* Paris 1910, p. 33.
[2] *Ibid.* pp. 12–42.   [3] *Istorie fiorentine,* Bk VIII, ch. lxxx.

Colonna and to create cardinals friendly to France. The sixth condition was to be revealed when the time was ripe. Bertrand de Got, having promised all these things, was elected without difficulty.

Villani's account is not only inaccurate in certain points of detail but is also contradicted by the facts. Our knowledge of the journeys made by Philip the Fair and Bertrand de Got [1] proves that at the time when the interview at St Jean d'Angély is alleged to have taken place, one was not far from Paris and the other at La Roche sur Yon. If, on the other hand, a pact had really been made between the two, it would be difficult to explain the laborious negotiations that later led to the resumption of the trial of Boniface VIII and the condemnation of the Templars.

Bertrand de Got [2] received the news of his election at Lusignan on 19 June while he was visiting his province. At once he retraced his steps and returned to Bordeaux. There he received the decree announcing his election, signified his acceptance and took the name of Clement. He arranged to be crowned at Vienne (Dauphiné) at the coming Feast of All Saints, and then announced his intention of going to Italy as soon as a final peace was concluded between France and England. [3]

A French embassy, however, raised objections to his plans; and the pope, to satisfy Philip the Fair, chose Lyons as the place for his coronation. He left Bordeaux on 4 September. By 1 November he had reached Lyons, having made halts on the way at Agen, at the monastery of Prouille, and at Béziers, Lézignan, Villalier, Montpellier and Viviers. On 14 November, Napoleone Orsini, who had become dean of the Sacred College on the death of his uncle Matteo, crowned Clement in the church of St Just, on French soil, in the presence of the cardinals, who had hastened there from Perugia, and of Philip the Fair and of a large number of prelates and high-born princes. A most unfortunate accident suddenly interrupted the progress of the magnificent procession as it made its way through the streets of Lyons; just as the papal procession was passing, part of a wall, overloaded

[1] Rabanis, *Clément V et Philippe le Bel*, Paris 1858, pp. 53–66. J. Boucherie, in *Archives historiques de la Gironde*, XXIII, 1883, p. 340; *Histoire littéraire de la France*, VOL. XXI, pp. 444–5.

[2] Bertrand was born at Villandraut (Gironde), the son of Béraud de Got, lord of Villandraut, Grayan, Livran and Uzeste; the date of his birth is unknown. He was educated in the convent of the Deffendi of the Order of Grandmont, in the diocese of Agen, and studied canon and civil law at Orleans and Bologna. He was successively canon of Bordeaux, of St Caprais at Agen, of Tours and of Lyons, and then vicar-general to his brother Béraud, the archbishop of Lyons. In 1294 he was entrusted with a diplomatic mission to England. On 28 March 1295 he was made bishop of Comminges and on 23 December 1299, archbishop of Bordeaux. Cf. Baluze, *Vitae*, VOL. II, pp. 31–175; Lizerand, *Clément V et Philippe le Bel*, pp. 23 f.

[3] C. Wenck, *Clemens V und Heinrich VII*, Halle 1882, pp. 169–70.

with spectators, collapsed and twelve people, including John, duke of Brittany, were killed.

The meeting between Philip the Fair and Clement V at Lyons was disastrous for the Church. Two weighty decisions emerged from the negotiations that followed: firstly, instead of making his way to Italy, the pope set off for Gascony; then on 15 December, he created nine French and one English cardinal, and reinstated Giacomo and Pietro Colonna in the Sacred College. Thus was accomplished in the senate of the Roman Church 'one of the most abrupt revolutions recorded in ecclesiastical history.'[1] The Italian element was reduced to a definite minority: it was to be even further reduced by the promotions of December 1310 and December 1312.

From the beginning of his reign, Clement V revealed characteristics that were to be evident throughout: a weak, impressionable personality, a vacillating diplomatist and a man of compromise, he was a completely unworthy opponent of Philip the Fair, who possessed an inflexible will and was accustomed to bring into play all the resources of a coldly calculating temperament. The pope was to use every stratagem and prevarication, only to have concessions wrested from him in the end. It was because of this that the scandalous trial of Boniface VIII came to be resumed, the outrage at Anagni pardoned and the Templars suppressed.

It is only fair to state, in Clement's defence, that he was a sick man during the whole of his pontificate. He suffered cruelly from a disease that is thought to have been cancer of the bowel or stomach. Under the effects of this disease, he became taciturn and lived as a recluse for months at a time, thus giving rise to the libellous rumours whose echoes came down to Villani and Albertino Mussato.[2] During the attack which lasted from August until the end of December 1306, he allowed no-one near him except four of his kinsmen, to the great displeasure of the cardinals, who did not succeed in approaching him until Epiphany 1307. From 1309, the attacks occurred at increasingly shorter intervals. In 1313 and 1314, the disease grew worse. Clement hoped to gain some relief from a change of air and planned to go back to his native country. Worn out by suffering, he died on 20 April 1314 at Roquemaure (Gard).

Except when he was contending with the king of France, Clement never lacked either energy or determination. He was the inevitable

[1] E. Renan, *Études sur la politique religieuse de Philippe le Bel*, Paris 1889, p. 100.
[2] *Istorie fiorentine*, Bk IX, ch. lviii. *De Gestis Henrici VII*, Bk III, tit. x, col. 606. The rumours reported by Villani, according to which the pope was alleged to have had improper relations with the countess of Périgord, daughter of the count of Foix, are without foundation. Cf. Lizerand, *op. cit.* pp. 375–6.

choice as arbitrator of differences in Europe. He reconciled rulers with each other or with their nobility and their people. In England, he freed Edward II from the vows he had made to his barons. In Hungary, his intervention in the question of the succession to the throne, in favour of Carobert, brought to an end a revolution that had lasted for fifteen years. He settled the question of the imperial crown. He was proud and imperious in his dealings with the Emperor Henry VII. At Poitiers, on 5 June 1307, he announced the excommunication of the emperor of Byzantium, Andronicus II Palaeologus. He upheld his right of suzerainty everywhere. He brought back Ferrara under his obedience and was harsh in his treatment of Venice which had tried to deprive him of Ferrara. Robert of Naples was happy to declare himself the pope's devoted son and to accept from him [1] the vicariate of Italy.

Under Clement, increasing emphasis was laid on the centralisation of the internal government of the Church. The choice of bishops was taken more and more out of the hands of cathedral chapters, who were compelled to respect the reservations of the Holy See. The list of benefices conferred directly by the pope grew so long that it caused disquiet to the ordinary collators.

Clement V was himself a man of letters and as such encouraged learning. He created universities at Orleans and Perugia. At Montpellier he codified the statutes of the Faculty of Medicine, while at Paris, Bologna, Oxford and Salamanca he ordered the founding of chairs of Hebrew, Syrian and Arabic.

This sick pontiff set great store on doctors. Peter von Aichspalt, who attended him, was raised to the archiepiscopal throne at Mainz. Arnold of Villanova found in him an effective protector.

But it is above all as a jurist that Clement V is known to posterity. He added a seventh book to the *Decretals*, bearing the name of *Clementinae*, and thus completed the compilation of the great code of ecclesiastical law, the *Corpus juris canonici*, to which certain Constitutions of his successors were later to be added, under the name of *Extravagantes*.

The works of art undertaken at his direction, though not numerous, are none the less remarkable: the collegiate church at Uzeste, and the impressive vaulting at St Bertrand de Comminges; the splendid cope given to that cathedral on the occasion of the translation of the relics of St Bertrand where seventeen historical scenes are represented, framed in medallions on a background embroidered with gold thread and covered with foliage and figures.

[1] Renan, *op. cit.* pp. 450–1.

Clement had a pleasing manner. He was affable by nature, and tried to win men's hearts by skilful compliments, and was lavish in his praises, especially to monarchs.

Unfortunately this affability degenerated into an easy-going good-nature. He had the all too human weakness of granting excessive favours to his kinsmen. July 1305 saw the beginning of a generous distribution of benefices to his nephews, friends and relatives. Five members of his family were each given a cardinal's hat; others occupied episcopal thrones that provided plentiful revenues. The laymen among them had no less generous a share in the pope's favours. They were provided with rectorates or with important offices in Church territories, and were content to accept the emoluments of these lucrative functions that they did not themselves perform.

At the papal court, Clement V's lack of supervision gave rise to regrettable abuses. Disorder and greed reigned to such an extent that the door-keepers and footmen would only allow access to the pope for a financial consideration. The religious who lived on the route of the progresses of the papal court were indeed unfortunate. The abbot of Cluny, Archbishop Egidio Colonna of Bourges, the inhabitants of Bordeaux, the Church in France—all groaned under the impositions to which they were subjected. Elsewhere, holders of benefices were no better treated. The total of the taxes raised by the collection of annates, fruits during vacancies, tenths, censes and common services, to name but a few, amounted each year according to the calculations of Ehrle [1] to about 200,000 florins. Of this vast sum 100,000 was sufficient for the modest needs of the court; the rest was laid aside, until in nine years' time, the cash in the papal treasury reached the figure of 1,040,000 florins. Clement V's will reveals that he lent 320,000 florins to the kings of France and England, while his nephew, the viscount of Lomagne, received 300,000 florins in return for leading five hundred knights on the crusade for the space of a year and a half or two years; 200,000 were left to his relatives, friends and members of his household, and 200,000 were intended for good causes in the south of France; only 70,000 were bequeathed to his successor.

[1] 'Der Nachlass Clemens V. und der in Betreff desselben von Johann XXII. (1318–1321) geführte Prozess,' *Archiv*, VOL. V, 1889, pp. 1–166.

CHAPTER II

John XXII 1316–34

CLEMENT V seems to have had some presentiment during his life-time of the dissensions that would arise in the Sacred College after his death. In 1311 he had published the Constitution *Ne Romani*, which laid down the conditions in which the conclave was hence-forward to be held, and made provision for the occasion when, if the cardinals were unable to agree, they might all leave the conclave simultaneously or successively. *Ubi periculum*, the earlier Constitu-tion of Gregory X (1274), had decreed that in the event of an impasse the governing body of the city where the conclave was gathered—and in the last resort the prince himself, according to the gloss of John Andreas—was to assume the right to compel the cardinals, by moder-ate coercion, to resume the preliminaries of the papal election at the point where they had been broken off, that is to say, all the cardinals save those who for reasons of health had a genuine dispensation. Moreover, the election was to be carried out strictly within the limits of the diocese where the pope had died, or at least in the place where, at the time of his decease, petitions and lawsuits concerning the apostolic see were heard.[1]

Towards the beginning of May 1314 the cardinals, in accordance with Clement's prescriptions, assembled at Carpentras where the Curia was established and shut themselves up in the bishop's palace. From the outset a sharp division was evident among them and three factions were formed. The most important of these was the Gascon party consisting of ten cardinals [2] who were confident of the support of the two nephews of the late pope, namely, Bertrand de Got, vis-count of Lomagne and Auvillars, and Raimond Guilhem de Budos. Their implacable opponents, seven in number,[3] formed the Italian party, which was itself divided into three groups. Between the re-markably united Gascon party and the disunited Italian one, there

---

[1] *Corpus juris canonici*, Bk I, tit. iii, col. 2, *in Clem.*; Bk I, tit. vi, col. 3, *in VI°*.
[2] Arnaud de Pellegrue, Arnaud de Faugères, Arnaud Nouvel, Raimond Guilhem de Farges, Bernard de Garves, Arnaud d'Aux, Guillaume-Pierre Godin, Raimond de Got, Vidal du Four, Guillaume Teste.
[3] Napoleone Orsini, Niccolò Albertini de Prato, Giacomo Stefaneschi, Francesco Caetani, Pietro and Giacomo Colonna, Guglielmo Longhi.

was a third faction, less coherent than the first and more united than the second, and consisting of cardinals of varying origin: three from Languedoc, the elder and younger Bérenger Frédol and Guillaume de Mandagout; one from Quercy, Jacques Duèse; two from Normandy, Nicolas de Fréauville and Michel du Bec; altogether six cardinals forming a French or Provençal faction.

The Italians, fully aware of their own weakness, joined forces with the Provençal party and cast their votes unanimously for Guillaume de Mandagout. This was an excellent choice, but pleased neither the two named Bérenger Frédol who were aiming at the papal crown themselves, nor the Gascons who wanted to elect one of their own number. Since all the opposing parties clung to their respective positions, not one of the candidates could obtain the required two-thirds majority.

While this discord was reigning in the conclave, serious disturbances broke out in the town of Carpentras. They began with brawling between Italian nationals employed at the papal court and the associates of the Gascon cardinals. Blows were exchanged and some deaths occurred. Taking advantage of this unrest, Gascon gangs led by the viscount of Lomagne and Raimond Guilhem de Budos made their way into the city on the pretext of removing the mortal remains of Clement V. On 24 July 1314, they took up arms, slaughtered some of the Italians, set fire to various parts of the town, attacked the houses where the Italian cardinals were staying and looted the dwellings of the townsfolk, the curial officials and the representatives of Italian banks accredited to the Holy See, making off with substantial booty of money, precious robes and other movable articles. They even besieged the conclave, with cries of 'Death to the Italian cardinals! Death! We want a pope! We want a pope!' Another body of armed men marched to the square in front of the bishop's palace, uttering threats of death and making ready to blockade the conclave. The Italian cardinals were so terrified that they made a narrow passage for themselves through a wall behind the besieged palace and fled from Carpentras.

The Gascon cardinals, annoyed at having their plans thwarted, returned for the most part to Avignon and thus revealed their secret intentions. Rather than give in, they had resolved to stand firm, even if a radical cleavage threatened, and to run the risk of schism. The Italians, in order to free themselves from any responsibility and to avert the danger, unmasked these dastardly plans of the Gascons in an encyclical letter, and declared themselves firmly resolved not to recognise anyone elected by the opposing faction, if an election were held in which they had not taken part. In addition, they threatened that they too would proceed to an election.

Almost two years were spent in fruitless discussion. Systematic obstruction by the Gascons prevented any agreement on the choice of a candidate and the place for the conclave. Despite the intervention of European powers, the threat of schism still hung over Christendom.

At last, in March 1316, the tension was eased. After they had exacted a solemn promise that 'no violence should be exercised against them, and that they would not be compelled to go into seclusion in order to proceed to an election,' the cardinals yielded to the persuasions of Philip, count of Poitiers, the leader of the French embassy, and set off slowly for Lyons. While confabulations were being held without result in the Dominican convent, called the Convent of Comfort, Louis X, 'le Hutin,' died. The count of Poitiers could not decide what to do. On the one hand, he did not like to leave Lyons without having seen a pope elected; on the other, he was impatient to reach Paris, where he was summoned by his own interests. His advisers decided that the promise made to the cardinals not to shut them up in conclave was nullified in view of the threat of schism.

On 28 June, troops sealed off the convent of the Dominicans where the Sacred College was assembled. The count of Forez told the cardinals bluntly that they would only regain their freedom when they had given a pope to the Church.

At the end of July they had still reached no agreement. The candidatures of Arnaud Nouvel, Guillaume de Mandagout, Arnaud de Pellegrue, Bérenger Frédol the elder and a prelate not a member of the Sacred College were all rejected in turn. But since the intrigues of Pietro Colonna had exasperated Napoleone Orsini, the latter had a meeting on 5 August with Giacomo Stefaneschi, Francesco Caetani and Arnaud de Pellegrue, the leader of the Gascon group. The name of Jacques Duèse, the favourite candidate of the count of Poitiers and King Robert of Naples, was proposed and accepted. The following day, 6 August, the cardinal-bishop of Porto was assured of eighteen votes. The dissidents, deciding that their opposition was useless and making a virtue of necessity, made over the balance of their votes to him, and on 7 August 1316 he was elected.[1]

In voting at Lyons for Jacques Duèse, the Gascon party had acted less from personal sympathy for him than from inability to do other-

[1] G. Mollat, 'L'Élection du pape Jean XXII,' *Revue d'histoire de l'Église de France* VOL. I, 1910, pp. 34–49, 147–66. The researches of E. Albe have established without any doubt that the story that John XXII was a cobbler's son must be regarded as nothing more than a fable. Though not of noble birth, Jacques Duèse was born into a rich bourgeois family at Cahors and baptised in the parish of St Bartholomew. After

C

wise and in despair of any other solution. It appears, too, that this candidature was accepted because of the pope's age—he was about seventy-two—and his sickly appearance. The Gascons, who bore with an ill-grace the set-back they had suffered in the conclave, expected shortly to be revenged. A page of the viscount of Lomagne denounced a plot hatched against the pope's life by the Cardinals Arnaud de Pellegrue, Guillaume Teste, Bernard de Garves and Bérenger Frédol the younger. The conspirators, so he alleged, planned to assassinate the pope in full Consistory and to wipe out the Cahors following.[1]

The enquiry into this perhaps imaginary conspiracy was without result. Later, the Gascons, especially the viscount de Bruniquel, Bishop Gailhard de Pressac of Toulouse and Arnaud de Pellegrue, were to be compromised in quite another way at the trial of Hugues Géraud, the bishop of Cahors.

This prelate, who had been guilty of peculation and simony, feared that all was lost when canonical proceedings were begun against him at Avignon. In order to escape punishment, he conceived the idea of cunningly contriving the death of John XXII in such a way that it would be attributed to his advanced age. Once he had decided on this crime, it remained to carry it out without arousing suspicion. Hugues Géraud made two stewards of the papal household, Pons de Vassal and Isarn d'Escodata, his accomplices; they agreed to put slow poisons, such as arsenic, into the beverages and dishes presented to the pope. Then he asked his treasurer at Toulouse, Aymeric de Belvèze, to procure harmful powders and wax figures with which he could practise sorcery, for in the efficacity of this there was general belief in the fourteenth century.

The messenger from the bishop of Cahors faithfully carried out his mission. He suborned the Jew, Bonmacip, who brought to Hugues Géraud everything needed to practise sorcery against his enemies. A wax image was first made of Jacques de Via, the favourite nephew of John XXII, who did in fact die on 13 June 1317. Hugues Géraud and his confederates lost no opportunity of attributing his death to their spells. Then it was the pope's turn.

To achieve their ends, Aymeric de Belvèze procured poisons from an apothecary at Toulouse, and bought three wax figures from the

studying in his native town and at Montpellier he became successively archpriest of St André at Cahors, canon of St Front at Périgueux and of Albi, archpriest of Sarlat, dean of Puy, bishop of Fréjus (4 February 1300), chancellor to Charles II of Anjou (1308), bishop of Avignon (18 March 1310), cardinal-priest of St Vitale (24 December 1312) and cardinal-bishop of Porto (May 1313).

[1] E. Albe, *Hugues Géraud, évêque de Cahors. L'affaire des poisons et des envoûtements en 1317*, Cahors 1904, pp. 131-3.

Jew, Bernard Jourdain. These images were baptised in the chapel of the archbishop's palace, in the presence of Gailhard de Pressac, of the viscount de Bruniquel and of half a score of witnesses, by Bernard Gasc, bishop of Ganos, vested with a stole. After this, each figure was given a strip of virgin parchment, on which were written these words: 'May Pope John die, and not another.' 'May Bertrand du Poujet die, and not another.' 'May Gaucelme de Jean die, and not another.' Then each figure, together with the poisons, was hidden in a loaf from which the inside had been scooped out, and which was carefully wrapped up and handed over to bearers who were leaving for Avignon under the escort of one Perrot de Béarn.

When they reached their destination, the mysterious appearance of the travellers aroused the suspicions of the papal police. They were arrested, their baggage seized and the incriminating images discovered. Interrogated concerning the instigators of the plot against the pope's life, the men from Toulouse supplied no information; they only knew those who had hired them. Hugues Géraud, instead of lying low, committed the amazing blunder of attracting attention by careless gossip. At the end of May 1317 the police arrested him in his turn and, with the assistance of the sergeants of the king of France, were successful in seizing his many accomplices. Criminal proceedings were begun, and Hugues Géraud was declared guilty of an attempt of assassination by poison and witchcraft made against the persons of the pope, Bertrand du Poujet and Gaucelme de Jean, guilty of regicide, and guilty of the murder of Jacques de Via. Then he was degraded from the episcopate and handed over to the secular arm, in other words, brought before Arnaud de Trian, the marshal of justice at the court of Avignon, who condemned him, as a murderer, to death by burning. Hugues Géraud died at the stake.[1]

The story of Hugues Géraud gives us some idea of the serious difficulties with which John XXII had to contend after his election. The court was disorganised because of the long vacancy in the Holy See; the apostolic treasury was exhausted by Clement V's fantastic legacies and by the extravagance of his nephews; the independence of the papacy was compromised by the intrigues of Philip the Fair; war was rumbling in Italy, and the East was threatened by the Turks; such was the situation in 1316. If the papacy was to recapture the authority it had lost during the previous pontificate and command the respect of the nations, it would have to strengthen the bonds that linked it to Christendom, become the leader of every great enterprise

[1] G. Mollat, 'Un Évêque supplicié au temps de Jean XXII,' *Revue pratique d'apologétique*, VOL. IV, 1907, pp. 753–67; E. Albe, *op. cit.*

for the public good, cause its judgment to be sought in cases of litigation and distribute its benefits judiciously wherever circumstances made this possible. For more than eighteen years John XXII endeavoured with remarkable determination to achieve this lofty purpose.

In the fourteenth century no power, even one essentially spiritual, could rule the world unless it was able to enforce its actions by the possession of territorial and financial property. John XXII acquired riches by creating a vast fiscal system which made available to him considerable pecuniary resources. Ecclesiastical benefices were subject to a variety of taxes: annates, fruits during vacancies, tenths, charitative subsidies, rights of spoil, etc.[1] Gold flowed into the Church's coffers so copiously that contemporaries believed the pope to have a huge treasury. Giovanni Villani in his *Istorie fiorentine* says that John XXII left at his death more than eighteen million gold florins and the equivalent of seven million more in church vessels, crosses, crowns, mitres, jewels and precious stones; in round figures twenty-five million gold florins. Galvano Fiamma improves upon Villani's figure and makes it twenty-two million, not counting the jewels. Matthias von Neuenburg is more conservative: he reckons the papal fortune at seventeen million gold florins. In reality the treasury deposit, at the time of the pope's death, amounted to about 750,000 florins.[2]

John XXII, a man of simple habits, sober way of life and personal frugality, reorganised his court from the moment of his accession, taking care to banish extravagance without incurring the reproach of miserliness. We learn this from a very interesting letter addressed to Philip the Tall, in which the pope invited the king to organise the expenses and regulate the various services of his court on the model of the papal one. Doubtless the model proposed was a convincing one, and the king acceded to the supreme pontiff's request.[3] Indeed, an examination of the registers of the Apostolic Camera gives the impression that the organisation of the papal court and the administration of its finances were carefully regulated, so that Müntz could without exaggeration call John XXII 'an incomparable administrator.'[4]

His gifts as an administrator are more particularly shown in the

[1] See below, Bk III, ch. 11.
[2] G. Mollat, 'Jean XXII fut-il un avare?' *R.H.E.* VOL. V, 1904, pp. 530–2; E. Göller, *Die Einnahmen der apostolischen Kammer unter Johann XXII*, ed. Görres-Gesellschaft, Paderborn 1910–37, pp. 122*–34*. On the value of the florin see K. H. Schäfer, *Die Ausgaben der apostolischen Kammer unter Johann XXII*, Paderborn 1911, pp. 53*–62*.
[3] Coulon, nos. 513, 1051.
[4] Müntz, in *R.Q.H.* VOL. LXVI, 1899, p. 14.

way in which he gathered all the machinery of Church government into his own hands. In the Constitution *Ex debito*,[1] John XXII extended papal reservations to include a large number of benefices whose collation he retained for himself. He bestowed bishoprics as he thought best, and almost did away with elections by cathedral chapters. In this way, the Holy See created a vast number of clients who aspired to ecclesiastical honours for themselves or their protégés. Foremost among these were heads of state, then princes, minor noblemen, prelates, corporate bodies such as universities, and lastly ordinary collators of benefices who had been deprived of their right of nomination. A kind of tacit agreement existed between these persons and the pope, which such a man as John XXII was able to exploit to his own advantage. The pope had the art of making his favours sought after, and many were obliged to beg for them.[2]

The movement towards centralisation, which was so emphatically imposed on the Church and which was to increase still more as time went on, was to give the papacy a power with which the governments of all countries had to reckon and negotiate.

Original as were the pope's views, they none the less brought with them inevitable consequences. In making the Church rich and powerful was there no risk of introducing a worldly spirit and neglecting the concern with souls? Had not Christ preached poverty and freedom from material goods? Some consciences were shocked by the new direction the Church was taking. Those most inclined to criticise were the Franciscans of the province of Provence whose wholehearted advocacy of poverty went as far as complete absence of worldly goods and actual begging. They were commonly given the name of 'Spirituals'. They became enthusiastic supporters of the apocalyptic speculations of Gerard di Borgo San Donnino, Pierre Jean Olieu and Ubertino da Casale, which had developed from the dangerously extravagant ideas of Joachim of Flora. These visionaries proclaimed that the era of the Holy Ghost had arrived, and the day of the Church, given over to avarice, pride and the delights of the flesh, was over; she had become 'Babylon, the great whore, who has ruined and poisoned mankind'; the pope was Antichrist. The official priesthood would be succeeded by monasticism, which would regenerate men and lead them back to the practice of Christian virtues: humility, chastity and above all absolute poverty.

Excitement increased when, at the request of the General of the Friars Minor, Michael of Cesena, John XXII cut short, without right

[1] *Corpus juris canonici, Extravagantes communes*, Bk I, tit. iii, col. 4.
[2] J. Haller, *Papsttum und Kirchenreform*, VOL. I, pp. 115–21, 133–53.

15

of appeal, the troublesome litigation which had for long divided the Spirituals and the Conventuals, concerning the form of the Franciscan habit and the lawfulness of their dues of corn, wine and oil from granaries and cellars. Most of the Spirituals refused to divest themselves of their short, narrow, patched gowns which were condemned in the Constitution *Quorundam exigit* (7 October 1317), and they denied the legitimacy of the provision of food. All the efforts made by John XXII to enforce obedience on these professed lovers of humility, were in vain. Confronted with an opposition spurred on by the notorious Bernard Délicieux, and the revelation of obviously schismatic tendencies, the pope was obliged to exercise his authority. The Bulls *Sancta Romana* (30 December 1317) and *Gloriosam Ecclesiam* (23 January 1318) declared the fraticelli, beghards, bizoches and brethren of the life of poverty to be excommunicate, and commanded them to dissolve the independent associations which, under cover of privileges granted by Celestine V, they were trying to form in Sicily, Italy and southern France. Those who resisted were seized by the Inquisition and imprisoned or burned alive.[1]

But soon the Holy See was involved in a conflict of a much more serious kind, not this time with a small band of fanatics, but with almost the whole Franciscan order. The dispute began in 1322 over an entirely theological issue: did Christ and the apostles practise poverty to the extent of possessing nothing, either in common or individually? John XXII, a man of an essentially practical nature, wished to dispose of the ambiguities dating from the somewhat obscure Constitutions of Nicholas III (*Exiit qui seminat*) and the Council of Vienne (*Exivi de Paradiso*). He consulted bishops, cardinals and theologians of repute.[2] When discussions began at Avignon, conflicting opinions were freely put forward. Meanwhile Michael of Cesena, acting with insolent audacity, did not await the Holy See's decision: on 30 May 1322 the chapter-general of Perugia declared itself convinced of the absolute poverty of Christ and the Apostles. John XXII could have struck at these dissidents without delay, but was content to revoke the Bull *Exiit qui seminat* which declared that all property of the Friars Minor, in lands, houses, furniture and money, belonged to the Roman Church, and that they had only the use of it (Bull *Ad conditorem canonum*, 8 December 1322). The dogmatic Constitution *Cum inter nonnullos* was published on 12 November 1323 and it condemned the declaration of the chapter of Perugia as heretical.

[1] J.-M. Vidal, *Procès d'inquisition contre Adhémar de Mosset*, Perpignan 1912, pp. 4–18.
[2] F. Tocco, *La quistione della povertà nel secolo XIV*, 1910, passim.

The pope's decisions unleashed a furious storm among the Franciscans. Some fanatical brethren considered that the apostasy of the official Church now seemed complete. Michael of Cesena, whose activities and violence of language had damaged his reputation, was summoned to Avignon to account for himself, and kept there as a kind of prisoner. During the night of 26–27 May 1328 he escaped, went to seek refuge at the court of Louis of Bavaria and joined the party of the antipope Nicholas V, the friar minor Pietro Rainallucci da Corbara. The conclusion of the schism on 25 July 1330 did not bring the Franciscan opposition to an end. Michael of Cesena was deprived of his dignities as General by the section of his order that remained faithful to John XXII; he died impenitent in 1348. However, the ranks of the rebels of whom he was the chief were eventually thinned.

John XXII was not neglectful of the spiritual well-being of Christendom, whatever the critics of the papacy might say to the contrary. He was, perhaps, an even more able reformer than his successor Benedict XII. In 1317 was published the Seventh Book of the *Decretals*, which Clement V had died too soon to promulgate; this was the beginning of the canonical work that the pope was to bequeath to posterity. The *Extravagantes* were for long to serve as a basis for ecclesiastical jurisprudence. The Bull *Execrabilis* [1], dated 19 November 1317, revoked the dispensations granted to the clergy by Clement V which allowed them to hold several benefices. This custom had led, especially in Spain and England, to notorious abuses, which were stamped out by John XXII with an energy of which his correspondence gives ample proof. Unfortunately he showed undue favouritism to his kindred, courtiers and cardinals and to the sons of kings and great lords. In the same way he carried to excessive lengths the practice of converting the revenues from benefices into salaries for officials of the papal court; this meant that prelates were encouraged not to comply with their obligations of residence.

The vast area of the diocese of Toulouse had not been conducive to the spiritual welfare of the faithful. As early as the beginning of the thirteenth century, Foulques de Marseille had recommended the division of his diocese as the most effective remedy against the spread of heresy. It would be easier, he thought, for several bishops to track down error than for a single prelate who had too vast a territory to govern. Rather late in the day, the papacy busied itself with carrying out this plan. On 23 July 1295, Boniface VIII had created the diocese of Pamiers. John XXII completed the work of his predecessor by

---

[1] *Corpus juris canonici, Extrav. Joan. XXII*, tit. iii, col. 1.

17

carving out of the magnificent territory of Toulouse the six bishoprics of Montauban, Rieux, Lombez, St Papoul, Mirepoix and Lavaur, which, together with that of Pamiers, constituted a new ecclesiastical province (1317–18).

This parcelling out was perhaps carried to rather extreme lengths. The bishoprics created by John XXII existed in a constant state of poverty. It had been imprudent to seize as a basis for territorial re-form the momentary prosperity of revenues subject to endless variations.

Other French dioceses were divided up, but in a less drastic fashion. Clermont lost the territory of St Flour; Albi that of Castres; Périgueux that of Sarlat; Poitiers those of Luçon and Maillezais; Rodez that of Vabres; Limoges that of Tulle; Agen that of Condom; while Narbonne gave rise to the dioceses of St Pons de Thomières and Alet (1317–18).[1]

In Aragon, on 18 July 1318, the province of Tarragona was divided into two archbishoprics: Saragossa, which took over five of the suffragan bishops, and Tarragona which kept seven of its former churches.[2]

In Italy, the making of the abbey of Monte Cassino into a bishopric (2 May 1322) seems to have been an unfortunate step; Urban V revoked it in 1367.[3]

On the other hand, the establishment of the ecclesiastical hierarchy in Persia and the creation of the archbishopric of Sultanieh greatly helped the expansion of Christendom.[4]

The increase of pastors throughout Christendom bears witness to John XXII's constant desire to keep a watchful eye on the spiritual well-being of the faithful. It was this same preoccupation that led him to inaugurate a lively reaction against the reign of Clement V, which was upbraided for its weak and even indulgent attitude towards heresy. The Inquisition had not found favour with Clement: it had its revenge under his successor. At no other time in the fourteenth century was it so active; never did it hand over so many victims to the stake. The Waldenses, refugee Catharists, fraticelli, beghards, and warlocks, magicians and sorcerers were all mercilessly persecuted. In Dauphiné, two inquisitors, the Friars Minor Catalan Faure and

[1] J.-M. Vidal, *Les Origines de la province ecclésiastique de Toulouse (1295–1318)*, Toulouse 1908, pp. 42–91 (reprinted from *Annales du Midi*, VOL. XV). J. Contrasty, *Histoire de la cité de Rieux-Volvestre et de ses évêques*, Toulouse 1936. (This work points out that John XXII wished, not to punish the bishop of Toulouse, but to put a term to the abuses brought about by the extent and prosperity of the diocese.)

[2] Cocquelines, *Bullarum, privilegiorum ac diplomatum Romanorum pontificum amplissima collectio*, VOL. III, pt 2, doc. XVI, p. 167.

[3] *Ibid.* pp. 185, 327.   [4] Mollat, no. 8187, 1 May 1318.

Pierre Pascal paid for their excess of zeal with their lives in 1321.[1]

The protection which John XXII extended to the Inquisition—and which was shown especially in the case of Bernard Délicieux—was by no means without discrimination. The pope, faithfully observing the Council of Vienne's decree *Multorum*, counter-balanced the influence of the Inquisitor by making the collaboration of the Ordinary compulsory. If he had any reason to suspect the procedure of certain judges of the Inquisition, he had no hesitation in withdrawing their right to hear cases and in handing such cases over to a more impartial tribunal. More than once his intervention prevented a miscarriage of justice and kept Inquisitors from avenging their hatred or private spite.[2]

John XXII was to act in the same way towards the religious orders as towards the Inquisition. His authoritarian temperament led him to interfere in their private affairs. We have already seen how he tried to bring the Franciscans back into line and to stamp out the disputes by which they were rent. His intervention in the grave crisis through which the Knights Hospitallers were passing was beneficial in a different way.

The Grand Master of the Hospitallers was Foulques de Villaret, an unjust man, a poor administrator, and fond of extravagance and ostentation. He had allowed disorder to creep into his congregation and contracted heavy debts. His knights, dissatisfied with him, had shut him up in the castle of Lindos at Rhodes, deposed him, and put in his stead Maurice de Pagnac (1317). The deposition of Foulques was valid, but public opinion remained on his side, for he was known as a brave soldier who had achieved resounding successes in the East for the Catholic cause.

John XXII after summoning both Pagnac and Villaret to Avignon, tried to gain time by appointing, as vicar-general, Brother Géraud de Pins. Realising that irremediable disaster was threatening the Hospitallers and that they themselves were powerless to deal with it, the pope took their interests in hand and saved them whether they would or no, without troubling to respect their prerogatives. 'Thus he renewed the general privileges of the order, and, from a disciplinary point of view, compelled the rebellious brethren to submit to the Master's authority, and the prelates to recall the knights to a less dissolute way of life, to less luxury in their dress, and to passive

---

[1] J. Chevalier, *Mémoire historique sur les hérésies en Dauphiné avant le XVIᵉ siècle*, Valence 1890, pp. 12–16.

[2] C. Douais, 'Guillaume Garric de Carcassonne . . . et le tribunal de l'inquisition (1285–1329),' *Annales du Midi*, VOL. X, 1898, pp. 5–45; J.-M. Vidal, *Bullaire de l'inquisition française au XIVᵉ siècle*, Paris 1913.

obedience. He ordered the chapters of priories to meet yearly and declared that no brother should benefit from two offices at once. In order to prevent the diminution of the Hospitallers' possessions, he forbade the Grand Master to allow any alienation of land, ordered that the fines should be exacted for alienations already authorised, and appointed judges to preserve the privileges of the order and to recover goods that had been sold. In collaboration with the chancellor, Pierre de l'Ongle, and the visitor, Léonard de Tiberti, . . . he took energetic measures to wipe out the debts that threatened the very existence of the order; starting on 21 July 1317, . . . he proceeded to a new method of appointing all the priors for a period of ten years from 1 February 1318. Sometimes his choice fell on former holders of the office, sometimes on new men, and it was always inspired by his determination to put experienced administrators in these posts. Since he was convinced that normal resources were inadequate to re-establish financial equilibrium, he instituted a special tax, which each prior was bound to pay over and above the usual commitments of priories; the rate for this was fixed in proportion to the importance of each priory.'[1]

Having decreed all these measures of reform, John XXII annulled the election of Maurice de Pagnac on 1 March 1319 and, after compensating him, reinstated Foulques de Villaret in his charge. The pope then obtained Villaret's resignation, appointed him prior of Capua, exempted him from the exercise of juridical powers over the order and caused his successor to be elected. It is thus to John XXII that credit must be given for saving the order of Hospitallers when it was about to founder, and so preserving for Christendom its most intrepid defenders against the Turks.[2]

At about the same period, the order of Grandmont was going through a similar crisis. The twenty-first prior, Jourdan de Rapistan, who had been leading a scandalous life and dissipating the riches of the community to pay for his wild extravagance, was deposed in 1315 by seven *definitores* (counsellors within the order) who in the following year elected in his stead the corrector of Louye, Hélie Ademar. Riots broke out among the partisans of the two rivals, and the order seemed about to break up.[3] It owed its salvation to John XXII, who, after insisting on the resignation of both claimants, reorganised it from top to bottom (17 November 1317).[4] The priory became the

[1] J. Delaville le Roulx, *Les Hospitaliers à Rhodes*, Paris 1913, VOL. I, p. 20.
[2] *Ibid.* pp. 12–28, 51–61.
[3] A. Lecler, 'Histoire de l'abbaye de Grandmont,' *Bulletin de la Société archéologique et historique du Limousin*, VOL. LVIII, 1908–09, pp. 478–82.
[4] Cocquelines, *op. cit.* VOL. III, pt 2, doc. XII, pp. 155–60.

seat of an abbey. The order, which had previously had one hundred and fifty-two cells or correctories, was reduced to thirty-nine conventual priories, whose priors were to be appointed by the Holy Father in the first instance. Subsequently these office-holders were to be elected. The number of visitors was increased from three to four.

Moreover, John XXII used the spoils of the Templars to create the order of Montesa in Aragon (10 June 1317) and that of Christ in Portugal (14 March 1319). Both of these were to carry on the struggle against the Moors.[1]

While John XXII continued to uphold Clement V's Constitution *Dudum a Bonifacio*[2] which restricted the privileges of the regular clergy, he defended the mendicant orders against the attacks of the secular clergy. A master of the University of Paris, Jean de Pouilly, had taught that the jurisdiction of prelates, bishops and humble priests came directly from God, and that as a result any privilege contrary to this jurisdiction, even though granted by the Holy See, was null and void. Very serious consequences resulted from these principles: since only the parish priest had the power to absolve his parishioners, absolution pronounced by the regular clergy, even those endowed with apostolic indulgences, was invalid, and the penitent was obliged to make a new confession to his own pastor. Realising the unrest caused by such theories, which constituted an unmistakable threat to the universal jurisdiction of the Holy See, John XXII summoned the Parisian master to Avignon. A theological debate took place in his presence, and the discussion put Jean de Pouilly to confusion. On 24 July 1321, his errors were condemned in the Bull *Vas electionis*.[3]

Doctrinal disputes were not brought to an end with the case of Jean de Pouilly. On 8 February 1326 sixty propositions, that a commission of eight theologians had selected from Pierre Jean Olieu's commentary on the Apocalypse, were censured.[4] In 1329, twenty-eight propositions drawn from the writings of the German mystic, Meister Eckhart, were censured; seven of them were marked down as heretical, and eleven as scandalous and suspect of heresy.[5]

It is a curious fact that a pontiff so zealous in stamping out all forms of controversy should have started one himself which had immediate repercussions. On All Saints' Day 1331, at the church of

[1] Baluze, *Vitae*, VOL. III, pp. 256–63. Mollat, no. 9053.
[2] *Corpus juris canonici*, Bk III, tit. vii, col. 2, *in Clem.*
[3] *Ibid. Extravagantes communes*, Bk V, tit. iii, col. 2. Denifle and Chatelain, *Chartularium*, VOL. II, p. 243, no. 798.
[4] Baluze-Mansi, *Miscellanea*, VOL. II, pp. 258–72.
[5] H. Denifle, 'Meister Eckehart's lateinische Schriften und die Grundanschauung seiner Lehre,' *Archiv*, VOL. II, 1886, pp. 416–640.

Notre-Dame-des-Doms, John XXII put himself on the side of a very few theologians and, contrary to the accepted opinion of learned theologians no less than the general belief of the faithful, preached the strange doctrine that the souls of the just, before the resurrection of the body, will enjoy no intuitive vision of God; they must remain *sub altare Dei*, created anew by the vision of Christ's humanity; after the last judgment they will be placed on the altar, and will contemplate the divine essence.

In a second sermon preached on 15 December, the pope developed this theory and declared that 'Before the resurrection of the body, departed souls possess neither eternal life, nor true beatitude, nor the beatific vision.'

On 5 January he deduced from his doctrine that neither the damned nor the devils live in Hell at present, and that this place of torment will only become their abode after the end of the world.

Public opinion was dumbfounded by these three sermons. The General of the Friars Minor, Guiral Ot, ranged himself on the side of the pope's teaching; but the supporters of Louis of Bavaria, Michael of Cesena, William of Ockham and Bonagrazia of Bergamo, priding themselves for once on their orthodoxy, hastened to proclaim John XXII a heretic. Cardinal Napoleone Orsini, who was living at Avignon, encouraged these erring Franciscans, and was busy intriguing with the Bavarian to depose the pope, to whom they mockingly referred as 'Jacques of Cahors.' Jacques Fournier, who was to become Benedict XII, and the German Ulrich then joined in the fray, and had no difficulty in proving that the pope, speaking as a private theologian and on a point of undefined doctrine, was quite free to uphold the opinion that seemed most likely to him. In a very short time, in any case, John XXII declared that he had only wished to speak as a private theologian.[1]

Far, indeed, from imposing his opinion on others, John XXII made every possible effort to clarify the doubt that had arisen in his own mind. He sought the opinion of the bishops and invited the most learned masters of theology to take part in the controversy. At his request, the famous theologian Durand de St Pourçain wrote a treatise in favour of the beatific vision but included in it ten or eleven propositions of doubtful orthodoxy; these were submitted to the scrutiny of several theologians and eventually not indicted.

In France, a regrettable incident gave rise to more spiritual unrest. Passing through Paris on his way to England, Guiral Ot was rash enough to preach the doctrine to which the pope adhered. Im-

[1] See below, p. 23, the recantation of John XXII.

mediately the University of Paris protested; the king was shocked by the incident. A gathering of prelates and masters of theology met at the castle of Vincennes on 19 December 1333 and roundly declared itself in disagreement with the doctrine put forward by Guiral Ot; its decision was forwarded to the papal court.

In Germany, the rebel Franciscans William of Ockham and Bonagrazia of Bergamo protested against the 'errors' put forward by 'Jacques of Cahors.' According to them, a heretic had usurped the pontifical throne. Meanwhile, in Avignon, Cardinal Napoleone Orsini was endeavouring by intrigue to hasten the convocation of a Council to judge the pope. It was at this juncture that John XXII fell seriously ill. He recanted on 3 December 1334 in the presence of his cardinals. His declaration of faith ends thus: 'In this manner we declare the mind that we have now and have had, in union with the Holy Catholic Church. We confess and believe that souls separated from their bodies and fully purged from guilt are above, in the kingdom of heaven, in paradise and with Jesus Christ, in the company of the angels, and that according to the universal law, they see God and the divine essence face to face and clearly, *so far as the state and condition of a separated soul permits.*' These last words really constitute 'a reservation, showing after all that there is a possibility that separated souls see God differently from those souls that are reunited to their bodies.' The pope was only partially renouncing his conviction, even while he humbly submitted himself to the decisions of the Church in a matter in which the doctrine had not yet been formulated.[1] At about the hour of prime on 4 December, the old man died: he had reached the age of ninety.[2]

John XXII was so much disparaged by his contemporaries and his memory has been so mercilessly attacked by his enemies,[3] that to try to sketch his portrait is perhaps foolhardy. However, even making some use of the writings of his detractors, it is possible to fix on the following characteristics as genuine. John XXII had a small, delicate physique and pale complexion, a gift of quick repartee, a peremptory and impetuous manner and an extraordinarily lively mind. He was a true son of Cahors in being astute and able to probe quickly into the secret plans of the politicians and place-seekers who tried to circumvent him. The account of the audiences granted to the ambassadors of King James II of Aragon are remarkably informative. For all they

[1] X. le Bachelet, in *Dictionnaire de théologie catholique*, VOL. II, 1905, cols. 657–69. Denifle and Chatelain, *Chartularium*, VOL. II, nos. 970–87. N. Valois, in *Histoire littéraire de la France*, VOL. XXIV, pp. 551–627.
[2] E. Göller, *Die Einnahmen*, p. 16*. The Archives of Vaucluse: collection of the metropolitan chapter.   [3] *Regesta Vaticana, 131*, fol. 59ᵛ, ep. 212.

were on their guard, these diplomatists contradicted themselves, to the great joy of the pope, who could not conceal his malicious laughter.[1]

John was not only blessed with energy and will-power, but possessed a toughness astonishing in a man of his age. His capacity for work was incredible. He was able to carry on simultaneously the most varied activities: thus, at more or less the same time he was striving to end the old enmity dividing the kings of England and France and which threatened at any moment to set them at each other's throats, and to settle the dissensions between quite minor country squires like those from Quercy, the lords of Castelnau, Thémines, Peyrilles and Gourdon. He dealt with the innumerable and exceptionally serious difficulties caused him by the Visconti in Milan, by Louis of Bavaria, the rebel Franciscans under the leadership of Michael of Cesena, the schism of Pietro da Corbara, and by the rebellion of the towns in the Papal States. At the same time he concerned himself with sending the West to conquer the Holy Places and to spread the knowledge of the Gospel to the very borders of Tartary. He not only reorganised the Church, but devoted his attention to the niceties of the negotiations carried on by the nuncios and legates that he sent to every part of Christendom, from Portugal to farthest Poland, and from Sicily to Scotland and Norway.

This characteristic energy of John XXII was shown in the government of the Church by vigorous action and sometimes by rigorous measures; but it did not degenerate into harshness or cruelty. Indeed, the pope would have been within his rights had he meted out severe punishments to the cardinals and prelates most deeply compromised in the trial of Hugues Géraud. His alleged harshness was in fact nothing more than an insistence on strict obedience to the orders of the Holy See. It is not borne out by the affable tone of John XXII's correspondence. He shows great delicacy of feeling in consoling the unhappy Queen Clementia on the untimely death of her son. He mourns the death of Philip V the Tall with sincere feeling and invites his widow to place her whole confidence in him, like a beloved daughter in her father.[2]

John XXII carried family affection and esteem for his compatriots to excessive lengths. He lavished worldly goods on his brothers and sisters, nephews and nieces, his kindred and all those who were connected closely or distantly with the Duèse family. Natives of Quercy

[1] H. Finke, *Acta Aragonensia*, Münster-Berlin, 1908–23, VOL. I, p. xviii; VOL. II, pp. 218, 797.
[2] Coulon, nos. 71, 1351, 1367. A. M. Huffelmann, *Clemenza von Ungarn, Königin von Frankreich*, Berlin 1911.

occupied all the offices and dignities of the Church: some were robed in cardinal's purple, others were given administrative offices in the court or the papal residence; some were legates and nuncios, others stewards, cup-bearers, scribes or clerks of the wardrobe. Pierre Duèse, the pope's own brother, received as much as 60,000 gold florins for the purchase of lands, one of which carried with it the title of viscount of Caraman.[1]

There are certain extenuating circumstances for this undeniable nepotism.[2] The conspiracies at the beginning of his reign had given John XXII a legitimate desire to surround himself with trustworthy and devoted friends. In order to make sure that his Italian policy would succeed, he thought it necessary to place those he could trust on the episcopal thrones of the peninsula. His chief reason for making the episcopate consist of his minions was the desire for a forceful centralisation of power. Moreover, those who enjoyed his favour did not prove unworthy of it; far from it. Such men as Bertrand du Poujet, Gaucelme de Jean, Bertrand de Montfavès, Gasbert de Laval and Aimeric de Châtelus, to name but a few of the most famous, rendered distinguished services to the Church.

[1] E. Albe, *Quelques-unes des dernières volontés de Jean XXII*, Cahors 1903, pp. 6–7.
[2] E. Albe, *Autour de Jean XXII*, Rome 1903–06, VOL. I, pp. 1–3, 57–9.

CHAPTER III

Benedict XII 1334–42

IN accordance with the directions of Gregory X, the cardinals, to the number of twenty-four, shut themselves up in conclave in the papal palace, on 13 December 1334, under the double guard of the seneschal of Provence and the rector of the Comtat-Venaissin. Seven days later, on 20 December at about the hour of vespers, Jacques Fournier was unanimously elected by ballot, and chose the name of Benedict XII.[1] His coronation took place on 8 January 1335 in the church of the Dominicans at Avignon.

The new pope came from Saverdun, a little town in the county of Foix, and was of humble family. He entered the Cistercian monastery of Boulbonne (Haute-Garonne) at an early age, and there soon made his profession. His paternal uncle, Arnaud Nouvel, brought him to the monastery of Fontfroide (Aude) of which he was abbot, and later sent him to the College of St Bernard in Paris. There Jacques Fournier attended lectures conscientiously, passed his theological examinations up to the doctorate and even held a chair. In 1311, he succeeded his uncle, who had been made a cardinal, as abbot of Fontfroide. Later, higher honours came his way: on 19 March 1317 he was appointed bishop of Pamiers, and on 3 March 1326, bishop of Mirepoix.[2]

As bishop of Pamiers, Jacques Fournier was noted for the zeal with which he pursued the Waldensian, Catharist and Albigensian heretics who had fled to his diocese, which had become a kind of Promised Land to heresy. In agreement with the Inquisitor of Carcassonne he set up a tribunal and set to work with vigour. Between 15 July 1318 and 9 October 1325, his court of justice sat for no less

---

[1] Villani alone relates the following anecdote. The cardinals had been split into two factions, a French party under Talleyrand de Périgord and an Italian one led by Giovanni Colonna. The French faction exacted a formal promise from their candidate, Jean de Comminges, not to take the Holy See back to Italy. Jean de Comminges refused, and the cardinals then transferred their votes to Jacques Fournier, although they did not regard him as a serious candidate. This move succeeded contrary to their expectations, and Jacques, as much surprised at his election as were those who had voted for him, is alleged to have cried out, 'You have elected an ass.' Cf. Muratori, VOL. XIII, col. 766. According to Matthias von Neuenburg (ed. Hofmeister, VOL. I, p. 126) Benedict only received two-thirds of the votes.

[2] Mollat, nos. 3206, 24542.

than three hundred and seventy days, and five hundred and seventy-eight witnesses and accused appeared before it. He was the terror of heretics, who in their turn showered insults and curses upon him. Some called him 'The Devil', or the 'Spirit of Evil'. Another said, 'May he fall over a cliff,' while yet another groaned, 'So long as he still remains alive, it means death for us all. He is a demon infesting the country.'[1]

The manner in which Fournier conducted interrogatories shows him to have been an expert inquisitor, extracting admissions with masterly skill, and showing himself unsympathetic and even harsh to the accused. Nevertheless, he was not blinded by his avowed hatred of heresy: he showed himself to be an upright judge, extremely punctilious, so conscientious that he insisted on being present at every session of the trial, and very rarely relied on his subordinates to carry out minor formalities. Once he had obtained confessions, he showed forbearance and consideration and was indulgent in allotting punishment and softening the harshness of the inquisitorial code: he only sent four Waldensians and one relapsed Catharist to the stake.[2]

His zeal had its reward: on two separate occasions, John XXII[3] congratulated him warmly on having rooted out heresy both in the diocese of Pamiers and in that of Mirepoix; on 18 December 1327 he made him cardinal-priest of St Prisca.

During his time as cardinal, Jacques Fournier earned the whole-hearted confidence and respect of John XXII. He was put in charge of examining the appeals which came up from the Inquisition to the court of Avignon; between 1330 and 1334 he appeared as judge in the actions brought against the German fraticello Conrad, the Inquisitor of Carcassonne, Jean Galand, the Breton priest Yves de Kerinou, the English Dominican Thomas Wallis and the knight Adhémar de Mosset.[4] His knowledge of theology was especially displayed at the time of the notorious controversies that arose concerning both the poverty of Christ and the beatific vision. John XXII, who guessed his ability, was anxious to have his opinion and gave him the opportunity to write several treatises. His works at this period include a treatise against the fraticelli, a refutation of the errors of Joachim of Flora and Meister Eckhart, a treatise on the doctrines of Michael of Cesena, William of Ockham and Pierre Jean Olieu, a treatise on the state of the souls of the righteous before the Last Judgment and

---

[1] J.-M. Vidal, *Le Tribunal d'inquisition de Pamiers*, Toulouse 1906, pp. 76, 77.
[2] *Ibid.* pp. 75–81; 115–19, 235, 243–6.   [3] *Ibid.* pp. 254, 255.
[4] Eubel, *Bullarium*, VOL. V, nos. 842, 857. Denifle, *Chartularium*, VOL. II, nos. 971, 973, 976, 979, 980, 986. J.-M. Vidal, *Un Inquisiteur jugé par ses victimes. Jean Galand et les Carcassonnais*, Paris 1903, pp. 28–30.

another on questions arising from the doctrines of Durand de St Pourçain.[1]

At a time when Christendom was threatened by heresy, the cardinals' eyes were naturally turned towards the man whom J.-M. Vidal has justly called 'The brightest theological light of the Sacred College.'

Benedict XII did not disappoint his electors. He speedily put an end to the discussions on the beatific vision, declaring that the souls of the just, since they have no sin to expiate, 'see the divine essence by intuitive vision and even face to face' immediately after death (Constitution *Benedictus Deus*, 29 January 1336).[2] He then undertook to root out the abuses that abounded in the Church, by inaugurating a series of reforms dealing with the papal court, the religious orders and the secular clergy.

'Abuses without number'—to use Benedict XII's own expression —had found their way into the higher levels of Church administration. Officers of the papal court were shameless in their behaviour. The marshal's subordinates in particular committed the most shocking malpractices: the least of their peccadilloes consisted in extracting huge gratuities from the common people. On 13 January 1335, a Bull ordered John of Cojordan to open an enquiry without delay. Those who were implicated did not wait for the result of the judicial enquiry, of which they could only too clearly foresee the outcome, but escaped punishment by fleeing from Avignon. The investigation, indeed, proved how well-founded were the complaints that poured in from every side. On 29 June 1335, the marshal's court was issued with detailed regulations which laid down the salaries to be paid and the powers to be invested in the officials.[3] The marshal, Arnaud de Lauzières, was dismissed in 1337.[4] One of his successors was convicted of being an accessory in the kidnapping of the ambassador to England Nicolino Fieschi in 1340 and was put in prison, where, in despair, he took poison: his corpse was for long denied burial. As for the sergeants-at-arms who had taken part in the outrage, they were hanged on a beam from the windows of Nicolino's dwelling.[5]

The other departments of the court were reorganised. A strict limit was placed on the field of action of the penitentiary.[6] To guard

---

[1] J.-M. Vidal, 'Notice sur les œuvres du pape Benoît XII,' *R.H.E.* VOL. VI, 1905, pp. 788–95.
[2] Cocquelines, *Bullarum* . . . VOL. III, pt 2, pp. 213–14.
[3] Theiner, *Codex*, VOL. II, doc. I. *Regesta Vaticana, 130*, fol. 6ᵛ, 85ʳ; *131*, fol. 41ᵛ.
[4] Vidal, no. 4109, in the registers of Benedict XII.
[5] E. Déprez, *Les Préliminaires de la guerre de Cent Ans. La Papauté, la France et l'Angleterre*, Paris 1902, pp. 305–12.
[6] Denifle, in *Archiv*, VOL. IV, 1888, pp. 209–20.

against the indiscretion of chancery employees the copying of the pope's secret correspondence was entrusted to a college of secretaries.[1] The presentation of petitions by officers of the court had become a source of illicit gain. Consequently, Benedict XII decreed that henceforward an official should register in a special volume all petitions bearing the *fiat* and the signature of the pope, and should himself bring them to the offices of the chancery.[2] In order to ensure that unworthy persons did not hold ecclesiastical honours, he compelled candidates to be subjected to an examination conducted by men of his choice, and excommunicated anyone who might try to send a substitute to this examination. Such substitutes would themselves lose their benefices, or, if they did not have any, would be declared unfit to receive them.[3] Moreover, the access of those, rich or poor, who wished to present a plea to the Holy See was facilitated by the Constitution *Decens et necessarium* which laid down the duties of procurators and advocates.[4]

On 10 January 1335[5] bishops and ecclesiastics in possession of benefices involving a cure of souls were bidden to leave Avignon before the approaching Feast of the Purification and to observe the conditions of residence in their benefices, on pain of incurring the sanctions of canon law.

Neither Clement V nor John XXII had made any attempt to guard against nepotism; but it had no hold on Benedict. Egidio di Viterbo has attributed a saying to him which, even if not authentic, conveys exactly the strictness of his attitude: 'The pope,' he is alleged to have said, 'must be like Melchisidek, who had neither father nor mother nor kindred.'[6] Not one of his relatives was made a cardinal. Guillaume Fournier, his nephew, was warned in a curious note from Cardinal Bernard of Albi that to come to Avignon would not put him in his uncle's favour. 'You must know,' he told him, 'that in our master natural affections have no voice.' Again, although the marriage of his niece Faiaga to the son of Arnaud, lord of Villiers was contracted at Avignon, the pope would not allow any pomp in its solemnisation.[7]

The religious orders had, in the course of the last centuries, lapsed

---

[1] E. Göller, *Mitteilungen und Untersuchungen über das päpstliche Register und Kanzleiwesen im. 14. Jahrhundert besonders unter Johann XXII und Benedikt XII*, Rome 1904, pp. 42–60.
[2] Baluze, *Vitae*, VOL. I, new edn. pp. 211, 228.
[3] Cocquelines, *op. cit.* VOL. III, pt 2, p. 288.
[4] M. Tangl, *Die päpstlichen Kanzleiordnungen (1200–1500)*, Innsbruck 1894, pp. 118–24.
[5] K. Jacob, *Studien über Papst Benedikt XII*, Berlin 1910, p. 42.
[6] Pagi, *Breviarium historico-chronologico-criticum*, VOL. IV, p. 117.
[7] Vidal, no. 7601.

greatly from their original zeal; Benedict tried to re-establish the religious life in all its integrity. Knowing how prejudicial to monastic discipline was the transference of professed religious from the mendicant to the Benedictine and Cistercian orders, he limited this practice by insisting that permission be first obtained from the Holy See.[1]

The fourteenth-century Church was caused much distress by the large number of wandering monks who had been turned out of their convents and, having no desire to go back, roamed the world in search of adventure, living as best they could at the expense of public charity. Benedict XII made every effort to cause these vagabonds to return to their monasteries. In the Constitution *Pastor bonus* (17 June 1335) he requested abbots to receive the runaways kindly and to reinstate them in their communities. If the abbot found that the behaviour of the delinquents had been too outrageous, or if their return to any particular convent was likely to cause trouble, then the pope granted the rebel monks permission to transfer to another convent of their order on condition that they performed a fair penance.[2]

The first order to attract the attention of Benedict XII was that of Cîteaux. As early as 1317–18,[3] John XXII had realised that reforms would have to be introduced, but the eloquence of Jacques de Thérines made the pope abandon his plans. Nevertheless, as we read the ingenious speech of Thérines in support of his order, we gain the unfortunate impression that work, as recommended by the primitive rule, is almost unknown, poverty abandoned, and monastic austerity scarcely a memory. The Constitution *Fulgens sicut stella* [4] laid down rules for the administration of temporal matters, curbed luxurious living and prescribed that chapters and visitations should be held regularly; all Cistercian monasteries were to maintain a certain number of theological students in appointed centres of study; and young religious were forbidden on pain of the strictest penalties to study canon law which would make them eligible for benefices. Despite the objections of the order, formulated in a long and interesting indictment,[5] Benedict himself made sure that his decree was carried out, and insisted that his commissaries should see that it was strictly applied. He hunted down monks who prevaricated, thwarted any resistance, deposed abbots, brought back the wandering monks by force to their monasteries and gave the abbot of Cîteaux extraordinary powers of jurisdiction.[6]

---

[1] Cocquelines, *loc. cit.* p. 203.　　　　[2] *Ibid.* pp. 201–03.
[3] N. Valois, 'Un Plaidoyer du XIVe siècle en faveur des Cisterciens,' *B.E.C.* vol. XLIX, 1908, pp. 352–68.　　　　[4] Cocquelines, *loc. cit.* pp. 203–13.
[5] Bibliothèque nationale, MS. Latin 4191, fol. 48r–63r.
[6] Vidal, nos. 2269, 2351, 2355, 6330, 6331, 7411, 7499 etc.

But Benedict's most famous reform was that which he imposed on the Benedictine order. After consultation with the six principal abbots of the order, those of Cluny, Chaise-Dieu, St Victor of Marseilles, Psalmody, Montolieu and Issoire, he promulgated on 20 June 1336, in agreement with his cardinals, the Bull *Summi magistri,*[1] known as the 'Benedictine Bull.' The thirty-nine articles, all very long and detailed, contained in this Bull may be grouped under four principal headings: the government of the order, the monastic life, the care of temporal matters and study. Benedict's reform was especially intended to unify and centralise the order: it recommended the triennial holding of provincial chapters, a practice that had lapsed somewhat despite the objurgations of John XXII; it divided the various houses of the order into thirty-five carefully circumscribed provinces. The wisest rulings dealt with study, which the pope wished at all costs to revive. In every establishment of any size a master was to teach grammar, logic and philosophy; no outsider was to be admitted to these lessons. After this initial instruction, one out of every twenty students was to be sent to the university to study theology, the Scriptures and canon law. Both the allowance granted to each student and the salary of the masters were carefully fixed, to avoid any argument. On 5 December 1340,[2] the pope completed the Bull of 20 June 1336; he explained certain points of detail which had not been understood or were obscure and he defined the rules that were to govern the holding of chapters. The whole Benedictine order was affected by the pope's reforms; in every province, by virtue of the apostolic authority, abbots summoned their chapters willy-nilly; commissaries-extraordinary curbed the luxury, extortion and debauchery which were bringing dishonour on the sons of St Benedict.

The elevation of Jacques Fournier to the papal throne had revived the hopes of the fraticelli who knew of the severity and even austerity of his personal life. Their hopes were dashed. In the Consistory of 23 December 1334[3] in the presence of the Generals of the great orders, Benedict XII severely criticised the conduct of the Franciscans. He reproached them harshly for their heretical tendencies, revolutionary spirit, contempt for the official Church and relaxation of discipline. On the other hand, he praised the purity of the Dominicans' faith and went so far as to declare that St Dominic's was the 'head' of all the other orders. This rebuke should have been enough to damp the ardour of the fraticelli; but they came to Avignon in great numbers and took the liberty of criticising the cardinals. The Bull

[1] Cocquelines, *loc. cit.* pp. 214–40.
[2] *Ibid.* pp. 288–91.   [3] Jacob, *op. cit.* p. 33.

Redemptor noster of 28 November 1336 [1] took away their last illusions: it condemned the fraticelli and all holders of doctrines suspected of heresy; prescribed for all Franciscans constant attendance at the divine office; insisted on uniformity of dress on pain of excommunication; and decreed, amongst other things, that novices should be trained in certain houses only and not in every convent. The new Constitution was promulgated at the chapter-general held at Cahors in June 1337 with Guiral Ot, the minister-general, presiding; it was put into force and had considerable influence on the subsequent legislation of the order.[2]

The Canons Regular living under the rule of St Augustine also had their share in the reforms. The Bull of 15 May 1339 [3] contains lengthy regulations intended for them, modelled on those already given to the Benedictines.

The only order to oppose the will of Benedict was precisely the one whose praises he had sung most loudly, the Dominican order. The chapters-general of London, Bruges and Valence, fearing the results of the application of the Constitution *Pastor bonus,* had used all their ingenuity to create as many obstacles as possible to prevent 'apostate' mendicants from entering the order of St Dominic, that is to say the wandering monks who had left their convents without their superiors' permission. Benedict XII summoned the General, Hugues de Vaucemain, to appear before him at Avignon, and there urged him to leave to the pope the business of administering the order and modifying its constitutions. Experience had proved that the observation of communal poverty was no longer practicable: begging had become less and less rewarding; the convents were reduced to bare necessities and able neither to feed their own brethren nor to maintain students at the universities. To relieve their distress, the friars made personal appeals for alms, and some were so successful in rousing the sympathy of the faithful by their appearance or their pleas, that with their well-filled begging bowls they could live a life of luxury little suited to their rule. By a strange anomaly, to quote the original remark of Father Mortier, 'Poverty remained communal and wealth became personal.' It is not difficult to realise how shocking such an unremittingly austere Cistercian as Benedict XII found this state of affairs, against which the chapters had legislated in vain. The pope's plan was simple: to do away with communal poverty, which was not essential to the rule and had only been introduced because it was con-

[1] Cocquelines, *loc. cit.* pp. 242–58.
[2] F. Schmitt, *Benoît XII et l'ordre des Frères Mineurs* (thèse de doctorat manuscrite soutenue à Strasbourg en 1956).   [3] Cocquelines, *loc. cit.* pp. 264–86.

sidered a means of attaining the apostolic life. The General, on the other hand, thought that it would be sufficient to concede partial authorisations, in accordance with the legal recommendations of Pierre de la Palud. He replied to Benedict's proposals with a firm demurrer. From that time a struggle began between the pope and the order, which was to last for five years. The meetings for discussion were sometimes so lively that the pope had attacks of fever, or so Galvano Fiamma alleges. When Hugues de Vaucemain died, Benedict hoped that he would at last see his views prevail; but he found that the other dignitaries of the order were just as implacably opposed to him as the late General. In vain did he hold certain friars prisoner, forbid chapter meetings, refuse to allow the election of a new General: he could not succeed in overcoming their obstinate resistance. The struggle only ended with the death of Benedict XII.[1]

Although Benedict XII is especially remembered in history for the reforms he imposed on the religious orders, the secular clergy were not forgotten. It is true that they appear less frequently in the papal registers; but this is because abuses were at that time less frequent among them than in the cloister. Numerous synods were held between 1334 and 1342.[2] On 18 May 1335, Benedict revoked all grants *in commendam*, and, on 18 December, all expectative graces granted until his time.[3] He insisted upon residence, and settled the conditions for admission to the canonicate.[4] One of his most salutary measures was the Constitution *Vas electionis*,[5] in which he fixed for a long time to come the maximum rate of procurations, that is, of those pecuniary dues levied on holders of benefices by bishops and minor prelates, abbots, archdeacons, archpriests or deans, at the time of a visitation. He gave his most powerful support to education, founding a university at Grenoble and promulgating new statutes for the Faculty of Law at Montpellier; in Italy he tried to set up a university at Verona and elsewhere he often intervened on behalf of students or teachers.[6]

Benedict XII seems to have been an energetic reformer. Before making any laws, he ordered enquiries and obtained the advice of competent persons. He was well informed of abuses, and in order

---

[1] Mortier, *Histoire des maîtres généraux de l'ordre des Frères Prêcheurs*, VOL. III, Paris 1907, pp. 87–167. The reform introduced into the order of Fontevrault should also be noted. Cf. Daumet, nos. 22, 23, 233, 265, 505, 913; Vidal, nos. 3994, 5047, 5165, etc.
[2] Hefele-Leclercq, *Histoire des Conciles*, VOL. VI, pp. 833–68.
[3] Vidal, nos. 2447, 2454.   [4] Daumet, nos. 667, 896. Vidal, no. 9149.
[5] *Corpus juris canonici. Extravagantes communes*, Bk III, tit. x, col. 1.
[6] Denifle, *Die Entstehung der Universitäten des Mittelalters bis 1400*, VOL. I, Berlin 1885, pp. 351, 354, 565, 634. Vidal, nos. 5122, 5123, 5166, 6265, 7416, 7435, 7438, 7539, etc.

to abolish them made decrees dealing with every minute detail. But to decree a reform is not to carry it out. We are therefore entitled to enquire whether the reforming work of Benedict XII was effective.

The 'Benedictine Bull' had the force of law until the Council of Trent. This Council also deleted from the statutes of the Dominican order the mendicancy that the pope had sought to suppress. By compelling the friars to study theology, which had rather fallen out of favour, was he not providing the Church with those who would defend the faith against the attacks of heresy? The measures against the Spirituals and the fraticelli bore fruit; the stake reduced the fanatics to silence, for the Inquisition pursued them relentlessly.[1]

Yet despite his efforts, the reformation attempted by Benedict XII only had limited results. The pope's reign did not last long enough to ensure the success of his work. His best reforms were more or less nullified by the extreme favour shown by Clement VI who all too readily granted dispensations to the religious orders.[2] For this reason, those reforms that were not abrogated were very quickly forgotten.

Benedict XII was himself a little responsible for these set-backs, because of the minute attention given to detail in his reforms, especially in those concerned with monastic organisation. He drew up a code of laws too complicated to be really effective. He increased penal sanctions against transgressors to an absurd extent and he placed an unbearable burden upon the monks. In ordering the meeting of chapters, he did not think of the expenses that would be incurred; and unfortunately the times were hard, and poverty reigned more often than prosperity in the cloister: war, pestilence and famine were soon to take their toll of the monasteries. Although he revoked all grants *in commendam*, he excepted the cardinals from the Constitution.[3] Yet it was they who, because of their exalted position, were best enabled to seize benefices and, as history bears ample witness, were the most avid to seek them. Although he curbed the excessive use of expectative graces, he extended the Holy See's reservation[4] to include a greater number of benefices than his predecessors, and thus was in danger of seeing the reappearance of the very expectative graces that he was rebuking. Finally, though he declared himself to be the restorer of morals among the clergy, he was regrettably lax in

---

[1] C. Douais, *La procédure inquisitoriale en Languedoc au XIVe siècle d'après un procès inédit de l'année 1337*, Paris 1900; F. Ehrle, 'Die Spiritualen, ihr Verhältniss zum Franziskanerorden und zu den Fraticellen,' *Archiv*, VOL. IV, 1888, pp. 1–190.

[2] U. Berlière, 'Les Chapitres généraux de l'ordre de St Benoît,' *Mélanges d'hist. bénédictine*, VOL. IV, Maredsous 1902, pp. 161–7; *Notes supplémentaires*, Bruges 1905, pp. 20–1. Déprez, no. 154.   [3] Vidal, nos. 2319, 2447.

[4] Vidal nos. 2417, 2418, 3984, 3985, 8178.

allowing bastards to take holy orders and seek their fortune in the Church.[1]

Seldom has any pope been more abused. His contemporaries accused him of avarice, hardness of heart, obstinacy, egoism and lack of generosity in the distribution of his favours. They reproached him with showing unmerited suspicion of his cardinals, hatred towards the mendicant orders and favouritism towards inferiors, whose part he would take against their superiors. Petrarch, in descriptions of Avignon that are doubtless fanciful, depicts Benedict XII laughed to scorn by a licentious court and greeted with jeers by his own entourage. In his *Epistles*, the guests at sumptuous feasts mock at the pope's abstinence. One chronicler depicts him as weak and characterless, always weeping and groaning. Peter of Hérenthals inserts in his chronicle an epigram of the day that is very uncomplimentary to the pontiff's memory:

> *Iste fuit Nero, laicis mors, vipera clero,*
> *Devius a vero, cuppa repleta mero.*[2]

Against these malicious anecdotes must be placed the accounts of other chroniclers who are full of praise for Benedict. They extol his austerity, his high-minded honesty, his sense of justice, his genius for reform, his hatred of heresy and his horror of nepotism.

It is not too difficult to disentangle the truth from such contradictory verdicts. In the first place, the evidence of Petrarch, Matthias von Neuenburg, Galvano Fiamma and the anonymous author of the eighth *Life* of Benedict XII edited by Baluze bears the mark of obvious prejudice. These clever men were only too pleased to feed the bitterness of the Italians, of the supporters of Louis of Bavaria and of the host of monks and parasites at the papal court who had let out cries of rage at the pope's innovations. Benedict shared the lot of every austere reformer. He was not greatly loved; on the contrary, he was decried, hated and libelled. He died, as he had been elected, at about the hour of vespers, on 25 April 1342.

Tall, with a high colour and a resonant voice; a good theologian, skilful in canon law and a respected commentator of Scripture;[3] a man with a high sense both of duty and of justice; energetic, tenacious, determined to put down abuses; unmoved by family affection,[4]

---

[1] See e.g. Vidal, nos. 1715–2088.
[2] Baluze, *op. cit.* p. 234. Contemporary comments have been collected by Jacob, *op. cit.* pp. 30–1, 154–5, and by Haller, *Papsttum und Kirchenreform*, VOL. I, pp. 121–3, 155.
[3] Vidal, 'Notice sur les œuvres du pape Benoît XII,' see above, p. 28, *n.* 1.
[4] On the family of Benedict XII, see Vidal, *Note sur la parenté du pape Benoît XII*, Foix 1929.

austere in his personal life, economical, and fond of restraint in art;[1] this was the real Benedict XII. As for his politics, though not as feeble as has been alleged, they lacked vision. His unbending character made him little inclined to compromise in that complicated game. As we shall see, only set-backs can be put to his account in this field.

[1] Guiraud, *L'Église romaine*, pp. 26–7. M. Cerruti, 'Il tetto della basilica Vaticana rifatto per opera di Benedetto XII,' *Mélanges*, VOL. XXXV, 1915, pp. 81–118. Dr Colombe, 'Les Grands Architectes du palais des papes à Avignon,' *Bulletin archéologique*, 1920, pp. 427–48. F. Pasquier, 'Un Mirapicien, architecte du palais des papes en Avignon,' *Bulletin périodique de la Société ariégeoise des sciences, lettres et arts*, VOL. XVI, 1923, pp. 54–6.

CHAPTER IV

Clement VI 1342-52

As soon as Philip VI received news of the death of Benedict XII, which had occurred on 25 April, he sent his eldest son to Avignon, charged, so certain chroniclers allege, with supporting the candidature of Pierre Roger, archbishop of Rouen. The duke of Normandy arrived too late to carry out his commission. The cardinals had gone into conclave on 3 May and had voted unanimously for Pierre Roger; according to Annibale di Ceccano and Raimond de Farges in their letters to Edward III, the election had been made on 7 May, 'by divine inspiration alone.'[1]

The choice made by the Sacred College was excellent in many respects. The archbishop of Rouen[2] had acquired a well-deserved reputation as an able theologian and was considered one of the finest orators of his day. At the assembly of Vincennes in 1329, his eloquent defence of ecclesiastical jurisdiction, which had been violently attacked by Pierre de Cugnières, made a favourable and lively impression on Philip VI. Favoured by Philip, who counted him among his councillors, and also by Edward III, whose subject he was by birth, this prelate seemed the very man to prevent a disastrous war between France and England.

The cardinals, however, had had other reasons for their choice. They were weary of the rigid, austere, autocratic government of Benedict XII, and had considered the opposite qualities that characterised Pierre Roger—his urbanity and gentleness, his pliant temperament and aristocratic airs. They hoped that under him they would enjoy a tolerant, easy-going and bountiful régime.

---

[1] Rymer, *Foedera*, VOL. II, pt 2, p. 123.
[2] The various stages in Clement VI's career are as follows: he was born in 1291 at Masmonteil, near Égletons (Corrèze), of Guillaume Roger, lord of Rosières, and Guillemette de Mestre; he entered the Benedictine monastery of Chaise-Dieu in 1301, and made his profession there. By special favour, John XXII conferred on him the mastership and the licenciate in theology on 23 May 1323. He was appointed prior of St Pantaléon (Corrèze) in 1321, and became prior of Savigny in the diocese of Lyons, prior of St Baudil in the diocese of Nîmes (24 April 1324), abbot of Fécamp (23 June 1326), bishop of Arras (3 Dec. 1328), archbishop of Sens (24 Nov. 1329), archbishop of Rouen (14 Dec. 1330) and cardinal-priest of St Neraeus and Achilleus (18 Dec. 1338). See Denifle and Chatelain, *Chartularium universitatis Parisiensis*, VOL. II, Paris 1891, p. 272.

Poor clerics seeking benefices, who had been driven from Avignon in the previous pontificate, felt their hopes rising anew. As Pentecost drew near, they were invited to present their pleas during the following two months. As may be expected, the call was quickly heard: a tidal wave of petitioners—a hundred thousand according to an eye-witness, the chronicler Peter of Hérenthals [1]—came flooding into Avignon. In order to distribute expectative graces generously among them, Clement VI had to abuse his right of reservation of benefices, to the great detriment of those conferring them in the ordinary way. Indeed, bishops were reduced to begging for the authorisation to confer benefices in their own dioceses. Such a one was the bishop of Geneva, who 'can no longer confer a single benefice because of the great number of those who put themselves forward armed with apostolic expectatives.' [2] It is significant that in this instance the pope confessed that he was himself overwhelmed with demands; he apologised, but granted the bishop only a limited permission. The repetition of similar incidents soon produced disquiet in the Church, characterised by a weakening of the power of the bishops and slackness in ecclesiastical discipline. It showed, too, how far the centralisation of the Church had increased. In 1344 Clement VI proclaimed that 'plenary powers of disposal of all churches, dignities, offices and ecclesiastical benefices are vested in the Roman pontiff.' [3] Careerists saw only too clearly the logical conclusion of this: since everything depended on the sovereign will of the pope, the surest way for them to acquire office in the Church was to seek their fortune at the court of Avignon and to gain favour with powerful protectors.

Clement VI was accustomed to live like a lord, and had modelled his conduct upon an emperor's maxim that 'No-one should go out from the prince's presence discontented,' and another saying that 'A pontiff should make his subjects happy.' [4] If he was reproached for his generosity, he used to say, 'My predecessors did not know how to be popes.' [5] These principles led him into dangerous ways beginning with the squandering of the wealth amassed by the parsimonious Benedict XII. The completion of the papal palace, the reconstruction of the abbey of Chaise-Dieu [6] at a cost of about 30,000 florins, the purchase of Avignon in 1348 at the stipulated price of 80,000 florins,[7] the upkeep of a luxurious court, and considerable loans to successive

[1] Baluze, *Vitae*, VOL. I, new ed. pp. 276, 298.
[2] Gräff, 'Clément VI et la province de Vienne,' *Bulletin de l'Académie delphinale*, ser. 5, VOL. II, 1908, p. 100.
[3] Rinaldi, *ad annum* 1344, §55.   [4] Baluze, *op. cit.* p. 275.
[5] *Ibid.* p. 298.   [6] Faucon, *Documents*, p. 4.
[7] J.-B. Christophe, *Histoire de la papauté pendant le XIVe siècle*, Paris 1853, VOL. II, pp. 467–71.

kings of France and the lords of southern France [1]—all these depleted the finances of the Holy See. By an unfortunate coincidence, the deficit occurred at a time when the revolt of the citizens of Bologna, the activities of Bernabo Visconti and the insurrection of the Papal States all called for vigorous intervention in Italy. Clement sought to remedy the disaster by bringing pressure to bear on the French clergy, who were already sorely tried by the Hundred Years' War. The income from taxes levied on Christendom was not sufficient to restore the balance of the papal budget. The deficit caused by Clement's imprudence was never restored in his lifetime, and the future, too, was burdened with very heavy charges. Innocent VI, Urban V and Gregory XI all groaned under the appalling financial situation they had inherited. The financial measures that they were obliged to take caused estrangement from their subjects: nearly all the responsibility for this rests with the extravagant Clement.

Apart from a few members of the clergy, his contemporaries did not find fault with his ostentatious way of life; indeed, so generous a pope seems to have been much admired. His court was the most civilised in Europe, the haunt of the highest nobility, enlivened with feasts, balls and tournaments. The finest figures of the time were to be found there: painters from Italy and Germany, French sculptors and architects, poets and men of letters, physicians, doctors and astronomers. A commission of scholars met in 1344 to try to reform the Julian Calendar. Jean des Murs and Firmin de Beauval (or d'Amiens), had come to Avignon. Long discussions took place and memoranda were prepared: special attention was paid to the Golden Number. Although the commission broke up without having found any practical means of rectifying the errors in the Calendar the initiative that had set it up was most praiseworthy.[2]

The festivities for which his court provided the setting did not make Clement VI unmindful of his duties as pontiff. He took pleasure in presiding at religious ceremonies, in preaching to his people and making speeches in memorable circumstances. His charity was boundless when the Black Death depopulated Europe in 1348 and again in 1349. This sickness had come from China by three different routes: by India, the Caspian Sea and Asia Minor; by Bokhara, Tartary and Constantinople; and by Baghdad, Arabia, Egypt and

---

[1] 592,000 florins and 5,000 crowns were advanced to the king of France between 26 November 1345 and the end of February 1350 (M. Faucon, in *B.E.C.* VOL. XL, 1879, p. 571). The count of Comminges borrowed 32,000 florins (A. Clergeac in *Revue de Gascogne*, VOL. V, 1905, p. 308).

[2] E. Déprez, 'Une Tentative de réforme du calendrier sous Clément VI . . . ,' *Mélanges*, VOL. XIX, 1899, pp. 131–43.

Africa. It was introduced into Italy by vessels which had put into the islands of the Archipelago; it devastated Florence, crossed the Alps, attacked France and gained a hold in Belgium, Holland, England, Denmark, Sweden and Norway, and as far as Iceland and Greenland. It is estimated that about forty million people died in this horrible epidemic.

Avignon suffered greatly from the Black Death. Our information concerning this critical time is derived from the memoirs of Guy de Chauliac, physician in the service of Clement VI. The sickness ravaged the town for seven months and manifested itself successively in two characteristic forms. The first showed itself in a persistent fever, accompanied by the spitting of blood: 'Men died of it in three days.' This form was particularly prevalent in the first two months and proved highly infectious. The other form which succeeded it, also caused fever, but was accompanied by 'abscesses and carbuncles in the external parts, chiefly in the arm-pit and groin; and men died of it in five days.' [1] On 27 April 1348, Louis Sanctus of Beeringen, Petrarch's beloved friend, wrote to his correspondents at Bruges that more than half the population of Avignon had died, and that more than seven thousand houses were shut up. In the cemetery bought by the pope, eleven thousand dead were buried between 14 March and 27 April. Since 25 January death had claimed a total of sixty-two thousand inhabitants. [2] Guy de Chauliac agrees with Louis Sanctus in his description of the wretched conditions in which the people of Avignon died. 'The people died without servants and were buried without priests. The father visited not his son, nor the son his father. Charity was dead, and hope cast down.' [3] The contagion was so much dreaded that the population was crazed by fear. As Boccaccio wrote, 'Men were infected by touching the sick, but it was not necessary even to touch them. The danger was the same if one were within range of their words or only cast one's eye upon them.' [4]

Clement VI remained at Avignon and was lavish in the distribution of benefits. He engaged doctors to care for the sick; carters and grave-diggers in his employ carried off the dead and buried them. Severe police measures prevented the infection from spreading further. Special indulgences encouraged the priests and the faithful to devote themselves to the service of those stricken by the plague. [5] The pope also instituted a special mass to implore an ending to the scourge. [6]

[1] E. Nicaise, *La Grande Chirurgie de Guy de Chauliac*, Paris 1890, p. 170.
[2] De Smet, *Recueil des chroniques de Flandre*, VOL. III, Brussels 1856, pp. 14–18.
[3] Nicaise, *op. cit.* p. 170.   [4] *Decameron*, Bk I.
[5] Baluze, *op. cit.* pp. 251, 284.
[6] J. Viard, ' La Messe pour la peste,' *B.E.C.* VOL. LXI, 1900, pp. 334–8.

People's minds were stricken with terror and very soon began to go astray: they attributed the plague to the sorcery of the Jews and accused them, as they had done in 1321, of poisoning the wells and springs where Christians drew their water. A dreadful persecution broke out against them. Popular fury handed them over to the stake in thousands, at Strasbourg, Mainz, Speyer, Worms, Oppenheim and many other places. Clement VI was perturbed, and took the Jews under his protection, declaring that anyone molesting them would be excommunicated (4 July and 26 September 1348).[1] What is more, those fleeing from persecution found a kindly welcome in his territories.[2]

In the hope of appeasing the divine wrath, bands of fanatics formed in Swabia, claiming that they could bring about the cessation of the pestilence by flagellations lasting for thirty-three and a half days. At the end of this time, the soul was judged to be cleansed of its impurity and to be once more in a state of baptismal innocence. This popular movement, developed by ill-informed piety, spread rapidly from the month of June 1349. Germany was overrun by bands of *flagellantes*. These fanatics, stripped of their garments to the waist, prostrated themselves in turn, face downwards with their arms stretched out in the form of a cross, while their companions walked round them in a circle. At a word of command, using whips whose thongs were provided with four iron spikes, they lacerated their bodies till they drew blood. After this, they all prostrated themselves on the ground in the form of a cross, saying strange prayers, sobbing and imploring divine mercy to come down upon the world. Then at another signal the flaggellations began again.

These fanatics were scarcely dangerous at first, but eventually became a public menace. Their blind zeal led them to acts of pillage and to persecution of the Jews; they threatened ecclesiastical property, shook off the authority of the Church and despised the ordinary means of salvation. When they reached Avignon, Clement VI, frightened at the revolutionary movement they were provoking, solemnly condemned them and ordered bishops and princes to dissolve existing associations and to imprison those who were recalcitrant (20 October 1349).[3] Most of the flagellants dispersed and were reconciled with the Church; those who persisted in their error died at the stake or languished in prison cells.

In the political field Clement VI showed qualities of the first order.

---

[1] Rinaldi, *ad annum* 1348, §33.
[2] L. Bardinet, 'La Condition civile des Juifs du Comtat-Venaissin pendant le séjour des papes d'Avignon (1309–1376),' *Revue historique*, VOL. XII, 1880, pp. 18–23.
[3] Rinaldi, *ad annum* 1349, §18–22.

The Hundred Years' War had compelled Benedict XII to abandon the dream long cherished by John XXII, of sending the French royal house to conquer the East. Clement made no attempt to take it up again, but this did not cause him to abandon the idea of a crusade. He evolved a bold plan by deciding to form a naval league between the Latin peoples of the East and the Venetians, against the Turkish corsairs which were infesting the Archipelago. He then proposed to take advantage of the weakness of the Greeks and Armenians to lead them to seek the alliance of the Latin league and to abandon their schism. The first part of this vast plan was begun. After laborious negotiations in the course of which Clement VI showed his qualities of patience and cunning, a league was made between the papacy, the Venetians, the king of Cyprus and the Knights Hospitallers. The capture of Smyrna on 28 October 1344 and the victory at Imbros in 1347 swept the Turkish corsairs from the Archipelago. The attempts at reunion with the schismatics were on the point of succeeding. Unfortunately, however, Clement VI did not succeed in carrying out the whole of his programme; the fault is not his, but must be attributed to the rivalry between the peoples of Genoa and Venice, as well as to the incompetence and indecision of the dauphin of Vienne.[1]

The fine qualities of diplomacy that Clement VI had thus displayed in the East were equally in evidence in the West. It was owing to his efforts that the war between France and England was broken off several times. The quarrel that had for so long caused disunion between the Papacy and the Empire came to an end soon after the death of Louis of Bavaria.

The pope died at Avignon on Thursday, 6 December 1352. Though he had suffered for some years from gravel, his death was caused by the rupture of an internal growth. He did not therefore meet his end as a result of a shameful disease brought on by the dissolute life that Matteo Villani, Matthias von Neuenburg and the monk of Melsa [2] gratuitously accuse him of having led.

A somewhat embarrassing account of Clement VI has, however, come down to us: that of Petrarch. 'I speak,' he says, 'of things seen, not merely heard.' [3] He attributed the most lascivious remarks to the pope which, if they were really made, would leave no doubt as to his illicit love-affairs. Some time ago Bartoli and later Piur made extracts of numerous passages in the works of Petrarch which form an over-

---

[1] J. Gay, *Le Pape Clément VI et les affaires d'Orient (1342–1352)*, Paris 1904.
[2] Matteo Villani, *Istorie fiorentine*, Bk II, ch. iv; Böhmer, *Fontes*, VOL. IV, p. 227; *Chronicon de Melsa*, VOL. III, p. 89.
[3] Epistle XIV (no title), in *Opera omnia*, Basle edition, 1581, p. 723.

whelming indictment of the morals of Clement VI.[1] In 1905, Douet used the same texts as sources for an historical novel, *Au temps de Pétrarque*, depicting the loose morals of the supreme pontiff and the vices of his chamberlains.

However positive Petrarch may be in his statements, he was not really in a position to censure the pope's conduct. His accusations must be considered unjust and unlikely. His avowed antagonism towards the Avignon popes provides the historian with a cogent reason for doubting the truth of his unsavoury anecdotes. In Clement VI he hated one who had been able to shed an unrivalled lustre on the Avignon papacy. He was so blinded by his hatred as to be unable to form a rational judgment of the leaders of the Church. As has been said,[2] 'The only people likely to believe him are those actuated by hatred of the papacy.'

Petrarch's conduct, moreover, seems incompatible with the feelings he expressed on the subject of the Avignon popes. If he despised them, why did he seek their favours? Why did he remain at a court whose morals caused him such horror? He ought logically to have fled from it.

Petrarch, indeed, seems to take pleasure in providing us with the means to attack him. He has written concerning Clement VI, of whom he spoke so ill: 'Clemens VI, egregius nunc Romulei gregis pastor, tam potentis et invictae memoriae traditur ut quidquid vel semel legerit oblivisci, etiam si cupiat, non possit. . . .'[3] We may well be surprised at such language. If Clement VI was really given up to immorality, as the Florentine poet alleges, he could not have been 'egregius . . . pastor.'

---

[1] Bartoli, *Storia della letteratura italiana*, VOL. VII, Florence 1884, pp. 85–112; P. Piur, *Petrarchas Buch ohne Namen und die päpstliche Kurie*, Halle 1925.
[2] R. Delachenal, *Histoire de Charles V*, VOL. III, Paris 1916, p. 494.
[3] *De rebus memorabilibus*, Bk II, ch. i.

CHAPTER V

Innocent VI 1352–62

ON 16 December 1352, the cardinals, twenty-five in number, withdrew to the rooms placed at their disposal in the papal palace at Avignon. They were anxious to take advantage of the modifications that Clement VI had made to the Constitution *Ubi periculum* which had regulated the holding of conclaves since 1274. They had curtains round their beds while they rested, and two members of their household, clerk or layman, to attend upon them. Their bill of fare was henceforward to include, at dinner and supper, as well as bread and wine, a dish of meat, fish or eggs, meat or vegetable soup, hors-d'œuvre, cheese, fruit and electuaries.[1] The Sacred College did not benefit from these concessions: on Tuesday 18 December at the hour of terce, Étienne Aubert was proclaimed pope, with the name of Innocent VI.

The election had not been uneventful. The candidature of Jean Birel, a native of Limoges, had been much discussed. Though venerated for his holiness, this worthy General of the Carthusians was not a suitable man to rule the Church; to choose him would have been to repeat the mistake made by the conclave in 1294 in electing Celestine V. Cardinal Talleyrand de Périgord succeeded in convincing his colleagues that in the critical circumstances prevailing in Europe, it would be unwise, if not actually dangerous, to appoint a second Pietro da Morrone as pope. This seemed sound advice and was accepted by the conclave.[2]

The Sacred College, yielding to oligarchic tendencies, and wishing perhaps to restrict papal power which was becoming more extensive every day, seized the opportunity of the conclave to work out a compromise. This compromise some of the members swore merely to observe, while others prudently inserted into their oath the following restrictive clause: *si et in quantum scriptura hujusmodi de jure procederet*. It was agreed that in no case should the number of cardinals

---

[1] Cocquelines, *Bullarum*, VOL. III, pt 2, p. 313; Constitution *Licet in constitutione*, 6 December 1351.

[2] Martène and Durand, *Veterum scriptorum*, VOL. VI, Paris 1729, p. 187. Souchon (*Die Papstwahlen*, pp. 55–66) has indicated that the speech attributed to Talleyrand de Périgord during the conclave is unlikely to have been delivered.

44

be more than twenty. The future pope undertook not to create any more until the present number had been reduced to sixteen. Cardinals were only to be chosen by the consent of all the survivors, or at least by a two-thirds majority. No cardinal was to be deposed or imprisoned without the unanimous approval of the Sacred College. A two-thirds majority would be sufficient to pronounce sentence of excommunication or ecclesiastical censure against him, to suspend his right to vote in a papal election, to take part in Consistories and to wear a red hat, to decree his temporary or permanent loss of benefices and seizure of goods before or after death. The same majority would be required to transfer, surrender or grant in fee-tail or for payment of rent the provinces, towns, fortified castles and lands belonging to the Roman Church; likewise, to appoint or dismiss the high officers of the court and of the Papal States. The offices of the marshal of the court and the rectors of the Church provinces were not to pass into the hands of a relative or ally of the reigning pontiff. The approval of the Sacred College was to be necessary to levy tenths or subsidies from kings or princes, or to deduct taxes from the clergy for the benefit of the Apostolic Camera. The latter was to hand over half its revenues to the treasury of the College in accordance with the terms of the regulation made in 1289 by Nicholas IV. Lastly, the cardinals were to be entirely free to express their opinions and to give their approval in the conduct of affairs.[1]

The conclave might have gone on for longer, had they not feared that the king of France might interfere in the election. Accordingly agreement was quickly reached on the person of the Limousin Étienne Aubert, a native of the village of Les Monts, near Pompadour. He was a lawyer of note, renowned for his teaching at the University of Toulouse. He was known to have the approval of the king of France, in whose name he had carried out the important duties of the *juge-mage* of the seneschal's court of Toulouse. He had been bishop of Noyon (23 January 1338) and Clermont (11 October 1340), and was elevated to the dignity of cardinal with the title of St John and St Paul on 20 September 1342, becoming bishop of Ostia and Villetri on 13 February 1352, and finally Grand Penitentiary.

The new pope was advanced in years, of a sickly disposition [2] and a rather wavering and impressionable personality, easily depressed,[3] and of a somewhat vacillating character. No doubt the Sacred College hoped to mould him easily to its wishes. This hope, however, was

---

[1] Cocquelines, *op. cit.* VOL. III, pt 2, pp. 316–18; Constitution *Sollicitudo pastoralis*, annulling the general sense of the compromise.
[2] His health caused anxiety at the French court from the time of his accession. See E. Déprez, *Innocent VI*, no. 4.   [3] *Studi storici*, VOL. XII, 1903, p. 331.

disappointed. On 6 July 1353 Innocent freed himself from the oath he had made to the conclave. He declared the oath null as being contrary to the *Decretals* of Gregory X and Clement V, which had forbidden the cardinals to deal with any other business except the election while the Holy See was vacant.[1] He did, however, grant the cardinals a slight compensation by allowing them to reserve certain dignities in both cathedrals and collegiate churches, secular and regular.[2]

Innocent VI was upright, just and animated by the best intentions; he upheld the traditions of Benedict XII and adopted salutary measures of reform. The clergy who had been drawn to Avignon by Clement VI's generosity soon took themselves off for fear of incurring excommunication for not residing in their benefices.[3] No-one could obtain an ecclesiastical charge without supplying real evidence of learning and merit. Those who were affected complained. 'This same Pope Innocent,' one chronicler declares, 'was harsh to the clerks, and it was for this that learning was in great wise diminished at Paris and elsewhere in his time, for he wished to grant no benefices to the clerks or to those who deserved them.' [4]

Scholarship was dear to this former professor of law. Innocent founded the college of St Martial at Toulouse and a Faculty of Theology at Bologna.[5]

The pope exercised his reforming zeal on various religious orders. His relations with the Franciscans in particular were very stormy. We can follow their course in the language used by St Bridget in speaking of Innocent VI. At first she had been full of enthusiasm at the election of this pontiff. 'Pope Innocent,' she wrote, 'is of sounder metal than his predecessors, and of a substance fit to receive the finest colours.' But as he began to take progressively more severe measures against the Spirituals and the fraticelli, the Swedish princess's writings show a diminution of praise, which gives place to bitter criticism. Even the death of the pope does not mollify her: 'Pope Innocent,' she says at this time, 'has been more abominable than the Jewish usurers, more treacherous than Judas, more cruel than Pilate; he has devoured the sheep and slain the true shepherds; and now at last, for all his crimes (Christ) has cast him into the pit, like a heavy stone, and has condemned his cardinals to be consumed by the same fire that devoured Sodom.' [6]

[1] See p. 9, *n.* 1 above.   [2] E. Déprez, *Innocent VI*, no. 267.
[3] Baluze, *Vitae*, VOL. I, new ed. pp. 343, 347.
[4] *Annuaire-Bulletin*, VOL. XX, 1883, p. 255.
[5] Fournier, *Les Statuts et privilèges des universités françaises*, VOL. I, Paris 1890, nos. 612–55. Cocquelines, *Bullarum*, VOL. III, pt 2, p. 323.
[6] *Revelationes*, Bk IV, ch. cxxxvi.

Indeed, on every hand the Inquisition was set in motion against the fanatical Franciscans, and tracked them down without mercy. At Avignon two friars died at the stake. Jean de Roquetaillade, another Franciscan from the convent of Aurillac, who had been incarcerated in the papal prison in the time of Clement VI, prophesied like a true disciple of Joachim of Flora. He recounted his prophetic visions and apocalyptic dreams in a book, the *Vade mecum in tribulatione*, and proclaimed a kind of modified millenarianism.[1] Falling into the error of the Spirituals, he virulently castigated the morals of the clergy and foretold that they would lose their property.[2] Innocent did no more than order this visionary to be put into confinement.

The Franciscans had not forgotten, either, that in the Consistory of 8 November 1357 the pope had listened to the archbishop of Armagh, Richard Fitz-Ralph, fulminating in the name of the clergy of Britain against the mendicant orders, attacking their privileges, and objecting to their encroachment on curial rights. Innocent, as it happened, made no pronouncement on the matter; he ordered both the archbishop and the mendicants, who had hastened to defend their cause, to be silent, and had the case examined by a commission of cardinals. The storm that threatened the English Franciscans only abated with the death of their spirited adversary. The chronicler spitefully adds that on the day that Richard Fitz-Ralph died the monks sang *Gaudeamus* rather than *Requiem*.[3]

Towards the middle of the fourteenth century the Dominicans had fallen into complete decadence. In an effort to increase the numbers in the convents decimated by the Black Death, local priors had encouraged the recruitment of novices by mitigating on their own authority the austerity of the rule. Poverty was no longer observed, and continual breaches of discipline had spread a spirit of insubordination among the members of the order. No longer able to enforce discipline and at the end of his tether, the General, Simon de Langres, had recourse to the Holy See. In 1360 Bulls were issued ordering the definitors of the chapter of Perpignan to visit the various houses of the order and to compel the friars, under pain of censure, to reveal existing abuses. Friars who boasted of their title of honorary chaplain to the pope in order to claim exemption from the jurisdiction of their superiors and to elude the observance of the rule,

---

[1] E. Brown, *Fasciculus rerum expetendarum et fugiendarum*, VOL. II, London 1690, pp. 494–508.
[2] F. Kampers, in *Historisches Jahrbuch*, VOL. XV, 1894, pp. 796–802.
[3] Baluze, *op. cit.* pp. 324, 337. In 1357, the archbishop of Armagh wrote a *Defensorium curatorum contra eos qui privilegiatos se dicunt*. See E. Brown, *op. cit.* VOL. II, pp. 466–86.

were told that the honours they enjoyed gave them no privileges, and that if they were recalcitrant, they ran the risk of imprisonment.

Infuriated by the reforms that Simon de Langres sought to impose on them with the help of the papacy, eight out of the fourteen definitors deposed him. When Innocent VI learned of this, he put Cardinal Francesco degli Atti in charge of an enquiry. On 22 June 1361, he reinstated Simon de Langres in his office and promised him support for his reform.[1]

The pope's relations with the Hospitallers were equally difficult. There had already long existed a strong party at the papal court that was very hostile to the Knights. They were upbraided for their slackness and lack of zeal against the infidel, for their luxury and their ill-used wealth. In 1343 Clement VI had threatened the Grand Master, Hélion de Villeneuve, that he would transfer the property of the Hospitallers to a new, more active and zealous order. On 24 August 1354, Innocent, who shared the prejudices of his entourage, warned the Grand Master, Pierre de Corneillan, to expect the arrival of a mission led by the Knight Juan Fernandez de Heredia, and instructed the nuncios to set forth the complaints of the Holy See against the order and the measures decreed for its improvement. The transfer of the convent at Rhodes to Turkish territory was to take place without delay, otherwise the Templars' property, previously added to that of the Hospitallers, would be handed over to a new order. On his own authority, the pope summoned a chapter-general to meet at Avignon. It accepted all that was imposed on it, including very severe disciplinary reforms, the suppression of the office of regional commander, and considerable restrictions on the Grand Master's prerogative.

But Innocent changed his mind. Under the pressure of Heredia, whose ambition it was to become Master, the pope gave up his plan of transferring the headquarters of the Hospitallers to Turkey and had some idea of causing the Knights to buy the Principality of Achaia. What was more, in order to overcome any opposition, he endowed the adventurer Heredia with the priory of St Gilles. Roger de Pins, the Grand Master, sent ambassadors to Avignon to present respectful objections to this appointment. The supreme pontiff paid no attention. It was only the opposition of Robert II of Taranto, titular emperor of Constantinople, to the transfer of the order to Achaia that compelled Innocent to give up his other plans as well.

Although the reforms that the pope sought to impose upon the Hospitallers were for the most part wise and well-conceived, his un-

[1] Mortier, *Histoire des maîtres généraux*, VOL. III, pp. 295–442.

limited confidence in Juan de Heredia could not but compromise their success. This knight had stirred up dangerous sedition within the order by his ambition and insubordination. In raising him to one of the highest offices in the order, Innocent was making a great mistake and giving rise to the belief that he was incapable of seeing through a well-hatched plot.[1]

The attacks made by lovers of poverty on the luxury of the court at Avignon were not all justified. Innocent VI strove to reduce his household and dismissed the parasites who were cluttering it. The cardinals, too, reduced their expenditure. As it happened they were all bowing to necessity as much as to a real desire for reform: the coffers of the papal treasury were empty, and in 1357 Innocent was complaining of poverty. His distress was quite genuine: on 5 November 1358 he was driven to sacrifice much of his silver and a great quantity of jewels and precious ornaments. He was reduced to extreme penury: works of art were sold for their weight in gold or silver without any account of the value of their craftsmanship.[2]

These financial troubles, brought on by the costly wars in Italy, were not the only ones to cause Innocent VI anxiety. The truce of Bordeaux on 23 March 1357 had led to the disbanding of the mercenary troops used by England against France, who now formed themselves into 'Companies.' France was overrun with soldiers who looted everything as they went, set fire to castles and villages, ransacked churches and monasteries and killed many nobles and country folk. The pope tried to put an end to this scourge by pronouncing an anathema against the Companies; but the Church's thunderbolts were of little avail against men without faith, whose only delight was in pillage, murder and arson.

Suddenly, in May 1357, Avignon was seized with fear. Gangs under the command of the notorious archpriest of Vélines, Arnaud de Cervole, were preparing to invade Provence. In vain did Innocent beseech the French government and neighbouring princes to keep their armed forces from joining the invaders. Wherever he turned, he received only fair words. Provence was invaded. At this news, the gates of Avignon were repaired in great haste on 6 July, look-outs kept a watch on the enemy's movements, and troops of cavalry and infantry guarded the city walls. Strong-points in the Comtat-Venaissin were put in a state of defence, and with the help of financial contributions from courtiers and inhabitants of Avignon the work of fortifying the town was begun and ramparts energetically constructed.

[1] Delaville le Roulx, *Les Hospitaliers à Rhodes*, Paris 1913, VOL. I, pp. 116–39.
[2] M. Faucon, in *Revue archéologique*, VOL. XLIII, 1882, pp. 217–25.

By the spring of 1358 the inhabitants of Avignon felt a temporary lessening of their anxiety. As there was nothing left to pillage in Provence, Arnaud de Cervole enrolled under the banner of the Dauphin and went off to fight against Étienne Marcel and the citizens of Paris in June and July. But as soon as the riots in Paris had been quelled, he appeared again in Provence, and was obviously determined to exact a high price for peace. Innocent VI agreed to act as arbiter between the bandit and the people of Provence. After insisting on the payment of an indemnity of 1,000 florins by the Holy See, the Archpriest Arnaud withdrew and by 29 September was in the Nivernais.[1]

The signing of the treaty of Brétigny on 8 May 1360 which ought to have brought peace to France, in fact became a source of further misfortunes. The mercenaries who had been dismissed and were now idle, reorganised themselves into Companies even more formidable than those of 1357. It is true that they were only soldiers of fortune; but they were seasoned professional troops, disciplined and skilful, and above all avid for booty. The gangs who were roaming the countryside of Beaucaire, having learned that a considerable sum of money would be taken to Pont St Esprit, on the left bank of the Rhône, seized that town during the night of 28-9 December. This news caused consternation to Innocent VI: the capture of Pont St Esprit cut off Avignon from the outside world and gave the enemy a favourable point from which to rob at their pleasure prelates, clergy and layfolk on their way to the Curia with well-lined purses.

Innocent VI's terror spread to the people of Avignon. As the ramparts were not complete, they hastily built wooden barricades, while armed patrols in the pope's pay kept watch on the approaches to the city, and artillery was placed on the ramparts. Innocent made use, too, of the spiritual armour of the Church and preached a real crusade. His appeal was heard, and help arrived from Aragon, Languedoc, Beaucaire, Gevaudan, Velay and Vivarais. Juan Fernandez de Heredia, the valiant castellan of Emposte, assumed command of the crusaders and besieged Pont St Esprit. Unfortunately he had neither money to pay his troops nor supplies to feed them. For their part, the besieged were hard-pressed and had just cause for alarm. Both sides were glad to come to an agreement which was in fact concluded towards the end of March 1361. In return for a payment of 14,500 gold florins, the Companies set off to fight in Italy

[1] H. Denifle, *La Désolation des églises, monastères et hôpitaux en France pendant la guerre de Cent Ans*, VOL. II, Paris 1899, pp. 188–211.

under the command of the marquis of Montferrat.[1]

The population of the Comtat-Venaissin and the neighbouring districts, alarmed by the presence of mercenaries on the banks of the Rhône, had sought refuge in Avignon. There they found appalling suffering and death. Famine and then plague wrought dreadful havoc: between 29 March and 25 July the epidemic accounted for seventeen thousand people, including nine cardinals.[2]

As well as acute anxiety over his own safety, Innocent had to endure bitter disappointments arising from his inept diplomacy. Although he nobly spent his life in preaching reconciliation and the re-establishment of peace in the world he saw war, discord and crime flourish on every side. Ingenuous and lacking in perspicacity, he was deceived by the kings of France, England, Navarre, Castile and Aragon, and by Bernabo Visconti. Overcome with grief, depressed by the turn of events, and worn out in spirit, Innocent VI went into a rapid decline. He died on 12 September 1362, asking that his remains should be buried in the Charterhouse at Villeneuve that he had founded in 1356 and where, amid all the upheavals of his life, he had enjoyed in the course of his reign a few hours of peace and quiet.

[1] Denifle, *op. cit.* pp. 385–98.
[2] E. Nicaise, *La Grande Chirurgie de Guy de Chauliac,* Paris 1890, p. 169. Baluze, *op. cit.* VOL. I, pp. 327, 340: VOL. II, p. 490.

CHAPTER VI

Urban V 1362-70

THE pontificates of Clement VI and Innocent VI had each in turn
had the effect of concentrating a Limousin party at the court of
Avignon. Naturally this party's one ambition was to keep for as long
as possible the advantages they had hitherto enjoyed, and their chief
interest was to support the candidature of one of their number for
the triple crown. On the other hand, the personal ambition of
Cardinal Guy de Boulogne and of Cardinal Talleyrand de Périgord
prevented any unity from developing among those who did not belong
to this party. The conclave, which began on 22 September 1362,
threatened to be a restless and stormy one. Some of the cardinals, not
knowing which party to join, thought they would delay the election
by voting without consulting each other and so wasting their votes.
The votes thus made without any previous agreement were all for
Hugues Roger, the brother of the late Pope Clement VI. To the surprise of everyone, when the result of the ballot was announced,
Hugues Roger was found to have been elected by fifteen votes out of
twenty.

This election displeased everyone, but their anxiety disappeared
when, through humility and fear of the burden placed upon him,
Hugues made it clear that he refused to accept office. The cardinals,
determined to be prudent after this mishap, distributed their votes
so carefully that it seemed impossible to agree on the name of any one
among them. Consequently the only course that remained was to
choose a prelate from outside the Sacred College. On 28 September,
Guillaume de Grimoard, abbot of St Victor of Marseilles and at that
time nuncio in the kingdom of Naples, was unanimously elected.[1]

[1] See Matteo Villani, *Istoria fiorentine*, Bk XI, ch. xxvi; Baluze, *Vitae*, VOL. II,
p. 356. Guillaume was born in 1310 at the castle of Grisac (Lozère), the son of Guillaume de Grimoard, lord of Grisac, Bédouès, Bellegarde, Montbel and Grasvillar, and
of Amphélise de Montferrand. He received the tonsure at the age of twelve and went to
study at Montpellier and Toulouse. After qualifying in civil law, he entered the
Benedictine priory at Chirac. He was professed at the abbey of St Victor at Marseilles,
then returned to Chirac and attended lectures at the Universities of Toulouse, Montpellier, Avignon and Paris. He received his doctorate on 31 October 1342 and taught
canon law in various universities. His success attracted attention and earned him the
charge of vicar-general to Pierre d'Aigrefeuille at Clermont and Uzès, and the titles of
abbot of St Germain of Auxerre on 13 February 1352 and of St Victor of Marseilles
on 2 August 1361, as well as several legations in Italy, in 1352, 1354, 1360 and 1362.

Messengers left for Italy with the utmost secrecy, with instructions to bring Guillaume back without delay. As soon as he received their message, the abbot of St Victor obeyed and set sail. He landed at Marseilles on 27 October, reached Avignon on the 31st and was enthroned on the same day.[1]

The coronation ceremony took place on 6 November without any of the customary pomp. Instead of riding through the streets of Avignon escorted by a brilliant procession of cardinals, princes and bishops, Urban V never left his palace.[2] Thus at the very beginning of his pontificate he demonstrated his horror of luxury and ostentation. On the throne of St Peter, he led the life of a monk faithfully carrying out the smallest details of his rule. He could never bring himself to leave off his monastic habit.

His day was extremely arduous. Having a very sensitive conscience, Urban made his confession before saying Mass, and would remain kneeling for a long time in the same place where he had acknowledged his sins, pouring out his soul in fervent prayer, reciting psalms or imploring God in his mercy to forgive him.

After reciting his office, the pope held audience and dealt with day-to-day affairs until his mid-day meal. He ate frugally, fasting every day in Advent and Lent and two or three times a week at other seasons. As he ate, he conversed amiably with his familiars, and made anxious enquiries about the health of people at court, or ordered help to be given to the needy.

Half an hour was given over to rest; then Urban would sign petitions, deal with his correspondence and spend some time in study. The catalogue of his fine library, drawn up in 1369, lists a vast number of works of Scripture, history, law, theology, philosophy and polemic. Such reading befitted a man well-versed in ecclesiastical lore, zealous for the sanctification of souls, whose heart was set on safeguarding the property and temporal rights of the Holy See, and who was anxious to bind his pontificate closely to that of his predecessors.[3]

After study came prayer, the recital of the Vespers of the Dead and the office of the day; then more audiences were given. As the day drew to its close, Urban liked to wander along the spacious covered walks of the palace or the pleasant gardens that he had had enlarged. At this hour he was pleased to have the company of cardinals and prelates of distinction.

[1] Prou, *Étude sur les relations politiques du pape Urbain V avec les rois de France Jean II et Charles V*, Paris 1887, pp. 3–7.
[2] J.-H. Albanès and U. Chevalier, *Actes anciens et documents concernant le Bienheureux Urbain V*, VOL. I, Paris 1897, p. 40.
[3] F. Ehrle, *Historia bibliothecae Romanorum pontificum*, Rome 1890, pp. 274–450.

At a given signal, conversation would be broken off and the pope went back to his apartments to sup, read a little and discuss what he had read with his gentlemen-in-waiting; he would speak of the consolations of the apostolic ministry, tell anecdotes from the lives of the saints, or bemoan the evil ways of the world. Then his confessor and his chaplains and attendants would join in reciting Matins. When it was time for bed, this holy man would stretch himself, fully dressed, on the bare ground.[1]

Urban's love of study made him a generous patron of literature and learning. He founded a *studium* at Trets: a centre of advanced study intended to prepare young men for the famous universities of the day. In 1365 the college of Trets was transferred to Manosque, a place in the Alps which seemed more suitable. Students came in great numbers, both there and to another *studium* set up at St Germain de Calberte in the diocese of Mende.

All the universities felt the salutary results of the pope's enlightened patronage: he supported as many as fourteen hundred students at his own expense. Urban drew up new statutes or revised the old ones at the Universities of Orleans, Orvieto, Toulouse and Paris. New universities were set up at Orange, Cracow and Vienna, as well as a school of music at Toulouse. Montpellier, that 'smiling garden of learning' as Urban called it, had a substantial share in his benefactions. After the plague of 1361 and the ravages of the Companies, the Faculty of Law was practically deserted, and the Faculty of Medicine, formerly so flourishing, had no more than thirty students. To bring back the students to these shrines of learning, the pope founded the College of St Benedict and the College of the Twelve Doctors. So dear were these foundations to his heart that before leaving for Rome he visited the building sites between 9 January and 8 March 1367, to make sure that his orders were being scrupulously carried out. It was a considerable undertaking, for the construction of the monastery and college of St Benedict alone involved the expropriation and demolition of about sixty buildings.[2]

Urban's encouragement of art was no less lively than that he gave to learning and letters. He was responsible for the alterations and embellishments made to the papal palace, for the fortifications of Avignon and most particularly for the restoration of the abbey of St Victor at Marseilles. In October 1365 the pope wished to come in person and admire the work of his architects: he went to Marseilles, consecrated the high altar in the church of his old abbey and loaded

[1] M. Chaillan, *Le Bienheureux Urbain V*, Paris 1911, pp. 32–9.
[2] *Ibid.* pp. 40–75.

it with splendid gifts, valuable reliquaries, jewels, tapestries and sacerdotal ornaments.[1]

In Lozère, especially, Urban proved to be a great builder. He constructed a cathedral at Mende, restored and beautified the priory at Chirac, founded the collegiate churches of Quézac and Bédouès, endowed a parish church at his native village of Grisac, had a bridge built over the Lot at Salmon, and gave evidence of his bounty at St Bonnet, Moriès, Montjézieu, Banassac, Montferrand, Marijoulet, Auxillac, Ispagnac and Florac.[2]

So generous a pope was bound to inspire love in his people. Indeed, in his lifetime he seems to have been highly esteemed, loved and venerated. Petrarch himself,[3] who did not tend to lavish compliments upon the Avignon popes, yields to the general feeling when he writes, on the occasion of the pope's journey to Marseilles: 'Recently, when you made your way to Marseilles, urged by your devotion and desire to see once more that humble nest whence divine Providence and your virtue have caused you to take flight to the highest honours, the people, who are devoted to you and cherish you, received you *not as a man, but as God himself*, whose vicar and representative you are. Marseilles welcomed you with boundless joy and infinite respect. I know not whether, moved by so touching a sight, you could restrain your tears, but the words that you let fall resounded pleasantly in our ears, and brought us sweet hope. Even if you had, as you have said, no other motive in going to Rome and Italy save that of thus arousing the devotion of the faithful, that should amply suffice to send you on your way.'

Contemporaries also made much of the reforms in the Church introduced by Urban. Petrarch has praised them magnificently in his ornate style. He says in one of his letters: 'I have learned, Holy Father, the great things you have done and which I expected of you. I have learned of your sending back to their churches those prelates that thronged the court of Rome. That is well and excellently done. For what can be more useless and more likely to cause a ship to founder than to see the sailors abandon oars and ropes, and all gather at the stern of the ship, and continually impede the pilot's movements? You have curbed the frenzied pursuit of benefices and forced these insatiably ambitious priests to be content with only one. That is as it should be. Was it not shameful to see some loaded with revenues while many others, far better than they, lived in want?

'I know that you have laboured hard to bring back modesty and

---

[1] *Ibid.* pp. 93–106.   [2] *Ibid.* pp. 107–18.
[3] *De rebus senilibus*, Bk VIII, Epistle 1. See Chaillan, *op. cit.* p. 105.

decency into the manner of dress. In that you are worthy of all praise, for the absurd fashions introduced in our day were no longer to be endured, when men who thought to make themselves appear fine and interesting were really bringing dishonour on themselves. How indeed were the monstrous novelties displayed before us to be endured?—shoes pointed like the prow of a galley, hats with wings, hair elaborately curled, with long pigtails, and men with ivory combs set on their foreheads, as though they were women? . . . It was right that you, who are the Vicar of the Sun of Justice, should restore justice to its full power, and cause these damnable practices to disappear. . . .[1]

Petrarch's praises, like the admiration of Urban V's biographers, have a certain element of exaggeration. It is obvious that they are inspired by the enthusiasm that seized hold of his contemporaries. It is true that Urban was a reformer; but he was only following the example of his predecessor, Innocent VI. His own work, which was far inferior to that of Benedict XII, only consisted in curbing the greed of court procurators and advocates, halving the rate of tenths, decreeing severe penalties in the Constitution *Horribilis* for the accumulation of benefices, regulating the services of the Apostolic Camera, and insisting on the holding of provincial councils.[2]

Moreover, Urban's merits have been praised beyond their deserts: genius cannot be ascribed to him. But he did have a happy combination of qualities, especially that attraction characteristic of sanctity and greatness of soul; and this made him universally popular. Even his virtues were not without some corresponding faults. Thus he followed his generous impulses with no thought for their consequences. He thought it necessary to indulge in excessive liberality, which involved the papal treasury in heavy debts and was to lead him to borrow from the cardinals and to decree financial measures that were oppressive for the clergy.[3] If he were rebuked for the gifts he made to students, he would reply: 'I hope that the Church of God may abound in learned men. I admit that all those that I am educating and maintaining will not be ecclesiastics. Many will become monks or secular priests, but others will remain in the world and bring up families. What of that? Whatever may be the state that they embrace, even if they were to take up manual labour, it would always be useful to them to have spent some time in study.'[4]

[1] *Op. cit.* Bk VII, Epistle I. See Chaillan, *op. cit.* p. 105.
[2] C. Samaran and G. Mollat, *La Fiscalité pontificale en France au XIVᵉ siècle*, Paris 1905, pp. 18–21, 231–6.
[3] Lecacheux, *Urbain V*, nos. 800–13.
[4] Albanès, *op. cit.* p. 414. Chaillan, *op. cit.* p. 207.

The policy of the pope was entirely one of appeasement, and achieved a success unknown in the time of Innocent VI. Its short-comings, however, were due to an excessive goodness and a certain inability to understand men. For example, the wise tactics used by Albornoz against Bernabo Visconti were frequently thwarted; in this the pope was guilty of an unfortunate lack of foresight in preventing the complete overthrow of the tyrant of Milan, and he was later to pay dearly for this mistake. Moreover, it must have been either extreme ingenuousness or idealism that led him to wish to send the Companies to conquer the Holy Land.[1]

Urban showed real courage and true perspicacity in carrying out a plan that shed glory on his pontificate: that of restoring the papacy to Rome. Only thus, he considered, could the order restored in the peninsula by Albornoz be made permanent. Moreover, at that time Avignon was none too safe as a place of residence. The Comtat was in constant danger from the depradations of the Companies, and the supposed wealth of the Curia excited the greed of bandits. Bertrand du Guesclin, under the pretext of trying to expel these bandits and to make an expedition against the Infidel, had obtained from Urban in 1365 not only a remission of tenths for the ecclesiastical province of Tours, but an enormous contribution to his warlike activities, valued by Cuvelier, with some exaggeration, at 200,000 francs. This was nothing less than a ransom.[2]

On 30 April 1367, Urban left Avignon; he spent two nights at the castle of Sorgues, stayed at Noves, Orgon, and Aix and reached Marseilles on 6 May. While he was waiting for a favourable wind, the cardinals made a last attempt to prevent his departure for Italy and went so far as to threaten to leave him. These tactics of intimidation did not succeed. In order to prove to the members of the Sacred College that he had no need of them, he raised Guillaume d'Aigre-feuille, who was barely twenty-eight, to the cardinalate, and assured them, according to Peter of Hérenthals, that he could produce other cardinals from underneath his cowl.[3]

On 19 May the fleet, composed of galleys from Naples, Pisa, Genoa and Venice, together with those of Raimond Bérenger, Grand Master of the Hospitallers, set sail, while the court and a certain number of cardinals took the land route under the protection of the Knights Hospitallers. On the evening of the 19th the fleet called at Toulon, on the 20th at Port-Olive near Nice, on the 21st at

[1] Albanès, *op. cit.* p. 68.
[2] Denifle, *La Désolation des églises*, VOL. II, pp. 485–8, 498–9.
[3] Baluze, *Vitae*, VOL. I, p. 403.

St Étienne, on the 22nd at Albenga, on the 23rd at Genoa. On the 28th they made ready to sail to Porto Venere, and were at Salsadas on the 31st, and Pisa on 1 June and Piombino on the next day. On 3 June they landed at Corneto, where a considerable crowd had gathered to greet the pope. On 9 June, after spending the night at Toscanella, the court entered Viterbo.

Urban V entered Rome on 16 October. Next year, as the heat of summer approached, he retired to the castle of Montefiascone. In this splendid residence, looking out on the magnificent prospect of the Apennines reflected in the deep waters of Lake Bolsena, the pope thought wistfully of the gentle countryside of the Comtat-Venaissin, for his subjects gave him little cause for satisfaction. Nevertheless, he reappeared among them on 21 October 1368, riding a palfrey whose bridle was held by the Emperor Charles IV. On All Saints' Day the Empress received the imperial crown at St Peter's, in the presence of her noble husband, who created some new knights and served at the altar as a deacon.

The series of solemn rites did not end there. In 1369, on 15 April, the canonisation of Eleazar of Sabran took place, and then the re-cantation of John V Palaeologus, emperor of Constantinople was witnessed,[1] on 18 October, in the church of Santo Spirito.

On 5 September 1370, Urban set sail from Corneto. The thirty-four galleys, supplied by the kings of France and Aragon, Queen Joanna of Naples and the people of Avignon and Provence, put into Marseilles on 16 September. Eleven days later, the court entered Avignon with great ceremony.

In the month of November, the pope had the first attacks of the sickness that was to prove mortal, and from that time he prepared himself for death. This came on Thursday, 19 December 1370 at about three o'clock in the afternoon, in the dwelling of his brother where, for humility's sake, he had desired to be taken, there to end his life of sanctity.[2] Five centuries later, on 10 March 1870, the Church acknowledged his merits by conferring on him the title of Blessed.

[1] Prou, *op. cit.* pp. 79–81. O. Halecki, *Un Empereur de Byzance à Rome*, Warsaw 1930, pp. 188–212. A. Vasiliev, 'Il viaggio dell' Imperatore bizantino Giovanni V Paleologo (1368–1371) e l' unione di Roma,' *Studi bizantini*, VOL. III, 1931, pp. 153–93.
[2] Chaillan, *op. cit.* pp. 196–209.

CHAPTER VII

Gregory XI 1370–78

ON 29 December 1370, as soon as the nine days decreed by custom for the obsequies of Urban V were over, the cardinals went into conclave; the next morning they unanimously elected as pope, Pierre Roger de Beaufort, son of Guillaume de Beaufort and Marie du Chambon. Cardinal Roger took the name of Gregory XI and was crowned by Guy de Boulogne on 5 January 1371. Born in 1329 he was then only forty-two years old.

The new pope had had a rapid career from one ecclesiastical honour to another. At eleven he was already canon of Rodez and of Paris, at nineteen his uncle, Clement VI, had made him cardinal-deacon of Santa Maria Nuova (28–29 May 1348). Instead of giving way to the charms of the ostentatious way of life at Avignon, the young man had gone to Perugia, there to attend the lectures of the famous jurist Pietro Baldo degli Ubaldi. Through this association with the master, he had acquired a profound knowledge of law and an unusually balanced judgment. His biographers tell us that Baldo was so proud of his disciple that he took pleasure in quoting his judicial opinions.[1]

In Gregory XI moral qualities of no common order were allied to a cultivated mind. Coluccio Salutati, who cannot be accused of being prejudiced in his favour, praises his prudence and discretion, his modest demeanour, his piety, goodness and affability, the uprightness of his character and his steadfastness of purpose in word and deed.[2] A sickly disposition and a delicate constitution had refined his features and added still more to his personal charm.

Though he did not rival the munificence of Urban V—indeed the sad state of his finances made it impossible—Gregory XI gave generous support to religious undertakings in Avignon: the convent of St Catherine, the house of the Penitents and the orphanage founded in 1366 by Jean de Jujon and transferred to the hospital of Notre-Dame-du-Pont-Fract. He also added fresh beauties to the palaces of Sorgues and Villeneuve, presented a huge clock to the town

---

[1] Baluze, *Vitae*, VOL. I, new ed. p. 460.
[2] *Epistolario*, ed. Novati, VOL. I, p. 143.

hall at Avignon, helped to mend the bridge of St Bénézet and ordered large-scale restoration work to be done on the Roman palaces.[1]

His marked taste for scholarship led him to seek out precious manuscripts and to enrich the papal library with many works by classical authors, as well as with books of ecclesiastical learning.[2]

The reform of the Church, which had claimed the attention of Innocent VI and Urban V, found no less zealous an advocate in Gregory. The Knights Hospitallers of St John of Jerusalem were at this time in a truly critical state. All their houses were suffering from the same evils: relaxation of discipline and unbridled luxury. Their debts had reached an alarming figure. Gregory instructed the bishops of the whole of Christendom to hold an enquiry and supported the Grand Master, Roger de Pins, in his work of restoring his order, and gave him continuous help.[3]

In the East, the pope, together with the General, Élie Raimond de Toulouse, came to the rescue of the Dominican missions which had been decimated by the pestilence. Of all the monks who had once filled the fifteen houses established in Persia, only three had survived. The Magdeburg Chapter had in 1363 more or less decreed the suppression of the wandering friars, by withdrawing their right to nominate a vicar-general and by attaching the convents of Pera, Caffa and Trebizond, where intending missionaries were trained, to the Greek province. Furthermore, the recruitment of novices was impeded by the Dominican priors of the houses in Europe, who were unwilling to see their young religious set off for the East. Gregory XI forbade any practice that might restrict the scope of the missions and in 1374–5 restored matters to the state they were in before the Chapter of Magdeburg. From that time forward, the wandering friars began once more to lead a virtually autonomous existence; their numbers rapidly increased, especially after Gregory XI had amalgamated them with the congregation of the United Friars of Armenia, composed of monks of the order of St Basil who had been converted to the Roman faith, and who had been officially recognised by Innocent VI on 21 January 1356.[4]

On 27 August 1373 Gregory introduced an important reform into the Dominican order in Europe. For the future they were to be allowed to hold chapters-general only once in two years. In order to

[1] Cf. E. Müntz, 'Les Arts à la cour des papes au XIVᵉ siècle,' *Revue de l'art chrétien*, VOL. XXXIV, 1891, pp. 183–90; M. Chaillan, *Recherches et documents inédits sur l'orphanotrophium du pape Grégoire XI*, Aix 1904, and *Notices et documents inédits sur la maison des repenties à Avignon au XIVᵉ siècle*, Aix 1904.
[2] F. Ehrle, *Historia*, VOL. I, pp. 451–574.
[3] Delaville le Roulx, *Les Hospitaliers à Rhodes*, Paris 1913, VOL. I, pp. 170–91.
[4] Mortier, *Histoire des maîtres généraux*, VOL. II, pp. 320–34, 442–53.

help the General to reform his order he stopped, from 18 November 1373, all privileges and dispensations hitherto granted to the friars by the Holy See or by its legates. A significant detail showing clearly the Holy See's hold on monastic institutions is the granting to the Dominicans of a 'cardinal protector,' normally resident at the papal court.[1]

The defence of the Faith was close to the heart of Gregory XI. He showed his indefatigable zeal in declaring war on heresy and in making use of the terrible weapons that were then at the Church's disposal. Not content with sending the Dominicans to win back Dauphiné, Provence and Lyonnais, which were full of Waldenses, he put an active leader, François Borel, at the head of the inquisitorial tribunals, with a special nuncio, Bishop Antonio of Massa Maritima, to assist him. Royal officials, who had shown a marked lack of co-operation, had to give way when Charles V issued a formal order for the application of the laws passed against heretics. The Inquisitor's activities were soon crowned with such success that prisons were inadequate to hold all those who escaped the stake or the sword, and the alms of the faithful were besought for the sustenance of those who were detained.

In Aragon, the pope encouraged Nicolas Eymerich who was hesitant to attack the converted Jews found guilty of sorcery or of heretical doctrine. The bishop of Lisbon was given a mandate to appoint the first Portuguese Inquisitor, Martino Vasquez. The bishops of Ajaccio and Mariana, assisted by Fra Gabriele da Montalcino, vigorously pursued the Catharists who had fled to the forests and mountains of Corsica. In Sicily, fraticelli and Jews were hard-pressed, while in Germany, beghards and flagellants were hunted down by the Inquisitors.[2]

Yet Gregory's efforts were not, in the last resort, successful. The Inquisition, despite the impetus it received, was moribund; public authorities were suspicious and jealous of it and no longer gave it much support. Discontent with the Church continued to grow, and heresy remained very much alive in spite of persecution. This was the time when Wycliffe was rousing Europe with his incisive writings and his thundering sermons, when the Bohemian priests Conrad of Waldhausen, Milicz of Cremsier and Matthias of Janow were castigating the disorders of the clergy without restraint. The spirit of insubordination with which these innovators were infusing the

---

[1] *Ibid.* pp. 397–9.
[2] H. C. Lea, *History of the Inquisition in the Middle Ages*, London 1888, VOL. II, passim.

Christian masses was a distant precursor of the separatist movement that was to culminate in the Reformation.[1]

At a time when war was raging with especial violence, Gregory continued to work as nobly as his predecessors had done to bring peace to Europe; in this he displayed a mastery which was worthy of Clement VI. His diplomacy was clear-sighted, versatile and active. It is true that the successes he achieved were mingled with bitter disappointments: plans for a crusade, though constantly put forward, were never realised; the momentary peace in Spain was soon broken by renewed discord; hostilities between France and England, briefly interrupted by truces, broke out afresh. Yet it is only fair to recognise that through the intervention of the Holy See many occasions of international friction were avoided, and that in France the renewed outbreak of war was postponed. As the causes of conflict, however, had not been removed, war was bound to recur.

In the Empire the papal policy triumphed, and peace was restored between Charles IV and Louis of Hungary, and between the dukes of Bavaria and the count of Savoy.[2]

In Italy, the crafty Bernabo Visconti suffered considerable reverses; Florence, haughty and jealous of the temporal power of the papacy, reaped only losses and insults from her audacious revolt; and the Florentine league that had been formed with such difficulty, broke up in the twinkling of an eye.

Gregory was a subtle diplomat, and knew how to play for time and watch the progress of events before embarking on any action, following his plans from afar and with determination, so that he could take energetic action when the moment seemed favourable. The firmness of his character and the versatility of his mind are nowhere better shown than in the way that he brought to a successful conclusion that undertaking which sheds lustre on his name: the return of the Holy See to Rome.

Having endured to the last moment the pressure to change his mind put upon him by the French court, his cardinals and those near to him, on 13 September 1376, Gregory boarded the ship which was to take him from Avignon. The papal flotilla went down the Rhône and then followed the Durance, called at Noves (14 September), and spent two days at Orgon. From there the company went overland, and reached Marseilles by way of Salon (17th–18th), Trets, St Maximin (19th–20th) and Auriol (20th–22nd).

[1] J. Trésal, *Les Origines du schisme anglican (1509–71)*, Paris 1908, pp. 2, 6–14.
[2] L. Mirot, *La Politique pontificale et le retour du S. Siège à Rome en 1376*, Paris 1899, pp. 11–17.

On 2 October, a sad day when 'Never were seen so many tears, lamentations and groanings,' the pope left the convent of St Victor of Marseilles and set sail in the galley of Ancona. When the breeze began to fill the sails, he was overcome by emotion and, tears running down his pale cheeks, he wept for his native land. Soon a heavy swell developed and the papal fleet was obliged to drop anchor at Port-Miou (3 October), and then at Sanary, Ranzels (3–6 October), Reneston, St Tropez (7 October), Antibes (8 October), Nice and Villefranche (9 October). When they were within sight of Monaco a terrible storm arose and the admiral was forced to turn back. Angry waves tossed the ships from side to side; the sails were torn, the ropes broke, the anchors dragged and the terrified sailors feared the ships would be wrecked.

On 17 October it was calm and they were able to put in at Savona, and then on the 18th at Genoa. They set off again on the 28th; but contrary winds prevented them from leaving Porto Fino until 4 November. They touched at Porto Venere on the 6th, stayed at Leghorn from 7 to 14 November, and put in at Piombino on the 15th. Another storm, more terrible than the preceding, scattered the fleet. One of the galleys from Marseilles under the command of Cardinal Jean de la Grange foundered and another ship also went to the bottom.

When the fine weather returned on 29 November they left Piombino. They lay at Orbitello from 30 November until 3 December and landed at Corneto on 6 December. After spending five weeks in this town Gregory put to sea again, and on 17 January 1377, landed from his galley which was moored by the banks of the Tiber near the church of St Paul-without-the-walls. He entered Rome to the acclamations of the crowd, which thronged around him, and admired the brilliant procession of dancers, singers, lute-players and trumpeters, of troops led by Raimond de Turenne, and of ecclesiastical dignitaries, knights and senators.

Gregory XI was not long to enjoy the success of his Italian policy. His health, always delicate and greatly impaired by the trials of his difficult journey, was unable to withstand the rigours of the Roman climate. At the very time when a European congress was meeting at Sarzana with the intention of restoring the balance of power in Italy, the last of the French popes died during the night of 26–27 March 1378, with a sombre presentiment of the divisions by which the Sacred College was soon to be rent, and the woeful schism that would afflict the Church.[1]

---

[1] Baluze, *op. cit.* VOL. II, pp. 742–3. P. M. Baumgarten, 'Miscellanea cameralia,' *Römische Quartalschrift*, VOL. XIX, 1905, pp. 163–8.

Book Two: Papal Relations with Christendom

CHAPTER I

The Papacy and Italy

'THE bark of Peter is in danger of sinking and the fisherman's net of breaking; instead of calm and peace, storm-clouds are piling up; disastrous wars are laying waste the lands of the Roman Church and the neighbouring regions; the sower of tares is loosing his sharpest darts against them.'[1] In these uncomplimentary words the cardinals, assembled at Perugia, summarised the true situation of Italy at the beginning of the fourteenth century. While the dissension that had so long raged between Guelphs and Ghibellines had lost none of its bitterness, the Guelph faction in Tuscany had split into two: the Whites and the Blacks. Benedict XI, striving to put right the mistakes of Boniface VIII, had tried in vain to reconcile them.

Perhaps the wisest plan would have been to deal with matters on the spot, as the cardinals advised Clement V on 9 June 1305. The pope, however, considered—and this view was shared by his successors—that before venturing beyond the Alps, it would be better to pacify the Italians and to establish the Church's authority firmly in its own territory.

Obstacles of every kind impeded the realisation of this vast programme: it was too sharply opposed to the Italian ambitions of the king of the Romans, the house of Anjou and the Hungarian princes to be fully successful. It thwarted still further the selfish plans of the republics of Venice and Florence, of the Visconti and other powerful local families, and the intrigues of carefree adventurers whose ambition was to carve out lordships themselves, to the detriment of the communes and the papacy. The Holy See, after exhausting every means of conciliation without achieving any success whatever, had to accept the necessity of waging war upon its rivals great and small. Had it not done so, its future grasp of temporal power, on which, in the Middle Ages, spiritual power depended, would have been heavily compromised. For nearly seventy years there was to be a succession of military operations and diplomatic negotiations which were eventually to result in the restoration of the papacy to Rome, its natural seat.

[1] D. Mansi, *Sacrorum conciliorum nova et amplissima collectio*, VOL. XXV, Venice 1782, col. 127.

67

1

Clement V's Intervention in Tuscany

The policy of the Holy See in Italy had up till this time favoured the Guelphs; Clement V seems to have wanted to change these tactics. Did he have a definite plan of campaign? Did he really cherish the far-fetched idea that he could bring peace to Tuscany? Or was he rather under the influence of cardinals with Ghibelline tendencies, such as Niccolò Albertini and Napoleone Orsini? Did he fear that in his absence Robert of Anjou might take advantage of the title of Captain-General given him by the Guelphs, to encroach upon the territorial rights of the Roman Church? It is very difficult to give an authoritative answer to the many problems raised by his complicated policy.

Clement V was by nature a vacillating diplomat; his object seems to have been to keep manœuvring flexibly among the various factions that were dividing Italy and each in turn seizing power or losing it according to the play of popular feeling or internal quarrels. In this way he hoped to prevent any of them from being crushed and to avoid the destruction of the balance of power among them. His actions were dictated by the turn of events, and were invariably characterised by opportunism and realism. On one essential point, however, Clement V was immovable: his chief preoccupation was always to preserve intact the temporal power of the Church.

While the cardinals were still in conclave at Perugia, they had begged the newly-elected pope to re-establish peace in Italy. Clement V lost no time in intervening, but he did so on the side of the Ghibellines and the White Guelphs, who were besieged within the walls of Pistoia, and at the precise moment when the Black Guelphs were preparing for a final assault. The town, which was entirely surrounded by entrenchments, was at the end of its resources when there arrived in Florence, in September 1305, two nuncios, Guillaume Durant, the bishop of Mende, and Pelfort de Rabastens, abbot of Lombez, who unexpectedly arranged a truce and summoned the belligerents to appear before them by proxy to conclude peace. The citizens of Lucca and Florence refused to submit to the sentence imposed upon them by the representatives of the Holy See at a time when decisive victory seemed at hand. Acting on the authority of the Bull of 11 November 1305, Guillaume Durant and Pelfort de Rabastens pronounced at Siena the excommunication of all those who did not abandon the siege of Pistoia, and threatened those who disobeyed their orders with a fine of 10,000 silver marks and deprivation of the fiefs and privileges granted them by the papacy. Robert of Anjou, who had sent troops to Florence, at once bowed to necessity. It was not a favourable moment for resistance, since his father, Charles II, was making ready to render homage to Clement V on the occasion of his elevation to the pontificate. The citizens of Lucca and Florence, who did not have to keep in the good graces of the papal court, lodged an appeal and intensified the siege: any man who attempted to leave the precincts of the town, which was now stricken by famine, had a foot cut off and any woman her nose. Thus mutilated, and forced to make their way back, they struck terror into the hearts of their fellow-citizens. The return of the Black Guelphs to Bologna on 1 March finally decided the besieged towns-folk to capitulate, which they did on 10 April 1306.[1]

This rebuff suffered by his nuncios at Pistoia did not prevent Clement V from pursuing his peace-making overtures. Cardinal Napoleone Orsini went to Florence to demand the return of the exiles: he was not received in audience.[2] At Bologna, where he negotiated the return of the White Guelphs, insults were hurled at him and he was robbed by brigands.[3] Together with the citizens of Arezzo, he tried to lead an armed expedition against the Florentines, but in vain.[4] The only weapon at his command—an entirely futile one—was to issue a flood of excommunications and interdicts.

The Guelphs, flushed with success, were prepared to carry on per-petual warfare with the Ghibellines and Whites, who were a constant source of anxiety to them. They conspired against Pisa, since she supported their enemies, and thought to weaken her power by helping James II, king of Aragon, to conquer Corsica and Sardinia, whose investiture had been granted to him by the pope on 29 October 1305. They promised him a gift of 50,000 florins (January 1309). But this offer came too late; Cardinal Niccolò Albertini had offered the lord-ship of Pisa to the king, and was doing his utmost to persuade Clement to give his consent, pointing out to the pope that, as the result of a gift made in the past by Charlemagne, the sovereignty of Tuscany had devolved upon him as pope. The pope hesitated; he was sceptical of the good faith of the Pisans and, despite the affirmations of three

---

[1] R. Caggese, *Roberto d'Angiò e i suoi tempi*, VOL. I, Florence 1922, pp. 35, 41.
[2] Villani, *Istorie fiorentine*, Bk VIII, ch. lxxxv.
[3] A. Veronesi, 'La legazione del cardinale Napoleone Orsini in Bologna nel 1306,' *Atti e memorie di storia patria per le provincie di Romagna*, VOL. XXVIII, 1910, p. 79.
[4] Villani, *op. cit.* Bk VIII, ch. lxxxix.

cardinals, was uncertain of his right to invest James II with the suzerainty of Pisa. To overcome the pope's objections, the Aragonese ambassador advised the payment of tribute to the pope and the loading of the College of Cardinals with gifts. The Holy Father appeared to be yielding, but had no intention of being concerned with the actual handing over of the city to the king of Aragon. James II, for his part, acted with caution: he treated Sardinia and Pisa as separate questions, considering that if the latter did not turn out well, he still had the resource of seizing the island he so ardently desired with the assistance of the Guelphs, with whom he was still laboriously negotiating.[1] Clement V had, in fact, seen the truth of the situation; the Pisans' only motive for beginning negotiations with James II was to insure against the loss of Sardinia. The plans of the Emperor to descend upon Italy interrupted the negotiations and prevented any Guelph expedition from being sent against the Pisans and renewed their courage.

2

The War with Ferrara, 1308–13

Although Clement V's intervention in Italian affairs was marked by a caution that history must occasionally find baffling, he revealed unexpected energy when the Venetians attempted to snatch Ferrara from him.

The popes had been suzerains of Ferrara since it had been given by the Countess Matilda to Gregory VII in 1077 and confirmed to Pascal II in 1102. The inhabitants, though directly subject to the Roman Church, enjoyed great liberty, and elected their own governors during the thirteenth century. The papacy allowed them to deal with their own affairs and had cordial relations with the marquises of the house of Este, Obizzo and Azzo, who governed Ferrara in 1264–93 and 1293–1308 respectively, and who favoured the Guelph party. But danger threatened from Venice, who wished to have for her own exclusive profit the right to convoy goods to northern Italy along the course of the Po. On 31 January 1308 Azzo d'Este died and war broke out over the question of the succession, which he had bequeathed to his natural son, Fresco.

The young man's uncles, Aldevrandino and Francesco, felt themselves slighted. They attempted to seize power, and sought the

[1] P. Silva, 'Giacomo II d'Aragona e la Toscana (1307–1309),' *Archivio storico italiano*, VOL. LXXI, 1913, pp. 23–57.

alliance of the Paduans to this end, while Fresco received help from Bologna and later from Venice, which feared interference from Padua. He was thus able to recapture Arquà, a stronghold that he had previously lost. Owing to one of those shifts of policy that so frequently occurred in the peninsula, once Fresco had achieved this success the Paduans joined the victor.

Humiliated by these reverses, Francesco d'Este engaged in intrigues at the court of Clement V and made his nephew out to be a usurper. The pope, without waiting to judge between the rights of the rival claimants, hastened to intervene; he was determined to take advantage of these events to regain the direct power over Ferrara which his predecessors had let slip. With this end in view, he sent to Italy two nuncios, Arnaud de St Astier, abbot of Tulle in the diocese of Limoges, and Onofrio de Trevi, dean of the church of Meaux, charged with re-establishing the authority of the Holy See in Ferrara.[1] The moment seemed a favourable one, for the people of Ferrara had soon become hostile to Fresco; moreover, it was important that energetic action should be taken, since Venice, in an effort to exploit the situation, was defiantly insisting on the prompt fulfilment of earlier commercial agreements which had been continually contravened, and was making ready for a punitive expedition. Fresco's submission to the will of the Venetian republic caused an outbreak of rebellion in Ferrara; but the dissidents were overcome with the help of the inhabitants of Bologna.

Arnaud de St Astier and Onofrio de Trevi left the Curia in May or June of 1308, and first visited Bologna so that they could find out the state of public opinion. While they were staying in this Guelph city, they called upon Fresco to hand over his power to them, and upon Venice not to impede their actions. Reckoning, however, that these requests might well meet with a refusal, they arranged alliances so that, if the occasion arose, they might take Ferrara by force. Bologna, Ravenna, Cervia, Mantua and Cremona replied to their advances, fearing that Venice might make a base at Ferrara and so obtain supremacy over the whole of the river Po. Only Padua remained outside.

From this point, Fresco's situation became critical. Hated by the majority of Ferrarese and abandoned by Bologna, he was terrified to see considerable military forces rallying under the banner of the Church, while his uncle Francesco joined the nuncios. Venice, on the other hand, quite underrated the effect of the coalition, and saw herself already victorious. Forbidding Fresco to obey the nuncios'

---

[1] *Regestum Clementis V*, no. 3570, Bulls dated 27 April 1308.

ultimatum, she sent him troops and offered him a pension for life if he would hand over Ferrara.

On 23 September 1308, Fresco received warning notice to resign his lordship within five days, on pain of incurring spiritual and temporal penalties. Upon this the Ferrarese determined to rebel, and during the night of 2–3 October 1308, Fresco was forced to flee to Castello Tedaldo while the Venetians retired into the upper town. The attempted attack by the allies came to nothing, and they had to resort to negotiations; but these too proved useless, and on 4 October both Fresco and the Venetians were declared excommunicated. During the night of the 5th, however, the Ferrarese opened the city gates to the papal army and the Venetians had to retreat into the citadel.

The coalition were unable to follow up this success: the Venetians, having cut off communications by the river, were able to starve out their enemies, already disheartened by the Venetians' many sorties and the fires they started in Ferrara. The ranks of the besiegers grew alarmingly thin, and the nuncios had to accede to the demands of Bernardino da Polenta, who insisted that he should be made podestà. To make matters worse, Fresco, having abandoned all hope of ultimate success, handed over all his rights to Venice.

Arnaud de St Astier made one last approach to the Venetians, requesting them to order their troops to retreat. He was answered with nothing but abuse, and wherever he went was greeted with cries of 'Death to the legate,' while a hail of stones rained upon him and his attendants. Accordingly the nuncio proclaimed sentence of excommunication upon the Venetians on 25 October 1308. Far from subsiding, the struggle between the papal troops and those of the republic became more bitter. From their strongholds in the township of San Marco and Castello Tedaldo, the Venetian garrisons inflicted such heavy losses on the Ferrarese that the nuncios were obliged to yield. The peace-treaty, concluded on 1 December, contained clauses which established in the main the division of authority between Venice and the Holy See; but in reality the power of the latter was only nominal; from the point of view of trade, Venice was predominant in the districts watered by the Po and its tributaries, in other words in the whole of northern Italy.[1]

The validity of the articles of the agreement, however, depended on their receiving papal ratification, and Clement V was not at all disposed to approve them. On 4 December, unaware that his nuncios

[1] See the well-documented work by G. Soranzo, *La guerra fra Venezia e la S. Sede per il dominio di Ferrara (1308–1313)*, Città di Castello 1905.

had signed the capitulation, he had published a Bull, threatening the Venetians with severe penalties if they did not give him back Ferrara.[1] Arnaud de St Astier and Onofrio de Trevi, affected by this document, found themselves in an embarrassing situation: they emerged from it with some skill by spreading abroad the contents of the Bull without reporting it to the Venetians; so it came about that the Ferrarese did not observe the agreements to which the Venetians attached supreme importance.

On 27 March 1309, Clement V, who had at last been informed of the capitulation agreed to by his nuncios, threatened Venice with his interdict and major excommunication if she did not hand back her conquests within thirty days.[2] Moreover, he appointed as legate Cardinal Arnaud de Pellegrue[3] who arrived at Asti[4] with two thousand men. The papal envoy carried out his mission with despatch, pronouncing against the Venetians the penalties with which they were threatened, and forbidding anyone to trade with their merchants: a disastrous measure for them. This done, he preached a crusade against the rebels. On 28 June 1309 Clement V, for his part[5] ordered that all Venetians living abroad should be arrested and their property confiscated.

Meantime the crusaders' anomalous army, consisting of men from Ferrara, Bologna, Romagna, Padua, Vicenza, Florence, Lucca and Siena, came together and conceived a cunning plan of attack: while one band of soldiers pressed hard upon the Venetians, shut up in their fortress at Castello Tedaldo, in the township of San Marco and in a tower on the further bank of the Po, others became bridge-builders for the occasion and completely blocked the river with boats, so that no supplies could reach the besieged. An army sent to help them suffered a reverse at Francolino and could not succeed in breaking up the blockade of boats. In Ferrara itself, the besieged Venetians tried to break out through the enemy lines on the night of 27–28 August; but after a bloody defeat costing them between two and three thousand dead, they abandoned first the fortress at Castello Tedaldo and then on 24 September that at Marcamo, which had been specially built to prevent free traffic on the Po.[6]

Venice, though conquered, did not ask for pardon but remained

---

[1] *Regestum Clementis V*, no. 5000.
[2] J. Lünig, *Codex Italiae diplomaticus*, VOL. IV, pt 2, pp. 1589–1600.
[3] His letters of appointment are postdated to the 22 May; see *Regestum Clementis V*, nos. 5024–54.
[4] *Chronicon Astense*, in Muratori, *Rerum italicarum scriptores*, VOL. XI, col. 184.
[5] *Regestum Clementis V*, nos. 5081–2.
[6] H. Finke, *Acta Aragonensia*, VOL. II, Berlin 1908, p. 657 (account of the battle by the leader of the papal army).

obstinately rebellious. This was to cost her dear: the consequences of the excommunication and the interdict pronounced against her caused irreparable harm. Venetians living abroad were incarcerated; Istria and Zara made themselves independent; earlier alliances were broken off and treaties that had been painfully negotiated were trampled underfoot; Venetian trade, formerly so flourishing, fell into a decline. The proud city bowed beneath so many misfortunes and resigned herself to negotiate an agreement with the Curia in September 1309, through the mediation of Philip the Fair of France.[1] She had a forlorn hope of safe-guarding part of the rights she had acquired over Ferrara through the surrender of Fresco d'Este. But Clement V was not to be moved; he declared to the delegates of the doge that their powers as representatives were insufficient, and insisted on unconditional surrender. In March 1310, the Venetian government agreed to submit to the pope's wishes, and to give Francesco Dandolo the necessary authority to sign the peace. Thorny discussions were begun with the three cardinals, and not concluded until 1313; on 17 February[2] Clement V gave solemn notice of the important act by which Venice renounced all the rights she held from Fresco d'Este and from the agreements accepted by Arnaud de St Astier and Onofrio de Trevi in 1308. The losers had to pay the cost of the war, amounting to fifty thousand gold florins, to compensate all the crusaders injured by them, and to give up, in part, the commercial advantages they had gained from the different agreements made with Ferrara before 1308. They had now lost all hope of imposing their supremacy on northern Italy.

The republican government was wise enough to realise how great a mistake it had made, and henceforth scrupulously observed the conditions laid down by Clement V.

The Roman Church had done a great service to those who lived on the banks of the Po, and had freed the Ferrarese from Venetian domination: now it had to govern with equity a population that was turbulent, unstable and always prone to sedition. The rivalry and ambition of the noble families were also to be feared, as were the discontent of the Ghibellines and the underhand manœuvres of Francesco d'Este, who was cherishing the hope of succeeding his nephew. The exercise of direct power, accepted on 27 January 1310,[3] with due ceremony depended for its success on the employment of competent, honest and judicious subordinates. Unfortunately the viscount de Bruniquel, who was appointed vicar-general on 19 May

---

[1] Baluze, *Vitae*, VOL. III, p. 103.
[2] *Regestum Clementis V*, nos. 9007–11.
[3] *Ibid.* no. 6316.

1310, made himself hated, and his officers committed malpractices deplored and condemned by the pope.[1] In July a revolt broke out in Ferrara and was harshly repressed: Cardinal de Pellegrue condemned to be hanged thirty-six well-known citizens found guilty of provoking the rising.[2] The murder of Francesco d' Este by the papal troops on 24 August 1312 heightened the popular excitement. The Church's cause seemed compromised to such an extent that Clement V chose to hand over the vicariate to King Robert of Naples.

It is an open question whether the government by Neapolitan officials was worse than that by the representatives of the Holy See, and whether it was characterised by 'barbarous cruelty, excesses, monstrous acts of horror, detestable infamy and obscenity'. The marquises of the Este family and other witnesses cite the following in support of their violent allegations: virgins violated and married women raped, widows reduced to prostitution, the bishop's palace transformed into a resort of depraved courtesans, and the cathedral itself turned into a den of thieves and a house of ill-repute. It is alleged that the people groaned beneath the crushing weight of new or greatly increased taxes, of the salt tax and the customs duties, and that money gifts were extorted from them by threats of imprisonment. Corrupt judges sold justice to the highest bidder, wronged the innocent and refused to listen to the complaints of the common people. Monasteries, churches and charitable institutions, it is said, were plundered, devastated and overwhelmed by unjust demands for money exacted even with violence. 'The poor, orphans and widows, more sorely tried by these afflictions, shed tears that ran down their breasts, beneath the gaze of the most merciful Creator.'[3]

The bombastic style of the indictment brought against the administration of the Neapolitan officials casts some doubt on the truth of its allegations. Should it not rather be considered as a lawyer's pleading, intended to mislead the Holy See as to the true nature of the troubles which occurred at Ferrara on 4 August 1317? On that day about the hour of nones, a sudden tumult arose and cries rang out, 'Death to the robbers! Death to the traitors!' An onslaught was made upon the feeble garrison, composed of Catalans, who fled headlong before the large numbers of their assailants and took refuge in Castello Tedaldo. The crowd forced them out and massacred them; the corpse of the castellan, Rostang, was hacked into small pieces. The fortress itself was partly burned and partly demolished. The sequel to this affair

---

[1] *Ibid.* nos. 6299, 6313, 6314, 6317, 8749.
[2] Villani, *Istorie fiorentine*, Bk IX, ch. iv.
[3] S. Riezler, *Vatikanische Akten*, Innsbruck 1891, pp. 39 and 55, nos. 51 and 72.

followed swiftly: on 14 August the people led the d' Este with honour to their palace, crying 'Long live the *Marchesi!* Long live the House of Este!' So this great family returned to power—a power that it was long to retain—as the result of a *coup d'état* engineered with the help of the Ghibellines who longed to see King Robert driven beyond the confines of northern Italy.[1]

3

The War in Lombardy[2] and the Legation of Bertrand du Poujet, 1316–34

The Roman expedition of the Emperor Henry VII had resulted in rekindling the hatred between Guelphs and Ghibellines so that the strife between them became more furious than ever. Upon his untimely death, the inhabitants of Pisa sought to be reconciled, and made peace with their enemies on 27 February 1314.[3] This truce, however, proved short-lived: the death of Clement V on 20 April 1314 and the prolonged vacancy of the Holy See renewed the courage of the Pisans. Uguccione della Faggiuola, their acknowledged leader, was an active and ambitious man, seeking glory and revenge. He established his authority by seizing Lucca on 14 June 1314, and then reorganised the Ghibelline league on stronger lines. His success was crowned by his glorious victory over the Guelphs at Montecatini on 29 August 1315. This secured predominance in Italy for his party and destroyed completely the praiseworthy enterprise begun by Henry VII, of establishing in various places vicars who would eventually put an end to the government by the lesser nobility. Matteo Visconti ruled over Milan, Piacenza, Tortona, Alessandria, Pavia and Bergamo; Can Grande della Scala over Verona and Vicenza; Passarino Bonaccolsi over Mantua and Modena; and the d'Este family over Ferrara. The province of Piedmont was ruled by Count Amadeus VI of Savoy, Theodore, marquis of Monferrat, Philip of Achaia and Manfred of Saluzzo; Lucca by Castruccio Castracani, after the downfall of Uguccione della Faggiuola; and Urbino by Federico da Montefeltro.

The ambition of all these nobles was to create for themselves small regional states. Had they relied on their own strength they would

---

[1] Riezler, *op. cit.* p. 39 (report made to John XXII by Bernard Gui and Bertrand de la Tour on 20 August 1317).
[2] This was the name given to northern Italy in the fourteenth century.
[3] R. Caggese, *Roberto d'Angiò e i suoi tempi,* VOL. I, Florence 1922, p. 201.

not, perhaps, have constituted too serious a threat to neighbouring cities and to the king of Naples, the nominal leader of the Guelphs; but when, on the other hand, they formed a bloc with Matteo Visconti, who, as Villani tells us, considered himself no less than a king,[1] they were in danger of disturbing the balance of power in Italy which the Roman Church had always sought to preserve intact. Moreover, Bologna and the Romagna were too attractive as booty not to prove tempting to the powerful and crafty master of Milan. Pope John XXII put an end to the cautious and opportunist attitude adopted by Clement V, and undertook to rally the Guelph party, which had always received support from the Church. To achieve this end, he made a personal attack on Matteo Visconti and his chief satellites.

Before adopting this extreme measure, however, the pope took over the Emperor's rôle and in his turn made a vague gesture of conciliation: he sent to Italy two men of value, the chronicler and Inquisitor Bernard Gui, and Bertrand de la Tour, the minister of the Franciscan province of Aquitaine.[2] They had a twofold mission: to proclaim the six months' truce promulgated on 12 March 1317[3] between the king of Naples on the one hand, and on the other, Amadeus, count of Savoy and his allies Philip of Achaia, the marquis of Saluzzo and Matteo Visconti; and to restore peace between Guelphs and Ghibellines. This last enterprise was doomed to failure from the start, as the recent expedition of Henry VII had only too clearly shown. Moreover, it seems unlikely that the pope was deluded by any false hopes, since as early as March 1317, he announced to King Robert that he intended to appoint a legate in Tuscany and Lombardy. His only reason for delay in naming a cardinal for this post was that he was uncertain whom to choose.[4] No doubt he wished to justify the armed intervention which he had already decided was inevitable. This valiant part remained to be played, if his efforts at peace-making proved unsuccessful.

The people of Piedmont, who had been severely tried by the rigours of war, were glad to welcome the nuncios, who had crossed the snow-clad Alps about Easter 1317. It was easy to persuade the enemies of the king of Naples to negotiate a lasting peace with him at Avignon.[5] It was evident from the start, however, that the task to be

[1] Villani, *Istorie fiorentine*, Bk IX, ch. cvii.
[2] For a short account of their careers, see *Histoire littéraire de la France*, VOL. XXXV, pp. 139–232, VOL. XXXVI, pp. 190–203.
[3] Mollat, VOL. I, no. 5133. See also C. Cipolla, *Lettere di Giovanni XXII riguardanti Verona e gli Scaligeri*, Verona 1908, no. 16.   [4] Cipolla, *op. cit.*
[5] See the nuncios' letters dated 18 April and published by S. Riezler, *Vatikanische Akten*, Innsbruck 1891, no. 50, pp. 22–3.

undertaken in Lombardy would prove arduous. Vercelli and Novara had recently been conquered by Matteo Visconti; here the nuncios declared that the people did not dare to tell them of their grievances, because spies kept a close watch on the citizens and the conqueror held them 'in his claws.' Full of apprehension, they wrote, on 18 April 1317, 'We are more afraid of the wiles of the fox than of the pride of the lion.'[1] Their forebodings were soon justified. When he was requested to allow the exiles from Milan to return home, to restore their property to families that had been despoiled and to set free political prisoners, Matteo Visconti replied in enigmatic terms: 'I will take counsel with upright men of experience and give you my answer.'

Accordingly a solemn assembly of the Ghibellines of northern Italy took place at Milan and decided upon a concerted plan of action. Visconti's reply was haughty: in the words of his spokesman, the cities that obeyed him enjoyed peace thanks to his efforts, and had no need of papal intervention; none were held prisoner save criminals who deserved to die but who were allowed to live by his mercy; the della Torre family were guilty of treason, and richly deserved a capital sentence under a decree of Henry VII. The delegates from the Ghibelline cities sang the praises of Matteo Visconti and of their common policy, and loudly abused the Guelphs. Some voices were raised to suggest that in Milan 'Fifty nobles would rather devour their own children than allow the della Torre to be freed.' One went so far as to say, 'If they had been beheaded, they would no longer be spoken of.[2]

Bernard Gui and Bertrand de la Tour reached Verona on 14 June 1317, and there met Can Grande della Scala, whom, in accordance with their instructions, they begged to break off hostilities with the people of Brescia and to give up his attempt to capture their city. But the tyrant—for it is thus that the Bulls were to refer to these potentates of northern Italy—had made common cause with the exiles and had agreed to be their overlord; therefore, not wishing to give up this authority, he forbade his protégés to sign the peace with their fellow-citizens who had immediately seen what such an action would entail. When he was urged to give up his warlike plans, he flew into a rage, and brutally declared: 'I shall do everything I think fit, and I will impose my will upon them; no man will dare to do anything against it.' Can Grande categorically refused to set free the captured citizens of Padua and Vicenza, and to renounce the title of vicar-general, bestowed on him for life by Henry VII. He cared

[1] Riezler, *op. cit.* pp. 23–4.   [2] *Ibid.* pp. 24–7 (nuncios' letters dated 23 May 1317).

nothing for the threat of excommunication; the papal sentences would not affect him, for eminent lawyers had assured him that they were worthless.

Passarino Bonaccolsi followed Can Grande's example and agreed to none of the pleas put forward by the nuncios: he continued to consider the exiled Mantuans as undesirables, to encourage the internal dissensions existing at Parma and Cremona, and to style himself vicar-general in the name of the Empire.[1]

Bernard Gui and Bertrand de la Tour were failing lamentably to carry out their mission. Then a very unwelcome piece of news reached them: revolution had broken out in Ferrara and the Este family had assumed power. The two nuncios, full of bitterness, painted the Italian situation in the darkest colours. The tyrants, they declared, greedy for new conquests, are the cause of the troubles that are ravaging the country; they oppress the devoted sons of the Church—meaning the Guelphs—and extort from the people the money they need to maintain large numbers of cruel and barbarous mercenaries who cause terror wherever they go. There is no justice, no equity. 'It is pitiful to see churches outside the cities made into desert places by war, lonely and despoiled of their riches.' Ever since the coming of Henry VII, good and praiseworthy though he was, the state of Italy has grown and still grows worse from day to day, because of the ferocity and lust for spoil of those who came in his train. It is generally agreed that peace will never come to Lombardy until 'an indigenous and hereditary' kingdom is set up, whose leaders will be capable of inspiring 'fear and love' and of destroying the unbearable yoke of the tyrants and spreading concord and justice around them.[2]

As a result of the setback that his nuncios had experienced, Pope John XXII decided to take the offensive against the Ghibellines, who were in his eyes guilty of disobedience. To this he was driven by his domineering and authoritarian temperament, and exceptional circumstances furthered his plans; for after the death of Henry VII the double election [3] of Frederick of Austria and Louis of Bavaria, on 19 and 20 October 1314, allowed him to act with complete freedom.

As soon as he was crowned, John XXII invited the two rivals to settle their quarrel by peaceful means (5 September 1316);[4] for several years, he preserved an apparently neutral attitude towards them, though his sympathies were rather with Frederick of Austria.

[1] *Ibid.* pp. 29–34 (nuncios' letters dated 15 July 1317).
[2] *Ibid.* pp. 36–9 (nuncios' letters dated 18 July and 20 August 1317).
[3] See below, Bk II, ch. II.
[4] J. Schwalm, *Constitutiones et acta publica imperatorum et regum*, VOL. V, no. 373. The pope made the same recommendation in 1320, *ibid.* no. 579.

James II of Aragon, Frederick's father-in-law, who had warmly embraced his cause,[1] deserved to be treated with consideration because he was working untiringly to bring to a peaceful end the discord between his brother, Frederick II, king of Trinacria, and Robert of Anjou. On the other hand, the pope had reason to fear the advances made by Louis of Bavaria to the Ghibellines, on whom, in the person of Cardinal Pietro Colonna[2] and four members of his family, he heaped favours.

Truth to tell, John XXII had no wish to see an end to the vacancy in the Empire, prolonged by the double election of 1314, and he prepared to reap the maximum advantage from it. Into the *Corpus juris canonici*[3] he inserted an act destined to have considerable consequences, in which he declared that, in the absence of a secular authority, the jurisdiction, administration and ordering of the Empire devolved upon him, since God had conferred on him, in the person of the blessed St Peter, the right to command both in heaven and on earth. He expressed astonishment that those who had received vicariates or offices from Henry VII should have continued in them without having either sought or obtained the permission of the Holy See. Others, he said, had recently taken up such offices, or, having formerly resigned them, had boldly taken them back. The perpetrators of such intolerable abuses would be deemed worthy of excommunication if they did not resign; and the same punishment would fall on those who obeyed them or lent them aid, counsel and assistance. All oaths of loyalty made to representatives of the imperial authority, together with pacts or agreements contracted with them, were to be considered invalid.

Though it did not mention him by name, the Decretal *Si fratrum* was directed against Louis of Bavaria who had, on 4 January 1315, nominated John of Hainault, the brother of Count William of Holland, as vicar-general in Italy.[4] John XXII pretended to be unaware of this nomination, and, on 16 July 1317[5] confirmed Robert of Naples in the vicariate-general conferred on him by Clement V. After this the pope claimed the right actually to govern the Empire

---

[1] Schwalm, *op. cit.* VOL. V, nos. 223, 226, 256, 311, 376. The Aragonese ambassador, Juan Lopez, advised his sovereign that all the cardinals favoured Frederick. *Ibid.* no. 260, p. 222.

[2] Louis of Bavaria calls him his 'very dear friend' in the privileges granted to him in 1315. See Schwalm, *op. cit.* nos. 289, 290, 333.

[3] Constitution *Si fratrum*, in *Corpus juris canonici, Extrav. John XXII*, tit. V. See also Schwalm, *op. cit.* VOL. V, no. 401: *Licet de jure sit liquidum et ab olim fuerit inconcusse servatum quod, vacante Imperio, cum in illo ad secularem judicem nequeat haberi recursus, ad Summum pontificem, cui in persona beati Petri terreni simul et celestis Imperii jura Deus ipse commisit, Imperii predicti jurisdictio, regimen et dispositio devolvatur.*

[4] Schwalm, *op. cit.* VOL. V, nos. 195–6.   [5] *Ibid.* no. 443.

during the interregnum and to exercise judiciary powers by special right. It may be that John XXII, influenced by the attitude of those around him—for the most part theologians, ardent supporters of the doctrine of the universal supremacy of the Roman pontiff—did not realise that the state of mind of his contemporaries had suffered great changes; it is possible, too, that he deliberately reacted against the new tendencies.[1] Though the Italians of the fourteenth century venerated the spiritual head of the Church this did not prevent them from disputing his right to make use of ecclesiastical penalties to uphold a political cause, such as that of the Guelphs, whom they accused him of favouring. Furthermore they would not acknowledge his claim to govern the Empire during the vacancy or to exercise judiciary powers;[2] in short, they were already making a clear distinction between temporal and spiritual authority. The author of the *Annales Mediolanenses*[3] expresses himself clearly on this point: 'Is Pope John XXII waging a just war against the city of Milan? It seems not, for he should not intervene in wars, but only in spiritual matters. . . . Moreover, no man acts with equity when he seizes another's property; since, then, the pope has no rights over this city, he is acting unjustly in attacking it.' This is why the events in Lombardy and the surrounding regions have such great importance; they foreshadow the birth of what has been called the spirit of the modern world long before the days of Machiavelli.

John XXII's first sanctions were directed against Matteo Visconti, Can Grande della Scala and Passarino Bonaccolsi, who had contravened the Constitution *Si fratrum*. On 16 December 1317, Inverard, abbot of the Benedictine monastery of St Euphemia at Brescia and administrator of the diocese, opened canonical proceedings against them. The Ghibelline leaders were in no way intimidated by the threats of excommunication and interdict made against those who did not cease hostilities against the Brescians within twenty days and, within thirty, restore the fortresses won from them;[4] they continued, too, to style themselves imperial vicars, except for Visconti, who took the title of duke of Milan, in the hope of disarming the pope: a hope which proved vain, for John XXII treated him as a usurper for not having asked his consent. On 6 April 1318 the three tyrants were cited to appear within two months.[5] Matteo Visconti had been excommunicated since the previous December, and the interdict

---

[1] N. Valois, in *Histoire littéraire de la France*, VOL. XXXIV, pp. 480–1.
[2] It should be noted that at Verona the secular and regular clergy except for the cathedral canons contravened the interdict pronounced against the town. See Cipolla, *op. cit.* no. 100, p. 117.
[3] Muratori, VOL. XVI, col. 697.
[4] Cipolla, *op. cit.* no. 28.
[5] *Ibid.* no. 30.

affected Milan, Vercelli and Novara, for the della Torre family had not been set free.[1] Here, indeed, the pope was asking the impossible, for to liberate the members of this family would inevitably have led to revolution in Milan and hastened the downfall of its new master.

Visconti, far from being dismayed by the anathemata of the Church, flouted them. Had he not reached the summit of power, since he kept the mastery of Milan for himself, while of his four sons, Galeazzo was master of Cremona and Piacenza, Marco of Tortona and Alessandria, Luchino of Pavia, and Stefano of Lodi, Como and Bergamo? Moreover, did not Voghera, Vercelli and Novara all obey him? When the families of Doria and Spinola were driven from Genoa by the Fieschi and the Grimaldi and called on him for help, Matteo Visconti put his son Marco in command of numerous German and Lombard bands who joined the mercenaries of the Ghibelline league in besieging Genoa by land and sea.[2]

The beleaguered city asked for help from John XXII, and the pope several times appealed to Matteo Visconti to raise the blockade but he replied that Genoa was on imperial territory and not subject to the Church. Then the Genoese called on Robert of Anjou to come to their aid, and he left Naples with a large fleet and an imposing army. The Genoese welcomed him with gratitude and on 27 July 1318 made him lord of the city for twelve years.

The king of Naples was not acting entirely out of disinterested devotion to the Guelph cause. He foresaw that if he were victorious he might be able to involve the Genoese in a campaign directed against Sicily. Moreover, he was glad to fight against the Spinola and the Doria, who were his personal enemies and had often joined Frederick II, king of Trinacria, in plotting against him.[3]

Robert of Anjou was aiming still higher. About September 1318, he revealed his distress to his kinsman, King Philip the Tall, of France. His forces were insufficient to combat the Ghibellines who were besieging Genoa. He could not rely on the help of his barons, for he dared not withdraw them from Apulia, which was constantly threatened with sudden attack by Sicily. 'Protected by the victorious standards of the lilies of France, to the sound of the trumpet and the clash of arms'—what a fine opportunity this would be to avenge the innocent blood of the king's brother Pierre and his nephew Charles, shed on the battlefield of Montecatini![4]

The pope's co-operation was no less to be desired: Robert went to

[1] A. Ratti, 'Intorno all' anno della scomunica di Matteo Visconti,' *Rendiconti del R. Istituto lombardo di scienze e lettere*, ser. 2, VOL. XXXVI, 1903, pp. 1050–67.
[2] Villani, *op. cit.* Bk IX, ch. lxxxviii.   [3] *Ibid.* chs. xci, xcii, cvii.
[4] Schwalm, *op. cit.* VOL. V, no. 505.

Avignon[1] and obtained it without difficulty. John XXII called upon Matteo Visconti to end the siege of Genoa. The tyrant did not deign to reply. Ten months of fighting by the Neapolitan forces that had entered the city were needed before the enemy could be driven back.

Meanwhile Can Grande della Scala was not giving up any of his plans of conquest. The Brescians, molested by his troops, feared that all was lost and saw their only chance of salvation in offering King Robert the lordship, which he willingly accepted on 28 January 1319. This more than compensated him for the loss of Ferrara, and enabled him to cut communications between Verona and Milan. Matteo Visconti immediately parried this blow by forming a league with Philip of Achaia.[2]

Can Grande della Scala also had designs on Treviso, and in the hope of seizing that city, formed a coalition with the count of Goritz, Guecello da Camino, and with Uguccione della Faggiuola, the lord of Lucca and Pisa. Faggiuola went so far as to take over the command of the attacking forces. John XXII was requested to intervene, and ordered the bishops of Bologna and Arras and Aimeric de Châtelus to draw up charges against the coalition (22 November 1318). The threat of ecclesiastical penalties did not deter the besieging forces from tightening their grip on the city. In their distress, the inhabitants sent ambassadors to Duke Frederick of Austria. But the remedy was worse than the disease for the king of the Romans forced the count of Goritz upon them as his representative! In the circumstances, a compromise with Can Grande was inevitably reached, and on 4 October 1319 the two antagonists signed a pact of friendship, making over Treviso to the count and Padua to Can Grande.[3]

In face of the ever-increasing effrontery of the Ghibellines, Pope John XXII realised that he must appoint a legate in Italy, and chose a compatriot, Bertrand du Poujet, who had been raised to the purple in 1316.

This man, who was to play a rôle of the first importance, was the subject of much controversy in the fourteenth century.[4] While the pope praised his activity, vigilance and discretion, and others emphasised his wisdom, generosity, sense of justice, literary gifts, learning and administrative ability, some Italians complained at length of

---

[1] His presence, as well as that of the king of France on 27 April and 9 May 1320, is attested by the account-books of the Apostolic Camera. See K. H. Schäfer, *Die Ausgaben der apostolischen Kammer unter Johann XXII*, Paderborn 1911, pp. 59–60.
[2] Cipolla, *op. cit.* p. 16.   [3] *Ibid.* nos. 36–40, pp. 45–56.
[4] See the evidence collected by Baluze, *Vitae paparum Avenionensium*, ed. Mollat, VOL. II, p. 221. For biographical studies, see E. Albe, *Autour de Jean XXII*, VOL. I, Rome 1902, pp. 168–82, and L. Ciaccio, *Il cardinale legato Bertrando del Poggetto in Bologna*, Bologna 1906.

his authoritarian personality and unbridled ambition, of the harshness of his character and of his disdainful and haughty manners.
Petrarch went so far as to make him out a fierce *condottiere*, a sort of
Hannibal marching at the head of his legions to conquer Italian territory; then, in his usual way, he changed his mind. In 1352 Petrarch
wrote, 'His life seemed very long to himself and was so according to
the natural law; but, if I am not mistaken, it was all too short for the
public weal.'[1] Giovanni Villani[2] has had his share in spreading the
legend of the cardinal's relationship with the supreme pontiff, and
until this very day historians have repeated his false reports without
attempting to verify them. This outburst of Italian feeling against
Bertrand du Poujet can no doubt be accounted for by the many years
he spent as legate among the Italians, and the resentment of those
whose policy he so firmly thwarted.

The cardinal was chosen as legate on 23 July 1319,[3] but did not
immediately leave the papal court: the troubled situation in northern
Italy caused anxiety lest he might find himself in a serious predica-
ment. The Bulls of this time[4] do not indicate exactly what this pre-
dicament was. It seems highly probable that owing to the intrigues
of Matteo Visconti the days of the envoy's life were likely to be
numbered so unsafe were the roads. He was not granted full spiritual
and temporal authority until 2 June 1320, and did not leave until
10 July.[5]

Bertrand du Poujet had an exceptionally difficult task before him
At the outset he issued a kind of ultimatum to Matteo Visconti,
calling on him to renounce the lordship of Milan and give it to Robert
of Naples, to recall political exiles to the city and to set free the della
Torre. Matteo's only reply was to cast into prison the chaplain entrusted with conveying John XXII's wishes.[6] As a result the legate
excommunicated him.

The pope, however, was not taken by surprise. He had foreseen
that the lord of Milan would only yield to force. Since the troops at
the legate's disposal—about eight hundred men[7]—were not in his

[1] *Opera*, Basle 1580, Epistle VII (no title); *Lettere famigliari*, ed. Fracasetti, Florence
1892, No. XI, 6.
[2] 'Per li più si diceva piuvicamente ch' egli era suo figliuolo, e in molte cose il somi-
gliava.' (*Op. cit.* Bk XI, ch. vi.) E. Albe (*op. cit.*) has unequivocally revealed the truth
and proved, moreover, that the cardinal was not the pope's nephew, but only related
to the family of La Pérarède, who had contracted matrimonial alliances with members
of the Duèse family. Bertrand was born at Castelnau-Montratier (Lot), the son of
Bertrand, lord of Poujet.
[3] Mollat, VOL. II, nos. 10203, 10204. See also Rinaldi, *ad annum* 1320, §10.
[4] Coulon, VOL. I, no. 1040, col. 897.
[5] Mollat, VOL. III, nos. 12112–50. See also Coulon, VOL. I, nos. 1041, 1044.
[6] Mollat, no. 12296. *Annales Mediolanenses*, in Muratori, VOL. XVI, ch. xcii, col. 698.
[7] Villani, *op. cit.* Bk IX, ch. cvii.

opinion sufficient, he followed the example of Robert of Anjou, and asked for help from France.

This twofold request for help was highly embarrassing to Philip the Tall, especially as he received at the same time a similar request from the Ghibellines. If he lent his support to the latter, he would alienate the papacy which had helped him to the throne and shown feelings of real friendship towards him. If, on the other hand, he made an alliance with the Guelphs, he would be supporting the interests of their leader, the king of Naples, which were not always identical with his own. All Philip the Tall did was authorise his cousin, Philip of Valois, count of Maine, to go to Italy. He compromised himself, however, with regard to the Empire by allowing his cousin to assume the title of Vicar-General, a title which had been conferred on Robert of Anjou by the Church, and subdelegated to the French king with the approval and confirmation of John XXII.[1]

In the month of April 1320, Castruccio Castracani, the tyrant of Lucca, and the people of Pisa, got wind of what was being planned at the court of Avignon. Their anxiety grew when they learned that a thousand horsemen, from Bologna, Florence and Siena, were concentrated at Reggio Emilia. Urged on by Matteo Visconti, who feared the worst, Castruccio Castracani created a diversion in order to prevent the invasion of Lombardy: he broke off his peaceful relations with Florence without the slightest provocation and made a surprise attack on Florentine territory.[2]

The French army,[3] fifteen hundred horsemen strong, reached Coni on 6 June and then pressed on to Asti. Without waiting for the promised reinforcements from the Florentines and their allies, they left that city on 2 August, intending to liberate Vercelli, which was being besieged by the Ghibellines. At Mortara they met with the Visconti army, which was coming to help the besieging forces. Rightly interpreting the secret wishes of Philip the Tall, who still hoped to have the Ghibellines on his side and to carve out a kingdom in the north of Italy, Philip of Valois parleyed with the enemy. Galeazzo Visconti, a master of persuasive tactics, soon won him over. The Visconti family, he pointed out, had always had friendly relations with the court of France. He would gladly take advantage of the good offices of Philip the Tall to settle the dispute with the papacy. As a final argument, he referred to the numerical superiority of his forces.

[1] Schwalm, *op. cit.* VOL. V, no. 577 (19 May 1320).
[2] Villani, *op. cit.* Bk IX, ch. civ.
[3] *Ibid.* chs. civ, cvii, cviii. See also P. Lehugeur, *Histoire de Philippe V le Long*, Paris 1897, pp. 211–16; J. Viard, *Philippe de Valois avant son avènement au trone, B.E.C.*, VOL. XCI, 1930, pp. 307–25.

According to Villani, presents and gifts accompanied this cunning speech. Béraud de Mercœur, suborned by Milanese gold, urged Philip of Valois to retreat. Philip heeded his advice and his troops moved off towards the Alps, while the Guelph reinforcements, reduced to relying on their own strength, dared not risk an encounter with the Milanese and dispersed; thus the French expedition came to a lamentable end. The count of Maine is said to have given the king the excuse that neither the pope nor Robert of Anjou had sent him money in time to pay his troops and those on whose help he had counted. If he did make these unjust statements, John XXII and Robert repaid him generously for the money he had spent.[1] The responsibility for the setback rested entirely upon him: it had been very unwise—unless it was a tactical manœuvre—to go prematurely into action.

The defection of the French army deprived Bertrand du Poujet of all his means of defence, and at the same time made the Visconti even more bold. With the help of Castruccio Castracani, they reinforced the siege of Genoa.[2] In August 1320, forty-two ships arrived from Sicily and, together with the twenty-two galleys of the Genoese exiles, made the blockade complete.

At this news, the small Franco-papal flotilla, which was in a Mediterranean port preparing for the crusade, changed its objective and under the command of the Admiral Ramon of Cardona sailed to attack the enemy squadron. When they approached, the Sicilians pretended to flee, and put in at the rich island of Ischia, which they laid waste. When the Neapolitan sails were sighted on the horizon, they made as if to retreat towards the south, and then, going about, they returned to renew the blockade of Genoa (3 September 1320). Ramon of Cardona pursued them, but the Franco-papal squadron fell into the hands of Admiral Corrado Doria. Despite this disaster, furious battles took place on 26 and 29 September. Discouraged by the resistance they encountered and the losses they had suffered, the Sicilians were disheartened and put out to sea again.[3]

On land, the Visconti were successful in their military operations. They seized Vercelli in April 1321, and Cremona on 5 January 1322.[4]

In this critical situation, John XXII recalled that Louis of Bavaria's rival had given undoubted evidence of friendship. Indeed, at one time, in June 1316, there was talk of a matrimonial alliance

[1] Schäfer, op. cit. pp. 59, 60, 172, 816.   [2] Villani, op. cit. Bk IX, ch. cix.
[3] Ibid. chs. cx, cxi, cxiii. See also Ch. de la Roncière, ' Une Escadre franco-papale (1318–1320),' Mélanges, XIII, pp. 397–418.
[4] Villani, op. cit. Bk IX, chs. cxxvi, cxxvii.

between his sister Catherine, and Charles, duke of Calabria, who had once been proposed as husband of Beatrice of Luxembourg.[1] By 1320, a political alliance with Robert of Anjou seemed likely: the seneschal of Provence, on 15 June, had been given authority to contract 'pacts, conventions, promises and obligations' with the representatives of Frederick of Austria, and to provide all necessary guarantees, after approval by the Holy See.[2] John XXII cajoled the prince, writing, 'We hold thee dear in our heart.' He set himself to force Frederick of Austria to fall in with his wishes, and suggested that he should dissociate himself from 'the great excesses and unconsidered acts' committed in Avignon by an emissary of Frederick II of Trinacria, who had dared to defy Robert of Anjou. If the pope disapproved of Frederick of Austria's friendly relations with Can Grande della Scala, he expressed himself tactfully and without anger; he was obviously handling him carefully.[3]

John XXII was able to show himself in a favourable light by dangling before Frederick of Austria the glittering hope of having his election confirmed, and of obtaining the archbishopric of Mainz for his brother,[4] provided that he came to the aid of Bertrand du Poujet. Matteo Visconti was soon able to tell the king of Trinacria, with whom he had made an alliance, that Duke Leopold would come to the aid of the Guelphs; this news caused violent reaction in the Ghibelline party, especially in Sicily.[5] In July 1321, James II of Aragon calmed his brother by informing him that this Guelph combination had failed.[6]

In 1322, John XXII took heart again, and was able with great joy on 21 February to advise the inhabitants of Brescia of the approaching arrival of the Austrians.[7] On 4 April, two thousand soldiers entered the town. Together with the papal army that was concentrated at Valenza and the reinforcements from Bologna, Florence and Siena, they constituted a serious threat to Milan. Matteo Visconti, knowing that the people were groaning under the consequences of the excommunication pronounced against him, took fright. While twelve notables parleyed with Bertrand du Poujet, other ambassadors were working hard to present their case skilfully to the leader of the Austrian expedition, pointing out the dangerous consequences that might result from a successful campaign against Milan: namely, the destruction of the Ghibelline party; as for the Holy See, they said,

---

[1] Schwalm, *op. cit.* VOL. V, no. 364.   [2] *Ibid.* no. 584.   [3] *Ibid.* no. 582.
[4] Villani, *op. cit.* Bk IX, ch. cxlii.
[5] Schwalm, *op. cit.* VOL. V, no. 625 (letters dated 1 May 1321, addressed to James II of Aragon, from Frederick II).
[6] *Ibid.* no. 626 (James II's reply, dated 30 July 1321).   [7] *Ibid.* no. 647.

once it was firmly established in northern Italy, the Emperor would find his way barred.[1]

John XXII suspected that Matteo Visconti, 'that pestilent and perfidious enemy of God and the Church'[2] was immobilising the Austrian troops at Brescia; moreover, he warned Duke Henry against Matteo's cunning, and urged him 'to accomplish what had been laudably and manfully begun,' for otherwise 'the divine Majesty would be offended, and the wrath of the Church unleashed.'[3] But exhortations to action and veiled threats were of no avail against the gold so cleverly distributed by the Visconti. On 18 May, the Austrians retreated as far as Verona, where Can Grande della Scala loaded them with honours and gifts.[4] In August, ambassadors were sent to the legate, in order to justify Frederick's conduct, and to conclude a treaty with him. They had chosen a favourable moment, for Ramon of Cardona, the leader of the papal army, was in an unfortunate position in the faubourgs of Bassignana: he had failed to conquer the fortress, and was now himself hard-pressed and besieged. It was agreed that, as surety, the ambassadors should receive the faubourgs and the fortress from the hands of the occupants. But the negotiations came to nothing, and these two pledges had to be handed back to Marco Visconti.[5]

This was yet another bitter blow for John XXII. Just as France had deceived him in 1320, so now in 1322 Austria was betraying him and dashing his hopes; he had in truth reaped nothing but disappointment in the field of foreign affairs. The pope showed his bitterness by ordering Bertrand du Poujet to annul the oaths of loyalty made to Henry of Austria in Lombardy on his brother's account, together with the pacts and alliances made by him to the detriment of the Church.[6]

In October 1322, however, more encouraging news reached Avignon: since the ninth of that month the important town of Piacenza had recognised the Church's authority. Its lord, Galeazzo Visconti, had abused the wife of a Ghibelline, Versuzzo de Lando, who took advantage of a chance absence of Galeazzo to bring in four hundred of Bertrand du Poujet's men, thanks to the complicity of a friend who treacherously opened one of the city gates. The legate set up his headquarters there on 27 November.[7]

---

[1] Villani, *op. cit.* Bk IX, chs. cxlii–cxliii.

[2] He refers to him thus in a letter addressed to the Brescians. See Schwalm, *op. cit.* VOL. V, no. 655 (20 May 1322).

[3] Schwalm, *op. cit.* VOL. V, no. 657 (letters of 24 May 1322).

[4] Villani, *op. cit.* Bk IX, ch. cxliii.   [5] *Ibid.*, chs. clviii, clxii.

[6] Schwalm, *op. cit.* VOL. V, no. 700 (30 November 1322).

[7] Bertrand du Poujet remained there until 21 November 1325. See *Chronicon Placentinum*, in Muratori, VOL. XVI, col. 493.

These events caused a sensation in Lombardy; they came at a time when the canonical proceedings brought against Matteo Visconti in 1317 by the bishops of Asti and Como, and, in 1320, by Bertrand du Poujet, were entering a new phase. The legate, cooped up in Asti, a town subject to King Robert, had for long not dared to venture beyond its confines. With such patience as he could muster, he had to wait for the monies brought in by the unwieldy financial system that John XXII had set up throughout Christendom[1] in order to engage a suitable number of German and Catalan mercenaries, who demanded heavy payment. All the cardinal could do was to begin new proceedings against the Ghibelline nobles who had not obeyed the summonses addressed to them to appear in Avignon, and who had remained excommunicate for three years. The Holy See had determined to apply strictly the Decretal *Quum contumacia* and inquisitorial methods;[2] these laid down that whosoever continued excommunicate for more than one year gave clear evidence that he despised the Church's penalties, and that consequently there rested on him 'a strong presumption of heresy'; in such circumstances, the judge 'could condemn the contumacious offender to major excommunication, and forbid all dealings with him. In obedience to the pope's commands, Bertrand du Poujet once more cited the guilty to appear, this time in order to answer the charge of 'the stain of heresy' of which they were 'suspect' and to present their defence, on 18 and 27 June and on 18 and 28 November 1320.[3]

The case against Matteo Visconti was made worse by depositions heard at Avignon in February and September 1320. A priest from Milan, Bartolomeo Canholati, told how, about the middle of the previous October, the tyrant had summoned him to his palace and had shown him 'a statuette of silver, longer than a man's palm, with the face and form of a man, bearing these letters engraved on its forehead: *Jacobus, papa Johannes*, and on its breast a cabalistic sign representing Saturn, with the word *Amaymon*, the name of a devil of the West. The head of the image was pierced and had a silver cover.' Then the tyrant had said, 'The pope is no more pope than I am God; if he were, he would not act as he does; he would not plunge the whole universe into error. He is doing his utmost to deprive me of my heritage and to bring me to nought; I shall strive to do the like to him. . . . Behold, Bartolomeo, this image that I have had made to

---

[1] Mollat and Samaran, *La Fiscalité pontificale en France au XIVᵉ siècle*, Paris 1905.
[2] *Corpus juris canonici*, Bk V, tit. II, ch. vii, in *VIᵒ*. See also Douais, *Practica Inquisitionis hereticae pravitatis auctore Bernardo Guidonis*, Paris 1886, pp. 109, 177.
[3] Mollat, VOL. III, nos. 12180, 12185–9, 14193–6, 14211–12. See also Cipolla, *op. cit.* nos. 45, 47, 49, 52.

bring about the pope's death; it must be submitted to fumigations. This thou canst do: do it then, with due solemnity; I will make thee rich and powerful.'

The priest begged to be excused, declaring that he knew nothing of incantations. In March 1320, since he was suspected of betraying Visconti's plans, he was cast into prison. But when a powerful intervention was made on his behalf, he was released and finally summoned to Piacenza. There Galeazzo Visconti questioned him on the reasons for the failure of the attempted bewitching of John XXII, and asked for his help in return for a substantial reward. As Bartolomeo was unwilling to reply, Galeazzo pressed him saying: 'Have no fear, but rather be sure that if thy soul were lost or damned' (for the clerk had given as excuse his fear of eternal damnation) 'thou couldst save it by doing what I ask. Consider now how the pope sows death throughout all Lombardy, and how many murders he causes. He who would put him to death would win eternal salvation. The pope has joined with the Guelphs; he causes them to return to their homes, but the Ghibellines he puts out. To kill him would be a work of piety. . . . Dost thou know,' he continued, 'that I have had Master Dante Alighieri come here from Florence for this affair. . . ? I would not for the world have him concerned in it; I would not reveal it to him for a thousand gold florins, for I wish thee to have charge of it; I have great faith in thee.' Bartolomeo Canholati pretended to agree, declaring that he must procure the necessary poisons at Milan, and had the image sent to him there. In this way he was able to put this evidence in the hands of the three examining judges appointed by the Holy See.

Others besides Bartolomeo Canholati gave evidence against Matteo Visconti. The archbishop of Milan and the Inquisitors collected many witnesses to speak against him and his son. Matteo was accused in particular of denying the resurrection of the body, divine providence and the existence of hell and paradise, of taking part in the Black Mass, and of bowing the knee at Soncino before the bones of Eccelino da Romano, an excommunicate and a rebel against the Church, and of having an elaborate service celebrated in his honour.[1]

The complete dossier is still preserved in the Vatican;[2] but the Holy See acted only upon the charges of maltreatment of members of the clergy at Milan and elsewhere, that is to say the levying of excessive taxes, the seizure of their goods, their imprisonment and

---

[1] Robert André-Michel, in *Mélanges*, Paris 1920, pp. 149–206.
[2] Vatican Library, Latin MSS. 3936, 3937; see the extracts published by Robert André-Michel, *op. cit.* pp. 184–205.

torture; the incarceration of the vicar-general of the Archbishop Gaston della Torre, who had refused to agree to the levying of taxes, and of the master-general of the *Humiliati*, who had forbidden his subordinates to make any payment and had been replaced by an outsider. The Bulls specify other misdeeds, such as the arrest of papal messengers and the seizure of the correspondence they were carrying.[1]

It is impossible to know whether the papal court believed the truth of the Milanese priest's revelations, for no official pronouncement was made on the subject. Whatever theory we may form, it is certain that people in the Middle Ages believed in the efficacy of magical procedures and sorcery. We have but to recall the notorious trials of the reign of Philip the Fair. It may well be that Matteo Visconti, like his contemporaries, deluded himself with the hope that he could be rid of one of his greatest enemies by unlawful means.

The tyrant's failure to appear at Avignon unleashed against him the full force of the papal anathema. Since he was suspected of heresy, excommunication was pronounced against whosoever gave him 'counsel, aid and assistance,' and Milan was laid under an interdict (23 January 1322). Moreover, on 28 January, indulgences were promised to those who took up arms against this enemy of the Church.[2] These extremely serious measures taken by John XXII were complicated by political consequences. Bertrand du Poujet had in fact invited the Guelphs and the doge of Venice to lay hands on all who abetted the Visconti, and to sequester their goods and chattels.[3]

Matteo could not count on the friendship of all the inhabitants of Milan; a party of malcontents headed by Francesco di Garbagnate compelled him to negotiate with the legate. A curious state of affairs had arisen: this Ghibelline's opposition to the peace proposals put forward at the beginning of 1322 through the intermediary of the Bishop of Parma had been so violent that it hampered his acceptance of Bertrand du Poujet's comparatively lenient conditions. The sudden change of attitude in April could only be explained either by the fear of the penalties imposed on the partisans of the Visconti, or by a revival of enmity. What happened was that twelve leading men of the party met the cardinal and obtained peace on condition that Matteo renounced his lordship. On their return to Milan, they fell foul of Galeazzo, who refused to ratify the agreement they had reached, and

---

[1] Riezler, *op. cit.* no. 216*a* and *d*, pp. 114, 116.
[2] Mollat, VOL. IV, nos. 16197, 16213; VOL. V, no. 20362. See also Riezler, *op. cit.* no. 356; Rinaldi, *ad annum* 1327, §7–11.
[3] Ciaccio, *Il cardinale legato Bertrando del Poggetto in Bologna*, Bologna 1906, document no. 1, p. 152.

so they roused the rabble with cries of 'Peace! Peace! Long live the Church!' Intimidated, Matteo resigned his authority in his son's favour on 23 May and died at Crescenzago on 24 June. In November a further riot broke out and on the 8th Galeazzo was forced to flee to Lodi. The twelve rectors, who had fomented it, begged the legate to join them. Bertrand du Poujet had the good sense not to heed them, and withdrew to Piacenza where he learned that Galeazzo had returned to Milan on 29 December.[1]

The appointment of rectors at Reggio and Parma caused the legate to begin more active military operations. The success of the preaching of the crusade gave him good reason for optimism. He had received troops both from Florence and from the della Torre, while Henry, count of Flanders, formerly a marshal in Henry VII's army, had offered his services and assumed command of the non-Italian soldiers. The king of Naples had sent the pope a renowned warrior, the Catalan Ramon of Cardona, who was given the rank of captain over all the troops. Gold was flowing in to pay the mercenaries.[2]

The campaign began about the end of February 1323. Tactics and strategy played but a modest part: we must not imagine slaughter and the clash of armies. Throughout the fourteenth century the war in Italy followed, with few exceptions, a uniform pattern, and consisted of the investment of enemy towns. The assailants' method was to lay waste the outskirts in order to starve the population and to prevent the arrival of help. They also had recourse to trickery, bribery and treason; the cities, beset by a spirit of faction, often remained only for a short time in the conqueror's hands, and changed masters frequently as a result of some unexpected revolution.

Hostilities began in February 1323. Tortona, Monza and Alessandria surrendered on 19 February, 27 February and 2 April respectively. In Genoa, the Neapolitans and Guelphs succeeded in driving the Ghibellines from the faubourgs. A victory on 19 April at Gargazzuola over Marco Visconti allowed the legate to press on with the siege of Milan (11 June). The troops of Ramon of Cardona were so numerous that the city was expected to fall without delay.[3]

While northern Italy was ravaged by war, on the far side of the Alps a victory over Frederick of Austria on 28 September at Mühldorf had secured the imperial throne for Louis of Bavaria. Only a few days before this memorable event, on 23 September, John XXII had been calming Frederick's fears, assuring him that the intrigues

---

[1] *Annales Mediolanenses*, in Muratori, VOL. XVI, col. 699; cf. VOL. XII, col. 727–9.
[2] See the accounts of payment published by K. H. Schäfer, *Deutsche Ritter und Edelknechte in Italien während des 14. Jahrhunderts*, Paderborn 1909, VOL. II, pp. 1–20.
[3] Villani, *op. cit.* Bk IX, ch. ccx.

of kings, princes and other persons that he so feared—a special envoy had been sent to reveal these fears to the court at Avignon—would not harm him; the imperial election would be carried out according to the rules of the strictest equity. When he was asked to give his support to the victor of Mühldorf, the pope, usually an extremely fluent speaker, was reserved and chary in his congratulations, begging Louis to show mercy to his conquered enemy, who had been taken prisoner, and offering his services to draw up peace between them. To the vital question of his support he replied in a laconic and enigmatic fashion: 'We shall proceed without delay to do what we think fitting.' [1] John XXII was in fact trying to evade the issue.

Many circumstances of various kinds lead us to suppose that the pope, before coming to any decision, made conditions which Louis of Bavaria did not accept. At the Avignon court, Louis' designs on Italy and the repeated appeals made to him by the Ghibellines were alike well known. At the very moment when the victorious papal forces were preparing to crush the Visconti and their allies, the Holy See had every reason to fear the arrival in Lombardy of the man who was the obvious supporter of the party that opposed the Church.

Since no agreement was forthcoming on the subject of Italy, Louis of Bavaria did not wait for the Holy See to recognise him as the king of the Romans, but immediately began to act as such. On 25 January 1323, he informed the Visconti, who had asked him for help, that within ten days plenipotentiaries would leave Munich, who would be competent to put right the critical situation into which the Visconti had been driven by Bertrand du Poujet. [2] On 2 March of the same year, German intervention in Italy became effective following the appointment of Berthold von Neifen count of Märstetten, as vicar-general; he began his duties immediately, with the aid of Count Berthold von Graisbach and Friedrich von Truhendingen. [3] The scope of his authority included Lombardy, Tuscany and the Marches of Treviso, in other words exactly the region where Robert of Anjou, in the name of the Roman Church, had the same prerogatives. It was inevitable that a conflict must very shortly break out.

In the month of April, the three representatives of Louis of Bavaria had a meeting at Piacenza with the legate Bertrand du Poujet and demanded the lifting of the siege of Milan, which was still invested by papal and Guelph troops. This they asked because they alleged that Milan was 'a city of the Empire.' The cardinal expressed his astonishment at such a request. Who would dream of giving help to the Visconti, who had been convicted of heresy? Did

[1] Schwalm, *op. cit.* VOL. V, nos. 673, 711.   [2] *Ibid.* no. 723.   [3] *Ibid.* no. 729.

Berthold von Neifen, Berthold von Graisbach and Friedrich von Truhendingen have specific instructions? When they were requested to divulge the content of these instructions, they made all manner of excuses, and withdrew.[1]

On 5 May 1323 a more serious incident occurred. In the episcopal palace at Mantua, Can Grande della Scala and Passarino Bonaccolsi, who had hitherto wielded power at Verona and Mantua in the name of the Empire and contrary to the Decretal *Si fratrum*, were now preparing—following the recent successes of the papal troops— solemnly to declare, in the presence of a large assembly, their sub- mission to the Roman Church. At this juncture, the three delegates of Louis of Bavaria arrived and presented their credentials, remind- ing the tyrants of their oaths of loyalty formerly made to Henry VII and consequently calling on them to come to the aid of the Milanese.[2] This dramatic intervention was enough to alter the peaceful intentions of Can Grande della Scala and Passarino Bonaccolsi, and the Ghibel- line league was swiftly re-formed on 28 June 1323.[3] Four hundred men at arms, brought into Milan by the imperial vicar, gave renewed courage to the besieged, who rushed to the attack. The papal army, reduced in size by the defection of the German mercenaries who went over to the enemy, and further decimated by sickness brought on by the heat of summer, had to retreat towards Monza on 28 July. Thus Louis of Bavaria's intervention in Italy had speedily brought all the pope's plans to nothing. But the aged John XXII did not lose heart; he set to work immediately to build up another armed force and pressed the Florentines to supply him with fresh troops.[4]

On many occasions the Church had had recourse to what con- temporaries called 'the papal arms,' as a last resort in exceptional circumstances. It was of these that John XXII thought in October 1323. He had plenty of grievances against Louis of Bavaria. In addi- tion to his meddling in Italian affairs, the pope held against him the fact that he had welcomed at his court those Franciscans who had rebelled after the publication of the Bulls dealing with apostolic poverty. In a Consistory, he proposed to initiate legal proceedings against Louis on various counts: he had 'aided and abetted' heretics and those who had rebelled against the Church; he had said to the legate of Lombardy, 'You are waging an unjust war against the Visconti, and I will come to their aid with arms'; he had no right to rule the Empire before his election had been examined and confirmed

[1] Villani, *op. cit.* Bk IX, ch. cxciv.
[2] Schwalm, *op. cit.* VOL. V, no. 742.   [3] *Ibid.* no. 753.
[4] *Ibid.* nos. 742, 753, 780. See also Riezler, *op. cit.* no. 330. (Circular letters sent by John XXII to the Guelph communes.)

by the Holy See. This last affirmation was contested by Cardinal Napoleone Orsini, who declared that Louis' victory at Mühldorf had given him the right to assume power, and that to act against him would be an 'unusual and dangerous' step. 'For seven years,' he added, 'you have plunged Germany into strife; you have never uttered one word of peace.'[1] Cardinal Pietro Colonna declared that election and coronation conferred the right to rule the Empire. The pope retorted, 'You speak in error! You speak in error! We will make a Decretal against your opinion.' 'Your Decretal,' replied Pietro Colonna, 'will give you no fresh power.' Whereupon Giacomo Caetani Stefaneschi exclaimed, 'Holy Father! Beware the fury of the Teuton.' At this, the pope brought the discussion to an end, with 'Fury! fury! The Teutons will have to suffer mine.'[2]

On 8 October Louis of Bavaria received a monitory, warning him to appear within the next three months at the court of Avignon and to refrain from exercising imperial sovereignty on pain of excommunication.[3]

Mischief-makers, foremost among whom was Napoleone Orsini, spread the rumour that these latest developments had been inspired by the king of France, who had been offered the Empire by Pope John XXII, and who was mysteriously plotting with the sovereigns of Naples and Bohemia. The ambassadors of Charles IV protested, however, that their master had not been informed of the pope's decisions, and had learned of them with deep regret. The plenipotentiaries from Aragon felt unable to decide who was telling the truth.[4]

Before the date of the summons had expired, a Bavarian embassy reached Avignon. They pointed out that Louis was being exploited by his enemies, and that he would prove his innocence and amend any errors, if he had really committed any. He 'humbly' begged for an extension of the time-limit.[5] On 7 January 1324, the pope granted a delay of two months, after a considerable show of reluctance, and after drawing up a list of charges relating to the actions of Louis of Bavaria in Italy.[6] When this time-limit expired, the duke, who had failed to comply with the orders of the Holy See, was solemnly excommunicated and threatened with loss of his rights if he did not, within the space of three months, refrain from styling himself king of the Romans and from ruling the Empire, unless his election had

[1] This was something of an exaggeration as is proved by the papal Bulls; see above, p. 93.
[2] Despatches from the plenipotentiary of the king of Aragon, in Schwalm, *op. cit.* VOL. V, nos. 788–90.   [3] *Ibid.* no. 792.   [4] *Ibid.* no. 801.
[5] *Ibid.* no. 834. (Text of the request, 4 January 1324.)   [6] *Ibid.* nos. 835, 839.

by then been confirmed.[1] On the same day, the crusade was once more preached against the Visconti;[2] and in April, Berthold von Neifen, Berthold von Graisbach and Friedrich von Truhendingen, who were responsible for the success of the Visconti and guilty of having fought against the papal army, were excommunicated.[3]

John XXII's active opposition to Louis of Bavaria fostered in Germany an agitation that was harmful to his own interests. The aberrant Franciscans who thronged his court advised Louis to imitate the methods of intimidation formerly employed by Philip the Fair against Boniface VIII. At Sachsenhausen, on 22 May 1324, Louis of Bavaria issued a public announcement replying to the judgments of John XXII against himself and his officers by counter-accusations of heresy, and he began a polemical campaign with the intention of appealing to world opinion. 'The pope's wickedness,' he declared, 'touches even Christ, the most blessed Virgin Mary, the Apostles and all whose lives have reflected the doctrine of perfect poverty as set forth in the gospel. Seven popes have approved the rule which God revealed to St Francis, and on which Christ by his stigmata set, as it were, his seal; but this oppressor of the poor, this enemy of Christ and the apostles, seeks by lying and subterfuge to destroy perfect poverty. . . .'

Louis added to these reproaches a vehement protest against the Holy See's claim to consider the Empire vacant and to rule over it, pretensions whose only purpose was to sow discord among princes, nobles and people in Germany. As for the Ghibellines in Italy, 'cruelly and inhumanly ill-treated, oppressed and unjustly slandered,' it was only right to come to their aid.[4]

The *Defensor pacis*, a work finished about 24 June 1324, had repercussions far different from those of the grossly exaggerated manifesto of Sachsenhausen. One of the writers who composed it, Jean de Jandun, was from Champagne, and the other, Marsiglio of Padua, was Italian by birth. They had become friends when they were both studying at the University of Paris, and both equally anxious to acquire honours and powerful protectors, they conceived the idea of drawing Louis of Bavaria's favourable attention to themselves by combining to write a book which, despite its confusion and obscurity, was boldly to declare the supremacy of the Empire and its independence of the Holy See. According to them, one of the reasons for the

---

[1] Schwalm, *op. cit.* VOL. V, no. 881.   [2] *Ibid.* no. 882.   [3] *Ibid.* no. 897.
[4] *Ibid.* nos. 909, 910. The so-called appeals of Nuremberg (18 December 1323) and Frankfurt (5 January 1324) were not made public. See Schwalm, *ibid.* nos. 824, 836. Cf. K. Zeumer, 'Zur Kritik der Appellationen Ludwigs des Baiern,' *Neues Archiv*, VOL. XXXVII, 1911, pp. 221–72.

disturbance of peace on earth was the papacy, 'a fiction' and a human institution, which had only acquired pre-eminence by cunningly supplanting throughout many long years priests, bishops, peoples, princes and the Roman Empire, and which had finally come to meddle in temporal affairs, to excommunicate those who disobeyed it and to encroach on lay jurisdiction. The Church had no powers of coercion, since the apostles taught that every man must submit to political leaders, except in matters of faith. The pope and the bishops could only exercise such powers with the consent of the faithful of a city, or of the community, or of the General Council or of their superior. Supreme authority in the Church was vested in the General Council, which consisted in theory of all the faithful, and in practice of their delegates, both clerical and lay, who must be learned and worthy; it could only be summoned by 'the faithful human legislator, who is subject to none'—in other words, the Emperor, to whom the Roman people, according to the *Defensor minor*, had transferred their legislative powers. The pope's only authority was that derived from the Council or the Emperor; he might be punished, suspended or deposed by them; his election was dependent on the people, their representative (the Emperor again) or the Council. In short, the supreme pontiff must lose the prerogatives he held most dear, and see them transferred to the Emperor.[1]

At first Louis of Bavaria was alarmed by the subversive doctrines put forward by these two writers from Paris. But it was obvious that a war to the death would henceforth be waged, and it would have been difficult for him to escape the pressure put upon him by his followers, who now included the avowed enemies of the pope. His hesitation was short-lived, however. Jean de Jandun and Marsiglio of Padua were soon to see their theories put into practice. Marsiglio of Padua was eventually loaded with honours, became Louis' physician and probably inspired his Italian policy.

John XXII took up the challenge to the papacy. On 4 July he declared Louis excommunicate, a sentence postponed by the Bull of 23 March. This sentence was more terrible than the preceding ones: Louis of Bavaria was deprived of any claim to the Empire and summoned, for the last time, to appear before the apostolic tribunal, on

[1] N. Valois, in *Histoire littéraire de la France*, VOL. XXXIII, 1906, pp. 568–87. H. Otto has suggested that there were two versions of the *Defensor pacis*, the first dating from 1324, and the second from before 1327 and differing from the earlier one, though it draws on it. M. R. Scholz admits that there are two versions, but has proved that the final one was completed in 1324 ('Zur Datierung und Überlieferung des "Defensor Pacis" von Marsilius von Padua,' *Neues Archiv*, VOL. XLVI, 1926, pp. 490–512). See H. Otto's reply, *ibid.* VOL. XLVIII, 1929, pp. 174–7. The *Defensor minor* has been published by G. Kenneth Brampton: *The Defensor minor of Marsilius of Padua*, Birmingham 1922. Brampton differs from N. Valois in making the date of composition 1342 and not *c.* 1328.

or about the Kalends of October. The pope again protested [1]—no doubt with a view to placating German opinion—that he had no intention of depriving the prince-electors of their electoral privileges.

Far from capitulating, Louis of Bavaria informed the Marquis d'Este and the Ghibellines in Lombardy and the March of Treviso that he was determined to advance into Italy during the course of 1325 at the head of two thousand 'valiant knights,' so that he might receive the imperial insignia, 'to the glory of God, the honour of the Holy Roman Church, the metamorphosis of the Empire, the consolation of the faithful and the happiness of the world.' [2]

But the diplomatic intrigues of King John of Bohemia, Charles IV of France and Duke Leopold of Austria prevented Louis of Bavaria from carrying out his intentions. When Leopold, the most steadfast champion of the cause of Frederick of Austria, died on 28 February 1326, Louis had complete freedom of action at Trent (January–February 1327) where, before a brilliant assembly of Ghibellines, he made a solemn oath to come to their help in Italy and to march on Rome. With the encouragement of bishops, prelates, friars minor, Dominicans and Augustinians, who were all in revolt against the Church, Louis declared 'the priest John'—for it is thus that the pope was now designated—to be heretical and unworthy of the triple crown. The struggle between Empire and papacy was entering a new phase. Until now, Louis had done no more than side with heretics; now he was himself preparing to make the schism complete.

The Ghibellines had put pressure on him by the offer of 150,000 golden florins, so that he might attack the Guelphs, whose activities were causing them some alarm.

After the siege of Milan had so disastrously been lifted, Bertrand du Poujet had undergone a distressing series of reverses, such as the loss of Pavia, Carrara (October 1323) and Casciano (12 November). In February 1324, during the engagement near the bridge over the Adda at Vaprio, his valiant captain, Ramon of Cardona, had been taken prisoner; and on 10 December the capture of Monza by the Visconti seemed to set a seal on his failure in Lombardy.[3] In 1325, the enemy pressed home the offensive against the papal forces, and their misfortunes reached a climax in the overwhelming defeat of the Florentines at Altopascio on 23 September, followed by that of the Bolognese at Zapolino on 15 November.[4]

[1] Schwalm, *op. cit.* VOL. V, no. 944.
[2] *Ibid.* no. 912. (Letters dated 26 May 1324, addressed to the archbishop of Trier.)
[3] Villani, *op. cit.* Bk X, chs. ccxxx, ccxxxviii, cclxx.
[4] R. Davidsohn, *Geschichte von Florenz*, Berlin 1912, VOL. III, pp. 740–3, 748. See also Villani, *op. cit.* Bk IX, chs. ccciv, cccxxi.

It was obvious that the allies of the Church were in grave danger. On 17 April 1326, John XXII appointed Giovanni Orsini as a second legate to Italy; he was to relieve Bertrand du Poujet in central Italy, south of a line passing through Pisa, Castello, Perugia, Urbino and the March of Ancona.[1] It must not be supposed that the supreme pontiff had lost confidence in Bertrand du Poujet; on the contrary, he praised his 'courage and prudence' and was anxious to allow him to concentrate his efforts on Bologna, which seemed ripe for capture. Thanks to the authorisation of the king of France, cardinal du Poujet was provided with a new captain-general—Hugues des Baux, a Provençal,[2]—and was thus able to seize a number of villages and strongholds. Then Modena on 5 June 1326, Parma on 30 September, Reggio on 4 October and Bologna on 8 February 1327, each in turn yielded to the Church.

The surrender to Bertrand du Poujet of the lordship of Bologna was complete and unconditional, a fact explained by the continual phases of anarchy from which the city suffered and which put it in a very disadvantageous position with regard to its enemies, the chief of whom was Passarino Bonaccolsi, and then Can Grande della Scala, Azzo Visconti and the Estense.

The cardinal used to the full the authority granted him and introduced fundamental reforms in Bologna. Thus he abolished the posts of *bargello* and gonfalonier together with the city council, which had until then had sovereign power. He replaced the podestà by a rector and instituted a 'provost of offices,' who acted as a kind of inspector of all communal administration. In other words the legate suppressed every trace of democratic government and instituted a form of absolutism, by reserving to himself the right to appoint and supervise all officials. The available documents give proof that his rule was a beneficent one. He put down abuses, compelled employers strictly to carry out their duties, introduced improvements into the whole administration of the city and indeed reorganised it. Despite his autocratic personality, he was careful and moderate in the power he exercised. Although his followers received ecclesiastical benefices in Italy, they were not appointed to any of the honorific posts, which remained in the hands of the original inhabitants or of trusted persons from cities obedient to the Church.

The fact that Bertrand du Poujet was a foreigner did him harm. The Pepoli family regretted the lordship which Romeo had held for

[1] Riezler, *op. cit.* no. 666. See also Mollat, VOL. VI, nos. 26398–438; Villani, *op. cit.* Bk IX, ch. cccxli.
[2] He was appointed on 1 July 1326. See Riezler, *op. cit.* no. 707, p. 290. The king of France was slow in giving his consent, *ibid.* no. 623, p. 269.

five years, and were jealous of the cardinal. From the months of September and October 1327 onward, they fomented plots against him. The Maltraversi faction were even more anxious to rouse public opinion against the cardinal, and hatched a more dangerous conspiracy in 1329. Bertrand had to take vigorous action: certain conspirators were beheaded and others exiled. Two lawyers who had objected to the papal government had their tongues cut out. Order reigned at Bologna, for fear of sterner measures to come.[1]

The possession of this city gave the Roman Church a considerable advantage: Bologna guarded the approach to the Apennines, and was one of the chief haunts of the Guelph party. John XXII decided to make it the centre of a huge state, whither he could transfer his court and from which he could direct Italian policy much better than he could in Rome, which was unsafe and too far from the centre of events. In order to provide a worthy dwelling for the pope, Bertrand du Poujet adapted for his use the magnificent fortress known as La Galliera which was first begun in 1330 for military purposes. Palaces were requisitioned to provide lodgings for the Sacred College. The inhabitants of Bologna, counting up the financial and commercial advantages that would accrue from the establishment of the papal court, and delighted at such unexpected good fortune, begged the pope to hasten his coming. Their ambassadors heard the pope, in full Consistory, declare his firm intention of coming within the year. Giovanni Villani [2] asserts that all these verbal demonstrations were intended to deceive, and that the promised arrival of the pope was an invention whose only purpose was to speed up the construction of an impregnable citadel, by means of which any attempted rebellion on the part of the Bolognese could be rapidly put down. It is well known that this author had a marked partiality for his native town, which has surely misled him on this occasion: too many documents prove that John XXII's plans for the future of Bologna were quite definite. For the rest, the proposed transfer of the papacy to Italy caused feelings to run high not only in Italian circles—no doubt it was on this occasion that Petrarch composed his twenty-third Sonnet, *Vedrà Bologna, e poi la nobil Roma*—but more especially at the court of France, where every effort was made to dissuade John XXII.[3]

The grandiose—and perhaps illusory—plan conceived by the pope demanded the annihilation or neutralisation of the Ghibelline party. The successes achieved by Bertrand du Poujet caused the Estense to negotiate an alliance with him. A Bull dated 5 December 1329 freed

---

[1] Ciaccio, *Il cardinale legato* . . . , pp. 31–76.
[2] *Op. cit.* Bk X, chs. cxcix, cc, ccxi.   [3] Rinaldi, *ad annum* 1332, §1, 8.

them from the spiritual and temporal penalties they had incurred after the *coup d'état* of August 1318; they then consented to give back the fortress of Argenta and to accept the title of vicars-general at Ferrara, upon payment of an annual tax of 10,000 gold florins.[1] Azzo Visconti, who had been driven out of Milan by Louis of Bavaria, declared his submission to the pope, who granted him the vicariate for the space of one year.[2] At Mantua, after the murder of Passarino Bonaccolsi on 16 August 1328, Luigi da Gonzaga grew more respectful.[3] The death of Can Grande della Scala on 22 July 1329 removed a dangerous enemy of the Holy See, and the friendly attitude of his successors, Alberto and Mastino, removed all cause for alarm.[4] The situation in northern Italy thus appeared more favourable. All that remained for Bertrand du Poujet was to pacify Emilia and Romagna.

Leaving his lieutenants to carry on the war in Emilia, he himself took on the task of compelling the obedience of the lords of Romagna who had made themselves independent of their master, the supreme pontiff. During their travels in Italy, Bernard Gui and Bertrand de la Tour, although not charged with making enquiries in the March of Ancona and in Romagna, had heard of the bad administration of the rectors and governors; they felt morally obliged to warn Pope John XXII, and advised him to act promptly, otherwise disasters similar to those at Ferrara would ensue.[5]

Aimeric de Châtelus, who had been appointed rector on 5 June 1320, had encountered the greatest difficulties in Romagna, in spite of his competent and equitable dealings. If he had cause to summon members of the clergy or laity before his tribunal, they would immediately give notice of appeal to the Holy See, and although the appeals were fictitious, they had the effect of impeding his action. If the court at Avignon decided anything in the rector's favour, the tyrants and communes did their utmost to molest any who dared to complain about them to him or to the pope. In order to improve this situation, Aimeric summoned a general parliament at Bertinoro on 12 November 1320; but this proved completely ineffective.[6] Except at Cesena, Bertinoro, Meldola and Castrocaro, his authority continued to be counterbalanced by local tyrants; Francesco de' Manfredi was in power at Faenza and Imola, the Polenta at Ravenna, the Malatesta at Rimini, the Ordelaffi at Forli, and the count of Cunio at

---

[1] L. Muratori, *Delle antichità Estensi ed italiane*, Modena 1717, pp. 80–1. See also A. Theiner, *Codex diplomaticus*, Rome 1861, VOL. I, nos. dccxxxviii–dccxxxix.
[2] Riezler, *op. cit.* no. 1222, p. 430.   [3] *Ibid.* no. 1286, p. 451.
[4] Cipolla, *op. cit.* nos. 102, 103, pp. 118–19.
[5] Riezler, *op. cit.* no. 50, p. 39. (Letters dated 20 August 1318.)
[6] Mollat, VOL. III, nos. 12166–75, 12218, 14321–3, 14343; VOL. IV, no. 16152.

Bagnacavallo. Writing from Cesena on 23 February 1321 to the Camerarius, Gasbert de Laval, Aimeric frankly admitted his power-lessness and painted a vivid picture of the behaviour of his perfidious subjects. If he gave any man an order, he would reply, 'I will do it, if it is my lord's will'; and this lord was the very tyrant who had usurped the rectoral authority. In his indignation with his subjects, this gallant man, who did not fail in his task, exclaimed, 'O vain-glorious province, always ripe for deceit, worthy of England for frivolity and treachery! Its inhabitants are more cunning and far subtler than the English, and in trickery, supreme among the Italians.' All things considered, his advice was to hand over the government of the province to the king of Naples.[1] The Holy See paid no heed and showed its confidence in Aimeric by appointing him archbishop of Ravenna on 24 September 1322, while allowing him to retain the dignity of rector.[2]

Bertrand du Poujet was to find that the severe assessment made by Aimeric de Châtelus of the people of Romagna was only too just. He wore himself out in taking castles. His temporary successes came to nothing, and one by one his conquests slipped from his grasp. As soon as they felt themselves too closely threatened, the lords made a show of submission, only to rebel at the first opportunity. He would have needed a powerful army to achieve a decisive victory, but the forces at his disposal were disseminated by his very successes, for was he not obliged to leave garrisons at the strongholds he had con-quered? This petty war of ambushes, skirmishes and sudden attacks into which the cardinal was forced could settle no problems but it dragged on until 1330.[3]

The year 1330 was a decisive one in the history of the Italian peninsula: the threat from the Empire which had hung over Italy for so long finally disappeared under concerted attacks from the Guelphs, Robert of Anjou and the Church. There can be no doubt that the many mistakes made by Henry VII and Louis of Bavaria, their heavy demands and their inability to carry out their ambitious plans, had all contributed to the crumbling of the authority of the Empire. From this time, the names Guelph and Ghibelline ceased to have any real meaning, and Italy was only to witness the conflict of regional interests between cities or tyrants desiring to extend their dominion over their neighbours. But the part that the Holy See had to play became, not simpler, but even more complex. Confronted with the revolutionary spirit, and with insubordination, discord, ambition and

---

[1] Fantuzzi, *Monumenti Ravennati*, VOL. V, Venice 1801, p. 391.
[2] Mollat, VOL. IV, no. 16305.   [3] Ciaccio, *op. cit.* pp. 77–116.

jealousy, those abiding evils devouring Italy in the fourteenth century, the pope had to oppose them with supreme skill, constant vigilance and a deep knowledge of affairs, if he was not to suffer a series of painful and mortifying experiences.

John XXII was the first to benefit from the effects of the events of 1330. He was greatly comforted by the friendly attitude of Azzo Visconti. Three proctors of Milan appeared before him with ropes around their necks, and promised to obey him. The pope gladly removed the interdict, which had lain upon the city for fifteen years, on reasonable terms: they must recognise him as the true pastor of the Church; promise not to show favour to any heretic or schismatic; give up their exactions from the clergy; restore the property and goods of the della Torre; and undertake not to invade any town or stronghold subject to the Church. Giovanni Visconti handed to the pope by proxy the cardinal's hat which he had been given by Nicholas V on 15 September 1329 and, in August 1331, received as token of his forgiveness, the bishopric of Novara.

Further sudden developments in the political situation in Italy took place in October 1330. The Brescians, besieged by Mastino della Scala, the tyrant of Verona, and fearing to be overthrown, had asked in vain for help from Robert of Anjou. In their distress they had recourse to a foreigner, a descendant of Henry VII, King John of Bohemia. This prince, thinking to add another kingdom to those he already possessed, hastened to accede to their request, and on 24 December he entered Brescia, which yielded to him.

When this news reached him from Italy, John XXII was gravely displeased, for he already had several grievances against the king of Bohemia. Indeed, this prince had offered to intervene, together with the archbishop of Trier and Duke Otto of Austria, in the hope of settling the conflict between the Holy See and Louis of Bavaria. An unforeseen occurrence—the death of Frederick of Austria on 13 January 1330—smoothed out all difficulties, at least so far as the self-appointed negotiators were concerned. They assured the pope that Louis of Bavaria was prepared to 'deport' the antipope, revoke his own acts 'threatening the sacred person of the pope and the Roman Church,' confess his 'excesses,' recognise the validity of the sentence of excommunication pronounced upon him, and throw himself on the pope's mercy. But the pope proved implacable and insisted, before he would consider any reconciliation, that Louis of Bavaria must give up his claim to the dignity of the Empire, from which he had been canonically degraded. This was the real source of conflict, for, while he begged for forgiveness, Louis had made it an express condition that he should 'continue in his state and dignity.'

While his ambassadors were parleying in Avignon, John of Bohemia became still more deeply involved, by making a written request for an interview with Azzo Visconti on the pretext of discussing with him imperial affairs, and by charging him to inform his 'faithful followers' to this effect. Emissaries even came to Milan and declared that John had full authority to reconcile him with Louis of Bavaria. Azzo replied that he scorned his advances and had no desire to make any agreement, whereupon the envoys suggested an annual payment of tribute, in return for which the Emperor would not invade the territories of Milan either in his own person or through a third party. As Visconti remained adamant in his refusal, it was suggested that he was acting in this way because of the pope, with whom he was negotiating. He replied: 'I am not negotiating for peace: I already possess it by virtue of a treaty.'

John XXII made no attempt to conceal his surprise at such proceedings. Who was 'bewitching' the king of Bohemia? Who was compelling him 'to persecute the Church, to mislead her devoted sons into disobedience, and to entice them into the sway of a heretic?' How could the king forget the benefits bestowed on his house by Clement V and by John himself?[1]

It seems clear from a reading of the reprimand addressed to John of Bohemia that John XXII believed him to be in collusion with Louis of Bavaria. At the same time the Chancery sent out a series of Bulls likely to satisfy the Gonzagas and the Visconti, and to keep them within the Church's fold: the interdict was lifted from Mantua as from Milan, Vercelli, Pavia, Novara and Bergamo, and from the castles, districts and lands situated beyond the confines of the county of Milan.[2] A kind of league was even made between Azzo and the Holy See: in case of German attack, the two parties agreed to join forces against the invader.[3]

Meanwhile it was rumoured in Italy that John of Bohemia had gone to Trent and there had summoned the rectors of the Lombard cities, with the pope's knowledge and consent. The pope, however, protested that this was not so.[4] Indeed, so little was he in agreement with this prince that he loudly proclaimed his displeasure when—following the example of Brescia—Bergamo, Cremona, Crema, Como, Pavia, Vercelli, Novara, Lucca, Parma, Modena and Reggio came one after the other under this foreign domination. John of Bohemia

---

[1] Riezler, *op. cit.* no. 1386*a*, p. 481. (Letter dated 21 September 1330.)
[2] *Ibid.* nos. 1407, 1416, 1422, 1434.   [3] *Ibid.* no. 1421.
[4] *Ibid.* no. 1428. (Letter from Azzo Visconti, dated 14 January 1331.)

had to defend himself from the charge of prejudicing the Church's interests, and suggested a settlement, under the aegis of the king of France. Although he humbly besought the goodwill of the pope, it was the argument at the end of his request that most impressed the Avignon court. After all, he said, 'was it likely that these Lombard tyrants would be more faithful and useful to His Holiness and the Holy Church than he himself, whose devotion they knew well?'[1]

Two ambassadors arrived in Avignon on 28 March 1331, and succeeded in changing the pope's feelings towards their master, and in persuading him of the latter's complete devotion. John of Bohemia had in fact thrown off this mask and shown his true purpose: he was no longer working for Louis of Bavaria, but for himself. His unlooked-for successes, achieved without striking a single blow, had embroiled him with the Emperor, and made clear to him the path he was to follow henceforward. Without the pope, he could not consolidate the advantages he had gained in Italy, and it therefore became imperative to have his approval. On 17 April, a political compromise was worked out at Castel Franco with Bertrand du Poujet. The king of Bohemia was to restore the towns of Parma, Reggio and Modena to the Holy See, which would give them back to him as hereditary fiefs, on the obligation of paying homage and swearing fealty.

But John XXII completely upset all these political plans. Thinking the pacification of Emilia, where the Ghibelline party had always been preponderant, an illusion, he judged it wiser to favour the establishment in northern Italy of a lay kingdom which should be a vassal of the Church. He remembered that the creation of the kingdom of Naples by his predecessors for the benefit of the house of Anjou had resulted in the complete overthrow of the Ghibellines in the south of the peninsula, and saw no reason why an operation of similar scope should not be successful in the north. The pope forgot that there was no similarity at all between northern and southern Italy: in the one the tyrants had made themselves masters, while in the other there had been no cohesion among the supporters of the Empire. He had also to reckon with Guelph susceptibilities, and especially with the reactions of the king of Naples; and for this the pope made provision. John of Bohemia had to undertake not to invade the kingdom of Naples or its possessions in Lombardy or Piedmont; to put Lucca and her territory into the hands of the Holy See until an agreement was reached between King Robert and the Florentines; not to accept the office of captain, overlord or any other position in Lombardy or Tuscany without the permission of the

[1] *Ibid.* no. 1449.

pope; and not to attack Milan or the surrounding district. If, by chance, he were himself attacked, he was free to defend himself; but in these circumstances the pope would give him no temporal aid. If John of Bohemia succeeded in subduing Lombardy, he was to compel obedience to the Church of all rebels, to restore to the clergy the goods that had been taken from them, to allow free elections to take place in cathedrals, collegiate churches and conventual houses, and to respect the privileges of the ecclesiastical court. He was, moreover, to promise never to join with Louis of Bavaria and to fight against him if Louis threatened the Holy See, her lands or her subjects.[1]

The pact of 17 April 1331 had been considered in the most minute detail by the papal diplomats, and aimed at avoiding any danger of reaction from either Guelphs or Ghibellines. These attempts at conciliating such divergent interests might well have borne fruit, had it not been for the fantastic ideas hatched in the imaginative brain of John of Bohemia. He was no longer content merely to have Italy; he was now casting envious eyes at the Empire, since it seemed that John XXII was driving Louis of Bavaria to abdication, and was working for a new election. The prince first reconciled himself with the king of Hungary, the Austrian dukes and the margrave of Misnen (September 1331) and visited the Emperor. Then at Fontainebleau, in January 1332, he promised to ratify any territorial encroachments made upon the Empire by Philip VI, and to give him the kingdom of Arles, provided that John himself were given complete freedom to intrigue for the imperial crown for a member of his family.[2] John of Bohemia even handed over to the king of France the recently acquired lordship of Lucca.[3]

The negotiations at Castel Franco, which were kept as secret as the scheming of John of Bohemia, aroused the suspicions of the Italians. The Bolognese believed that the Holy See had betrayed them, despite their submission to the Church 'in perpetuity' made in 1331–2, and feared that their city might be handed over to the king. John XXII protested that he would never give up the seisin of Bologna or of its county, and that only stern necessity had prevented the fulfilment of his openly declared intention to transfer to that city: he was detained in Avignon by the organisation of the crusade; 'sinister' events occurring in France—the opening of hostilities with England—were preventing his departure.[4] Guelphs and Ghibellines alike feared the

[1] Riezler, *op. cit.* no. 1457, pp. 505–09.   [2] *Ibid.* nos. 1478, 1510.
[3] Robert of Anjou made such a lively protest that Philip VI never took possession. See L. Mirot, 'La Cession de la ville et du comté de Lucques par Jean de Bohême à Philippe de Valois en 1332,' *Mélanges Henri Hauvette*, Paris 1934.
[4] Ciaccio, *op. cit.* doc. XLII, XLIII.

intervention of the king of Bohemia, and at Ferrara in September 1332 they formed a league, into which entered the Estense and the Scaligeri, Luigi Gonzaga, Azzo Visconti, the communes of Perugia, Siena, Florence, Orvieto, Volterra, Colle San Geminiano, Prato and San Miniato, as well as the king of Naples who was wronged by the treaty of Fontainebleau. The members of the league resolved to help Azzo Visconti to take Cremona and Borgo San Donnino, the della Scala to seize Parma, Luigi da Gonzaga to enter Reggio and the Florentines to recapture Lucca.

The league of Ferrara astounded the Italians. The alliance of the leaders of the Guelphs with the Ghibellines of northern Italy, against whom they had fought for so long, did, however, prove justified. In place of the Holy See which was keeping aloof, following the compromise of Castel Franco, it fell to the league to preserve the political balance in Italy, which was being shaken by the immoderate ambition of John of Bohemia.

Scarcely had it been formed when the league of Ferrara took action. As early as October, Azzo Visconti attacked Cremona and then Modena, and in November 1332 took Pavia. The Estense joined in the campaign, but Charles of Bohemia (John's son), on 25 November before the walls of the castle of San Felice, fought a hard battle with them from nones until vespers, and inflicted considerable losses upon them in killed and prisoners. In February 1333, the legate, Bertrand du Poujet, seized Consandolo in the commune of Argenta and began to besiege Ferrara. He was determined to have the Estense at his mercy, and he dissuaded the Florentines from sending help to tyrants who were as much their enemies as those of the Church. They replied that in their view John of Bohemia was the common enemy, and that it was unseemly to have any dealings or to enter into any alliance with him. Florence, in fact, suspected the legate of plotting with the king to enter her city and to subject her to the fate of the Bolognese; she accordingly sent troops to the Estense, with instructions to take the sea-route and land at Genoa and from there advance on Milan and Verona. Robert of Anjou, who was a member of the league, had no desire to fight against the Church: his soldiers camped on the Florentine frontier near Lucca.[1]

The wisest plan was obviously to dissociate the affairs of the Church from those of the king of Bohemia whom the members of the league wished to drive from Italy and who had already lost Brescia in July 1332 and Bergamo in September. But since Bertrand du Poujet's forces were markedly inferior in number to those of the

[1] Villani, *op. cit.* Bk X, chs. ccvii, ccix, ccx, ccxiv, ccxv.

Guelphs and Ghibellines combined, he drew up a plan of campaign with John against the Estense at Bologna on 3 April 1333. All available forces, under the command of Count Jean I of Armagnac, made a concerted attack on Ferrara. Fighting began before the city walls on 14 April; after a prolonged struggle and much skilful manœuvring, the allies were left in command of the field, and took back to their camp a large number of prisoners, including Jean d'Armagnac himself and the cavalry sent by Bologna and Romagna.[1]

On 18 June at Argenta, the papal troops had a further set-back, though a less serious one, and they maintained their positions. Soon they were to bear the brunt of the war alone, for John of Bohemia, disappointed of his hopes, made a truce with the league, and in October set off to return to his own kingdom. The papal forces inevitably succumbed in this unequal struggle, for, as ill-luck would have it, all the lords of Romagna rose in rebellion.[2] On 23 November, the Estense besieged Argenta, a strategic point of prime importance, and the key to the whole Bolognese area.

A truce was signed, and when it expired on 1 January 1334 the allies met again at Lerici. Some were in favour of a prorogation; others—the Florentines and Mastino della Scala—expressed the view that it was unwise to allow the legate time to regroup his forces. The war-party won the day, and they divided the spoils of their conquests in anticipation.

Bertrand du Poujet showed no skill in handling this situation. Instead of being conciliatory he was 'hard' and thus antagonised both Guelphs and Ghibellines. John XXII urged him to be moderate, and himself intervened. Bertrand de Déaulx, the archbishop of Embrun, was sent to Italy as nuncio-extraordinary to retrieve the disaster suffered by the Church. As the pope sadly remarked, 'All our gains have been brought almost to nothing.'[3]

The papal envoy had an interview with the members of the league on 7 March 1334 at Peschiera. He demanded that the league should be dissolved, the siege of Argenta lifted, and the count of Armagnac and the other captives freed without a ransom. Mastino della Scala replied, through the intermediary of one of the Florentine ambassadors, that the league would be dissolved if Parma were no longer subject to the king of Bohemia and if Ferrara were restored to the Estense in return for the payment of the usual tribute, a small due would be paid for the possession of Argenta.

Before confirming this advantageous agreement, Bertrand de

---

[1] Villani, *op. cit.* Bk. X, ch. ccxvii. See also Galvano della Fiamma, *Opusculum de rebus gestis ab Azone, Luchino et Johanne Vicecomitibus ab anno 1328 usque ad annum 1342,* ed. C. Castiglioni, p. 13; *Corpus chronicorum Bononiensium,* VOL. II, pp. 424-7.
[2] *Ibid.* ch. ccxxvi.   [3] Ciaccio, *op. cit.* doc. CXXV–CXXVIII (17–19 October 1333).

Déaulx insisted on conferring with the legate. While he was on his way to Bologna, the inhabitants of Argenta, who had been reduced to a state of famine, capitulated on 8 March.

Instead of favouring a peaceful approach, Bertrand du Poujet persisted in having recourse to arms, and ordered his troops to advance towards Ferrara. To make matters worse, Bologna, where a seditious spirit had been at work for several months, rose against him on 17 August.

The rising broke out at the time of vespers. Obizzo d'Este and some of the notables of Bologna, had prepared the plan. They had agreed that armed bands should invade the countryside around Cento and Pieve and lay it waste, with the intention of compelling the legate to withdraw his troops from the city. When the armed bands had arrived some of the conspirators begged Bertrand du Poujet to help the countryfolk. He replied, 'What can I do? Well-nigh all my men have gone back to the army near Ferrara, except the few soldiers charged with guarding Bologna.' The traitors pressed him further: 'No men are needed here: send your soldiers to fight those who are burning and pillaging the countryside.' The cardinal agreed and ordered his men to go. Then the populace, roused by Brandiligi Gozzadini, seized first the square in front of the palace of the commune, and then, with cries of 'Long live the people! Death to the legate and the people of Languedoc!' rushed out to the cornmarket, where the marshal and the papal officers were, and set it on fire. The archbishop's palace, occupied by the Frenchman Bertrand Tissandier, was attacked by the flames. A systematic slaughter of the French was begun: one was disembowelled and the dogs ate his flesh. Their property was pillaged on every side. The rioters, helped by Ferrarese, then went to besiege Bertrand du Poujet who had retreated into the citadel of La Galliera. Shouts rang out, of 'Death to the legate! Death to the unjust and cruel tyrant!' The siege continued for ten consecutive days. But the Florentines, who were now inclining towards reconciliation with the Church, entered Bologna, parleyed with the insurgents and agreed to take the cardinal away under escort. While this party was leaving by a secret gate, the people rushed upon the citadel of La Galliera and rased it to the ground.[1]

Thus John XXII's grandiose scheme crumbled miserably. The restoration of government by the commune in Bologna, which followed immediately, made it impossible for the Holy See to return to Italy.

---

[1] Villani, *op. cit.* Bk XI, chs. v, vi. *Corpus chronicorum Bononiensium,* pp. 419, 432–7. See also a letter written by a Frenchman from Bologna on 22 March 1334, published in *Not. et extr. des mss.,* VOL. XXXV, pt 2, 1897, p. 419.

The pope had been the victim of the imprudent alliance contracted with the king of Bohemia, under pressure it is true from Bertrand du Poujet who had but little insight into the state of affairs. It had also been a mistake to quarrel with the Florentines, who until 1332 had always supported any military operation undertaken by the legate. An even greater misfortune had been to adhere to the treaty of Frankfurt, concluded with Philip of Valois on 7 December 1333. Robert of Anjou, who was wronged by this treaty, allowed the papal army to be defeated in Emilia and thus contributed indirectly to the loss of Bologna.

4

Benedict XII and His Policy of Appeasement

The failures that had so relentlessly dogged John XXII during the last years of his pontificate showed his successor the way he should follow. Since the members of the league had made some show of moderation at Peschiera in 1334, it was advisable to satisfy them and prudently to exploit their conciliatory attitude, provided that this proved sincere. Moreover, Benedict XII, who had been elected pope on 20 December 1334, did not possess John XXII's pugnacious temperament; on the contrary, he declared that he hated war. He was above all a monk; one who had imbibed in the Cistercian cloister a love of study, austere behaviour, respect for the monastic rule and dislike for any relaxation of ecclesiastical discipline. Since his appointment as bishop of Pamiers on 19 March 1317, and later during his episcopate at Mirepoix, dating from 3 March 1326, he had been noted for his zeal in hunting down heretics, Catharists or Albigensians, who abounded in these dioceses. From the time he became cardinal, his talents as a theologian, displayed during the theoretical controversies which disturbed his predecessor's pontificate, had attracted the attention of the Sacred College. The combination of qualities such as these made him little inclined to the complicated game of politics, nor did they fit him to venture into the difficult paths of appeasement, which demanded versatility, a profound knowledge of the Italian way of life and an unusually broad outlook.

From the year 1335, Azzo Visconti felt it necessary to reconcile his family with the Church.[1] It may be questioned whether his reasons were religious ones. Galvano della Fiamma,[2] his panegyrist, after

---

[1] Galvano della Fiamma, *Opusculum de rebus gestis ab Azone, Luchino et Johanne Vicecomitibus ab anno 1328 usque ad annum 1342*, ed. C. Castiglioni, p. 15.
[2] *Ibid.* pp. 19, 22, 33–5.

extolling his affable manner, peaceful nature and generosity, decked him in all the Christian virtues and depicted him as the benefactor of the religious orders; according to him, Azzo's piety was as great as his faith. It must be admitted, however, that worldly interest provided the chief motive for Azzo's actions and led him to reconciliation with the Church as the means to consolidating his conquests and to furthering his designs in Pisa and Genoa.

Benedict XII gave a favourable reception to Azzo Visconti's request for the winding up of the legal enquiry into the heresy of deceased members of his family. Though this enquiry was gathering dust among the files of the Inquisition, it still constituted a considerable menace to himself, and caused the interdict to weigh heavily on the Milanese. The names of Matteo and of Galeazzo were still sullied, and their mortal remains were still not lying in consecrated ground.

The noted lawyer from Bergamo, Alberico da Rosciate, presented to the papal court a lengthy memorandum which aimed at establishing the nullity of the inquisitorial proceedings on account of a formal defect, and at making them appear a weapon contrived for political purposes against the Visconti. The accusations of heresy, he alleged, were bound to fall because they were inconsistent and lacked incontrovertible proof.[1]

The occupation of Piacenza in 1337 by Azzo impeded the progress of negotiations, and roused the suspicions of Benedict XII, who had no wish to be deprived of a valuable weapon in order to contain Milanese ambition within reasonable limits. By the end of the year, however, the pope's discontent was appeased: a commission of cardinals, consisting of Bertrand du Poujet, Pierre des Prez and Annibale di Ceccano, was given the task of sifting the evidence of heresy. In December, Benedict XII was hard to please: far from accepting the contention of Alberico da Rosciate, he spoke of ordering the reopening of a full-scale enquiry. The lifting of the interdict would then be more easily granted: the affected towns would pay a *componendum* of 200,000 florins and a yearly tax of 40,000. In the end, Alberico agreed to the sums of 50,000 and 10,000 respectively.

The conditions to be imposed on Azzo himself gave rise to delicate negotiations, which had the following results: Azzo was to receive 'the vicariate, government and administration of the city, district and county of Milan,' and of the towns of Piacenza, Lodi, Crema, Caravaggio, Martinengo and Castelnuovo on a hereditary basis, without payment of tax—but only during the vacancy of the Empire; he was

---

[1] The memorandum has been published by C. Capasso, *La signoria viscontea e la lotta politico-religiosa con il papato nella prima metà del secolo XIV*, Pavia 1908, pp. 83–96.

to restore to the clergy the goods of which they had been deprived, and expel notorious heretics. One vital clause was aimed at Louis of Bavaria. Azzo was to consider as heresy Louis' pretension to depose the pope, he was not to recognise Louis as Emperor nor to come to his aid, 'he was not to receive whosoever might come to Italy either in the name of the Emperor, or of the King of the Romans, or with the powers of an administrator.'[1]

The death of Azzo Visconti on 16 August 1339 prevented the realisation of the proposed agreement with the Roman court. Giovanni, bishop of Novara, and Luchino Visconti, the uncles of Azzo, resumed the negotiations, which on 15 May 1341 reached a conclusion.

Marsiglio of Padua had formerly held the archbishopric of Milan from the Antipope Nicholas V. Before Marsiglio died on 10 September 1328, he had sown evil doctrines in his diocese, and traces of his subversive teaching were still to be found there. The Visconti promised to acknowledge Benedict XII as the true Vicar of Christ and to obey any prescriptions imposed upon them with regard to making good the culpable excesses formerly committed to the detriment of the Church. They declared that the Emperor had no prerogative to instal or depose the Roman pontiff, and they undertook to root out so far as they were able all heretics and notorious schismatics to be found in their lands. At this time when the conflict with Louis of Bavaria was still unresolved, Benedict XII received positive assurance that the Visconti would not, either directly or indirectly, give counsel, aid or succour either to Louis or to any antipope. The Emperor, his messengers or his subjects were only to be received with the consent of the Holy See. On the other hand, nuncios and faithful subjects of the Roman church were to be assured of welcome, protection and defence in the territories of Milan, so long as their mission was of a peaceful nature. The local clergy were not to pay taxes, were to be exempted from custom duties and from tolls and were to live peacefully in their parishes. The pope, for his part, granted the Visconti and their heirs in perpetuity the title of Vicars of the Church in Piacenza, Lodi, Crema, Caravaggio, Martinengo, and Castelnuovo Bocca d'Adda, on condition that they took an oath of fealty and made an annual payment of 10,000 florins. Of Milan, Brescia, Bergamo, Como, Vercelli and Cremona, the Visconti were granted the general vicariate temporarily, so long as the Empire, from which these cities were held, remained vacant. Novara was handed over on the same conditions to the local bishop, because there the temporal power was joined to the spiritual. As a sign of penitence, the Milanese were to expiate their

[1] Capasso, op. cit. pp. 72–81.

past sins by building two chapels in honour of St Benedict, and endowing them with sufficient ornaments, sacred vessels and vestments for two officiating priests; furthermore they were, in one day, to distribute alms to two thousand poor persons.[1]

Azzo died without issue on 16 August 1339, and the implementation of the proposed agreement was thus postponed, and not completed until 15 May 1341. Though peace had been achieved, from a religious point of view,[2] in all the cities of northern Italy that had been compromised by the schism brought about by Louis of Bavaria, the heresy trial affecting the Visconti family was still in progress; only Luchino and Giovanni were no longer molested. The Holy See gave them some slight satisfaction, while reserving to itself the right to cause them serious embarrassment if they should violate agreements they had entered into with the pope. It was not until 13 March 1353 that Innocent VI declared a complete annulment of the inquisitorial proceedings begun during John XXII's pontificate against the deceased Matteo, Galeazzo, Marco and Stefano.[3]

Alberto and Mastino della Scala obtained pardon much more quickly than Azzo Visconti. Benedict XII granted them the vicariate of Parma, Verona and Vicenza for a period of ten years, on condition that they made an annual payment of 5,000 florins, and he made over to them the additional territories of Magnano and Capria in the Veronese area as hereditary fiefs, in return for the payment of an annual tax of one golden mark and the giving of liege homage. The supreme pontiff's graciousness in overlooking a past that had been full of misdeeds was not without a utilitarian motive. The state of the papal finances no longer allowed expenses on the vast scale of those incurred by the war in Lombardy; the frugal Benedict XII preferred to create vassals who would provide him with military retainers. Thus the Scaligeri undertook to provide him with two hundred horsemen and three hundred foot-soldiers, who would ensure peace in Lombardy, in the March of Ancona, in Romagna and in the districts of Bologna and Ferrara (1 September 1339).[4]

The other 'tyrants' of northern Italy also received satisfaction: the Gonzaga accepted the vicariate of Mantua, and the Estense that of Modena, Comacchio and Argenta.[5]

The peace-making activities of the Holy See also extended to Pavia

---

[1] Rinaldi, *ad annum* 1341, §19–27, 29–33. See also Vidal, *Lettres closes de Benoît XII*, VOL. I, Paris 1919, no. 286a–g; Galvano della Fiamma, *op. cit.* pp. 42–3.

[2] Vidal, VOL. II, nos. 9161–75. (Bulls dated 15, 16 and 23 May 1341.)

[3] Capasso, *op. cit.* pp. 97–100. (Text of the Bull, in which the different stages of the trial are set out at length.)

[4] Vidal, VOL. II, nos. 7533–7. Rinaldi, *ad annum* 1339, §61–7. (Bulls dated 1 September 1339.)　　　　[5] *Ibid.* no. 7454. See also Baluze, *Vitae*, VOL. I, p. 231.

and the Riviera. In the Consistory of 11 February 1338, Genoa and Savona begged to receive pardon,[1] and, on the 22nd, Albenga did likewise.

Benedict XII's policy of appeasement appeared at first sight successful. After more than twenty years of discord, it seemed that peace reigned at last between the Church and the Ghibellines. Whereas Matteo Visconti, Can Grande della Scala and Passarino Bonaccolsi had disdainfully rejected the title of vicar at the hands of John XXII, the tyrants who had succeeded them had in effect recognised the validity of the contention always upheld by John: that as pope he had the right to govern the Empire while it was vacant; a contention opposed with equal vigour by Henry VII, Louis of Bavaria and, in the *Defensor pacis,* by Jean de Jandun and Marsiglio of Padua. The honour of the vicariate had been dearly bought. On the spiritual side, the complete healing of the schism caused by Nicholas V was easily achieved. All the cities that had made a pact with Louis of Bavaria and the Antipope Pietro da Corbara, or waged war against Bertrand du Poujet, had repudiated their past misdeeds and besought the pope's mercy. The sentences of excommunication and interdict, formerly despised, had produced genuine effects, and the populations of the cities rejoiced at being freed from them. A continuator of the Martinian Chronicle, however, remarked that contemporaries —doubtless the Guelphs are meant—condemned Benedict XII's actions: the granting of the vicariate to 'avowed oppressors of the liberty of the Roman Church' appeared monstrous to them.[2] These critics were not entirely wrong: contrary to the pope's intentions, the favours granted to the tyrants only served to consolidate their independence and to free them from papal authority.

The final settlement of accounts after the revolt at Bologna, which incurred the censure of some Italian critics,[3] was long delayed. On 27 February 1335, Benedict XII declared bitterly that the rebels still showed no inclination to be obedient, and that the mediation of the king of Naples had been of no avail. He announced, however, that he was prepared to receive the Bolognese 'joyfully and readily,' but his chief preoccupation was 'to uphold and preserve intact the rights of the Roman Church.' Although he did not say it in so many words, he did not at that time envisage any possible solution other than the subjection of the city of Bologna, in accordance with the grant made in perpetuity to John XXII in 1331–2.[4] The Pepoli, the chief

---

[1] Rinaldi, *ad annum* 1340, §69–71. Vidal, *Lettres closes,* VOL. I, nos. 286*b*, 1674–6.
[2] Baluze, *op. cit.* VOL. I, p. 239.   [3] *Ibid.* p. 237.
[4] Vidal, *Lettres closes,* VOL. I, nos. 76, 121. (Letters dated 27 February 1335, addressed to the Florentines, and 20 March, to the king of Naples.)

instigators of the revolt, had other ideas, and on 28 August 1337 they achieved their ends. Taddeo seized power, but prudently styled himself 'Keeper (*Conservatore*) of peace and justice' lest he incurred the enmity of Benedict XII. The pope was not deceived; he summoned the Pepoli to appear at Avignon within the next two months, together with a large number of Bolognese and the members of the town council. A Bull of 2 February 1338, couched in acrimonious terms, recounted in detail the 'shocking excesses' committed in March 1334. The pope 'blushed' to tell of them. The former judge of the Inquisition awoke in him and he castigated the criminal actions of the insurgents, emphasising the deeds of cruelty that had been perpetrated, and recalling the horrible case of Bertrand de Glar, a member of the bishop's household, who had been 'disembowelled and hacked into pieces, and whose flesh had been given to dogs to eat,' or again, that of the vice-marshal, Olivier Bérald, who was bound with iron fetters and many times put to torture.[1]

As by 2 March 1338, no-one had answered the summons to appear, excommunication was pronounced against the contumacious, and Bologna was placed under an interdict, together with its University, to which the teaching of the ablest lawyers of the day attracted a large and cosmopolitan body of students. As such canonical sanctions would have caused a wholesale exodus of the students, Taddeo Pepoli advised his fellow-citizens to make peace with the Holy See. By 13 October they appeared to have settled their differences.[2] When, on 30 December, Guigone da San Germano, who had been sent expressly by Benedict XII, read aloud before the assembled populace of Bologna, the clauses of the convention agreed at Avignon by its representatives, violent protests cut short his speech. To be directly subject to the Church, to swear an oath of vassalage, to allow the supreme pontiff to meddle with the machinery of the city's administration—all this was equivalent to subscribing to the loss of their dearest liberties: the Bolognese demanded changes or modifications to the conditions drawn up in the Consistory court after mature deliberation. The pope's reply was intransigent and he ordered the nuncio to leave if the Bolognese did not ratify, without more ado, what their representatives had already agreed.[3] On 4 March 1339, the ecclesiastical penalties which had been in abeyance since the previous 13 October were again inflicted on the city. This compelled the inhabitants to reopen negotiations at Avignon. This time Benedict XII

---

[1] Theiner, *Codex diplomaticus*, VOL. II, doc. LII.
[2] *Ibid.* doc. LXIII. See also Vidal, VOL. II, nos. 6422–9, 6472–4.
[3] Vidal, *Lettres closes*, VOL. I, no. 2186.

slightly mitigated his demands, and agreed to lift the interdict on 14 June 1340. Beltramino Paravicino, the bishop of Como, took possession of the castles in the Bolognese district in the name of the Holy See, received the oath of fealty from the citizens and accepted the keys of the city. These he restored on 21 August to Taddeo Peopoli, who accepted the title of 'Administrator of the rights and property of the Church at Bologna' for a period of three years; in addition a tribute of 8,000 florins was to be paid.[1] Until his death on 29 September 1347, Taddeo lived on good terms with the papal court and pursued a policy favourable to the Guelphs.

As a result of the reverses suffered by Bertrand du Poujet, the lords of Romagna had rebelled against the pope's authority. Benedict believed that he was capable of restoring order here, in the richest province of the Church States, without having recourse to war. He first turned to the communes of the larger towns and warned them that 'the troubles, molestations and oppressions that they had been compelled to endure without surcease' came 'from those who, not content with exercising their rights within just limits, could neither live in peace nor allow others to enjoy a tranquil existence.'[2] In this way Benedict XII, without mentioning any names, was inviting his subjects to break with the turbulent lords of Romagna, and to help the papal officials in their delicate task of administering the territory. To the lords, 'those fomentors of trouble and invaders of the Church's estate,' he spoke in his usual acrimonious tones, and threatened to take 'the necessary measures' if they failed to restore to the treasurer of the province what they had fraudulently acquired.[3]

In urging obedience to the apostolic representatives, Benedict XII was assuming that they possessed rare qualities inspiring respect in those they governed, in particular equity, probity, tact, savoir-faire, and above all perseverance. The insubordination of the people of Romagna made their task difficult. The treasurer, Guillaume Truelle, weighed down with anxiety, longed for his recall and bewailed the fact that his friends had not yet succeeded in obtaining it for him.[4]

Benedict XII determined that he would supply his States with rectors and with capable and honest officials. On 13 September 1335, he appointed only Frenchmen, all of them clerks. On their appointment, they received instructions containing some unusual clauses: they were required to investigate the misdeeds and malversations of

[1] Vidal, *Lettres closes*, VOL. II, nos. 8241–8, 8356, 8359. Theiner, *op. cit.* VOL. II, doc. XC.
[2] Vidal, *Lettres closes*, VOL. I, nos. 345–50. (Letters dated 22 June 1335.)
[3] *Ibid.* nos. 353–6.
[4] H. Otto, 'Benedikt XII als Reformator des Kirchenstaates,' *Quellen*, 1928, p. 91.

their predecessors, and to communicate their findings to the archbishop of Embrun, Bertrand de Déaulx. Benedict XII had singled
out for authority this trustworthy man, who had previously negotiated
the abortive agreement at Peschiera, and who had lost his belongings
in the rising at Bologna; to him he entrusted the task of inspecting the
States of the Church, of pointing out existing abuses and of introducing well-chosen reforms.[1]

Benedict XII, as authoritarian as John XXII and even more imperious, allowed his nuncio little freedom of action. He directed everything from Avignon and in the last resort made all the decisions. He
harried the archbishop with recommendations, indicated his course of
action in the minutest detail, and did not scruple to ignore his advice,
when he thought the moment favourable for military action.

The news he received from Italy persuaded the pope to promulgate on 10 July 1336 two beneficial Constitutions.[2] The rectors were
forbidden to promote their brothers, nephews or any relations by
blood or marriage to be marshals at their court of justice. Every six
months the judges were to give the rectors an account, in public
session, of their activities. If, for the sake of gold, favours or any other
reason, the rectors failed to punish their misdeeds, they themselves
would incur suitable punishment. The second edict restrained the
greed of certain rectors and treasurers, who amassed illicit profits by
paying wages to third parties with 'no aptitude or capacity' for com-
manding mercenaries or executing judgments. Anyone who repeated
such avaricious dealings for a second time was to pay to the Apostolic
Camera double the amount of what he had received.

But neither the pope's administrative reforms nor the threats made
to the lords of Romagna were put into full effect. Francesco Ordelaffi,
the tyrant of Forlì, was the most formidable cause of trouble.
Obsessed by the desire to round off his territory, in the spring of
1335 he attacked the fortress of Meldola, which was defended by
a ridiculously small garrison: two hundred foot-soldiers and one
hundred horsemen. The treasurer, Guillaume Truelle, feared the
worst: he was short of money, could not pay his soldiers and foresaw
their desertion. Florence, warned of this by Benedict XII, came to
his help, raised the siege in September 1335 and reached a 'dastardly
and intolerable' compromise with Ordelaffi. The fate of the stronghold seemed so little assured, so precarious, that the pope begged the
Florentines to remain on the alert. In September 1336 he feared a
fresh attack, and spent 4,000 florins in buying corn, foodstuffs and
weapons of defence. In May 1339 the threat became more definite:

[1] Vidal, *Lettres closes*, VOL. I, nos. 527–66.   [2] *Ibid.* nos. 979–80.

Eustachio da Polenta joined forces with Ordelaffi and together they prepared to march against Meldola. Had the Florentines not intervened, the fortress would once more have been besieged; but though it was saved, Francesco Ordelaffi took two other strongholds, Elmez and San Casciano, by storm. With an insolent disregard of proceedings begun against him by Raimbaud Romandiola, bishop of Imola, who had been made rector on 15 March, this perfidious tyrant soon reduced Cesena, Bertinoro, Meldola, Castrocaro and Castelnuovo.[1]

In the March of Ancona the situation was far worse than in Romagna. There was hardly one town council[2] that troubled to pay the various taxes and dues essential to the normal workings of public affairs. To the lords, Benedict XII uttered a sharp rebuke: he branded 'the countless injustices, the offences, the manifold excesses, the detestable acts too many to enumerate, the usurpations' that they had committed to the detriment and reproach of the Church. The rector of the province called on them to restore, within a fixed time, the goods and the rights that they had seized, to cease from molesting the papal officials or the 'faithful' of the Holy See, and to keep the peace. If they persisted in their insubordination, they would be summarily required to appear before the court at Avignon, on pain of excommunication and seizure 'of their goods, rights, jurisdictions, privileges, liberties and immunities, real and personal.'[3]

His correspondence reveals how deeply wounded Benedict XII was by the conduct of his subjects. The austerity of the Cistercian rule, by which he had been profoundly influenced, had inspired him with a respect for justice and a hatred of abuses. He was roused to anger by the acts of insubordination committed against the Roman Church, 'who yet feels a maternal affection for her sons . . . and who, by charitable exhortations rather than by the scourge, is ready to gather in her bosom, with loving patience' those who have offended against her.

The petty tyrants of the March of Ancona did not respond to the pope's generous appeal. Mercennario di Monteverde, a past master of 'bad faith, villainy and illicit machinations,' disappointed his hopes without the least compunction. When the interdict affected his territory because he had not restored to the Church the castles of Sant' Elpidio, Monsolmo, Montegranaro, Montefiore dell' Aso and Monte Santa Maria, in the diocese of Fermo, or paid the fine, as he had agreed under oath to do, he pretended to make amends, sending representatives to Avignon, who promised all that was required of

---

[1] Vidal, *op. cit.* VOL. I, nos. 351–8, 450, 598, 624, 766, 1022, 1354, 1066, 1355, 2241, 2389, 2465, 2488 and 2497. See also Theiner, *op. cit.* VOL. II, doc. LXXVI, LXXXII.
[2] See the long list in Vidal, *Lettres closes*, VOL. I, nos. 213–56. (Bulls dated 13 May 1335.)   [3] *Ibid.* nos. 257–77.

them; but he fulfilled none of these undertakings. By March 1339, Benedict XII's patience was at an end. He told Francesco Silvestri, the bishop of Florence, who had acted as his spokesman in dealing with the rebel, that he had no desire to negotiate any agreement, either in his own person or through an intermediary, until Fermo and the fortresses illegally occupied were effectively and truly restored. In May, he ordered the penalties previously imposed to be increased in severity.[1]

5

Clement VI and Giovanni Visconti

Benedict XII's policy had been one of appeasement, because of his reluctance to shed Christian blood on the field of battle. He was very parsimonious, and had economised to the point of meanness in the expenses of maintaining a sufficiently large band of mercenaries to preserve peace in Italy, preferring to spend his financial resources in good works and in constructing the forbidding palace whose majestic towers still overlook the town of Avignon. Moreover, the tyrants, great and small, whose crafty intrigues he had not known how to or had been unable to restrain, had taken advantage of his inexperience in worldly matters and his tendency to be merciful, to laugh at him and to grow ever more impudent. When Clement VI succeeded to the papal throne on 7 May 1342, the supremacy of the Church had almost ceased to be recognised in Romagna and the March of Ancona. By 1350, the condition of the Papal States had grown still worse. Giovanni and Giacomo Pepoli, who had taken over the government of Bologna after the death of their father Taddeo on 29 September 1347, were planning to free themselves from the tribute they owed to the Apostolic Camera, and so become independent. Subsequently, on 17 February 1350, Giovanni de' Manfredi seized Faenza. The Malatesta family extended their territories considerably. In addition to Rimini, Pesaro, Fano and Fossombrone, they laid hands on Ancona, Osimo, Sinigaglia, Jesi and Ascoli. As for Francesco Ordelaffi, he boasted about his brilliant conquests. In short, if the papacy wanted to save its States from complete disintegration, speedy action would have to be taken. Clement VI revived the warlike policy of John XXII and sent out an army under the command of Niccolò della Serra and Marshal Rostang Cavalier of Avignon. The troops consisted for the most part of eleven hundred and fifty cavalry

[1] *Ibid.* nos. 823, 1109, 1515, 2272, 2368.

supplied by Duke Werner of Urslingen. Lesser contingents came from Mastino della Scala, the marquis d'Este, Giovanni Visconti and the Pepoli. Supreme authority was in the hands of the Limousin Astorge de Durfort, a nephew by marriage of the pope and rector of Romagna since 1347.[1]

The papal army first attacked Giovanni de' Manfredi and defeated him on 20 May 1350. Then, instead of marching on Faenza, which was nearby and would at that time have been easy to take, they laid siege to Solarolo, which did not capitulate until 6 July. As the military operations proceeded, the attitude of the Pepoli seemed equivocal. Astorge de Durfort suspected that they were trying to come to an agreement with the enemy, and he set a trap for Giovanni. He invited the latter to confer with him, and Giovanni came, quite unsuspecting, to the camp at Solarolo. He was received with honour, and then arrested and imprisoned at Imola, where he was promised his freedom if he handed over Bologna to the Church. Astorge de Durfort went immediately into action, joined with the reinforcements sent by Mastino della Scala, invaded the region of Bologna and threatened its capital. His success seemed assured, when misfortune befell him: in vain did he appeal time and again to Avignon for funds, so that he could pay his soldiers; Clement VI sent him nothing. The pope, accustomed to living like a great lord, had soon made large inroads into the treasure amassed by the parsimonious Benedict XII. The completion of the improvements to the Palais des Doms, the reconstruction of the abbey of Chaise-Dieu, the purchase of Avignon in 1348, the upkeep of a luxurious court, the considerable loans he had agreed to make to the kings of France and the nobles of Southern France—all these had exhausted the finances of the Holy See. The great effort he had made to pay the German mercenaries could not be renewed, and Astorge de Durfort had no alternative but to hand over his prisoner to them as a pledge.

Giovanni Pepoli lost no time in paying his captors. He was set free on 29 August and went with all haste to confer with Giovanni Visconti, the lord of Milan since the death of his brother Luchino on 24 January 1349. There was everything to fear from such a development.

During Luchino's lifetime, Giovanni Visconti co-operated with him, and appeared to have no interest in succeeding to power. The two brothers avoided all friction with Clement VI, Luchino because he hoped to secure the succession for his young son, Giovanni in the

---

[1] The lists of the payments made to the Germans have been published by K. H. Schäfer, *Deutsche Ritter und Edelknechte in Italien während des 14. Jahrhunderts*, VOL. II, Paderborn 1909, pp. 137–52, 191–200. (These date from 1350.)

hope of snatching it more easily for himself. As a result, the pact made with Benedict XII in May 1341 had been scrupulously observed: moreover the Visconti had marched into the Trentino against Louis of Bavaria and the margrave of Brandenburg; they had recognised the papal candidate, Charles IV, as Emperor, and had come to the aid of the rector of Romagna and the archbishop of Ravenna against the rebels at Forli. It is true that the truce that Cardinal Guillaume Court had compelled them to make with their enemies in 1342[1] had been broken; but Clement VI had merely protested, and refrained from taking coercive action. Giovanni, having become sole master of Milan, was thus able to unite the temporal power to the spiritual, since the pope, carrying the spirit of appeasement to extremes, had been rash enough to confer the archbishopric upon him, on 17 July 1342. A subtle diplomat, utterly unscrupulous and coldly calculating, Giovanni at first made some pretence of pacifism: treaties were signed with the marquis of Montferrat, Luigi Gonzaga, Pepoli and the count of Savoy; his nephew, Galeazzo, married a sister of the count of Savoy, and his other nephew, Bernabo, a daughter of Mastino della Scala; military expeditions ceased for the time being. Nevertheless, Clement VI guessed Giovanni's secret plans, and moreover demanded that the troops encamped at a short distance from Genoa and in Piedmont should be disbanded. The pope gave an evasive reply to a request that the heresy trial of Giovanni's father, Matteo, begun under John XXII, should be reconsidered.

Giovanni Visconti was no great churchman. If we are to believe his relative Alcherio, abbot of San Pietro of Lodi, he only celebrated Mass once in his whole life.[2] Neither religious sentiment nor ecclesiastical discipline caused him the least embarrassment. He was essentially a sceptic, although in order to curry popular favour and the sympathy of the clergy, he increased the number of spectacular processions, the amount of alms given to the poor and the number of charitable foundations. He was handsome and attractive to women, and behaved like a prince: pages, chaplains, secretaries, singers, musicians and knights made the number of his court up to six hundred persons. In the outhouses of his palace there were large numbers of horses for riding, falcons, hawks and hunting-dogs. Guests gathered at his table for 'royal and continual' banquets.[3]

---

[1] Rinaldi, *ad annum* 1342, §17.
[2] G. Biscaro, 'Le relazioni dei Visconti di Milano con la Chiesa. L' arcivescovo Giovanni, Clemente VI e Innocenzo VI,' *Archivio storico lombardo*, series 6, VOL. LV, 1928, pp. 44–5.
[3] Galvano della Fiamma, *Opusculum de rebus gestis ab Azone, Luchino et Johanne Vicecomitibus ab anno 1328 usque ad annum 1342*, ed. Castiglioni, pp. 11, 48.

The ambition of this so ostentatious prelate was to carve out for himself a real state in northern and central Italy. Commercial and financial considerations also urged him to extend his territories as far as Genoa and so ensure access to the Mediterranean. The occupation of Bologna was of capital importance to him. His plan was to make this city his headquarters, and from there to invade the Church's lands and, since Florence was rousing the Tuscan communes against him, to reduce her to impotence. The Guelphs were no longer a force to be reckoned with: the death of Robert of Naples on 20 January 1343, had deprived them of a leader who, if not powerful, was at least still able to influence public opinion.

Giovanni Pepoli's journey to Milan caused alarm in Florence, and she offered to mediate with the Bolognese. Astorge de Durfort, guessing that it was the intention of the Florentines to establish themselves and to supplant both the Visconti and the Church, refused their far from disinterested offers, and persisted in his intention of reducing the Pepoli to a state of complete helplessness. This was the cause of the sale of Bologna by Pepoli to Giovanni Visconti on 16 October 1350.[1] On 23 October, Giovanni's nephew, Galeazzo, entered the city with twelve hundred horsemen, and two days later was made its lord.

The acquisition of Bologna, one of the greatest successes of the Viscontis' policy of expansion, had been arranged with the utmost secrecy. In order to achieve his end without hindrance, Giovanni carried his duplicity to the point of sending ambassadors to Avignon, to discuss with the papal court the return of the city to papal authority. When the real truth was known, Clement VI made use of the spiritual weapons at his disposal to regain Bologna. A summons, on 18 November 1350, to appear within forty days, a threat of excommunication on 4 February 1351 if the guilty party persisted in ignoring it, suspension *a divinis*, the loss of all power, both spiritual and temporal, the promulgation of the interdict—all the accumulated thunder of the Church did not dismay the archbishop of Milan; on the contrary, his defiance only increased the more.[2] But the accusations of heresy, made in full Consistory, by Alcherio, abbot of San Pietro of Lodi, appeared highly compromising. While he was bishop of Novara, on many occasions and before many credible witnesses, Giovanni had declared that the host consecrated by the priests was only a piece of unleavened bread and that the wine, also consecrated by them, was nothing but the pure juice of the grape. When friends

[1] Ch. Gherardacci, *Historia di Bologna*, pt 2, Bk XXII, ed. A. Sorbelli, Bologna 1933.   [2] Theiner, *Codex diplomaticus*, VOL. II, doc. CCII, CCV.

asked him why he did not celebrate Mass, he had replied, 'I prefer to eat tasty dishes, and to drink good wine.' On the first—and last—occasion that he did say Mass, the host slipped from his hands; as none of those present could find it, he had unleavened bread brought to him, and proceeded without more ado to the elevation, saying that that would do just as well.[1]

Astorge de Durfort, thinking that his cause was not irremediably lost, and with the help of the marquis d' Este and Mastino della Scala, made one last effort. He won a victory on 26 November before the walls of Bologna, but did not succeed in penetrating the fortifications: his troops were too greatly outnumbered by the enemy to force an entry. Clement VI, who was living on loans, could send neither soldiers nor money. Visconti took advantage of this forced inactivity of Astorge de Dufort to strengthen Bologna with a powerful garrison, and seized the offensive. Bernabo, who had replaced Galeazzo, bought from the mercenaries of the Church the castles in Romagna which they had received in surety for their wages, and took them into his service. On 17 February 1351, Astorge de Durfort, to his shame, was obliged to dismiss those who were faithful to him and to withdraw to Imola. There the Milanese besieged him by way of reprisal. If, as the chronicler Matteo Villani alleged,[2] Clement VI had intended to make a kind of principality for him—a suggestion which is not proven—he must have been deeply disappointed.

Disaster might perhaps have been averted, if the pope had succeeded in forming a league against the Visconti. But the policy both of the lords and of the communes, consisting as it did in nothing but the pursuit of their private, paltry and selfish interests, prevented him from realising his own wider aims. Since Florence had not supported him, Clement VI decided to do without her co-operation and modified his policy completely. In order to prevent the loss of the Papal States, in September 1351 he entered into negotiations with Giovanni Visconti who, for his part, needed peace to carry out his plans for the conquest of Tuscany. As soon as Florence had wind of these discussions which were taking place at Avignon, she tried by every available means to thwart them and threatened to appeal to the Emperor. Her ambassador, Pietro Bini, many times approached several of the cardinals and declared to them that any agreement with the Visconti would turn to the shame (*vergogna*) of the Church.[3] The gold, the intrigues and the promises of the representatives of the

---

[1] See the texts published by G. Biscaro, pp. 44–5, in the article cited above, p. 121.
[2] *Cronica di Firenze*, Bk I, chs. li, lvi.
[3] See the despatch sent from Florence on 6 November 1351, published by A. Sorbelli, *La signoria di Giovanni Visconti a Bologna*, Bologna 1902, doc. XII, p. 344.

master of Milan—according to Matteo Villani [1]—carried the day at the court of Avignon. On 27 April 1352 a Bull declared non-proven the allegations previously made in Consistory by the abbot of San Pietro of Lodi, though they had been made under oath; it likewise annulled all the proceedings begun against Giovanni, his nephews and his allies, the Pepoli and the Gonzaga, on condition that Bologna and the castles that had been conquered in Romagna and in the county of Imola should be restored; if any Milanese troops had invaded Imola they were to be withdrawn; a war indemnity of 100,000 florins should be paid; and Mastino della Scala and Obizzo d'Este, who had come to the aid of Astorge de Durfort, should not suffer any reprisals. On 28 April, the archbishop of Milan was granted the vicariate of Bologna for a period of twelve years, in return for an annual payment of 12,000 florins, and the active service of three hundred horsemen in the ranks of the papal army during four months of the year, or a payment equivalent to their wages. If he died, his nephews Bernabo, Matteo and Galeazzo would enjoy the rights granted to him. However—and this clause was of capital importance —the grant of the vicariate, which dated from 29 June, was to cease at the end of the twelve years; Bologna would then revert to the Church. [2] When the pact agreed upon in Avignon had been ratified, Guillaume de Grimoard, the future Urban V, took possession of the town, and then solemnly handed it over to its new vicar on 6 September 1352. Thus Clement VI preserved by a fiction the principle of his dominion over Bologna.

The Florentines had bitterly disapproved of the peace planned between the pope and the archbishop of Milan; in December 1351 they changed their minds. The fires, devastations, looting and raids in Tuscany during the fruitless campaign of Giovanni Visconti da Oleggio [3] from 28 July until 17 October, and the fear of a fresh Milanese invasion led them to beg Clement VI to include them, together with the Sienese and the Perugians, in the treaty that was being prepared. [4] Clement VI might well have hardened his heart against them for not having helped him in 1350, but he generously forgot his grievances and informed the Signory that, on his instructions, the Visconti accepted in principle a truce to last one year. [5] But when Florence learned this happy news, it put her in an embarrassing position; for Charles IV, in accordance with a pact recorded in a

---

[1] Villani, *op. cit.* Bk III, ch. i.
[2] Theiner, *op. cit.* VOL. II, doc. CCXX, CCXXI, CCXXXIX; see also Sorbelli, *op. cit.* doc. XIX, p. 351.
[3] For details of this campaign, see Sorbelli, *op. cit.* pp. 115–31.
[4] Despatch of 17 December 1381, *ibid.* doc. XIV.   [5] *Ibid.* doc. XLV.

diplomatic agreement, had promised to enter Lombardy and bring Giovanni Visconti's power to an end. Ambassadors were sent to discuss with him, and all turned out well. The Ghibellines had urged him not to come to Italy, and Charles IV had heeded their advice. He could scarcely respond to the original appeal of the Florentines now that the Church, without whose help no expedition could be made, had become formally reconciled with the tyrant of Milan. Although the Florentines' reply to Clement VI was slow in coming, it was in the affirmative. Giovanni Visconti was no less anxious than they for a truce that would deprive Charles IV of any excuse for crossing the Alps. It was true that this prince was not greatly to be feared, but as far back as men could remember, any imperial invasion had 'convulsed' Italy. Moreover, the lords in Lombardy and Romagna, no less than the Venetians, were threatening to form a coalition against the Visconti, whose policy of conquest was causing alarm.

The initiative thus taken by Clement VI bears the mark of his political genius. It allowed his successor to restore harmony between the Tuscan cities and the archbishop of Milan, and to cause a peace treaty to be signed at Sarzana on 31 March 1353.[1] All cause of future conflict seemed to have been removed. On the one hand, the archbishop undertook not to meddle in Tuscan affairs, unless the Holy See requested him in writing to send help to defend the Patrimony of St Peter; on the other, Florence and her allies promised to have no part in the affairs of Bologna and Lombardy. For the papacy, too, peace offered equally great advantages: the pope was reconciled with Florence and the Guelph party, while Giovanni di Vico, the prefect of Rome, was deprived of help from Milan, and the way was thus left open for the Church to win back her States. It is to Innocent VI, who succeeded to the triple crown on 30 December 1352, that credit must be given for finding the right man to achieve this great task: Gil Alvarez Carillo Albornoz.

6

Albornoz and the Conquest of the Papal States

Albornoz had been chosen to head the legation to Italy on 30 June 1353 [2] because of the reputation he had gained. He was descended, on his father's side, from Alfonso IV of Leon, and, on his mother's, from King James of Aragon; he had been at the court of Castile and

---

[1] The text of this treaty is in Ughelli, *Italia sacra*, VOL. IV, Venice 1719, pp. 222–49.
[2] A. Theiner, *Codex diplomaticus*, VOL. II, doc. CCXLII.

earned the favour of Alfonso XI. His elevation to the dignity of archbishop of Toledo on 13 May 1338 and his appointment as chancellor of the kingdom made him a man to be noticed. Benedict XII had made him legate when the crusade was preached against the Saracens in Andalusia, and he distinguished himself at the battle of Tarifa on 30 October 1340: when he saw that the Christians' courage was flagging, under a vigorous harrying from the infidel, he rallied them, and it was his energetic intervention that won the day. In 1342 Albornoz took part in the siege of Algeciras and in that of Gibraltar in 1349. He had thus given obvious proof of his military talent. Under Pedro the Cruel, like all the courtiers of Alfonso XI, he fell into disgrace, and was obliged to retire to Avignon towards the end of 1350; there on 17 December Clement VI made him cardinal-priest of St Clement, as a reward for his gallant behaviour.

The Papal States, which Innocent VI wished his legate to restore to his sovereignty, were divided into seven provinces: (1) the district of Benevento; (2) the Campagna and Maremna; (3) the Patrimony of St Peter, bordered by the Tiber, the Paglia, the Fiora and the Mediterranean Sea, to which had been added the county of Sabina, the land called *Terra Arnulphorum* (a mountainous district extending from Spoleto to the river Nera), and the towns and dioceses of Narni, Terni, Rieti, Amelia and Todi; (4) the duchy of Spoleto; (5) the March of Ancona, together with the districts of Urbino, Massa Trabarea and the territory of Sant' Agata; (6) Romagna; and (7) the city and county of Bologna.

The administration[1] of every province, with certain exceptions, was in the hands of a rector,[2] appointed by the pope directly or through the intermediary of a legate. The Bull, announcing the appointment of a new holder of the office, laid down the precise limits of his authority, which might be reduced by former or subsequent privileges of exemption. When he took up office, the occasion was marked by the holding of an assembly, called a *parlamento*, where oaths of obedience were taken by prelates, delegates of churches and of chapters, nobles, castellans and representatives of the communes and lesser territories. A banquet was held at their expense.

The assembly met, normally at the place where the rector resided,

[1] K. H. Schäfer has given a concise account of the administration of the Papal States, using material from the account-books of the treasurers, in *Deutsche Ritter und Edelknechte in Italien während des 14. Jahrhunderts*, VOL. I, Paderborn 1909, pp. 16–44. See also C. Calisse, 'Costituzione del Patrimonio di San Pietro in Tuscia,' *A.S.R.S.P.*, VOL. XV, 1892, pp. 5–70.

[2] On 8 August 1318, Guillaume of Balaeto, archdeacon of Fréjus, combined the offices of rector of Benevento and of the Campagna. See Mollat, VOL. II, nos. 8322, 8327.

at irregular intervals as the necessity arose, usually in order to arrange for an equitable distribution of the extraordinary subsidies required to meet the expenses of war. The communes duly sent good men and true to represent them, the greater communes four, the lesser one or two. These discussed current affairs, undertook obligations and took cognisance of papal decisions. Letters of convocation, addressed to them by the rector, threatened defaulters with penalties.

There was no freedom of trade. The rector drew up a tariff of selling prices, and permitted or forbade exports. He minted a special coinage known as the *papalino*, bearing the pope's effigy, and fixed its rate of exchange in relation to other currencies in circulation. The rector also saw to it that the property of the Holy See was maintained in good order, and opposed evictions. He had no right to make a grant of even the smallest piece of the demesne lands.

During the fourteenth century clergy were generally chosen as rectors. If the Holy See preferred a layman—as Clement VI did—a vicar-general was also appointed to deal with spiritual matters. Sometimes the rectors chose as assistants vice-rectors or vicars who governed parts of the province that were very distant or scattered. They also had counsellors.

A treasurer and vice-treasurer took care of financial administration. The pope or the rector prescribed the actual payments. The revenues came from many sources: fines for murder, mortal injury, adultery, insults, riotous behaviour, disturbances of the sabbath; the cense, duties, taxes on hearths and horses; subsidies raised at Christmas, Easter and at certain other feasts from abbeys, convents, communes, castles and territories; tolls and dues of the seal; levies on the income of officials and banks; farms of castellanies and of real estate; profits from prisoners; legacies and inheritances; confiscation of goods; taxes for the maintenance of troops, etc.

A court of justice considered appeals, and consisted of two judges, one to judge laymen and the other clergy. In the March of Ancona, three tribunals operated, dealing respectively with criminal, civil and appeal cases. Clerks of the court kept records of the proceedings. Advocates or procurators fiscal defended the interests of the Holy See.

Outside the rectoral court, magistrates functioned in the name of the feudatories, of the communes or the castellans, but on the instructions of the rector, who always reserved to himself the right to intervene and to stop proceedings. In this way, different forms of jurisdiction were superimposed one on the other. It was the rector who had to settle conflicts arising between communes and feudatories, or any body possessing judicial authority. It was he, too, who had to deal with the execution of sentences, with perquisitions, confiscations and arrests.

A marshal had command of a body of horsemen and foot-soldiers, varying in number, and he had a constable at his orders. He carried out police duty.

A captain-general was in charge of the army. His troops consisted of feudal militia supplied by feudatories owing military service, and militia from the communes, recruited in proportion to the number of inhabitants. The communes provided their recruits with arms and victuals, shouldered the expense of constructing or repairing the walls of their cities, and undertook to guard the means of communication. Under Albornoz, they provided the money needed to pay the *condottieri*.

The fortresses scattered over the territory of the province were occupied by garrisons in command of castellans.

The organisation of the administrative framework was simple, and sufficed to ensure the smooth running of local interests. Like all mediaeval institutions, it left loopholes for arbitrary action, especially in judicial matters, though the subjects of the Holy See could appeal to the pope against sentences imposed by the tribunals of the rectors. The Vatican registers show only too clearly how venal were the papal officials. During the pontificate of Clement V the Gascons, who held these offices, indulged in scandalous extortions and made themselves hated. John XXII and Benedict XII repressed such abuses by useful reforms and by appointing officials of greater integrity and capability. In the time of Urban V and Gregory XI, the treasurer, Angelo Tavernini, a native of Viterbo, amassed untold wealth—18,000 gold crowns in bullion—acquired fiefs, practised usury and ill-treated his debtors; in fact a riot broke out against him at Viterbo in 1374. Apart from this unfortunate incident, the situation in the Campagna and in the Patrimony of St Peter, which at the beginning of the fourteenth century had for long been deplorable, was greatly improved.

The Romans had taken advantage of the absence of the papacy to extend their sphere of influence, and were drawing financial and material benefits from neighbouring territories. If citizens or country-folk refused to obey these illicit demands, a cavalry attack soon made them see reason.[1] The rector of the Patrimony, Guitto Farnese, reckoned that in 1320 his receipts had fallen by half. He declared that those under his jurisdiction were reduced to such despair that, if their defence were not undertaken, they would be in total submission

[1] A. de Bouard, *Le Régime politique et les institutions de Rome au moyen âge (1252–1347)*, Paris 1920, pp. 175–6, 211–20, 308, 324–5.

to the Romans. 'Holy Church,' he concluded pessimistically, 'will in the end have no alternative.' [1] Fortunately towards the end of the pontificate of John XXII, the king of Naples, honoured by the title of Senator, succeeded in preventing the Romans from violating the rights of the Holy See. Indeed, before the arrival of Albornoz the position of the Papal States, from the administrative and financial point of view, was not bad, as is shown by the normal collection of taxes and revenues everywhere except in the March of Ancona. [2] The legate consequently allowed existing institutions to remain, and contented himself with minor improvements and modifications.

The situation in the political field was a confused one. Church lands were divided into two categories, according to whether they were immediately or mediately dependent. The first category consisted of all places not infeudated and free from all seignorial subjection; these were designated in the texts as *manuales* or *in manu Ecclesie*, and formed the *domanium* or demesne; the second was made up of all those that the Holy See had ceded as fiefs to barons, churches, monasteries or individuals, or in the form of conditional or long-term leases.

Conditions of tenure of lands directly subject to the Church varied greatly. Over some the Holy See exercised power that followed a feudal pattern; some communes enjoyed only a modified form of liberty, and could not choose their podestàs; others, such as Bologna, Ancona and Perugia, elected their own. Where the Church made the appointments, she granted them to suitable persons who were compelled by their oath of loyalty to give guarantees and to render an account of their administration when their letters of commission expired; or else she farmed them, putting them to auction and granting them under surety to the highest bidder. This farming had the advantage of avoiding any apparently feudal concessions; but its drawback was that the holder of the farm tended to try to make the maximum profit and to bring pressure to bear on the inhabitants. [3]

In no province of the ecclesiastical states did the rector have an easy task; he had to compel individuals, barons and communes to fulfil their duties, and to assure to them the enjoyment of their respective rights: he was in theory a factor for peace and cohesion. During the fourteenth century his authority was whittled down in many ways: by the jealously guarded independence of which the communes boasted; by the manifold privileges of exemption, with which the Holy See was far too lavish; by the infidelity of the

[1] See *A.S.R.S.P.* VOL. XVIII, 1895, pp. 453–67.
[2] See the balance-sheets, published by Schäfer, *op. cit.* VOL. I, pp. 16–44.
[3] G. Ermini, 'Caratteri della sovranità temporale dei papi nei secoli XIII e XIV,' *Z.S.S.R.G.Kan.* VOL. XXVII, 1938, pp. 315–47.

feudatories in carrying out their duties; and by the growth in some important cities of a tyrannical régime in the hands of barons or opportunist adventurers. The Italians had a fanatical hatred of foreigners. One of them wrote to Cardinal Giovanni Orsini in 1326: 'The French are of all men the worst; they hold everything in scorn save their own nation, and will have dealings with none save those willing to join them in committing folly.'[1] In a word, anarchy reigned throughout the Papal States.

To accept the office of legate to Italy was an heroic gesture. Albornoz left Avignon on 13 August 1353. The prospects were depressing, for the active troops at his disposal were inadequate and his financial resources meagre, at a time when the art of warfare had made great strides. Ballistics had progressed as a result of the use of firearms; iron bombards, mounted on wooden carriages and furnished with rammers, fired iron balls weighing up to five pounds, while the foot-soldiers had muskets and guns of a very rudimentary type with which they caused considerable casualties. Side-arms had also become much longer and constituted a more formidable means of attack. Engineers (*ingignerii*) directed sapping operations, the hurling of stone projectiles by means of complicated machinery, and the construction of wooden towers for attacking fortresses and beleaguered cities. The formation of the Great Companies was even more important: instead of forming bands of from twenty to a hundred men, the mercenaries grouped themselves under a single leader and thus gained cohesion and strength. Duke Werner of Urslingen, had as many as two thousand, three hundred and seventy-five horsemen and one hundred and twenty-five officers under his command, and spread terror wherever he went. The author of the *Istorie pistolesi* alleges that he had, written in letters of silver upon his coat, the motto *Duca Guarnieri Signore della Gran Compagnia, nemico di Dio, di pietà e di misericordia.*[2] The name of Fra Moriale was no less feared. (His real name was Montréal de Grasse and he came not from a family of the Rhineland but from that of the lord of Bar and was therefore a Provençal.) Although Albornoz himself had several Great Companies in his pay, and owed them many victories, he was in constant fear that they might desert or cease to give service when there was any delay in paying their wages.[3]

Before beginning to fight against the usurpers of Church lands, the legate set to work to prevent any alliance among them, and to separate the powerful Giovanni Visconti from their faction. To this

[1] H. Finke, *Acta Aragonensia*, VOL. I, Berlin 1908, no. 335.
[2] Muratori, VOL. XI, col. 489.   [3] Schäfer, *op. cit.* VOL. I, pp. 67–95.

end, he went to Milan. The archbishop received him with ceremony and promised to give all the help that was asked of him against his former allies: his considerable influence, subsidies and even troop reinforcements. He was master of Bologna, and for the moment it suited him to be on friendly terms with the Holy See. From Milan, Albornoz went to Parma, Piacenza and Pisa, where he was greeted enthusiastically. On 2 October, the Florentines, now reconciled with the Church, gave him five hundred cavalry, and the able condottiere Ugolino di Montemarte. On 11 October the people of Siena gave him one hundred more, and those of Perugia two hundred.

On 20 November, Albornoz entered the territory of the Patrimony of St Peter, which Giovanni di Vico, the prefect of Rome,[1] was trying to seize for himself. Deceitful and cunning, consumed by ambition, Giovanni had begun his restless career by murdering his brother Faziolo in 1338. He had been skilful in exploiting the discontent roused by the activities of papal officers, and pursued his plans of personal aggrandisement in a remarkably deliberate manner. He was *de facto* lord of Viterbo, and bought Vetralla from the Orsini in 1345 despite Clement VI's protests; he seized Bagnorea, Toscanella and Piansano and inflicted a crushing defeat on the rector, Bernard du Lac, in July 1346. He was temporarily weakened by the war waged upon him by Cola di Rienzo, and agreed, in 1348, to a peace lasting for three years. In November 1351 renewed hostilities broke out. Either by ruse or by force of arms, Giovanni di Vico became master of numerous localities: in August 1352 he entered Orvieto; in April 1353 he conquered the papal forces, and in June he captured the important towns of Corneto and Toscanella.

This fortunate conqueror regarded the legate's arrival as dangerous; he came to meet him outside the walls of Orvieto and promised to restore the cities he had conquered. Giovanni di Vico carried his deception to the point of appearing at Montefiascone and swearing to Albornoz the feudal oath of obedience to the Holy See. But the moment he realised how paltry were the reinforcements under the legate's command, he threw off the mask and reopened hostilities.

Despite their numerical inferiority, the papal armies began their campaign in December 1353. They seized Civitella d'Agliano on 20 December, but were unsuccessful in their siege of Orvieto and had to retreat, while the enemy carried out successful forays in the Church lands and reduced Montefiascone, where the legate had set up his headquarters, to a state of famine.

[1] This was a purely honorary hereditary title, given to the members of the Ghibelline family of di Vico.

This was one of the bitterest hours in the life of Albornoz. His sufferings 'crucified' him. He was so greatly afflicted by insomnia that he could not study, or even read. He tells us that prayer gave him renewed courage, and 'his sorrow turned to joy.' Innocent VI, who had been warned of his plight, sent sums of money which saved the situation by enabling him to engage new troops, and even to entice eight hundred mercenaries away from the enemy.

By 10 March 1354, Giordano Orsini, the rector of the Patrimony, had approached Orvieto at the head of a powerful army, and was investing the city that proved difficult to take. He seized the convent of San Lorenzo, which provided him with a firm base and made it easier for him to harry the enemy.

While the siege of Orvieto was in progress, the towns of Toscanella, Graffignano, Abbadia al Ponte, Montalto, and Canino yielded to the Church: Corneto alone resisted the assaults to which she was subjected during March and April 1354. On 21 May, reinforcements ten thousand strong were sent by the Romans and Viterbo was encircled. This town was protected by massive fortifications, and obstinately resisted attack. Even when they had stormed the walls, the assailants had to fight for each yard. After exhausting engagements lasting for a fortnight, Giovanni di Vico, who had sneaked into the town, was reduced to begging for peace.

The treaty was signed at Montefiascone on 5 June. It re-established the Church's suzerainty at Corneto and Viterbo, and declared Orvieto and Piansano to be also subject to the Holy See. Vetralla was to remain as a fief to Giovanni di Vico, provided that the pope did not purchase it for 10,000 florins. The legate stopped all canonical proceedings against the vanquished di Vico and his supporters, and restored all his goods and rights that had been forfeited. But he and his brothers were compelled to make an oath of obedience to the Holy See, and his son Giambattista was handed over as a hostage.[1]

The terms of the treaty were put into immediate effect: Albornoz arrived at Orvieto on 9 June and stayed there until 12 July, during which time he received the submission of the inhabitants. He reached Viterbo on 26 July, and laid the foundation-stone of the citadel which was to be the official residence of the rector of the Patrimony of St Peter. He succeeded in arranging that Giovanni di Vico, in return for the vicariate of Corneto, should not set foot in Viterbo for ten years.

Innocent VI did not approve of the treaty of Montefiascone; he had wished Giovanni di Vico to receive harsh treatment, and viewed with disfavour the granting to him of the vicariate of Corneto. Albornoz

[1] Theiner, *op. cit.* VOL. II, doc. CCLXVII.

considered that it would be dangerous to carry out the pope's orders, and more politic to postpone the recapture of Corneto until later. It seemed to him much more important to bring peace to the Patrimony by summoning a solemn parliament at Montefiascone. On 30 September the barons swore an oath of fealty in the presence of the rector, Giordano Orsini, and undertook to fulfil the feudal obligations that they had hitherto transgressed. In a similar manner, the Church's rights in relation to the communes were defined in such a way as to obviate any future disputes. Albornoz, moreover, promulgated constitutions and ordinances which were completely recast in 1357.[1]

The submission of Giovanni di Vico had unexpected repercussions in the Patrimony of St Peter, and gave his partisans matter for thought. The lords of Vitozzo resisted no longer. It is characteristic of the respect and confidence inspired by the legate, that Amelia, Narni, Terni and Rieti, which had for long defied the Church, begged him and the pope as private individuals to accept their overlordship for life.

On 7 January 1355, well pleased with his good work, Albornoz left Orvieto and made his way to Foligno. In his skilful hands, the task of the pacification of the duchy of Spoleto was achieved without too much difficulty; now it only remained for him to deal with the lords of Romagna and of the March of Ancona.

In the Patrimony, his subordinates succeeded in restoring order. Corneto was occupied on 19 June 1355, and Civitacastellana capitulated in 1358. It is true that in the legate's absence, Giovanni di Vico began his treacherous activities once more, and constantly encouraged revolt among the lesser lords of the Patrimony. His death in September 1363 freed the Church from a constant source of anxiety, and eventually in 1366 the Brancaleoni, the last of the dissidents, submitted.[2]

[1] At the time of the parliament of Montefiascone, Albornoz had compiled a list of the rights and titles of the Roman Church in the Patrimony of St Peter. See P. Fabre, 'Registrum curiae Patrimonii beati Petri in Tuscia,' *Mélanges*, VOL. IX, 1889, pp. 298–320.

[2] We have drawn here on the excellent studies by M. Antonelli: 'Una relazione del vicario del Patrimonio a Giovanni XXII in Avignone,' *A.S.R.S.P.* VOL. XVIII, 1895, pp. 447–67; 'Estratti dai registri del Patrimonio del secolo XIV,' *ibid.* VOL. XLI, 1918, pp. 59–85; 'Vicende della dominazione pontificia nel Patrimonio di San Pietro in Tuscia della traslazione della sede alla restaurazione dell' Albornoz,' *ibid.* VOLS. XXV, XXVI, 1903–04; 'La dominazione pontificia nel Patrimonio sugli ultimi anni del periodo Avignonese,' *ibid.* VOL. XXX, 1907, pp. 269–332, VOL. XXXI, 1908, pp. 121–68, 315–55; 'I registri del tesoriere del Patrimonio Pietro d' Artois (d' Artis) (1326–1331),' *ibid.* VOL. XLVI, 1923, pp. 373–88; 'Di Angelo Tignosi vescovo di Viterbo e di una sua relazione al pontefice in Avignone,' *ibid.* VOL. LI, 1928, pp. 1–14; 'Nuove ricerche per la storia del Patrimonio dal 1321 al 1341,' *ibid.* VOL. LVIII, 1935, pp. 119–57; 'Notizie umbre tratte dai registri del Patrimonio di San Pietro in Tuscia,' *Bolletino della R. Deputazione di storia patria per l' Umbria*, VOL. IX, 1903, pp. 381–98, 409–506; VOL. X, 1904, pp. 31–9.

THE POPES AT AVIGNON

Whilst Albornoz was subduing Giovanni di Vico, Innocent VI was not idle. Regular proceedings were begun against the Malatesta. This had the effect of annoying the Florentines, who would not be able to extend their influence in Tuscany any further if the Church became a strong territorial power in their immediate neighbourhood. In order to parry the blow aimed at the Malatesta, the Florentines intervened many times on their behalf. Innocent VI refused to be intimidated by their demands, or to grant any kind of pardon. On 4 July 1354, he summoned the Malatesta to appear at Avignon, and on 12 December excommunicated them for having ignored his summons.[1]

Innocent VI dealt severely with the Malatesta in the hope that Charles IV, who had entered Italy and already reached Udine by 14 October 1354, would help him to restore the authority of the Church in her own States. His hopes proved vain. Charles IV's only purpose during his campaign in the peninsula was to sell at the highest possible price the title of imperial vicar to those who desired it, and liberty to the independent cities. His chief preoccupation was to balance his budget in advance. In the cruel words of Matteo Villani, he behaved like a cheapjack hastening to the fair.[2] After arranging a four months' armistice between the Lombard-Venetian league and the three Visconti, Bernabo, Galeazzo and Matteo—their uncle Giovanni had died on 5 October—Charles received the Iron Crown at the church of St Ambrose in Milan on 6 January 1355, and then took the Mediterranean coast road as far as Rome. He was solemnly crowned Emperor on 5 April by Cardinal Pierre Bertrand de Colombiers, and crossed the Alps again in haste, without giving any help to the Church.[3]

Meanwhile Albornoz began by holding discussions with the lords of the March, with the object of isolating the Malatesta. He succeeded in winning over Gentile da Mogliano, the tyrant of Fermo, Ridolfo da Varano, Niccolò da Buscaretto, the Simonetti and the Ottoni. But the last-named, guessing his plan, and perceiving the danger that they were themselves incurring, persuaded Gentile da Mogliano to be false to the undertakings he had given to the legate, and were themselves reconciled with the Ordelaffi. Thus the coalition of barons that the cardinal had tried to break up by his diplomacy had in fact been strengthened and he had to have recourse to arms.

The campaign began in spring. During the military operations success alternated with defeat, and Galeotto Malatesta seemed to

---

[1] Theiner, *op. cit.* VOL. II, doc. CCLXXXIII.
[2] *Istorie fiorentine*, Bk IV, ch. xxxix.
[3] E. Werunsky, *Der erste Römerzug Kaiser Karls IV. 1354–1355*, Innsbruck 1878.

have the best of it. On 29 April 1355, the papal cavalry under the command of Ridolfo da Varano made a surprise attack on the enemy camp, which was strongly entrenched near Paderno, and captured it after a violent battle. The capture of Galeotto Malatesta facilitated the invasion of the March: the siege of Rimini and the devastation caused in its outskirts frightened the prisoner and led him to agree, first to a truce on 2 June, and then, five days later, to a peace-settlement at Gubbio, where Albornoz was living. Galeotto gave back to the Church the territories he had usurped, and promised to pay tribute annually and to supply an armed contingent. In return, the sentence of excommunication was lifted, and he received for ten years the vicariate of Rimini, Pesaro, Fano and Fossombrone.[1]

The rest of the March was speedily conquered. Fermo was taken on 12 June and its lord, Gentile da Mogliano, was convicted of treachery and punished by banishment and loss of goods. Shortly afterwards, the counts of Montefeltro offered their submission, and Ancona opened her gates to the forces of the legate, who ordered an impregnable fortress to be built there. Albornoz left Gubbio on 20 June and completed the pacification of the country at a parliament held at Fermo on 24 June. He made this town the seat of the court of the new rector, his kinsman Blasco Fernandez.

Once again the legate used the technique that had produced invaluable results in the Patrimony of St Peter. Instead of crushing the vanquished, he forgave them generously and bound them to the Church by real and profitable bonds. Galeotto Malatesta showed himself by no means ungrateful: he was promoted to the rank of gonfalonier in the papal army, and put his sword and military talents at the legate's disposal.

Only one tyrant offered any invincible resistance: Ordelaffi, lord of Cesena and Forli, renowned for his bravado and for his acts of brigandage and cruelty. In July 1355 he had succeeded in routing the legate's troops. Secretly encouraged by the Visconti, and supported by the Manfredi of Faenza, Ordelaffi proved so serious an obstacle that on 17 January 1356 the pope had a crusade preached against him in Italy and Hungary.[2] The pope's voice was heeded, and subsidies and reinforcements arrived in such profusion that Galeotto Malatesta was able to march against Cesena. The siege of the town began in May, but was interrupted in August as a result of military operations undertaken against the Great Companies whom the

---

[1] Theiner, *op. cit.* VOL. II, doc. CCCXXIV.
[2] J. Wurm, *Cardinal Albornoz, der zweite Begründer des Kirchenstaates*, Paderborn 1892, pp. 117–21.

Visconti had surreptitiously taken into their pay. Ordelaffi took advantage of this respite to ravage the surroundings of Rimini. Towards the end of the year, on 20 November, the Manfredi treacherously deserted him and were reconciled with Albornoz. The campaign began again in the spring of 1357: in April simultaneous attacks were made on Cesena and Forli. In the absence of her husband, the intrepid Cià degli Ubaldini herself organised the defence of Cesena and rallied the spirits of the besieged citizens; but she was forced to capitulate on 21 June.

Just as the campaign was progressing favourably, it was brought to an abrupt end by the invasion of the March by bands of mercenaries intent on pillage and led by Count Conrad von Landau. Although the forces at his disposal were numerically superior to those of the German leader, the legate preferred to buy off the invaders, and on 5 September his representatives paid them 5,000 florins, on the condition that there should be no further attacks until 28 January following.[1] In this way the papal army had rid itself of a great source of anxiety, while reserving its forces for the assault on Forli.

At the court of Avignon, the emissaries of Bernabo Visconti, alarmed by the rapid succession of victories won by Albornoz, continually spread malicious gossip about him which was spitefully exploited by the cardinal's enemies, who were jealous of his success. The subjection of Bologna to Giovanni da Oleggio led to a suspicion that the Holy See would regard as obsolete the convention of 1352,[2] by which the vicariate of Bologna had been granted to the Visconti, and would simply decree the return of this city to the Roman Church. Accordingly, Milanese ambassadors had many times tried to persuade Innocent VI to allow their master to resume his authority at Bologna under the pope's aegis. They pointed out that to prolong the siege of Forli at this moment, when the papal coffers were depleted, would gravely compromise the balancing of the budget of the Apostolic Camera. If their requests were favourably received, Milanese troops would immediately join the ranks of the papal army, and Francesco Ordelaffi would shortly be rendered powerless.

Albornoz, who had for long been well aware of Visconti's perfidy, took a course opposed to his suggestions, and set himself to separate the problems of Forli and of Bologna, which Visconti had combined to serve his own ends. He was determined not to decide the fate of Bologna until he had reduced Ordelaffi to submission. He realised

---

[1] Schäfer, *op. cit.* VOL. I, p. 49.   [2] See above, p. 124.

that Bernabo would make little attempt to fulfil the undertakings the advantages of which had been so warmly commended to the pope by Visconti's ambassadors. His agents had warned him that his adversary, far from intending to take sides against the lord of Forli, was secretly encouraging the latter to resist and that the offers made at Avignon were no more than pretence, deceit and barefaced lies.

But Innocent VI thought otherwise. He allowed himself to be deceived and ordered Albornoz to negotiate with Visconti for the cession of Bologna. The legate did not feel himself bound to comply with the orders he received from Avignon, nor could renewed entreaties from the pope break his obstinate intention of ignoring them. Innocent VI yielded to the pressure put upon him by those who were jealous of the legate, and resolved to replace Albornoz by the abbot of Cluny, Androin de la Roche, newly returned from Germany where he had failed to persuade Charles IV to grant a faculty for the Holy See to levy a tenth on ecclesiastical property. On 17 March 1357, at Ancona, Albornoz received a curt note, dated 28 February, informing him of the imminent arrival of Androin, who would bring important instructions.[1]

The fact that he had not yet received the official status of nuncio did not prevent the abbot of Cluny from behaving like one: he entered Milan with great pomp, and Bernabo Visconti showered every attention and honour upon him. At Bologna, naturally enough, he did not succeed in persuading Giovanni da Oleggio to hand over the city to the Church and was obliged to ask the archbishop to pronounce an interdict. On 1 April he met Albornoz at Faenza and revealed to him the purpose of his mission.[2]

Convinced that to allow Bologna to become subject to Bernabo Visconti was a serious mistake, Cardinal Albornoz demanded to be recalled immediately for reasons of health. Innocent VI at once agreed, but begged him to postpone his departure until Forli had yielded. But Albornoz's pride had been hurt, and he insisted on an immediate recall. This reply filled the pope with sudden apprehension. Androin's lack of success at Bologna and the tidings that war had again broken out with Ordelaffi had sufficed to change the mind of the pope who was old and unstable of purpose. He now felt that no good would come of Albornoz's departure and, on 1 May, begged him to delay his return to Avignon until Androin de la Roche had fully acquainted himself with Italian affairs. Fearing that the legate

---

[1] E. Filippini, 'La prima legazione del cardinal Albornoz in Italia,' *Studi storici*, VOL. V, 1896, p. 501, doc. XL.
[2] Villani, *Istorie fiorentine*, Bk VII, ch. lvi.

might already have set off, the pope despatched a Bull in great haste on 6 May, granting full powers to Androin.[1]

The peoples of Italy were no less alarmed than the pope at the prospect of Albornoz's departure. At the general assembly at Fano, which met from 29 April to 1 May 1357, the hope was expressed that he would agree to remain in Romagna until the following September. They placed so high a value on the legislative code, known as the *Constitutiones Aegidianae* [2]—which the legate had drawn up and which, apart from a few subsequent additions, was to govern the Papal States until 1816—that they were unwilling to have so wise a prelate leave them. Androin de la Roche himself, dismayed at the weight of responsibility on his shoulders, added his plea to those of his subjects, and Albornoz at length yielded to their common entreaties. All this was displeasing to Bernabo Visconti, who once again began his intrigues at the papal court. With characteristic cunning and lavish promises, he took advantage of the alarm which the pope felt at the news that the Great Companies were approaching the walls of Avignon, and craftily suggested that if his views on Bologna received support, troops would be sent from Milan to defend the pope. This was sufficient to cause a complete change in the pope's unstable attitude, and he immediately sent word to Albornoz that he must have an interview with Bernabo.

This papal intervention was ill-timed. On 28 June, the legate had joined the league which Mantua and Ferrara had formed against Visconti as early as 1355. He flatly refused to accede to the wishes of Innocent VI, and determined to leave Italy, though not before he had vainly tried to make a surprise attack on Forli.

The attitude of Albornoz was enough to change the pope's point of view once more and, filled with sudden alarm, he wrote to Albornoz asking him to reverse his decision.[3] But this letter from the pope had no effect on the legate, who had already set out for Avignon, after

---

[1] Filippini, *op. cit.* p. 507, doc. XLIII.

[2] The *Constitutiones Aegidianae* are divided into six books. In the first Albornoz states the task he has set himself, and justifies it by reproducing the Bulls whereby Innocent VI granted him full powers in the Papal States. The second deals with the officials in these states; the third lays down regulations appropriate to Church lands. The fourth is a penal code and the fifth a code of civil law. The sixth book deals with rights of appeal. The *Constitutiones Aegidianae,* originally intended for the March of Ancona, were extended by Sixtus IV, Leo X and Paul III to all the Papal States. They were revised in 1538, when jurists incorporated regulations promulgated by popes and legates since the time of Albornoz. The first edition appeared in 1473 at Jesi and the second in 1481 at Perugia. See F. Ermini, 'Gli ordinamenti politici ed amministrativi nelle *Constitutiones Aegidianae,*' *Rivista italiana per le scienze giuridiche,* VOL. XV, 1893, pp. 69–84, 196–240; VOL. XVI, 1894, pp. 38–80, 215–47. P. Sella, *Costituzioni Egidiane dell' anno MCCCLVII,* Rome 1912. A. Zonghi, *Aegidianae Constitutiones Marchiae Anconitanae Perusii 1481,* Fabriano 1907.

[3] Theiner, *op. cit.* VOL. II, doc. CCCXXX.

handing over all his authority to Androin de la Roche on 23 August 1357 at Bertinoro.

Until this date, the abbot of Cluny had been content to follow the directives of Albornoz, in accordance with the express instructions he had received. He was a simple and credulous man, with little knowledge of arms, and quite without any sense of diplomacy; he was faced with a much more able enemy, who combined cunning with valour. As soon as he took over the direction of affairs, everything was in jeopardy: as winter drew on, he was hard-pressed by the enemy and was obliged to raise the siege of Forli; when the war was renewed in April 1358 he was no more fortunate. Two forts, intended to cut off all communication between Ordelaffi and the outside world, were constructed, one between Forli and Faenza and the other at Ponte a Ronco, between Forli and Cesena, but they proved quite ineffective. An attack on the town, on 17 June, was so badly organised that it failed lamentably. Though Meldola was taken on 25 July after a siege lasting twenty-four days, this did not compensate for the reverses experienced by the papal army. In July Forli was entered by the company commanded by Count von Landau which had been hired by Ordelaffi to put out of action the forts which were causing him some inconvenience. In August German mercenaries approached from Tuscany and threatened to invade the March of Ancona. Androin de la Roche despatched troops against them, renewed his attempts to bribe them off and sent his agents to and fro to keep an eye on their progress. But the mercenaries crossed the passes in the Appenines and by September they had harvested the corn and the grapes, and had supplied Forli with victuals and fresh troops. Then, on some trivial pretext, the marquis d'Este and Giovanni da Oleggio recalled to their own standards the mercenaries who were fighting in the ranks of the papal army. Nor was the news from the Patrimony exactly reassuring. In short, in a few months the work so painfully accomplished by Albornoz seemed gravely compromised by the incompetence of Androin de la Roche.[1]

At length Innocent VI realised how great a mistake he had made, and that there was only one man who could be sure of conquering

---

[1] Matteo Villani (*op. cit.* Bk VIII, ch. ciii) criticises him in severe terms: 'Esso abbate era huomo molle e poco pratico e sperto e sè nell' arme e sè nelle baratte, che richeggiono li stati e le signorie temporali . . . per tanto era poco ridottato e meno ubbidito, parendo loro che suo semplice governo poco atto fosse ad acquisto, e pericoloso a sostenere le terre che la Chiesa havea reconquistate nella Marca e nella Romagna.' There were complaints from Italy about the administration of Androin de la Roche, who justified his conduct of affairs in a memorandum published by me in *Revue d'histoire de l'Église de France*, VOL. II, 1911, pp. 391–403.

the Papal States: on 18 September 1358 Albornoz once more took up his duties as legate.[1] He left Avignon on 6 October, and was at Genoa on 5 November and Pisa on 13 November. Then he spent a month in Florence and arrived about 23 December in the March, where Androin de la Roche handed over to him the direction of affairs.

The bands of mercenaries under the commands of Conrad von Landau and Anechin von Bongartz were a source of great anxiety to the cardinal.[2] After fighting under the banner of the Church, they had now engaged in Ordelaffi's service. At one moment Albornoz thought of making terms with them; but the Florentines, for whom they constituted an equally serious threat, opposed this scheme, and gathered such an impressive force that the adventurers were intimidated and took themselves off to seek their fortune elsewhere. This move was fatal to Ordelaffi, who, left to his own resources, capitulated on 4 July 1359. The legate, following his favourite method, overlooked his crimes, and treated him with moderation, granting him the vicariate of Forlimpopoli and Castrocaro for ten years, in recompense for the loss of Forli.

In 1360 a unique opportunity arose to intervene at Bologna, where the vicariate had fallen to Giovanni da Oleggio. At the beginning of March, Niccolò Spinelli appeared at the court of Albornoz and suggested the restoration of the city to the Church, since his master, who had tried to become independent and had been driven to the last extremity by Bernabo Visconti, could no longer make any attempt to govern it. Without waiting to consult Innocent VI, the cardinal hastily accepted this offer, and granted Giovanni da Oleggio the vicariate of Fermo and the title of rector of the March of Ancona. On 17 March, the cardinal's nephew, Blasco Fernandez, entered Bologna and there took up the duties of rector.[3]

Bernabo Visconti protested to the pope, and did his utmost to have the legate's troops withdrawn. But despite the intrigues of his many partisans at Avignon, the reply he received caused him the greatest vexation. He was told that, since the annual tribute had not been paid as it should have been according to long-standing agreements, he had forfeited *ipso facto* all rights to Bologna, which in consequence reverted in the normal manner to the Church.

Bernabo Visconti, in a fit of rage, determined to have recourse to

[1] E. Werunsky, *Excerpta ex registris Clementis VI et Innocentii VI Summorum pontificum historiam S.R. Imperii sub regimine Karoli IV illustrantia*, Innsbruck 1885, pp. 469–73.   [2] Schäfer, *op. cit.* VOL. I, pp. 89–93.
[3] L. Sighinolfi, *La signoria di Giovanni da Oleggio in Bologna (1355–1369)*, Bologna 1905.

arms: he thought that victory seemed assured, since the legate had neither the troops nor the money to join battle and offer effective resistance. Innocent VI, once he realised the true situation, wrote urgently to the Emperor, to Louis of Hungary, to the cities of Italy and even to the king of England. Germany alone heeded his appeal; and even she sent only inadequate help. Moreover, Charles IV demanded a high price for his support. About the month of May 1359, he had asked for the abolition, or at least for a new version, of the Decretals *Romani principes* and *Pastoralis cura,* originally promulgated by Clement V. These Charles considered not so much an attack on the rights of the Empire as a blot on his grandfather's memory. The prince was also well aware that William of Ockham had used specious arguments to attack the validity of his election in 1346. That famous controversialist had claimed that since Henry VII had contravened the Apostolic Constitutions at the time of his expedition to Rome in 1313–14, he was tainted with heresy, and consequently his descendants to the third generation were disqualified from holding any office.

Innocent VI was loath to modify the text of two Constitutions that formed part of the *Corpus juris.* He was anxious, too, to have his revenge for the publication of the Golden Bull of 13 January 1356, which had settled the question of the vacancy of the Empire without consulting him; this was contrary to the doctrine professed by all his predecessors from the time of Clement V, since it set aside and passed over the papal court's claim to approve and confirm the election of the king of the Romans. He countered Charles IV's demand by a very polite plea of exception, with the excuse that so delicate a matter demanded a decision of the Consistory Court.[1] Towards the end of September 1360, the Emperor took advantage of the pope's difficulties to renew this demand. This time the pope yielded to his request in order to obtain military help; nevertheless he profited by the occasion to display all the resources of his legal knowledge: it was as former professor of Toulouse University and sometime *juge-mage* of the king of France for the region of Toulouse that he declared on 1 February 1361 that, though Henry VII had acted without consideration towards King Robert of Naples, he had none the less been an obedient son of the Church. Clement V had not wished to sully his memory in publishing the Constitutions *Romani principes* and *Pastoralis cura,* but only to affirm the rights of the papacy. The pope prudently passed over in silence the doctrine of the Church's supremacy over the Empire but did not hide his feelings about the

---

[1] *Monumenta Bohemiae,* VOL. II, Prague 1907, p. 995.

two Decretals which he continued to regard as fundamentally decisive.[1]

Meanwhile Bernabo Visconti was rapidly going into action. The province of Bologna was invaded. The leaders of the little papal army were resisting at Bologna with difficulty, but not without courage. To avoid, or at least to postpone, disaster negotiations were begun through the intermediary of Niccolò Acciajuoli. To the pope's suggestion of granting to Bernabo an indemnity of 80,000–100,000 florins, that powerful noble merely replied, 'I want Bologna.' But Innocent persisted in his refusal, and hostilities broke out with renewed force.

Suddenly, in the middle of September, it was rumoured that the Hungarians were coming in great numbers to the aid of the Church. The Milanese army immediately lifted the blockade of Bologna, and abandoned its siege equipment. On 30 September 1360 seven thousand Hungarians were arrayed before the city walls. Their undisciplined hordes frightened the papal supporters who disbanded them having no money with which to pay them. Nevertheless, their timely arrival had caused the enemy to retire so that Albornoz was able to enter Bologna in triumph on 15 October and to reward Niccolò Acciajuoli with the title of rector. But the joy of the inhabitants was short-lived, for the Milanese army soon reappeared before their city walls. The legate did his utmost at the beginning of 1361 to prevent the enemy from receiving help from Aldobrandino, the marquis d'Este, by dazzling the latter with vague promises that he might eventually be granted the vicariate of Bologna. On 15 March he went to solicit the help of the king of Hungary; but the king was under pressure from Visconti's ambassadors, who were lavish with money and gifts, and would not agree to the proposed conditions. Bernabo, for his part, appealed to the arbitrament of the Emperor. The landgrave of Leuchtenberg, chosen as arbitrator by Charles IV, decreed that the war must cease before any equitable decision could be made, but Bernabo refused to obey. Indignant at this evidence of bad faith, the Emperor took away his title of imperial vicar, deprived him of all his privileges, and pronounced sentence of outlawry and banishment against him.

In the meantime a ruse conceived by Albornoz proved extremely successful. Profiting by the absence of Bernabo, he sent to Bileggio, the leader of the Milanese army, a messenger who claimed to have

---

[1] F. M. Pelzel, *Kaiser Karl IV., König in Böhmen*, VOL. II, Prague 1781, no. 298; see also W. Schefler, *Karl IV. und Innocenz VI. Beiträge zur Geschichte ihrer Beziehungen 1355–1360*, Berlin 1912, pp. 143–6.

come from Galeotto Malatesta, the commander of the papal forces. This messenger suggested that they should betray the cause of the Church and join together in a military operation in order to hand over Bologna to Visconti. Bileggio fell into the trap and divided his forces on the supposed advice of Malatesta. After a crushing defeat at the bridge of Rosillo on 16 June 1361, he hastily retired into the Milanese district. This victory cost the life of the brave Blasco Fernandez, but it had at least saved Bologna.

But it was to be expected that the enemy would return. On 16 April 1362, Albornoz succeeded in meeting this threat by contracting a defensive and offensive alliance against Bernabo with the della Scala, and the Estense and with Francesco da Carrara. After this the campaign began again in the Bolognese district, with some success on both sides. It was, however, interrupted for a time by the death of Innocent VI on 12 September.

The very day after he was crowned—7 November 1362—Urban V hastened to confirm Albornoz's authority.[1] In spite of his gentle disposition, the pope did not hesitate to summon Bernabo Visconti to appear at Avignon on 28 November.[2] Ambassadors from Milan came to present their respectful homage to the pope on the occasion of his elevation to the pontifical throne. French plenipotentiaries joined them to discuss in general terms (*in genere*) the possibility of peace. 'Knowing the usual knavery of the Milanese,' wrote Urban to Albornoz on 1 February 1363, 'we replied that we would only enter into negotiations if the castles of the Bolognese district were first restored to the Church, and the molestation of the clergy and their property discontinued.'[3] As Bernabo Visconti did not fulfil the two conditions submitted to his ambassadors, the supreme pontiff condemned him for heresy on 3 March, in an open meeting of the Consistory Court and, since he 'despaired of his conversion,' launched a crusade against 'this perfidious and most cruel enemy' and urged the Estense, the della Scala and Francesco da Carrara to fight against him.[4] On 4 May, a Bull forbade 'All dealings, direct or indirect, hidden or public,' with the excommunicate Bernabo; it was forbidden for anyone to provide him with 'troops, grain, wine. victuals, cloth, wood, iron, arms, horses, ships, merchandise of any sort, or money.'[5]

In this way Urban V repeated the series of measures formerly

---

[1] A. Theiner, *op. cit.* VOL. II, doc. CCCLXVII. See also Lecacheux, VOL. I, Paris 1902, no. 126. [2] Theiner, *op. cit.* VOL. II, doc. CCCLXIX.
[3] Lecacheux, VOL. I, no. 194.
[4] Theiner, *op. cit.* VOL. II, doc. CCCLXXV, CCCLXXVIII; see also Lecacheux, VOL. I, nos. 223–6. [5] Lecacheux, VOL. I, no. 414.

adopted by John XXII against Matteo Visconti. He set out in detail
the accusations of heresy, basing his allegations on the fact that since
Visconti had not replied when summoned to appear by Innocent VI
and himself, he was guilty of contumacy, and had, moreover, for
a year and more made no secret of his contempt for the various
sentences of excommunication pronounced against him.[1] But the
'evil-doer'—for it was thus that the pope described him [2]—remained
quite unmoved. After the defeat inflicted on him by the members of
the coalition at Solarolo on 5 April, he pretended to talk peace but at
the same time played an underhand trick on Francesco da Carrara
by getting the Venetians to declare war on him over some disputed
Paduan territories.[3] But he took fright when a crusading army from
Germany, Poland, Austria and Hungary came to the help of the
Church, before setting off for the East. Albornoz was preparing to
crush his enemy, when a letter dated 26 November 1363 deprived
him of all authority in northern Italy and transferred his powers to
Androin de la Roche.[4]

What had happened? The danger he was in had led Bernabo
Visconti to think again. Ambassadors promised, in his name, to give
back the castles in the Bolognese district, and that of Lugo in the
diocese of Imola, and to destroy the forts which they held in the
Modena area, in return for a sum of 32,000 gold florins; after this,
peace would be signed. But he would only hand back his captures to
a new legate, and only with him would he discuss a treaty.[5]

So Urban V sacrificed the one man who might have completed the
downfall of Visconti to what he believed to be right for the Church.
To organise a crusade was his dearest hope and he had the chimerical
scheme of sending the Great Companies to the East, and by so doing
freeing France and Italy from their excesses. But the conquest of the
Holy Land was only possible if peace reigned in Italy. To achieve
this end he agreed in February 1364 to a humiliating treaty, which
guaranteed to Bernabo Visconti an indemnity of 500,000 gold florins,
on condition that he restored all his gains in Romagna and the district
of Bologna.

Urban V could have tried to spare the feelings of Albornoz, but
he was niggardly both of praise and of consolation, and merely bade
him carry out his duty. Moreover, vexatious orders to Albornoz
abounded: he was to dismiss his nephew, Gomez Albornoz, not
because he had failed as rector of Bologna, but because he was

[1] Lecacheux, VOL. I, no. 734.
[2] *Ibid.* no. 557. (Letters sent to the king of France on 5 August 1363.)
[3] *Ibid.* no. 547.   [4] *Ibid.* no. 681.   [5] *Ibid.* nos. 701–02, 724.

doubtless uncongenial to Bernabo Visconti; he was to hand over to Androin de la Roche all prisoners taken during the war; and he was continually reminded that he must observe the conditions of the peace-settlement, as though he were suspected of evading them.[1]

Albornoz saw with sorrow the collapse of all the work he had so painfully accomplished, and asked for his recall through the intermediary of his faithful representative at the papal court, Niccolò Spinelli. This Urban V refused to grant, and instead made him legate to the kingdom of Naples on 13 April 1364.[2] Despite his reluctance to remain where he was, the cardinal did not take up his new appointment until August 1365; in the interval, he gave generous assistance to Androin de la Roche, so that the 'shameful treaty'—for so Matteo Villani describes it—with Bernabo Visconti was speedily put into effect. He also contended with the Companies, who were unemployed now that the war had ceased, reconciled Florence and Pisa and settled the dissensions that had arisen between the Romans and the inhabitants of Velletri.[3] Towards the end of 1364, his life was endangered by a serious illness brought on by his distress at the news that the pope had taken further action against him: he was deprived of his legatine office in Romagna, and Petrocino Casalesco, archbishop of Ravenna, replaced him as vicar-general in temporal affairs. The ostensible reason for this was that the cardinal could not deal with the Church's interests simultaneously in Naples and in Romagna.[4] But the true explanation was quite different: it was that at Avignon the group of cardinals who heeded the malicious suggestions of Bernabo Visconti had accused Albornoz of having impeded the carrying out of the treaty of February 1364 in Romagna, of having contravened the supreme pontiff's orders as to the use of revenues from the Papal States, and even of having used them to his personal advantage.

Full of indignation, the legate again demanded to be recalled, declaring that he could not remain at his post while such accusations were being levelled at him, that he was hated by too many people and that he was old and must think of the repose of his soul. In these circumstances Urban V showed the nobility of his character: he called together the College of Cardinals and emphatically rebutted the malicious allegations that had been disseminated concerning his worthy and faithful servant. On 30 January 1365, he wrote an admirable letter to Albornoz, rallying his courage, praising his zeal in the

[1] *Ibid.* nos. 707, 736, 982, 1003. [2] *Ibid.* no. 885.
[3] *Ibid.* nos. 1070, 1110, 1250-2, 1485, 1486.
[4] *Ibid.* nos. 1316, 1382, 1447, 1504.

Church's cause, pointing out that his presence in Italy was essential and begging him, in the name of holy obedience, to go to Naples.[1]

The cardinal bowed respectfully to the wishes of the Holy Father, who had made a handsome apology: he left in August for the court of Queen Joanna. In January 1366 he was back in the Papal States without having achieved anything worthwhile. He had been received with great ceremony, but the queen's courtiers had proved so obstructive that not one of his orders was executed.

The whole of 1366 was taken up with negotiations. Italy was over-run by the Great Companies, the Companies of Sterz and of St George and the so-called White Company; they had not been disbanded, in spite of the ecclesiastical sanctions imposed on them by the Holy See. On 19 September 1366, Albornoz succeeded in forming a league against them, between the Church, the queen of Naples and the cities of Florence, Pisa, Siena, Arezzo and Cortona. It was thanks to Albornoz that peace was brought to the Papal States, so that the supreme pontiff could at last return to Rome. The death of Albornoz on 22 August 1367, brought about a complete change of attitude on the part of Urban V who, during the cardinal's lifetime, had constantly thwarted his skilful policy. Androin de la Roche contrived to muddle through the complexity of Italian politics so long as he had Albornoz at his elbow. After the cardinal's death, the abbot of Cluny, who was better fitted for devoutly singing matins in his cloister, gave immediate and repeated evidence of his incompetence. Too late the pope realised how culpably indulgent he had been towards Bernabo Visconti; he dismissed his legate and replaced him by Anglic Grimoard. Androin at first refused to resign, but Urban V threatened to excommunicate him if he did not comply; whereupon he finally submitted.

7

Rome and the Papacy: Urban V's Return to Italy

The commune of Rome had achieved its independence in 1144. During the fourteenth century, its relations with the papacy were affected by repercussions of contemporary events. In the hope, no doubt, of bringing Clement V back to the city, the Romans made him a senator for life; but he carried out his duties, indirectly, through chosen intermediaries. After Henry VII's expedition to Italy, the pope, unable by himself to restore order to the city which had been

[1] Lecacheux, VOL. I, no. 1535.

much disturbed by bloody street fighting between Guelphs and Ghibellines, delegated his authority on 14 March 1314, together with his office of imperial vicar-general during the interregnum, to King Robert of Naples.[1] But the title of captain-general of the Papal States did not increase that prince's reputation. Robert's authority was not sufficient to impose itself both on a turbulent nobility and upon the people. Violent brawls were constantly breaking out between the Orsini, Colonna, Caetani and Savelli. The situation grew worse when the populace, displeased that John XXII was continuing to evade the question of returning to their city, greeted Louis of Bavaria with transports of joy in 1328. But when six months had elapsed, the Romans realised their mistake, and having driven the Bavarian out with shouts and jeers, they humbly presented the pope, in his private capacity, not only with the office of senator, but with 'the syndicate' (i.e. the control of the administrative tribunal whose members were called syndics and had the task of supervising municipal officers of all grades), the captaincy and the 'rectorate' of Rome, with permission to have third parties act for him.[2] When he received the same honours,[3] Benedict XII considered that he was strong enough not to have recourse to the good offices of the king of Naples, as his immediate predecessors had done: henceforth the municipal officials were directly appointed by the Holy See. Thus, on the ruins of the democratic régime set up in the twelfth century and organised in the thirteenth by Brancaleone degli Andalo, was established seignorial rule.

Liberty raised its head again in 1339, when the people drove out the papal senators and divided the rectorate between an Orsini and a Colonna. But Benedict XII annulled all the revolutionary acts they had formulated, and became even more authoritarian. It was a sign of the times that in 1340 the city militia was fighting under the banner of the Church. The capitulation of the Romans followed inevitably from their inability to remedy their unfortunate financial position and to provide their fellow-citizens with the means of livelihood.[4] Nevertheless, internal unrest continued; disturbances occurred more frequently; the tyranny of the lords became more intolerable, and their palaces became dens for bandits who attacked passers-by, stripped peasants and pilgrims of their goods and

[1] J. Schwalm, *Constitutiones et acta publica imperatorum et regum*, Hanover 1906–11, VOL. IV, no. 1164.
[2] A. de Bouard, *Le Régime politique et les institutions de Rome au moyen âge, 1252–1347*, Paris 1920, p. 327. (Letters from John XXII dated 16 September 1332.) The pope subdelegated Robert of Naples on 15 March 1333: *ibid.* p. 328.
[3] A. Theiner, *Codex diplomaticus dominii temporalis Sanctae Sedis*, VOL. II, doc. XLII.
[4] De Bouard, *op. cit.* pp. 68, 165, 179, 185–6.

committed the worst acts of brigandage. In short, Rome was in a state of complete anarchy.

The plight of his fellow-citizens so moved a man of obscure birth, the son of an innkeeper and a laundress, that he determined to free his native city from the despotism of the nobles, and to restore order. We may well wonder whether he was a statesman or a fool, a hero or an impostor, a mountebank or a charlatan. Clement VI, while recognising his intellectual gifts, his powers of oratory and his skill in warfare, described him in November 1348 as 'a madman and insane,' suspect of schism and heresy, who had committed against Church, Emperor, nobles and common people a series of acts so impertinent and full of 'conceit' that 'never in the course of history have we read of such folly.'[1] The pope was an orator himself, and may have been exaggerating. According to one of his latest biographers,[2] Cola di Rienzo was by no means unbalanced, but a precursor of modern times, a man who, unlike the humanists and artists of the Renaissance, formed opinions on the state, the church, society and human personality based on a mystic inner sense of renewal, which ultimately derived from a religious ideal and the cult of antiquity.

From Cola's correspondence, written in a vivid, incisive and pungent style, we undoubtedly gain the impression of a man inspired, absolutely convinced of his mission and the part he had to play. He declares that he acts only with the inspiration of the Holy Ghost, who directs him, comforts him in all he does and gives him invincible courage, that he may bring back to Rome her vanished splendours. So guided, he declares that no fear can appal him—the future was to give the lie to this—though the whole world, Christians, unbelieving Jews and pagans, should oppose him. His one dream is to die for the love of justice and the honour of God and the Church.[3] When he was solemnly given the insignia of a tribune, he ordered that five crowns of leaves and one of silver should each in turn be placed on his brow, to denote the gifts of the Holy Ghost.[4] Cola also had visions. Two days before the bloodthirsty fighting that took place on 20 November 1347 outside Rome, near the gate of San Lorenzo, Boniface VIII appeared to him, urged him to engage in battle against the Colonna and assured him of victory.[5]

[1] Speech made in Consistory on 17 November 1348; see K. Burdach, *Vom Mittelalter zur Reformation. Forschungen zur Geschichte der deutschen Bildung*, VOL. II, Berlin 1929, pt 5.
[2] P. Piur, *Cola di Rienzo. Darstellung seines Lebens und seines Geistes*, Vienna 1931.
[3] K. Burdach and P. Piur, *Briefwechsel des Cola di Rienzo*, Berlin 1912, pp. 47, 55.
[4] *Ibid*. p. 130.   [5] *Ibid*. p. 179.

The pious sentiments displayed by Cola di Rienzo and his belief that the Holy Ghost reigned within him were the result of his connections with that off-shoot of the Friars Minor who, calling themselves fraticelli, or Spirituals, proclaimed that the era of the Holy Ghost had come, and the age of the official church was over. Cola had let himself be carried away by the apocalyptic dreams of these aberrant monks, who were in love with a strange mysticism and passionate admirers of the ideas of Joachim of Flora. Yet he had no desire to practise the absolute poverty so vigorously professed by these visionaries: on the contrary, he lived in an atmosphere of dazzling luxury, calculated to impress the Romans who loved ostentation. His gifts of oratory, his resonant voice, attractive smile and fine presence won him the favour of the populace. Assiduous reading of Livy, Seneca, Cicero and Valerius Maximus, together with a knowledge of the monuments of the ancient world, had given him a lively admiration for classical Rome: he resolved to bring her to life again, and cherished the hope of creating an Italy freed from the Empire and from the temporal power of the papacy.[1]

There is something of the miracle in the rise to power of such a man. Sent by his compatriots on an embassy to Clement VI, Cola di Rienzo so impressed the pope that the latter conferred on him the office of notary to the City Chamber, on 13 April 1344.[2] This office placed him in the limelight, and Rienzo increased his popularity by making virulent speeches against the nobility, and by having allegories painted on public monuments, thereby rousing public opinion to a frenzy. At the same time he was secretly preparing for the day of revolution by clandestine meetings which took place on the Aventine Hill.

A chance happening hastened the execution of his plans. Stefano Colonna, not realising the danger that threatened his party, had led the city militia outside the walls of Corneto to get provisions. Thanks to his absence revolution broke out, on 20 May 1347, in a strange manner, under the guise of a procession. An impressive cortège led Cola di Rienzo to the Capitol. There, before the populace who had been summoned by the tocsin, this skilful orator gave one of his most eloquent speeches and roused the enthusiasm of his hearers. Decrees were read out and submitted to the approval of the crowd, and were greeted with wild applause. By agreement with the Apostolic vicar, Raimond de Chameyrac, bishop of Orvieto, the overlordship of

[1] There can be no doubt of this, as is shown by the memorandum addressed in 1350 to the archbishop of Prague. See *ibid.* p. 241.
[2] Theiner, *op. cit.* VOL. II, doc. CXXXIX.

Rome was conferred on Rienzo; his authority was everywhere recognised, without a drop of blood having been shed. The Roman lords
left the city in haste. Stefano Colonna, when he came back from
Corneto, did not even try to launch an offensive.

The government of the new master of Rome began under the most
favourable auspices. Justice and equity reigned; the reorganisation
of the city militia was accomplished without conflict; the wise
administration of finance and the suppression of crime succeeded in
spreading well-being and security throughout the city.

Clement VI was alarmed by the revolution of 20 May 1347. The
numerous letters which the tribune addressed to him, in which he
unblushingly boasted of his almost divine mission, aroused the pope's
fears still more. In vain did Cola show himself increasingly respectful;[1] Clement was not to be deceived. He doubtless approved of the
new constitution which the Roman people had established without
his consent,[2] but he played his part cleverly: his correspondence
shows that though he made skilful use of Cola di Rienzo to put
down the tyranny of the prefect of Rome, Giovanni di Vico, and the
influence of the nobility, he feared the authority that this same
Rienzo had acquired, and was secretly undermining it by means
of his lieutenants who had remained in Rome.

His victory over Giovanni di Vico in 1347 filled the tribune with
pride. In his mad vanity he called himself 'Nicolas, by the authority
of our most merciful Lord Jesus Christ, stern yet merciful tribune
of liberty, peace and justice, liberator of the holy Roman republic.'
The official acts were dated thus: 'Given at the Capitol, where we live
with an upright heart, under the reign of justice,' or again, '. . . since
justice has once more come down from heaven.'[3] Cola di Rienzo
struck a new coinage, surrounded himself with regal splendour and
harried the nobility. His ultimate object was to unite all the cities of
Italy into a single state with Rome as its centre. To this end, he asked
them to send him ambassadors.

On 1 August 1347, the delegates of twenty-five cities appeared
before the tribune. Instead of discussing questions of Italian politics
with them, he did nothing more than provide them with the spectacle
of imposing ceremonies. A magnificent procession accompanied him
to the baptistry of St John Lateran, where he bathed in the font
where, according to legend, Constantine was baptised. This strange
ceremony was not a sign of madness: Rienzo had conceived it as a

---

[1] Burdach-Piur, *op. cit.* pp. 56, 147, 149.
[2] J.-B. Christophe, *Histoire de la papauté pendant le XIVᵉ siècle*, VOL. II, Paris 1853,
pp. 473–7 (documents). [3] Burdach-Piur, *op. cit. passim.*

symbol of the rebirth that he hoped to bring about in Italy. After-wards he had the arms of knighthood conferred upon himself, and, through a notary, published a series of extravagant decrees, which in their execution would have been injurious to the Holy See. Since Rome, he said, was once again possessed of world jurisdiction, all privileges contrary to this conception were annulled. He summoned Louis of Bavaria and Charles of Bohemia, as well as all the electors of the Empire, to appear before the tribune on the following Whit-sunday [1] thereby openly questioning the election at Rense on 11 July 1346. To emphasise the full extent of his authority, Cola di Rienzo brandished a naked sword, and thrust it alternately in three different directions, shouting 'This is mine!' The Apostolic vicar, Raimond de Chameyrac, immediately perceived the serious implications of these gestures and protested, but the voice of the notary who read his hastily composed manifesto was drowned by the noise of trumpets. Moreover, the tribune made no secret of his future intentions, and told the papal representative that he would govern Rome without any help from him.

These events in Italy caused some anxiety at the papal court. Anxiety there was redoubled when it was learned that Cola di Rienzo had come to an understanding with the king of Hungary to drive the queen of Naples out of her states, and to place her kingdom, as well as the county of Provence, in subjection to the Roman people. On 12 October 1347, Clement VI sent orders to Bertrand de Déaulx, the legate in Italy, to go to Rome and persuade the tribune to give up these plans, which would be disastrous for the rights of the Church. If he refused, the cardinal was to excommunicate him, urge the Romans to reject his authority and put their city under an interdict.[2]

Bertrand de Déaulx took up residence in the Vatican without delay and summoned Cola, who appeared before him clad in armour, with a silver crown on his head and a steel sceptre in his hand. 'You sum-moned me,' said the tribune arrogantly; 'what do you want of me?' The legate replied, 'I bring you instructions from our lord the pope.' 'What are they?' asked Cola. Bertrand felt his courage fail, and was silent. Quite at ease, the tribune turned on his heel and walked away with a contemptuous smile. As for the timid cardinal, he fled with all haste to Montefiascone.[3]

The Roman nobility, who had felt themselves ill-treated since the revolution of May 1347, had not been inactive: they were conspiring

---

[1] F. Papencordt, *Cola di Rienzo e il suo tempo*, trans. T. Gar, Turin 1844, doc. pp. 7–9.　　　[2] Theiner, *op. cit.* VOL. II, doc. CLXXXII.
[3] *Vita di Cola di Rienzo*, ed. A. M. Ghisalberti, VOL. I, Florence 1928, ch. xxxii.

to bring about the downfall of their enemy, and were stirring up public opinion against him. Cola di Rienzo felt that his authority was threatened; instead of acting prudently, he aroused the enmity of the people by his despotism, his luxurious way of life and his eccentric behaviour. Bertrand de Déaulx, plucking up courage again, declared him excommunicate and encouraged the count of Minervino to attempt a counter-revolution. On 15 December 1347, cries rang out, of 'Popolo! Popolo! Down with the tribune!' The bell of the Capitol was tolled. No-one came forward to defend the government. Cola di Rienzo feared that the populace was in revolt; he removed his insignia of power and retired within the walls of the castle of Sant' Angelo, from which he soon set out in the direction of Città Vecchia. The nobles at once came back to Rome and Bertrand de Déaulx, who also reappeared, rescinded all the decrees of the fugitive leader, re-established the old form of government and appointed Luca Savelli and Bertoldo Orsini as senators.

As soon as the nobles returned to the city, disturbances broke out. The safety that had existed in the streets for several months rapidly disappeared. Internal dissension between noble families and their supporters broke out with unprecedented violence. Weary of the quarrels that caused daily bloodshed in their city, a group of Romans met on 26 December 1351 at Santa Maria Maggiore and decided to confer authority on a respected plebeian, Giovanni Cerroni by name, who was immediately summoned from his home and brought in triumph to the Capitol. The populace, flocking to the sound of the tocsin, ratified Cerroni's election without more ado. Thus a revolution was again accomplished, as it had been in May 1347, as though by magic, without the least opposition from the aristocracy and without bloodshed.

Clement VI, glad to be rid of the danger created for him by Cola di Rienzo's pretentions, confirmed Cerroni in his offices of senator and captain until Christmas 1353, and even made him a gift of 14,000 gold florins.[1]

But Cerroni had no statesmanlike qualities. Though he brought peace to the Romans for a while, he lacked firmness and had no knowledge of the art of war. His prestige disappeared after a disastrous campaign against Giovanni di Vico, and he resigned in September 1352 and prudently withdrew to the Abruzzi.

Terrible disorder again broke out in Rome, and the streets ran with blood. The people rose against the nobility, whose constant turbulence was again disturbing the city, and, on 14 September 1353,

---

[1] Theiner, op. cit. VOL. II, doc. CCXXIII–CCXXV.

elected Francesco Baroncelli as 'second tribune and august consul.' Innocent VI had no liking for innovation, and decided to oppose Baroncelli with Cola di Rienzo, who was being held in semi-captivity on the first floor of the Tour de Trouillas at Avignon.[1]

Since his fall from power, Cola di Rienzo had many times tried to regain control of Rome. The few seditious risings fomented by him had been easily suppressed. Pursued by the papal officers sent to arrest him, he fled into the Apennines, to Monte Majella, on whose precipitous slopes some of the fraticelli had taken refuge. There he lived for nearly two years with these aberrant friars and came under their influence, delighting to read the *Oraculum angelicum*, which had been drawn up in the thirteenth century by the followers of Joachim of Flora.[2] Fra Angelo, a pious hermit, revealed to Cola God's supposed intentions for him. The time, he said, was drawing near when the Holy Ghost would begin to reign in this world. Cola di Rienzo was the chosen one, destined to assist in the reform of the Church and to regenerate the world with the help of Charles IV[3] the Emperor. Rienzo lost no time in crossing the Alps and, disguised as a Franciscan, arrived without difficulty at Prague where the imperial court was residing. In July 1350, he appeared before Charles IV and warmly urged him to come over to Italy, begging that he himself might receive the title of imperial vicar of Rome. The Emperor asked to have his plan in writing, and Cola made out an elaborate statement full of the apocalyptic visions of the hermits of Monte Majella. The effect of this memorandum was to land Rienzo in gaol, and later Charles IV handed him over to the pope, who in turn sent him to Cardinal Albornoz on 24 September 1353. The latter thought it unwise to allow Rienzo to return to Rome, where a rising had deposed Francesco Baroncelli, and only authorised him to come as far as Perugia.

In this city lived Brettone and Arimbaldo, the brothers of the condottiere known as Fra Moriale. Cola di Rienzo persuaded them to lend him money, which enabled him to hire five hundred mercenaries and to march on Rome, armed with the title of senator, which had been granted him by Albornoz. The expedition was successful, and he entered the city on 1 August 1354, amid the acclamations of the populace.

Their enthusiasm was short-lived. Instead of governing with wisdom and moderation, Cola di Rienzo behaved like a tyrant. The

[1] Dr. Colombe, 'Nicolas Rienzi au palais des papes d'Avignon,' *Mémoires de l'Académie de Vaucluse*, VOL. XI, ser. 2, 1911, pp. 323–44.
[2] Burdach-Piur, *op. cit.* VOL. II.   [3] *Ibid.* VOL. I, pp. 193–7.

beheading of Fra Moriale, who had helped him to regain power, alienated public opinion, and a series of arbitrary arrests brought about his downfall. On 8 October 1354, the Roman populace made an assault on his palace in the Capitol and set it on fire. Cola di Rienzo escaped from the blaze and, disguised as a peasant, mingled with the throng. But he was recognised, seized and dragged off to the Lion's Cage, half-way up the staircase of the Capitol. Cecco del Vecchio thrust a sword into his heart, a notary cut off his head and the populace mutilated his corpse.

After the tragic end of Cola di Rienzo, the government was taken over by a council of thirteen citizens, although the pope as a private individual had been granted the office of senator for life. But Albornoz intervened, forbade the introduction of a new régime and appointed Orso Andrea Orsini and Giovanni Tebaldi di Sant' Eustachio as senators. From this time, the Romans enjoyed an era of comparative peace. The legate's presence in Italy had the effect of subduing the aristocracy, who dared not stir up trouble as they had done in the past. Moreover, Innocent VI greatly reduced their influence by abolishing the custom by which, for more than a century, the dignity of senator had been especially reserved for the Roman nobles. From the autumn of 1358 only one senator was appointed and he was a non-Roman. The pope hoped in this way to keep the Church lands intact from the depredations of the Roman militia which was again active. The people were willing to welcome these reforms, but set up an organisation known as 'The Seven,' reformers who took over the municipal government; thus they hoped to safeguard their independence and prevent the decay of democratic principles.

Ever since 1305 the Romans had constantly urged—at more or less frequent intervals—the return of the papacy to their city. Major obstacles prevented Clement V and his successors from granting their wishes: apart from other reasons, the almost constant warfare in Italy was sufficient to explain their protracted stay in Avignon. When Albornoz had restored order in the Papal States and succeeded in overaweing the Roman nobility, everything conspired to invite the pope to return to the banks of the Tiber. His presence was necessary to consolidate the peace so painfully achieved, for there was still a risk that Rome might fall prey to revolution. Innocent VI realised that a return should be made, but his age and infirmity made it impossible for him to attempt such a journey.[1] Urban V, on 23 May 1363, wrote to the senator and the people of Rome: 'As to our coming, we have expressed our inmost desire, *in all sincerity*, to your

[1] Martène-Durand, *Thesaurus novus anecdotorum*, VOL. II, Paris 1717, col. 946–7.

ambassadors. Weighty obstacles, which we have told them of, have prevented us from achieving it; let us hope that the Almighty will dispose of them.'[1]

Foremost among the impediments which the pope invoked, without mentioning them specifically, was undoubtedly the war against Bernabo Visconti, then at its height and depleting his financial resources. An overland journey would be dangerous, and the sea-voyage could not be arranged overnight: to charter a fleet involved long and complex negotiations, while the problem of providing the transport necessary to bring sufficient supplies to Rome for the papal court was almost insoluble. The surrounding countryside had almost nothing to offer, and barrels of wine, cheese and salt fish (cod, herring and eels) had to be brought from France. Moreover, the palace of the Vatican was unfit for habitation: extensive repairs were needed to the roof; doors and windows were either missing or crumbling away. A team of carpenters, locksmiths, masons and marble-cutters had still not completed their task when the pope did finally disembark at Corneto. Judging by the vast cost of the repairs —15,569 gold florins—the papal palace must have been in a lamentable state.[2]

But the material difficulties were as nothing compared with the problem of overcoming the hostility of almost all the members of the Sacred College. We need not attach much importance to the slanders spread abroad by Petrarch, who depicts the cardinals as concerned at the prospect of no longer being able to enjoy the Beaune wines;[3] but it is true, nevertheless, that those who had lived in Avignon had little enthusiasm for leaving the charms of that country, the sunny skies of Provence, the green countryside of the Comtat-Venaissin and their luxurious dwellings, for a desolated land subject to miasma, an inclement climate, makeshift living quarters and a city that only a few years before had been given over to revolutionary disturbances. In vain had Petrarch disparaged Avignon which he described as 'unholy Babylon, Hell on earth, a sink of iniquity, the cess-pool of the world. There is neither faith, nor charity, nor religion, nor fear of God, nor shame, nor truth, nor holiness, albeit the residence within its walls of the supreme pontiff should have made of it a shrine and the very stronghold of religion. . . . Of all the cities I know, its stench is the

---

[1] Theiner, *op. cit.* VOL. II, doc. CCCLXXXII.
[2] J. P. Kirsch, *Die Rückkehr der Päpste Urban V. und Gregor XI. von Avignon nach Rom*, Paderborn 1898, pp. xii, xxix-xxx, 103–65.
[3] See *Rerum senilium*, Bk IX, ch. i, in *Opera omnia*, Basle 1581, pp. 845–6. The papal court did set a high value on Beaune wine: the captain of an Italian vessel transported as many as sixty-five barrels from Arles to Corneto in 1367. See Kirsch, *op. cit.* p. 5.

worst. . . . What dishonour to see it suddenly become the capital of the world when it should be but the least of all cities.'[1] He even made use of a favourite image in fourteenth-century heretical circles and identified Avignon with the harlot of the Apocalypse, 'Arrayed in purple and scarlet, and decked with gold and precious stones and pearls; having a golden cup in her hand, full of abominations and the filth of her fornication.'[2]

But the cardinals enjoyed living on the banks of the Rhône, and despite the invectives of Petrarch preferred to be there, where their well-being was assured; many were under the influence of the king of France, Charles V, who disapproved of the departure of the Holy See; others lent a favourable ear to the suggestions of Bernabo Visconti, who also had no wish to see them go.[3] The Emperor thought otherwise: after coming to an agreement with Giovanni Visconti in February 1364, he suggested that he himself might escort Urban V to Italy. The pope politely declined the offer;[4] he followed the example of his predecessors in not caring to accept a patronage that might prove compromising, or to support an expedition to the peninsula which, as the Florentines had repeatedly warned him, was sure 'To give rise to unheard-of doings, unfortunate incidents and wrongful acts.'[5] Furthermore, the moment was not propitious, for the Great Companies were infesting the Patrimony of St Peter and the Campagna. Charles IV took the matter up again when he made a short stay in Avignon from 23 May until 9 June 1365. Painstaking discussions were held and resulted in a practical decision: soldiers were to be sent to attack the Turks who had seized Adrianople; it was hoped that Louis I of Hungary would supply provisions for the troops.[6] This proposition was very congenial to Urban V, for the emperor of Constantinople, John V Palaeologus, had recently declared his intention of reconciling the orthodox church with the papacy, believing that the West would help him to withstand the Turkish danger. If the Latin and Greek Churches were to be united —and this would be no easy matter from the theological and liturgical points of view—then the Holy See must be at Rome. Urban V realised this. The first preparations for the return to Italy were made

[1] De Sade, *Mémoires pour la vie de François Pétrarque*, VOL. I, Amsterdam 1764, pp. 25–7. [2] Epistle XVI (no title) in the Basle edition, p. 729.
[3] Theiner, *op. cit.* VOL. II, doc. CDXVII, CDXXI. (Letters of the pope written with the object of appeasing the wrath of Bernabo Visconti after the pope's departure had been announced.) [4] Rinaldi, *ad annum* 1364, §11.
[5] Davidsohn, 'Tre orazioni di Lapo da Castiglionchio, ambasciatore fiorentino a papa Urbano V e alla curia in Avignone,' *Archivio storico italiano*, ser. 5, 1920, p. 229.
[6] G. Wenzel, *Monumenta Hungariae, Acta extera*, VOL. II, no. 472. See also Lecacheux, VOL. I, no. 1849.

in the autumn: a Bull of 10 September 1365 gave orders to repair the Vatican palace, and another on 13 November to lay out the adjacent gardens as vineyards and orchards.[1]

In the month of June 1366, the pope informed the cardinals, the Emperor, Bernabo Visconti, the Romans and the king of France of his irrevocable decision to leave Avignon.[2] The Florentines did all they could to keep him to his resolution. Lapo da Castiglionchio, speaking in their name in full Consistory, made a speech that was both eloquent and florid, saying, 'Rome summons her spouse who will also be her saviour; Italy hopes to prostrate herself at your feet. . . . Do not allow yourself to be detained by anxiety about events beyond the Alps or by the sweetness of your native soil. Think rather of Italy, bereaved by the absence of the supreme pontiff. . . . Put aside all private affection. Arm yourself with justice; let the divine will inspire you; think how you may reform the world and the Roman Church. . . . You will see how people and princes come to greet you. . . . You will hear rising to the upper air the shouts of those who applaud and encourage you. The golden age will come again, and erstwhile happiness be born anew.' After describing the marvels lying hid in Christian Rome, the Florentine envoy ended on a solemn note: he warned Urban V that if the pope continued to absent himself, the Roman Church would lose Romagna, the March of Ancona, the Patrimony of St Peter, the duchy of Spoleto and others of her lands.[3]

In Paris, the royal court, dismayed at the news from Avignon, made one last effort to keep the papacy within its grasp. A solemn embassy came to the Curia about the end of April 1367. It consisted of the count of Étampes; of the chancellor of Dauphiné, Guillaume de Dormans; of the major-domo of the royal palace, Pierre de Villiers; of the lord of Vinay and of several others. Ancel Choquart, master of the Court of Requests to Charles V, read a turgid speech to the pope, thick with quotations from biblical, juridical and classical sources in the scholastic manner, setting forth the reasons against his departure for Rome. The author recounted an imaginary dialogue between the pope and his devoted son Charles. 'Lord, where goest thou?' asked the son. 'To Rome,' replied the father. 'There thou wilt be crucified,' concluded the son, who then respectfully showed him the risks he would run. A peremptory argument closed the speech: 'Ought you not, most Holy Father, to think especially of

---

[1] Kirsch, *op. cit.* p. 265. See also Theiner, *op. cit.* VOL. II, doc. CDVIII.
[2] Theiner, *op. cit.* VOL. II, doc. CDXIII-CDXIX.
[3] Davidsohn, in the article quoted, pp. 240–6 (text of the speech).

settling the disputes in every part of France, and bringing peace to those in whose midst you have been living, lest you be like the hireling who "seeth the wolf coming, and leaveth the sheep and fleeth," since he cares so little for the sheep entrusted to him?'[1]

But Urban V remained unshaken in his resolve: he left Avignon on Friday, 30 April 1367, and reached Viterbo on 9 June. There he was to remain during the heat of summer in the fortress that Albornoz had built, waiting for the repairs to the Vatican palace to be, if not complete, at least sufficiently advanced for him to live there.

Urban V's arrival at Viterbo caused universal rejoicing in Italy. 'Nobles, magnates, prelates and delegates from the communes' came to pay him homage. But relations between the citizens of Viterbo and the people of the court deteriorated on 5 September. The cardinals' servants polluted the water of the Gruffols fountain, and this caused fighting and bloodshed. The people rose in arms, stretched chains across the streets, and seditious cries rang out, of 'Death to the Church! Long live the people!' Some rioters made their way into the lodging of Cardinal Guglielmo Bragose, killed a major-domo and a servant, threatened the cardinal's life and forced him to hand over his red hat and to pay a ransom of 300 francs. Étienne Aubert escaped secretly from his house, and disguised first as an Augustinian and then as a Dominican, succeeded in taking refuge in the papal citadel, which was besieged for two days. Fortunately help arrived from Rome and quelled the tumult. Gibbets were set up opposite the mansions that had been attacked, and there seven of the worst offenders were hanged.[2]

Urban V thought that this augured ill for the future, and began to say that tribulation was in store for the Church. The ultramontane party also exploited this incident, pointing out that Italy did not provide a safe shelter for the papacy. Petrarch, stung to the quick, declared that the Viterbo riot was nothing but a *motiuncula*, a skirmish of very little importance.[3]

When Urban V resolved to leave Viterbo, his escort was made up of two thousand men-at-arms led by Niccolò, the marquis d'Este, the count of Savoy, Ridolfo da Varano and the Malatesta. The exclusion of foreigners made it clear that his entry into Rome on 16 October was that of an Italian prince. Whether or no the Romans appreciated this papal gesture, their joy knew no bounds. Public and religious life took on a new intensity, with magnificent processions through the

[1] This speech has been printed by Du Boulay, *Historia universitatis Parisiensis*, VOL. IV, Paris 1673, p. 396, under the name of Nicolas Oresme.
[2] Baluze, *Vitae*, ed. Mollat, VOL. I, pp. 364, 388, 409; VOL. IV, p. 132.
[3] *Opera*, p. 853. The reference occurs in a reply to Jean de Hesdin; see also p. 1063.

streets, brilliant feasts to welcome the queen of Naples and the king of Cyprus (in Lent 1368), churches restored and abuses hitherto rampant now put down.[1] The humanist Coluccio Salutati wrote enthusiastically to Petrarch: 'If you were at Rome you would see ruined temples rise again by ceaseless toil, and I know you would rejoice. Your piety of soul would bless him who had rebuilt the Lateran, restored St Peter's and roused the whole city.'[2]

When the pope, to escape the summer's heat, went to the castle of Montefiascone, the Romans began to be alarmed. Their anxiety increased when, on 22 September 1368, only one Roman, Francesco Tebaldeschi, was elevated to the cardinalate, as compared with six Frenchmen and one Englishman. Neither Urban's return to the city, nor the crowning of the empress, nor the recantation of John V Palaeologus allayed their fears. Their ill-humour prompted them to injudicious action. Whilst Francesco di Vico was renewing hostilities against the Church in the Patrimony, the Romans made common cause with the people of Perugia, who had driven the papal legate from their city in the spring of 1370. Perugia even had the audacity to hire the mercenary bands of the condottiere John Hawkwood and to send them to attack Viterbo, whither the pope had retreated. Even when Hawkwood yielded, the situation remained much the same, for Bernabo Visconti, who was anxious for the pope to leave, had hired mercenaries in Tuscany. It seemed certain that the Patrimony of St Peter must shortly be invaded. There was no help to be had from the Emperor or the king of Hungary.

Perhaps the unrest among his subjects had an unfortunate influence upon the pope: or perhaps he obeyed the suggestions of 'whisperers' who made no attempt to disguise their opinion of those subjects. In any case, the strong animosity between Italians and French led them into venomous abuse of each other. Petrarch in his *Apologia*, acting as spokesman for his compatriots, describes the ultramontane party as haughty, flighty and barbarous (in other words ignorant, brutal, cruel and stupid), as gluttons and drunkards, braggarts and liars. The French rebutted these insults and defended themselves with equal liveliness and spirit.[3] Urban V may well have regretted leaving his own country where he was universally liked, and have desired to return, and so be rid of the discord that surrounded him in Italy. It is very likely that he felt unsafe in Rome, for the news of his departure, at the beginning of October 1369, was given from

[1] Baluze, *op. cit.* VOL. IV, pp. 132–3.
[2] *Epistolario*, ed. Fr. Novati, Rome 1891, p. 61.
[3] H. Cochin, 'La grande controverse de Rome et d'Avignon au XIVᵉ siècle,' *Études italiennes*, VOL. III, 1921, p. 13.

Viterbo where he was protected by a solid fortress. The pope declared that he was ready 'to work with all his might' to bring to an end the war which had broken out again between the kings of France and England, and to go wherever this might most easily be achieved.[1]

The Romans begged Urban V to reconsider a decision that was painful to them. To their ambassadors he said, on 22 May 1370: 'My sons, you are welcome. The Holy Ghost brought me to this region; now He takes me to other regions for the honour of the Church. If I am not with you in body, I shall be there in spirit.'[2] An official document dated 26 June begins by praising the Romans, but ends with a discreet reference to their recent aberrations and their intrigues with the Perugians. Urban V asked them to continue in their virtuous frame of mind, 'So that, if we or our successors decide for adequate reasons to return to Rome, we be not deterred by any troubles that may exist there.'[3]

Peter of Aragon, the Franciscan of royal blood, and Bridget of Sweden both did their utmost to persaude the papacy to remain in Italy.[4] But the misfortunes they foretold had no influence on Urban, and at the end of September 1370 the court entered Avignon with great pomp.

There was bitter disappointment throughout Italy. Petrarch spoke in his country's name, saying, 'Yes, I am bound to confess that I had borne many evil sons. . . . I was wounded with mortal sores; you came to me to bathe my wounds; . . . and began to pour in oil and wine. And then, before my wounds were bound up or the balm had touched them, you left me! You had begun to cut away the rotten flesh with steel, and then, cutting deeper, you perhaps found parts that might have been healed.'[5]

8

The Final Return of the Holy See to Rome and the War of the Otto Santi

With Urban V's return to Avignon it seemed as though the Holy See were likely to remain for ever on the banks of the Rhône. His successor was elected on 29 December 1370; according to Coluccio Salutati,[6] he combined intellectual culture with many rare qualities:

[1] Baluze, op. cit. VOL. I, pp. 374–5.   [2] Ibid. VOL. IV, p. 136.
[3] Rinaldi, ad annum 1370, §19.   [4] Ibid.
[5] H. Cochin in the article quoted, p. 12.
[6] Epistolario, ed. F. Novati, VOL. I, Rome 1891, p. 143.

prudence, circumspection, piety, goodness; a friendly manner, an upright character, a mind always consistent in word and deed. But would his sickly temperament and delicate constitution make him unlikely to show energy and a spirit of determination? Would this subtle diplomat and past-master of prevarication have the courage to venture into Italy? But Gregory XI dashed the hopes of the Limousins who wanted to stay in Provence. As he wrote to Edward III of England: 'Since we were first elevated to the supreme pontificate, we have always had a heart-felt desire, which constantly remains with us, to visit the Holy City, chief seat of our authority, and there and in the surrounding countryside to set up our dwelling and that of our apostolic court.'[1] For various reasons an early departure was desirable. After the death of Albornoz, Urban V and Gregory XI had scrupulously pursued the policy of that great statesman. They followed his example in keeping the nobles friendly by granting them vicariates or fiefs, on condition, in the latter case, that they did not build any fortresses or restore those that had been damaged or destroyed; on the other hand, in the Patrimony of St Peter they built citadels at Corneto, Montalto, Norchia and Canale. The chief communes were given papal vicars, who had express instructions to conform to local regulations and not to impose any tax or law without the consent of delegates of the communes. Jealously-guarded privileges softened the rigours of the sovereign's acts, and exemptions from rectoral authority led to easier settlements in litigation. Thus the bonds that kept lords and communes subject to the Holy See were strengthened. As the system of government by vicars extended, the Papal States came to resemble an Italian monarchy, and served as a rallying point for the towns and lordships of the peninsula, against the threat of Bernabo Visconti's ambition. If he were not to lose his supremacy and the benefit of Albornoz's conquests, the pope must move to Italy and govern his subjects directly.[2]

Moreover, the restoration of the papal monarchy had inevitably caused anxiety in Siena, Pisa and Florence. Gregory XI protested that his intentions were peaceful, and denied any attempt to increase his hold on Tuscany, but the Florentines remained jealous of the Church. The slightest movement of papal troops in the area around Tuscany caused them lively apprehension, and they regarded the occupation of Perugia in 1371 by Cardinal Pierre d'Estaing as a sure sign of plans for further conquest. When Géraud du Puy, abbot of

[1] Delachenal, *Histoire de Charles V*, VOL. III, Paris, p. 589.
[2] M. Antonelli, 'La dominazione pontificia nel Patrimonio negli ultimi venti anni del periodo Avignonese,' *A.S.R.S.P.* VOL. XXX, 1907, pp. 269–332; VOL. XXXI, 1908, pp. 121–168, 315–55.

Marmoutier, ruled the city as vicar, Florence was even more alarmed, for she feared the energy and warlike qualities of the Holy See's representative, and believed—or pretended to believe—that she was likely to be doubly attacked, from Bologna in the north and Perugia in the south. The powerful republic coveted Tuscany, and was angry to see the continued extension of the Holy See's zone of influence; she feared that she might suffer the fate of Perugia.

Gregory XI saw clearly where his duty lay: on 9 May 1372 he informed the cardinals in Consistory that he intended to return 'very shortly' to Rome.[1] The extreme delay in carrying his plans into execution is due not so much to his alleged weakness of character or natural indecision, as to obstacles that arose perforce out of the circumstances. The coffers of the treasury were empty. While he waited for the arrival of subsidies from the bishops,[2] the pope ordered the Camerarius to arrange a loan of 50,000 gold florins, for which his jewels were to be the security.[3] He had to hire mercenaries in order to finish the campaign against Bernabo Visconti in Piedmont. Florence did not join the league that Gregory XI strove to form in 1371–2 with Count Amadeus VI of Savoy, the marquis of Montferrat, Niccolò d' Este, the lords of Carrara, the queen of Naples and the king of Hungary. In 1373, Giovanni Albergotti, the bishop of Arezzo, succeeded in leading the army of the Church to victory at Pesaro and Chiesa, in seizing Vercelli and in forcing Ossola, Pianello, Piacenza and Pavia to yield.[4]

Encouraged by these successes in Piedmont, the pope announced his departure to the kings of England, Aragon, Castile, Navarre, Portugal and France.[5] 'The welfare of the Christian faith, the interests of our spouse, the Roman Church, the state of papal territory and the public weal,' he wrote, 'all press us to return to holy Rome.' Autumn seemed the best time for the journey.

On 6 September 1374, the date for setting out had not yet been settled, but the cardinal of Sant' Eustachio stated that it shortly would be. Avignon at that time presented an unusual spectacle, as preparations for departure were seen on every hand. Cristoforo da Piacenza told Luigi da Gonzaga of the comings and goings of ambassadors, messengers and men-at-arms. Some time before, the

[1] Despatch sent from Cristoforo da Piacenza to Luigi Gonzaga, in *Archivio storico italiano*, ser. 5, VOL. XLIII, 1909, p. 41.
[2] L. Mirot, *Lettres secrètes et curiales de Grégoire XI*, VOL. I, nos. 1083, 1086–8, 1093–1094, 1100–19, 1160, 1175–7, 1248, 1472–7, 1824–32, 1940, 1941.
[3] *Ibid.* no. 1393 (24 September 1373).
[4] G. Romano, 'La guerra tra i Visconti e la Chiesa (1360–1376),' *Bolletino della Società pavese di storia patria*, VOL. III, 1903, pp. 412–37.
[5] Mirot, *op. cit.* nos. 1738–43.

supreme pontiff had said in Consistory: 'We shall never have done with the Milanese, if we do not cross into Italy'; now their plenipotentiaries had been driven out 'like dogs' and when they eventually were admitted in audience, Gregory himself informed them that a crusade was to be preached against Bernabo Visconti.[1]

Autumn went by without any definite developments. But far from abandoning his plans for departure, in February 1375 the pope invited the Perugians to get ready accommodation for the court, and in March the inhabitants of Arezzo, Pisa, Florence, Siena and Genoa were told to assist Bertrand Raffin, clerk to the Apostolic Camera, to buy provisions.[2] On 5 June he sent word to the queen of Naples, asking that the six galleys 'generously' placed at his disposal should be sent to Marseilles on 1 September.[3] On 8 July this order was countermanded. That day, couriers had brought news that the kings of France and England had made a truce for a year and had agreed to begin negotiations for peace on 14 September, the feast of the Exaltation of the Holy Cross. To his great 'annoyance,' the pope was obliged temporarily to put off his departure, but only for 'a few days.'[4] On 28 July Gregory changed his mind again. He now thought that the whole winter should be spent in working out 'a peace most essential for all Christendom.' He proposed to set out in the following spring,[5] and told the Romans on 2 August 1375 that Charles V and Edward III had 'begged' him to ensure the success of their negotiations by staying in Avignon; he added: 'If we had been residing in Rome, we should have returned here.'[6]

Other things besides politics were discussed at Bruges. A disquieting disagreement existed between the papacy and England on the question of benefices and the 'anticlerical legislation' typified by the Statute of Provisors (1351) and that of *Praemunire* (1353). Moreover, when, in 1372, the Avignon court proclaimed a caritative subsidy at the rate of 100,000 florins, made necessary by the Italian wars, Edward III had forbidden his clergy to make any payment at a time when he was himself about to ask them for financial assistance. An embassy led by the bishop of Bangor had come to Avignon and protested with some acerbity against the papal tribunals' activities with regard to the English, and against the reservation of benefices, expectative graces and apostolic provisions. Concessions were made on both sides in December 1373, but it was agreed that discussions

---

[1] *Archivio storico italiano*, ser. 5, VOL. XLIII, 1909, pp. 53–4 (despatches dated 5 June 1373 and 4 February 1374) and p. 56.
[2] Mirot, *op. cit.* nos. 1801, 1833–9.
[3] *Ibid.* no. 1911. (Letter dated 5 June 1375.)
[4] *Ibid.* nos. 1932–5. [5] *Ibid.* no. 1939. [6] *Ibid.* no. 1942.

should be begun, at either Calais or Bruges, which, it was hoped, would arrive at a satisfactory agreement.

Negotiations proceeded slowly at Bruges during the years 1374 and 1375; the results were made public in six Bulls, dated 1 September 1375. These results, however, evidently appeared negligible to both Gregory XI and Edward III, since further attempts were made to reach an agreement in the last months of 1375 and in 1376, but were never implemented.[1]

The pope was detained in Avignon for perfectly adequate and legitimate reasons; but they did not impress the Romans. A rebellious spirit was at work among them, and in all the Church lands, especially at Corneto, Orvieto and Todi. Gregory was obliged to warn his subjects that this seditious spirit was bound to delay his return, and would mean that when he did come, he would have to chastise them.[2]

It was not only in Rome that the news of the pope's delay in returning was unfavourably received. General discontent grew in Italy. It was thought that Gregory XI was trying to avoid fulfilling his promises; the reasons he gave were regarded as mere subterfuges to escape the necessity of an enterprise distasteful to his court. Florence exploited the situation with some skill, in order to seize the offensive against the Church. She had been driven to action by the cessation of hostilities in Piedmont following the truce with Bernabo Visconti, signed on 4 June 1375. The republic feared the consequences of the Holy See's return to Rome and the renewed importance of that city. By a fresh outbreak of war she hoped that both would be made impossible.[3]

Such inexcusable aggression had to be justified and coloured with some fallacious pretext. Florence unjustly accused the pope's followers of having encouraged the formidable leader of the mercenaries, John Hawkwood, to invade her territory, and bitterly reproached Gregory XI with having hampered the export of corn from the Papal States at the expense of Florence. Coluccio Salutati ungraciously wrote: 'What had the Florentines done to the Church, that, at a time when they were stricken by famine, they were unable to trade in corn with the Church lands despite so many apostolic letters? It is a principle of imperial law that he who refuses food is guilty of killing. O inhuman cruelty, O cruel inhumanity! That of all peoples one, and that a staunch and Christian one, should be denied the food it

[1] E. Perroy, *L'Angleterre et le Grand Schisme d'Occident*, Paris 1933, pp. 17–50.
[2] Mirot, *op. cit.* nos. 1986–90. (Letters dated 2 and 3 November 1375.)
[3] Mirot, 'La Question des blés dans la rupture entre Florence et le S.-Siège en 1375,' *Mélanges*, VOL. XVI, 1896, p. 187.

needs and was promised, while others, even foreign nations, receive supplies publicly and openly.'[1]

Like the rest of his compatriots, this distinguished humanist was giving a tendentious explanation of Gregory XI's behaviour. Long before Florence had made her request, trade agreements had been reached with Marseilles, Pisa, Montpellier, Lucca and Rome, on condition that local resources allowed such trade to be carried on. This caused some alarm among the inhabitants of Romagna and the Patrimony of St Peter, lest their stocks became seriously depleted, and they protested violently. This led Géraud du Puy, vicar-general of the Patrimony, to forbid the export of grain, except to the Luccans and Romans. October 1374 was therefore a bad moment at which to ask for supplies of food. It was not Gregory XI who refused to grant them, however; Géraud du Puy, after several requests to satisfy the Florentines, was wrong in taking up a hostile attitude and so providing them with the grounds for a treacherous attack on the Church.

With equal disregard for truth, Florence alleged that Cardinal Guillaume de Noëllet, the legate in Romagna, had instigated the rebellion of Prato in 1375.[2]

Florence showed rather more skill in exploiting the discontent caused by the administration of Church lands by papal officers. Whether these were Frenchmen or not, they had incurred the dislike of the Italians; the Limousins, whose birth, customs and language were all foreign, and so automatically suspect, if not hated, were arrogant in their dealings with subordinates, and abused their authority; the Augustinian Luigi Marsigli who had come under the influence of the fraticelli, described them as 'miserly, dissolute, importunate and shameless.'[3] It is only too true that many of these Frenchmen regarded Italy merely as a place where they could rapidly amass a fortune. Gregory XI did all he could to put right such abuses. The Vatican registers show many signs of his efforts; but they also prove how well-founded were the complaints of the populations of the Italian cities.

Florence took advantage of the general discontent caused by the misgovernment of the legates and rectors, to cause trouble in the Papal States. While making a hypocritical show of her feelings of veneration for the pope, she brandished her red flag, on which the

---

[1] *Epistolario*, VOL. I, p. 216, translated into French by Mirot in the article quoted above, p. 181.
[2] A. Gherardi, 'Di un trattato per far ribellare al comune di Firenze la terra di Prato nell' anno 1375,' *Archivio storico italiano*, ser. 3, VOL. X, pt. I, pp. 3–26.
[3] See the text published by E. Dupré-Theseider in *I papi di Avignone e la questione Romana*, Florence 1939, p. 180.

word 'Liberty' shone in letters of gold, and so caused the Italians to rise up against the French. 'Now is the time,' she proclaimed, 'to revive the liberty of old! . . . Let all peoples unite with Florence! Tyranny will vanish.'[1]

The towns and villages of the Papal States, which had long resisted the intrigues of the Florentines, now rushed to join them. In October 1375 Orte and Narni were the first to join a league formed by the Florentines, and drove the papal officers from within their walls. In November, Città di Castello and Montefiascone rebelled. Francesco di Vico returned to Viterbo on 18 November and proclaimed himself its lord. The fortress to which the papal garrison had fled withstood a lengthy siege, but was taken by storm on 14 December and rased to the ground. On 7 December the Perugians had risen and compelled their vicar, Géraud du Puy, to flee. Finally, during the night of 19–20 March 1376, Bologna made herself independent. Thus within a short time, the Church had lost all her domains.[2]

All the rebels formed themselves into a league which at first seemed powerful, but rapidly disintegrated. Certain cities were more frightened than attracted by the effrontery of Florence, and her attempts at negotiation with the Venetians, the Genoese and the Neapolitans came to nothing. The Emperor Charles IV and King Louis of Hungary refused to listen to the proposals of her ambassadors. Bernabo Visconti held aloof, though he might have joined the league. Even amongst its members there was hardly any unity. Once the restraint imposed by the officers of the Church was removed from the rival cities and factions, old quarrels were revived. Each tried to snatch some coveted piece of land from a neighbour.

Florence was placed under the ban of Christendom on 31 March 1376, a mortal blow for the league. In addition to the interdict upon the city, Gregory XI invited all European monarchs to expel Florentine merchants from their lands and to confiscate their property. All trade with them was forbidden.

Did the republic of Florence, threatened with complete ruin, ask Catherine of Siena about June 1376 to beg Gregory XI for mercy? Raymond of Capua tells us that the Eight 'summoned her to Florence' and 'having gone to meet her, asked and required her with many prayers to come to Avignon into the pope's presence, there to treat for peace between them and him. She set out and came to Avignon

---

[1] L. Mirot, *La Politique pontificale et le retour du S.-Siège à Rome en 1376*, Paris 1899, p. 48.
[2] Antonelli, in the article quoted (see p. 161), pp. 121–68. See also O. Vancini, *La rivolta dei Bolognesi al governo del vicario della Chiesa (1376–1377)*, Bologna 1906, pp. 17 ff.

where I met with her. I was interpreter between her and the supreme pontiff, he speaking Latin, she Tuscan. I bear witness before God and man that this gentle pontiff, in my presence, with me as intermediary, gave peace into this virgin's hands, saying, "So that thou mayest see that I desire peace, I place it simply in thy hands; but do not forget the honour of the Church." For the Florentines did not desire peace, but only to destroy the Church. When the ambassadors arrived, the Saint ran to meet them and offered them peace. They answered her that they had no authority to treat with her.'[1]

This account by Raymond of Capua, of which the final version was written in 1395, can scarcely be accepted, despite its detail and precision.[2] It is difficult to see how the Eight, who were carefully guarded, could have had an interview with Catherine outside their city. If they did indeed entrust her with an official mission, how can one explain the silence of every contemporary source—narrative, diplomatic, documentary or epistolary. The scornful reply of the Florentine ambassadors is sufficient reason for rejecting this theory. Moreover, the Saint makes no allusion to this occasion in a letter dated 28 June, in which she gives a short account of her interview with the pope. Even if we are to believe that she really used the words ascribed to her by her confessor, no doubt Gregory XI was speaking ironically in his reply.[3] He was far too well acquainted with the tortuous policy of the Florentines to entrust peace negotiations to a humble religious, whose orthodoxy must have been in some doubt, since a commission of bishops subjected her to an exacting interrogation.

It was now too late for conciliatory intervention. On 20 May 1376, Breton mercenaries, hired with great difficulty through skilful negotiations on the part of Cardinal Robert of Geneva, left the Comtat-Venaissin, which was very glad to see them go. They amounted to as many as 10,000 men, under the command of Jean de Malestroit and Sylvestre Budes. The troops crossed the Alps and made their way into Lombardy, where Galeazzo Visconti greeted them as allies, supplied them with plentiful provisions, and, in order to give some satisfaction to the Florentines, tried to hire them for his own service; but the Bretons, faithful to their undertakings, were not enticed by alluring offers.

Florence was disappointed, and soon began to fear. She sounded

---

[1] *Legenda major*, §421–2, translated into French by R. Fawtier, *Ste Catherine de Sienne. Essai de critique des sources. Sources hagiographiques*, VOL. I, Paris 1921, p. 172.
[2] Fawtier, *op. cit.* VOL. I, pp. 173–80.
[3] *Revue d'histoire de l'Église de France*, 1940, p. 100. This suggestion comes from E. Jordan.

the alarm among her allies and called for help, whilst at the same time she put on a false appearance of confidence for the benefit of the Bolognese, who feared the worst and were unwilling to make peace. All efforts to snatch the Bretons and John Hawkwood, the leader of the English mercenaries, from the Church's service were unsuccessful. The enemy advanced, and soon appeared before the walls of Bologna. They had no hope of taking the city by storm, for it was well protected by high ramparts. The legate Robert of Geneva ordered the surrounding districts to be laid waste. Acts of the most horrifying pillage took place, together with killings, fires and whole-sale destruction. It was thought that the consequent shortage of food would produce famine in Bologna, and that this would drive her to desert the Florentine league. But they met with stubborn resistance, for the besieged city was waiting for help to be brought by the count von Landau and Ridolfo da Varano. Their courage was restored, too, by a minor victory at the beginning of July on the banks of the Panaro.

At this point, Robert of Geneva, realising that his army was inferior in numbers, tried to combine the Breton troops with those of Hawkwood, so that they could closely invest Bologna. But the English leader, though nominally in the Church's employ and ap-pointed by the Church, refused to leave Faenza, which belonged to him. He was unwilling to break the truce that he had recently made with Bologna, and was proposing to have an interview with the marquis d'Este about the sale of Faenza.

The legate then hoped to take Bologna by a trick: a plot, hatched by the Maltraversi faction in collusion with the marquis d'Este almost succeeded, but was discovered on 11 September and followed by very severe repressive measures. The city, in fact, remained im-pregnable. Worse still, Ascoli fell into the hands of the Florentines and, by an ironical trick of fate, the countryside, ravaged by constant raids, could no longer keep the Bretons supplied with food. They retreated in January 1377 and concentrated their forces in the neigh-bourhood of Cesena, Forli, Faenza and Rimini.

Meanwhile the Romans had formed the erroneous impression that, despite his clear affirmation, Gregory did not wish to settle in their midst. The pope was perfectly well aware that by tarrying longer in Avignon he was acting to the great detriment of the Church, as he declared to Edward III in a letter fixing his final departure for the beginning of September 1376.[1]

Some recent writers, with an inadequate knowledge of the course

[1] L. Mirot, *Lettres secrètes*, nos. 1986–90.

of events, and without consulting the Vatican archives, have drawn a misleading and, indeed, entirely fanciful picture of Gregory XI. The numerous postponements until better days of the papal court's departure, and the repeated contradictory orders shown in the Bulls, have been ascribed to the pope's weakness of character, indecision, lack of willpower and the pressure brought to bear upon him by the duke of Anjou and the cardinals, who were opposed to the journey to Rome. It is true that the speech that Froissart ascribes to the duke might well have impressed the supreme pontiff. 'Holy Father,' he is supposed to have said, 'you are going to a country and amongst people where you are little loved, and leaving the fountain of Faith and the kingdom where the Holy Church has more authority and excellence than anywhere in the world. By your fault the Church may fall into great tribulation, for if you die there, which is very likely, from what your master physicians tell me, the Romans, who are foreigners and traitors, will be lords and masters in the Sacred College, and by force will create a pope to suit themselves.'[1] Cardinal Giacomo Orsini took it upon himself to reply to the effect that the long absence of the Roman pontiff had been harmful to the Papal States. 'Who has ever seen a kingdom well directed and wisely governed in the prince's absence? It is certain that if the king of France left his kingdom and went to Greece, his own realm would not be well governed. I cannot foresee how peace can come to his domains, if the pope does not reside in his own see.' The cardinal's speech, delivered in the name of Gregory XI, amazed all the courtiers. Pierre Flandrin declared to Cristoforo da Piacenza that the Holy Father was more firmly resolved than ever to depart.[2] The same informant tells us that when the people of Avignon sought to dissuade him, they were told: 'Last year I thought I would die, and I consider that the sole cause of my sickness was that I was not living in Italy.' Moreover, the pope imposed 'perpetual silence on all men whosoever' on the subject of the impediments which might hinder his return to Rome.[3]

The truth was that Gregory XI always remained master of himself, acting with prudence and seeking to attune his acts to the circumstances of the time and the well-being of the catholic world. He had a unique opportunity to put an end to the disastrous war which set France and England in arms against each other, and which was hindering the preparations for a crusade. The pope's presence in Avignon greatly lightened the task of the legates, who were wearing

[1] Froissart, *Chroniques*, Bk IX, pp. 49–50.
[2] *Archivio storico italiano*, ser. 5, VOL. XLIII, pp. 71–2. [3] *Ibid.* p. 70.

themselves out at Bruges in their efforts to bring about a peaceful settlement.

The admirers and disciples of St Catherine of Siena have built up another and very persistent legend: they have attributed to her an outstanding rôle in the return of the papacy to Rome. As one of them has written, 'It was a woman's will that won the day.'[1] Others have given a tendentious interpretation to a passage in the *Legenda Major* where Raymond of Capua describes the influence of his penitent in the matter of the journey to Italy thus: '*Ipsa eum inducente.*' This expression, vague in itself, does not permit us to conclude that St Catherine's intervention was of overwhelming importance.[2]

It is true that the urgent exhortations she addressed to the supreme pontiff suggest that the virgin from Siena was profoundly convinced that his courage was failing and needed a vigorous stimulant. She set herself to confirm him in his resistance to the pleas of those around him, saying: 'Be the true successor of St Gregory; love God; have no ties with kinsmen, friends or temporal necessity. Fear nothing from the present storm, nor from those spoiled members who have rebelled against your authority. God's help is at hand; have dealings only with the good shepherds, for the bad ones have caused the rebellion. Remedy these evils, and act in Jesus Christ. Forward! Finish what you have begun! Tarry not, for delay has caused many ills, and the devil is using all his wiles to put obstacles in your path. Raise the standard of the true cross, for by it you will have peace. You will console the poor of Jesus, who await you with longing. Come, and you will see the wolves turn to lambs. Peace, that war may cease! Resist the will of God no longer, for the hungry sheep are awaiting your return to the see of St Peter. Vicar of Jesus, you must take your own seat once more. Come without fear, for God will be with you. Do not await the time, for the time waits not. Respond to the Holy Ghost. Come like the Lamb, who will put down his enemies with an unarmed hand, using only the weapon of Love. Be of good courage: save the Church from division and iniquity; the wolves will come like lambs to your bosom and beg for mercy.'[3] Catherine added this advice: 'Come like a man who is courageous and without fear; and above all, take care, for the love of life itself, that you come not with a military following, but come bearing the cross in your hand, like the gentle Lamb of God.'[4]

[1] J. Calmette, *L'Élaboration du monde moderne* (Collection *Clio*), Paris 1939, p. 216.
[2] N. Maurice Denis-Boulet, *La Carrière politique de Ste Catherine de Sienne*, Paris 1939, pp. 113 ff.
[3] L. Mirot, *La Politique pontificale et le retour du S.-Siège à Rome en 1376*, Paris 1899, pp. 93-4.   [4] See the translation by E. Cartier, VOL. I, p. 171.

St Catherine of Siena's words of encouragement may well have been needed. Gregory was beset by every sort of obstacle just before he set sail. Of these one of the most serious was the shortage of funds. In vain did the pope address repeated appeals to Christendom, demand extraordinary subsidies and pledge his jewels; the sums needed to meet the considerable expenses of the journey were not forthcoming. Before he could embark, the king of Navarre and the duke of Anjou had each to agree, in August 1376, to lend him 30,000 and 60,000 florins respectively.[1]

After a stormy voyage, Gregory reached Corneto on 6 December 1376, and entered Rome on 17 January. Far from following the advice of St Catherine, he came to his people accompanied by an escort of two thousand men under the command of Raimond de Turenne. The Saint had promised that the pope's arrival would disarm the rebels; but it was armed force—not gentleness—that overcame them.

The mercenaries of Robert of Geneva, some encamped inside Cesena and some in its suburbs, behaved with their usual licence. In the course of a brawl, started by them, four butchers were killed. The enraged populace rose in arms and cried 'Death to the Bretons! Death to the pastors of the Church!' In the streets of the city more than four hundred were killed. The survivors went to join the legate, who had taken refuge in the citadel; but there, reduced as they were to a small contingent, they knew the pangs of hunger. The garrison, at the end of their resources, seemed on the point of surrender, when the cardinal sent messengers bidding Hawkwood come to his aid. The English condottiere arrived with all speed. When he entered Cesena, the Bretons came out from their retreat, and made ready to avenge the death of their comrades. The carnage was appalling. To the cries of the legate 'Blood! Blood!' it is said that the followers of Sylvestre Budes replied with shouts of 'Strike! Strike! Kill! Kill!' The soldiers massacred the populace. More than four thousand corpses littered the streets and filled the ditches of the town to overflowing after this battle of 3 February 1377.

This cruel punishment inflicted on the inhabitants of Cesena still casts a dark shadow over the reputation of the man who authorised it. But we must not judge Robert of Geneva by modern humanitarian standards, but according to the customs of his day. If his troops had fallen into the hands of the besieging forces, their lot would have been a tragic one; those who had been taken prisoner by the Bolognese

[1] L. Mirot, 'Les Rapports financiers de Grégoire XI et du duc d'Anjou,' *Mélanges,* VOL. XVII, 1897, pp. 113–41.

in 1376 had their eyes put out and their hands cut off, according to an anonymous Florentine writer.[1] The Florentines, however, did their best to exploit this slaughter and to rouse general indignation. But the foreign princes [2] did not deign to acknowledge the letters they received; the Italian cities were drawing closer to Rome; the Bolognese betrayed their allies and on 19 March 1377 signed a truce with the legate, which on 4 July became a firm treaty of peace; and Romagna and the Marches submitted to the Church.

The legate's successes caused as great anxiety to Bernabo Visconti, as Hawkwood's plans to sell Faenza to the marquis d'Este. This crafty character now made overtures to Florence, not because he intended to embrace her cause, but in pursuit of his own dream of dominating the whole of Italy. Hawkwood, freed from his obligations to the papal party, was persuaded to go over to the pay of the league on 1 May 1377. This defection was counterbalanced in June by that of Ridolfo da Varano who served under the banner of the Church. Unfortunately his promotion to vicar-general roused the jealousy of Sylvestre Budes, who had formerly beaten him in battle.

Gregory XI, aware of the Breton leader's discontent, sent him to Tuscany and Umbria, with the idea of making a direct attack on Florence. The republic, aware of the danger that threatened her, prepared to occupy the approach routes made by the valleys of the Tiber and the Paglia, and the strongpoints of Perugia, Assisi and Orvieto. With this end in view, Hawkwood sent reinforcements to the borders of Tuscany to bar the road to the invader. There ensued a guerrilla war in the course of which the papal army experienced both successes and reverses. After taking Spello on 8 August 1377, it attacked Francesco di Vico, who had indeed been excommunicated on 17 April of that year. But the prefect of Rome attacked Montefiascone and took Raimond de Turenne prisoner. Then the Breton bands rushed upon Bolsena and massacred its inhabitants. They recaptured Montefiascone, and Francesco di Vico, utterly defeated, begged for mercy and made peace on 30 October 1377. His reconciliation with the Church ended for a time the need for pacification in the lands of the Patrimony of St Peter, a pacification which had been facilitated by the rewards meted out to the barons who had remained faithful, and by the punishment inflicted on the rebels. Thereafter, fighting tended to be concentrated around Assisi, Perugia and Foligno, and diminished considerably.

[1] 'Diario d' anonimo fiorentino,' *Archivio storico italiano,* ser. 3, VOL. VI, 1876, p. 311.
[2] Letter addressed to Charles V and inserted in the *Annales Mediolanenses.* Muratori, VOL. XVI, col. 764–7.

But now discord broke out among the soldiers of the Church whose leaders were jealous of each other. Worse still, there was no money to pay them, and there was talk of reducing their wages when they were re-enlisted; hence the discontent. Moreover, Malestroit, Budes and Raimond de Turenne were refusing to join in forming a single army to march on Florence, at the very moment when Hawkwood was taking advantage of this tense situation to invade the Church lands. All seemed lost, when at last the pope succeeded in scraping together the necessary money and hiring the Bretons once again. These tiresome contretemps had the unfortunate effect of ruining the plans for the expedition against Florence.[1]

Nevertheless, in the long run the consequences of the interdict upon the city made themselves felt. The people grew discontented with the eight burghers, the Otto Santi, who were obstinately carrying on the war. Moreover, the Florentines, deserted by all their allies, were tired of fighting alone against the Church. They were anxious for peace and accepted, though unwillingly, the mediation of Bernabo Visconti. A truly European congress met at Sarzana with the object of restoring the balance of power in Italy. Representatives of the two belligerents and of the mediator sat side by side with ambassadors from the Emperor, the kings of France, Hungary and Spain and Queen Joanna of Naples. The meetings resulted in the triumph of Gregory XI's policy; his skilful tactics had succeeded in isolating Florence and forcing peace upon her.

9

Sicily, the Kingdom of Naples and Hungary up to the Great Schism of the West

Ever since the Sicilian Vespers in 1282, southern Italy had been divided into two: the island of Sicily, governed by the house of Aragon, and the kingdom of Naples, ruled over by the princes of Anjou. But neither Charles II of Anjou nor the Roman Church accepted this situation, or believed that it could continue indefinitely. Their efforts tended towards a single end: to weaken the Aragonese conqueror through diplomatic means, and so pave the way for his downfall by armed force. In order to separate King James II of

---

[1] For the military operations, see the well-documented articles by L. Mirot, 'Sylvestre Budes (13??–1380) et les Bretons en Italie,' *B.E.C.* VOL. LVIII, 1897, pp. 589–614; VOL. LIX, 1898, pp. 262–303.

Aragon from his brother Frederick, who called himself Frederick II of Sicily, Boniface VIII confirmed James in 1296 in the possession of Sardinia, recently seized from the Pisans.[1] In March 1297, the isolation of the hated prince was completed as a result of the marriage of Robert of Anjou with Yolande of Aragon. Military operations could thus be begun with some chance of success. The campaign began well, with the naval victory over the Sicilian fleet on 4 July 1299 at Capo Orlando and the rapid conquest of Catania and the adjoining territory;[2] but unfortunately Robert of Anjou, whom his father had promoted to the rank of leader of the expedition, was of a taciturn and melancholy temperament, which did not express itself in action, and which prevented him from exploiting the advantages that had been gained. The war pursued an uneventful course, to the great displeasure of the impetuous Boniface VIII. He appealed to Charles of Valois, and this led Charles II on 9 May 1302 to make the French prince captain-general in Sicily. The pope had been too hasty in judging the merits of Charles of Valois; he was bitterly disappointed by the peace treaty signed on 24 September 1302 at Caltabellotta, by which the Angevin loss of Sicily was confirmed.[3] All he could do was to declare imprescriptible, the rights of the house of Anjou and refuse to recognise Frederick II by the title of 'King of the island of Sicily' which had been granted to him by Charles II but only as 'King of Trinacria' (the name Sicily was not to be used).[4]

The popes who succeeded Boniface VIII modelled their conduct upon his intransigent attitude: until 1372, they treated the Aragonese kings of Sicily as enemies, always regarded them as usurpers and gave moral support to every Neapolitan effort, however unfortunate, to regain the island.

As soon as he became pope, John XXII gave Guillaume Méchin, bishop of Troyes, and Pierre Tissandier the task of making Robert of Anjou and Frederick II sign a truce.[5] The two nuncios had the good fortune to promulgate such a truce for six months, and then to prolong it for a further three years. On 24 June 1317, Frederick gave back Reggio Calabria and various Calabrian castles that he had conquered.[6] But he indulged in a piece of insulting behaviour that infuriated the pope: a messenger who had come to Avignon to discuss peace terms seized the opportunity of Robert's presence to defy him in his own house. By way of reprisal, the pope excommunicated the

[1] I. Villani, *Istorie fiorentine*, Bk VIII, ch. xviii.
[2] *Ibid.* ch. xxix.   [3] *Ibid.* ch. xlix.
[4] Rinaldi, *ad annum* 1303, §24–9. (Bulls dated 21 May 1303.)
[5] Letters dated 14 March 1317, in Mollat, VOL. I, nos. 5136–8.
[6] *Ibid.* no. 5509.

prince for having broken the truce that he had sworn, under oath, to observe, and the whole of Sicily lay once more under an interdict.[1] But far from mending his ways, the king of Trinacria refused either to beg to have the ecclesiastical censures relaxed, or to pay the dues he owed to the Roman Church; he even forced the clergy to violate the interdict, making apostates and schismatics welcome in his lands and allowing them freedom to preach. There is an unmistakable note of anger in Benedict XII's invitation to him to come back into communion with Christendom, and without more ado 'restore' Sicily to the house of Anjou.[2]

This inflexible attitude of the papacy is easily explained. In former times Urban IV had handed Sicily over to the Angevins; consequently, the Holy See was obliged to give loyal support to its vassal's rights against all invaders.

Robert of Anjou was not lucky enough to recapture the lost part of his kingdom. All the expeditions he organised came to nothing, through lack either of energy or of sufficient resources to hire an adequate number of mercenaries; or because of the anxieties arising from the vicissitudes of Italian politics. His last days were darkened by grievous bereavements: his son Charles, duke of Calabria, and his brothers, the princes of Taranto and of Durazzo died in rapid succession. His only remaining direct heirs were his grand-daughters, Joanna and Maria. From this time, the old man's only thought was to make his kingdom secure for his descendants. One of his fears was that the branch of the Angevins that had succeeded to the throne of Hungary would thwart his plans. John XXII shared his anxiety: he believed, as did Robert, that the best way of ending the quarrel was to contract alliances between the two houses. In 1332 it was agreed that Joanna should marry either Louis, the elder son of King Carobert, or, if he were not available, the younger son, Andrew. If the princess were to die, her sister Maria would take her place. At the eleventh hour, these arrangements were modified: on 26 September 1333, Joanna was solemnly betrothed to Andrew, while Louis was promised to Maria. The marriage of Joanna and Andrew took place on 22 or 23 January 1343.

Before his death, Robert foresaw something of the dissensions which were to arise after he was gone. The princes of the blood and the leading figures of the court, gathered round his deathbed, were made to promise that his grand-daughter should be recognised as

[1] Mollat, VOL. III, no. 12206. See also Rinaldi, *ad annum* 1320, §14–16. (Bulls dated 23 July 1320.)
[2] Rinaldi, *ad annum* 1335, §51. (Bulls dated 4 May 1335.)

undisputed sovereign; but he still felt some doubt as to the sincerity of oaths made in such sad circumstances. Consequently, as a precautionary measure, his will arranged for the setting up of a regency council to give Joanna advice in governing the kingdom until she should reach her majority; in this way he made sure that she should not have as guardians either the Roman Church, with which he had not always seen eye to eye in matters of religion and politics, or the princes of Taranto and Durazzo, who had opposed the Hungarian marriage and coveted the royal crown for themselves. Clement VI could have protested against these clauses of the will attacking the rights of suzerainty exercised by his predecessors, and declared them invalid; but he contented himself with having nothing to do with the actions of the regency council ordained by Robert of Anjou, and waiting until the time was ripe to intervene.[1]

The king had no sooner breathed his last, on 20 January 1343, than the widows of the princes of Taranto and Durazzo, Catherine de Courthenay and Agnes of Périgord, began their intrigues, which were to prove fatal to their house. Although Robert of Anjou had in his will promised the hand of Maria, Joanna's sister, to Louis of Hungary or else to a French prince, Agnes of Périgord used her cunning to persuade Clement VI to issue a Bull authorising her son Charles to marry one of his close kinswomen, whose name was not revealed. Armed with this dispensation, Charles became betrothed to Maria on 26 March 1343, and then carried her off, or arranged for this to be done, perhaps with the connivance of the young queen. There was much indignation at this scandalous behaviour. Joanna herself changed her attitude and forbade her followers to be present when the marriage was solemnised on 24 April. Clement VI did his utmost to appease her anger, which was perhaps not altogether sincere. Joanna may well have been anxious to ward off in advance the resentment of Catherine de Courthenay, who was jealous of this union, by which her nephew would have the throne if Joanna died without issue.[2]

Catherine was determined to take her revenge. We cannot be sure whether it is true that she conceived the revolting plan whereby Filippa Catanese, Joanna's lady-in-waiting, encouraged her sensual tastes and excessive love of pleasure, and caused her to feel an aversion for her husband. We have no exact knowledge either of the character of Andrew of Hungary or of his wife's feelings for him; but

[1] E. G. Léonard, *La Jeunesse de Jeanne Ier, reine de Naples, comtesse de Provence*, VOL. I, Paris 1932, pp. 109–56, 193–226.
[2] F. Cerasoli, 'Clemente VI e Giovanna I di Napoli. Documenti inediti dell' Archivio Vaticano (1343–52),' *A.S.P.N.* VOL. XXI, 1896, pp. 7–14.

we do know that she was very careful to exclude him from public affairs.

This state of things caused some indignation at the Hungarian court. Elisabeth, the queen mother, came to Naples in July 1343 and tried to overcome her daughter-in-law's resistance, while ambassadors in Avignon claimed that Andrew should be given the title of king of Sicily and Jerusalem, and be allowed to play an effective part in the government of the country. But Clement VI was wary of the ambitions of the Hungarian rulers, and saw that it would be most unwise to give any encouragement to the creation of a powerful dynasty at the very gates of Rome. He received the envoys from Naples and Hungary with deference, and reserved his decision until later. His mind was, in fact, firmly made up: unless the Holy See acted with energy and good sense, the young queen and her regency council would soon find themselves quite incapable of thwarting the secret, but easily imagined, Hungarian plans to take possession of the kingdom sooner or later, and incompetent to deal successfully with the difficulties of foreign policy, and to prevent the squandering of public monies. In vain did Joanna and the families of Durazzo and Taranto try, openly or secretly, to upset the papal plans when they became known. Clement VI's reply was uncompromising: the setting up of a regency council was illegal; its members were liable to excommunication if they dared to govern the country; the pope alone, as suzerain during the queen's minority, could act as her guardian, an office which was to be put in the hands of Cardinal Aimeric de Châtelus-Marcheix,[1] a skilled diplomatist, a gifted administrator and one well-versed in Italian affairs (17 October and 28 November 1343); Andrew of Hungary was only to be crowned king as consort; nothing at all was said about his share in the government (19 January 1344).[2]

The choice of Aimeric de Châtelus was obviously an excellent one. This clear-sighted man was well able to avoid all the pitfalls laid for him by the Neapolitan court, who were anxious to prevent him from arriving promptly. Despite the many obstacles cunningly put in his way, he made a solemn entry into Naples on 20 May 1344. In spite of all resistance and the many attempts at negotiation made in Avignon by the cardinal of Périgord, who was acting for his sister Agnes, Joanna I made an oath of obedience to the Holy See on 24 August and paid homage on 28 August; thereafter, it was the legate who really governed the kingdom of Naples; but he acted in agreement with the members of the regency council who had been

---

[1] See above, pp. 101–02.   [2] Léonard, *op. cit.* VOL. I, pp. 299–302, 322, 339.

previously dismissed by Clement VI. But the situation remained delicate; he felt that he was suspect and even unwanted, and often begged to be recalled, thus seconding the queen's own dearest wishes.

Then suddenly the pope changed his mind; he decided that Joanna was sufficiently mature to wield authority without his help or that of her grandfather's servants. Certain restrictions were laid down, but they were of no practical significance (19 November 1344).[1]

This untimely decision by the court of Avignon bore immediate fruit: feeling that she was now free of the legate, and disregarding the pope's advice, the queen agreed to 'many alienations of her goods and rights.' Then discord between her husband and herself broke out, though this was not so much due to the fault of the couple themselves, as to the insidious and treacherous intrigues of those around them. As a result, Aimeric de Châtelus, instead of going, extended his stay in Neapolitan territory until 24 May 1345. Meanwhile Clement VI, uncertain as to whether Aimeric was on his way home, appointed as nuncio Guillaume Lamy, bishop of Chartres, with instructions to reform the abuses which the pope's informants had criticised. For his part, acting on instructions he had received, the legate published a Bull at San Germano, on 30 May 1345, dated from the preceding 30 January, revoking all the alienations that the queen had rashly made since her grandfather's death. Those who had benefited from her generosity were, on pain of excommunication, to give back what they had received; and he even went further than the sanctions issued under Clement VI's edict, by depriving those who opposed him of their goods and fiefs. But unfortunately Joanna persisted in her aberrations, despite the repeated exhortations of the pope.

Meanwhile it became evident that the question of the coronation of Andrew of Hungary could no longer remain in abeyance, for the veiled threats of the Hungarians were daily becoming more pressing. Clement VI acted with authority: he declared that the ceremony should take place, but specified, among other harsh and humiliating conditions, that Andrew must give up all hope of wearing the crown, except 'as his wife's husband.' If she died without issue, the kingdom must pass to his sister-in-law, Maria. But the papal letters [2] despatched on 20–21 September 1345, failed in their purpose: on the night of 18–19 September, at the castle of Aversa, Andrew was preparing for bed when a voice called to him. Wondering who it could be, the prince dressed hastily, put on his shoes and went out into a

[1] Cerasoli, article cited, pp. 238–42.   [2] Léonard, *op. cit.* VOL. I, pp. 461–4.

corridor adjoining the nuptial chamber, whence the sound had come. There conspirators leapt upon him and strangled him.[1]

The murder of the prince gave Clement VI much cause for anxiety. The king of Hungary, annoyed at the way in which the question of his brother's coronation had been dragged out at the Curia, took his revenge on the pope by seeking to ally himself with Louis of Bavaria and Edward III of England. Clement wished at all costs to avoid the danger of an invasion of the State of Naples, and for this reason wanted to see justice promptly carried out. After solemnly condemning in Consistory the crime committed at Aversa, the pope announced proceedings against its unknown perpetrators on 1 February 1346, and reserved to himself the right to punish them. The time for action had come; shortly afterwards an embassy arrived and insisted imperiously that King Louis of Hungary should be invested with the kingdom of Naples, and suggested that the Holy See should forbid Joanna to remarry. But Clement VI was not to be intimidated: he remained immovable, and would accede to none of their demands.

At Naples, the situation was growing complicated. Joanna returned to the city about 24 September 1345, shut herself up in the palace of Castelnuovo and on Christmas night gave birth to a son. He was named Charles Martel to please the Hungarians, and the pope agreed to act as his godfather.[2] The birth of this heir was highly displeasing to the ambitions of the royal princes. Louis of Taranto gained the queen's favour and begged for her hand. His brother Robert, and his cousin Charles of Durazzo, sank their differences to unite against their more favoured rival, and fomented a rising which took place on 6–10 March 1346. The people of Naples, who accused Joanna of having conspired with Andrew's murderers, rushed through the city crying, 'Death to the traitors! Death to the shameless queen!' The queen was besieged and compelled to surrender. She handed over a considerable number of those suspected of the murder of her husband to the justiciar Bertrand des Baux, to whom the pope had delegated the duty of holding an enquiry; this took place on 3–4 June 1346.

Catherine de Courtenay, with a complete disregard for the rules of decent behaviour, took up residence in Castelnuovo which Louis of Taranto had been compelled to leave. She set to work to unite in marriage Joanna and her favourite son Robert; he had already been put in power by a royal act of 26 April 1346. A petition was even

---

[1] Léonard (*op. cit.* pp. 465–73) has given a novel reconstruction of the course of these tragic events, using as his chief source the allocution of Clement VI given in Consistory on 1 February 1346. (See Baluze, *Vitae*, VOL. II, pp. 368–9.)
[2] Cerasoli, article cited, pp. 429–31.

sent to Avignon, begging for the necessary dispensations for consanguinity, at the same time as other emissaries were informing the
pope of the queen's loathing for her cousin. Clement VI, taken aback
at such contradictory overtures, remonstrated that the first of them
was singularly ill-timed, since at that very moment Louis of Hungary
was insisting that the queen, whom he accused of adultery and
murder, should be deposed. The Hungarian ambassadors, moreover,
had proposed that the government of the kingdom should be transferred to Stephen, governor of Transylvania, until Andrew's child
should come of age; they threatened Joanna with dire consequences
if she dared to marry Robert of Taranto or any other prince.[1] French
diplomatists, on the other hand, supported the demand for a marriage
dispensation; like the pope, they feared that the king of Hungary
would seize the kingdom of Naples.

Faced with such an alternative, Clement VI played for time. He
promised Louis of Hungary that he would only grant a matrimonial
dispensation for 'grave and reasonable cause.' He assured him that
Joanna could not be deprived of her States, since she had not as yet
been declared guilty or brought to justice. As for the child Charles
Martel, his welfare would be the concern of the bishops of Padua
and Monte Cassino. On 4 November 1346, the pope, in public Consistory, excommunicated Andrew's unknown assassins, confiscated
their goods and charged Bertrand de Déaulx with the setting up of
an enquiry, which was to investigate even the queen and the royal
princes.[2]

To Joanna, the pope announced his intention of working in her
best interests; the same two bishops, of Padua and Monte Cassino,
had ready secret powers authorising them to grant the required marriage dispensation should the occasion arise. At the same time, he
reproached the queen for cohabiting with Robert of Taranto, a state
of affairs likely to rouse the vindictive anger of Louis of Hungary. For
the rest, his nuncios were charged to compel her, under threat of
ecclesiastical censure, to conform to the admonitions made previously
to this date.[3]

The capital sentences were ostensibly carried out at the beginning
of August 1346; but the court of Naples turned a blind eye, so that
some highly-placed nobles escaped any form of punishment. Truth
to tell, Robert of Taranto, who had seized power for the time being,
was prevented by his lack of energy and good sense from adequately

---

[1] Rinaldi, *ad annum* 1346, §53–6.
[2] Cerasoli, article cited, pp. 438–40, 452–3.
[3] *Ibid.* pp. 443–4, 446–8, 455, 459.

sustaining this rôle, and only succeeded in compromising the queen further by continuing to live under the same roof. Bertrand de Déaulx had been appointed legate many months earlier, and his presence now became imperative. Meanwhile, the bishops of Padua and Monte Cassino undertook the delicate task of persuading Robert of Taranto to leave the royal palace.

But Joanna resolved this tense situation in an unexpected fashion: while the prince was away, in October 1346, attending his mother's funeral, she seized the opportunity to have his 'flunkeys' put out of the palace; and when Robert tried to return, he found the doors shut in his face.

The legate's arrival seemed likely at first to improve matters. Young Charles Martel, as heir to his mother's throne, received his subjects' homage in January and February 1347; edicts were issued proclaiming that all demesne lands illegally alienated should be restored, the country put into a state of defence and brigandage suppressed. But these various measures, all eminently desirable, and taken on the advice of Clement VI, remained unimplemented, for Joanna did not deign to carry them out. In the same way, she paid no heed to the warnings she received from Avignon, and would not agree to give up her intention of an exceedingly hasty second marriage with Louis of Taranto. France supported her in this, and insisted that a marriage dispensation should be granted. Once more Clement VI fell back on the policy of temporisation in which he excelled. He was still afraid that if this marriage took place, Louis of Hungary might be driven to invade the kingdom of Naples.

In other ways, too, Joanna was causing the papal court dissatisfaction. It was suggested that she should send Charles Martel to Provence, where he would be out of all danger. The surest way of giving the lie to the accusation that she and the princes of Taranto and Durazzo had had some share in the murder of Andrew of Hungary, was to appear before the legate who was to hold the enquiry. Unfortunately, Bertrand de Déaulx acted spinelessly, or rather, was unfaithful to his essential duty. Whether he was convinced that his efforts were useless, or thought the situation already lost, or whether he was simply giving way to cowardly feelings, he failed to obey the directives he received from Avignon. Instead, he left the royal palace, took refuge in the convent of San Severino and finally retired to Benevento. Clement VI, seeing that he was receiving so little support, did his utmost to postpone the Hungarian invasion, begging the king of France and Charles IV, king of Bohemia, to intervene. He also wrote a letter to the legate, in which he made no attempt to disguise his displeasure, and tried to rouse his dormant zeal; but without result.

When the pope learned of the forthcoming marriage of the queen with Louis of Taranto, and the rumour of a proposed union between young Charles Martel and the daughter of Charles of Durazzo, he was uncertain how to act: should he lend these unions the sanction of his authority? What, indeed, could he do against a *fait accompli*? Clement VI was determined to ensure that Charles Martel would succeed to the kingdom, and to strangle the covetous ambitions of Louis of Taranto; he announced that even if Joanna died without issue, the throne was to descend to her sister Maria, or her heirs. The pope's opposition to the prince was made even more clear by his order of 21 June 1347 to the legate, Bertrand de Déaulx, to keep the necessary marriage dispensations secret, and not to have recourse to them unless absolutely necessary.[1]

Despite these measures the dreaded Hungarian invasion took place; by 24 December 1347, Louis of Hungary's army, advancing rapidly through northern and central Italy, had come as far as Aquila without any difficulty. Clement VI, after vainly imploring the local nobility to oppose Louis's advance, was obliged to give way before it: not one of his threats to excommunicate the king if he intervened in arms was put into effect. Joanna, betrayed by the princes, fled from Naples on 15 January 1348, leaving her son behind, went by ship to Provence and hastened to Avignon. Clement gave a chilly reception to this somewhat untimely eagerness, for she was living as the mistress of Louis of Taranto, and was popularly suspected of regicide. Nevertheless, she was solemnly received at the papal court about 20 March 1348, and authorised to marry her lover. The pope had been informed by intermediaries that the queen would not consent to appear at an enquiry into the murder of Andrew of Hungary; he therefore merely went through a form of judicial procedure, which had no practical consequences, since the queen left Avignon on 24 July 1348 without having answered the summons to appear before the cardinals, Bertrand de Déaulx, Guillaume d'Aure and Gailhard de la Mothe. Some time before, on 30 March, Louis of Taranto had actually been awarded the Golden Rose.

Clement VI's attitude left no doubt as to his real feelings: he regarded Joanna as innocent,[2] since Louis of Hungary had produced no proof of her guilt, and since the circumstances in which the

---

[1] Cerasoli, article cited, pp. 465–74, 668.
[2] Léonard (*op. cit.* VOL. I, pp. 476–84), has shown that there is no proof of the queen's guilt and that grave suspicion rests on Louis of Taranto.

murder at Aversa had taken place were in her favour: it was difficult
to believe that if she had planned the crime beforehand, she would
have had it committed almost before her eyes. Clement VI sided
with her, while at the same time he treated the invader with some
respect. Though determined to do nothing to help Louis of Hungary
to gain the throne of Naples, to which he was still obstinately laying
claim, the pope began diplomatic negotiations with him, and used
every device to make them drag out as long as possible. Time and
Louis's blunders gave effectual help to the cause which the pope had
at heart. The people of Naples soon turned against Louis of Hungary
when they saw the atrocities committed by his troops, and Charles
of Durazzo illegally beheaded, cruel tortures inflicted on the nobles
suspected of the murder of Andrew, and the royal princes interned
in a Hungarian stronghold. On 18 June 1348, the barons rose against
him, and urged their queen to return; at the same time, it seemed
likely that Venice was preparing to cut off any attempt he might
make to retreat. The king made a sudden departure in the last days
of May 1348.

The happy outcome of the Hungarian invasion allowed Joanna to
return to her lands. The journey involved heavy expenses, and it was
hard to find anyone willing to lend the money. As early as April 1348,
the queen had suggested to the pope that she should sell to the Holy
See the town of Avignon and the lands attached to it; the city was
finally and perpetually handed over on 9 June at a price of 80,000
gold florins, and the pope formally took possession on 23 July.[1] The
Emperor Charles IV willingly ratified the deed of purchase.

Louis of Hungary had left troops in the kingdom of Naples under
the command of experienced leaders. Did this point to an early
return? Clement VI, fearing this, sent two legates, Annibale di
Ceccano and Guy de Boulogne, to Naples and Buda respectively,
charged with persuading the two courts to end hostilities. The cardinals speedily carried out their mission, and procured the signing of
an armistice in July 1349. On Louis of Hungary's side this was merely
a pretext to get rid of the gullible Guy de Boulogne, whose presence
prevented him from making ready for a fresh military venture, and
to keep Joanna from taking adequate security measures. In April
1350 troops landed unexpectedly on the coast of Apulia and soon
appeared before the walls of Naples. By a curious irony of fate, the
husband whom she had so recently married had soon snatched the
unfortunate Joanna's authority from her, and was even threatening
her life. Clement VI decided to come to her aid, and in July 1350,

[1] J.-B. Christophe, *Histoire de la papauté pendant le XIVe siècle*, VOL. II, pp. 467–71.

galleys from Provence entered the Bay of Naples. They had on board a special nuncio, Raymond Saquet, bishop of Thérouanne, and a masterful character named Hugues des Baux. While the nuncio was parleying with the Hungarians, Hugues blockaded Castelnuovo and compelled Louis of Taranto to hand over the government of the country to his wife; then, at the beginning of September 1350, they both concluded a truce with Louis of Hungary, who agreed to leave the kingdom of Naples at the same time as Louis of Taranto and Joanna. During the armistice the pope was to make an enquiry into the real part that the queen had taken in the murder of her first husband: if her guilt became apparent, she was to lose her lands which would pass to the Hungarian prince; but if her innocence was proved, she would pay him 300,000 gold florins as an indemnity, to compensate him for the loss of his conquests.[1]

This time the truce was punctiliously observed, at least in one of its vital clauses: on 17 September, Louis of Hungary left for Rome, while Joanna and Louis of Taranto went to Gaeta. In February 1351, Clement VI revoked the agreement, by allowing the Neapolitan queen and her consort to return to their capital; but by 20 February the political situation had completely changed, for Louis of Taranto had once more seized power after the murder of Hugues des Baux, and succeeded in ridding the kingdom of many of the Hungarian garrisons who were in occupation. Louis of Hungary was no longer a force to be reckoned with, and Clement VI had every prospect of successfully negotiating an agreement with him. When discussions began, no mention was made of the judicial enquiry into Joanna's conduct, and the war indemnity was reduced to 200,000 florins. The queen and her husband readily accepted the agreed conditions; the question of paying this enormous sum of money almost compromised the whole plan, but in the end Clement VI agreed to vouch for it, having exacted promises of repayment from the court of Naples, and peace was concluded in October 1351. Louis of Hungary undertook to hand over to the pope or his representatives 'the lands and fortresses of the kingdom of Sicily still occupied' by his troops, shifted on to him the responsibility for punishing the king's murderers, and promised to release Louis and Robert of Durazzo from prison. At the eleventh hour, the king nobly agreed to forgo the stipulated indemnity of 200,000 florins, since he said that his sole object in going to war had been to avenge the violent death of his brother Andrew.[2]

[1] Cerasoli, article cited, pp. 693–6. See also Rinaldi, *ad annum* 1352, §1–2.
[2] Cerasoli, in *A.S.P.N.* vol. XXII, pp. 12–18.

Clement VI gave the archbishop of Braga, Guillaume de la Garde, and Pierre de St Martial the task of making sure that the evacuated lands were handed over in accordance with the treaty. Then he saw to it that Joanna and Louis of Taranto took official possession of the throne of Naples, by authorising their solemn coronation which took place on 27 May 1352. It is impossible to verify the statement, made only by Matteo Villani,[1] that before the ceremony was performed the pope gave the queen absolution. On the other hand, we know exactly the conditions to which Louis of Taranto had to agree beforehand. Not only had he to promise to respect all the prerogatives exercised by the Roman Church as sovereign ruler, but also to renounce the crown if Joanna died before him and left direct heirs. If the heirs died, he was to succeed them, and would thus oust both Maria of Durazzo and her descendants and Robert, the leader of the house of Taranto.[2]

It cannot be denied that Clement VI showed a certain partiality in his dealings with Joanna I; but he was after all only doing his duty as suzerain: she had the invaluable advantage of knowing that she could rely on his constant support and much wise advice. He did not show any annoyance when this advice proved useless, and protected her, as her recent biographer has justly remarked, 'from her bad advisers, from her cousins, from the king of Hungary, from her husband, from almost the whole of Italy and from public opinion.'[3] It is true that his recognition of her union with Louis of Taranto was both unenthusiastic and tardy; but he had not shown too overt a hostility to Louis's coronation.

Despite the difficulties of the political situation at home, Joanna, like her grandfather, continued to maintain a state of hostility with the kings of Trinacria. There were two distinct phases in the military operations: in the first, the Neapolitans seized the offensive and took advantage of the disorganisation following the death of Peter II on 15 August 1342 to seize Milazzo and the Lipari islands and to blockade the harbour of Messina. In the second, John of Aragon, Louis's tutor, recaptured these towns and threatened Naples, at the time when danger from Hungary was increasing. Where circumstances varied so greatly, papal diplomacy was influenced by events as they arose: during the period of Neapolitan victories, in 1343, 1344 and 1345, Clement VI warmly supported the Sicilian demand for an armistice, for he considered that Joanna was playing a dangerous game, and deplored the continuance of the interdict upon Sicily,

---

[1] *Istorie fiorentine*, Bk II, ch. xxiv. See also Muratori, VOL. XIV.
[2] Léonard, *op. cit.* VOL. II, pp. 307–35, 354–60.   [3] *Ibid.* p. 388.

for it was seriously disrupting religious life; but he met with nothing but refusals. When the Catalan forces triumphed, he was equally unsuccessful in imposing a three-year truce, which he suggested on 5 July 1346; on the other hand, he raised no objection to the recapture of Milazzo. The death of John of Aragon in April 1348, however, made it possible for the two enemies to come to terms; but now it was the turn of the Holy See to refuse to accept the draft treaty, alleging that it was prejudicial to the Roman Church. However, although all efforts at reaching an understanding came to nothing, they at least succeeded in preparing the ground for the negotiations which eventually resulted in the peace settlement of 1372.[1]

Innocent VI, who was somewhat vacillating and easily frightened, was inordinately influenced by the cardinal of Périgord, an ally of the Durazzo family. From the first, Innocent's tone in writing to Louis of Taranto was aggressive, bitter and abrupt, and readily became threatening; but when the time for action came, he avoided the issue. This may have been due to a lack of energy or to a change of mood on his part; or he may well have felt himself powerless to act, for he knew from experience that Louis of Taranto thwarted his policy at almost every turn, and either took no heed of his exhortations, or else did precisely the opposite. It was not surprising, therefore, that Innocent VI should hope for Louis's downfall and favour the Durazzo faction. He tried, for example, though in vain, to insist that the daughters of Joanna's sister Maria should be made wards of Louis of Durazzo; he opposed the projected marriage between Robert of Taranto and this same Maria, who having been forcibly married to Robert des Baux, had had him put to death in her presence in 1353; he made enthusiastic overtures, on the other hand, to Giovanni Visconti, in the hope of obtaining the hand of his niece for Robert of Durazzo. Innocent VI did not confine himself to threats: as during the past three years he had received neither the cense due to the Roman Church nor the homage of the Neapolitan rulers, in January 1355 he excommunicated them and proclaimed an interdict upon the kingdom. These rigorous measures coincided with the open revolt of Louis of Durazzo.

But it is not true to allege, as did some of his contemporaries, that the pope carried his displeasure with Louis of Taranto to the extent of consenting to the invasion of Provence by the Great Companies under the command of Arnaud de Cervole: the parties in collusion

[1] Léonard, *op. cit.* VOL. I, pp. 280–8, 389–92, 447–52, 488, 569–70, 577–9, 685–6; VOL. II, pp. 139–41.

were the dauphin, Robert of Durazzo and Cardinal Talleyrand of Périgord. Innocent VI's vigour in tackling the scourge of war is in itself sufficient proof that he had no hand in the conspiracy. Moreover, the tension between Naples and Avignon slackened in the autumn of 1357, when a marriage dispensation was granted to Maria of Durazzo and Philip of Taranto, and at the same time, Louis being dangerously ill promised to mend his ways. These good resolutions, however, went by the board when his health improved, and bitter-sweet exchanges took place between him and the Curia. When it became known that Gil Albornoz had been appointed legate to the kingdom of Naples, the situation was immediately altered, for Louis of Taranto, realising that he had better appease the pope's anger, adopted a humble attitude and even sent his grand seneschal Niccolò Acciajuoli to Avignon to pay off the greater part of the overdue cense to the Roman Church. At this Innocent VI relented, lifted the interdict from the kingdom of Naples and granted various other lesser favours. Acciajuoli—perhaps deliberately—did not carry out the most important part of his mission, which was to see that Louis of Taranto paid homage together with the queen, and received assurance that, in the event of the queen's death, he should have Calabria and Sicily for his share. Fresh disturbances continued to break out between Avignon and Naples until the prince's death on 26 May 1362. The chief reason for the pope's hostility towards him was no doubt the fear that the establishment of too powerful a kingdom close to the Papal States would jeopardise their rehabilitation so brilliantly effected by Albornoz. This would explain his favourable attitude towards the Durazzo family, whose incessant intrigues weakened the authority of a sovereign who was in any case unfit to govern.[1]

The situation became even more complex on the death of Louis of Taranto. His brothers, fearing that the queen would now marry Louis of Durazzo, hastened the latter's end. Urban V advised Joanna to marry Philip, son of John II (the Good) of France. But the queen rejected this suggestion, saying that she would live the life of a hermit rather than submit to such a union.[2] She had lived in constant discord with Louis of Taranto, and thought that in James III, king of Majorca, she had found the ideal husband.

In 1372, peace was at last made between the courts of Naples and Sicily; but only at the expense of Joanna's capitulation. By proxy, Frederick III undertook to pay liege homage to her and her lawful

[1] Léonard, op. cit. VOL. III.
[2] Cerasoli, 'Urbano V et Giovanna I di Napoli. Documenti inediti . . . (1362–70),' A.S.P.N. VOL. XX, 1895, pp. 73–5.

heirs, to pay the annual cense of 3,000 ounces of gold, the equivalent of 15,000 Florentine florins, to the Roman Church, and to bear the title of king of Trinacria only, allowing the queen to retain that of sovereign of Sicily. The island of Lipari, at that time in the hands of the queen, was to remain hers for life and to revert to the king after her death.[1]

The text of the agreement which, according to the terms of the act, had to be submitted to the Holy See for confirmation and approval, was considered defective at Avignon. Gregory XI was displeased that it made no mention of the direct jurisdiction to which the Church laid claim, and declared that it contained much superfluous matter, while omitting details of vital importance. He produced instead an extremely lengthy version, which aimed at defining the rights of the supreme pontiff in minute detail, and made provision for all kinds of future eventualities.

According to this agreement, dated 31 October 1372, the two contracting parties recognised the papacy's direct dominion over Sicily, and paid the pope liege homage, according to the formulary laid down in the Bull. Frederick was to pay homage, too, to Joanna I, her legitimate descendants and her successors. The rules governing his own succession were rigorously defined: if he had no legitimate heir, the throne was to revert to Joanna and her successors, or, if there were none, to the Roman Church; if a daughter succeeded him she was only to marry with the consent of the Holy See, a Catholic, not suspect to the Church but filled with devotion to her, and not an enemy of Joanna I or of her successors. If the inheritance fell to a minor of less than eighteen years of age, the Holy See would act as his guardian. Frederick was forbidden to accept, without the express consent of the supreme pontiff, the imperial crown, the title of king of the Romans or of king of Germany, or the overlordship of Lombardy or Tuscany, in whole or in part under pain of losing Trinacria, which would then revert to Joanna or to the Roman Church. If, however, such an acceptance were approved, Frederick was to emancipate his son, and hand over to him the rule of Trinacria. If his heir were a daughter she could not marry the Emperor, the king of the Romans or of Germany, or the governor of the whole or of any part of Lombardy or Tuscany; if she married any one of these, she would forfeit her claim to Trinacria.

There were also religious clauses, abolishing innovations formerly introduced into Sicily by Frederick II. Elections were again to be free; ecclesiastical cases were to come under the jurisdiction of

[1] Rinaldi, *ad annum* 1372, §5.

188

ecclesiastical courts, and the clergy were to remain exempt from civil justice; the goods and rights of the Church in Sicily were to be completely restored within the space of three years.[1]

Hard as they were, by 16 January 1374 Frederick III had accepted all the terms laid down by Gregory XI. The only proviso was that the internuncio at that time resident in Sicily should be instructed to crown him with the royal diadem. The coronation took place on 30 March 1375.[2]

The capitulation of 1372 assured the Roman Church of complete sovereignty over the island of Sicily. This was a result of capital importance, for during the reign of Innocent VI a messenger from the duke and duchess of Bavaria had suggested that Frederick III should appeal to the Emperor, as suzerain of Naples and Sicily, to deal with the Sicilian problem.[3] The diplomatic agreement contained no innovations and incorporated most of the clauses to which the princes of Anjou subscribed when paying homage to the pope. Joanna, for her part, was bowing to the necessity of defending her crown. It was as though the house of Anjou were under a curse from heaven. The queen and her sister Maria lost their children. Maria herself died in 1366, and Robert and Philip of Taranto in 1364 and 1373 respectively. Louis of Hungary made no attempt to conceal his impatience to succeed his sister-in-law.

Faced with so dire a threat, Joanna, who had been widowed for the third time by the death of the king of Majorca in Roussillon in 1375, contracted by proxy, on 28 December 1375 at Avignon, a fourth alliance with Otto of Brunswick, a baron of no great lineage, but noted for his bravery as a leader of the mercenaries.[4] But this could not save the kingdom of Naples from anarchy. The nuncios sent there by the Holy See remained powerless, prophesying catastrophes which did indeed take place when revolution broke out in 1381.[5]

[1] *Ibid.* §6–24. [2] *Ibid. ad annos* 1374, 1375 §19.
[3] Léonard, *op. cit.* VOL. III, p. 491.
[4] Sauerland, 'Drei Urkunden zur Geschichte des Herzogs Otto von Braunschweig und der Königin Johanna I von Neapel,' *Quellen*, VOL. VIII, 1905, pp. 206–16.
[5] Cerasoli, 'Gregorio IX e Giovanna I di Napoli. Documenti inediti . . .,' *A.S.P.N.* VOL. XXIV, 1899, pp. 325–8. E. Martin-Chabot, 'Le Registre des lettres de Pierre Ameil, archevêque de Naples (1363–1365), puis d'Embrun (1365–1379),' *Mélanges*, VOL. XXV, 1905, pp. 273–84.

CHAPTER II

The Papacy and the Empire

1

Henry VII and the Italian Expedition

WITH the assassination of Albert of Hapsburg on the banks of the Reuss, on 1 May 1308, the question of the German succession arose. Philip the Fair having no hope of securing the imperial throne for himself, tried to seize it for his brother, Charles of Valois, and hastened to canvass the votes of the prince electors on his behalf. To realise his ambitions and extend his hegemony to imperial soil, he had to have the support of the papacy. The king of France, with characteristic impulsiveness, requested this support in the course of his second meeting with the pope at Poitiers.

The election of Henry of Luxemburg as king of the Romans on 27 November 1308 gave rise to complications in Italy. Clement V gave a cordial welcome to the ambassadors who had been sent to Constance on 2 June 1309 to request that the election be confirmed. He was anxious to set Henry against Philip the Fair, whose ever-increasing protectiveness he found somewhat oppressive. On 26 July, a Consistory of unusually solemn character was held in the convent of the Dominicans at Avignon. The meeting began with the reading of the act giving authority to the ambassadors; then Cardinal Napoleone Orsini made known the terms of the oath they were to take. Next the pope declared that Henry VII possessed all the qualities required for holding the imperial office, and as a General Council was shortly to be held in Vienne in the Dauphiné, he announced that the coronation ceremony would take place at St Peter's in Rome on 2 February 1312. He himself would consecrate the Emperor; if he were prevented from doing so, he reserved to himself the right to postpone the date.[1]

The pope's over-hasty action annoyed Philip the Fair, and French plenipotentiaries dared to protest formally in December 1310. But Clement V justified himself with eloquence: his approval of the

[1] J. Schwalm, *Constitutiones et acta publica imperatorum et regum*, Hanover 1906–11, VOL. IV, nos. 293–9.

election of Henry VII had not been lightly granted; Henry's ambassadors had waited a long time for a reply; the affair had dragged on for eight weeks; in face of the repeated German requests for a decision, he could in all conscience delay it no longer. Moreover, all the cardinals save one had approved what he had decided.

The French did not persist in their objections; but they pointed out to the supreme pontiff the dangers that would beset the Church in the future. Clement protested that Henry's promotion would help the pacification of Italy, given up as she was to discord, and secure honour and protection for the Church. Moreover, he added with a smile, 'I will straightway show you that which will cause you joy.' Thereupon the Camerarius, Bertrand de Bordes, showed to the representatives of Philip the Fair the acts of procuration delivered under the seal of the king of the Romans.[1]

The dangers foreseen by the French chancery were by no means illusory. Henry VII came of an obscure family, and thought that by gaining the imperial crown and restoring the rights of the Holy Roman Empire he would acquire the authority he lacked. His first thought was to march on Italy, and the announcement of his imminent arrival[2] roused great enthusiasm among the Ghibellines. Ready in speech and pleasant in manner, zealous for justice and filled with the best intentions, magnanimous and chivalrous, Henry none the less suffered from strange illusions as to the mission that he ingenuously believed he was destined to fulfil. His dream was to restore peace to the Italian peninsula, but he forgot that previous expeditions to Italy by the emperors had only succeeded in rousing the mutual hatred of the factions who afflicted the cities.

Did Clement V hope 'to restore imperial power under the protection of the Church,' as R. Caggese[3] has suggested, or as Davidsohn[4] has supposed, to use imperial power to re-establish papal authority? Some of his actions seem to give equal support to both hypotheses. Henry VII had requested to be accompanied on his expedition by a legate *a latere*; on 27 June 1310 the pope chose[5] one of his kinsmen, Cardinal Arnaud de Faugères, and charged him, in September,[6] to make his way to the Italian frontier to meet the prince, receive him with all due honour, and assist him 'with zeal' in his noble enterprises. Clement, moreover, urged both the subjects of the Empire

[1] *Ibid.* no. 514, pp. 472–3.
[2] *Ibid.* nos. 361–79 (May–August 1310).
[3] R. Caggese, *Roberto d' Angiò e i suoi tempi*, VOL. I, Florence 1922, p. 118.
[4] R. Davidsohn, *Geschichte von Florenz*, VOL. III, Berlin 1912, p. 414.
[5] Schwalm, *op. cit.* VOL. IV, no. 390.
[6] *Ibid.* no. 437.

and the peoples of Lombardy and Tuscany to support the prince in his attempts at pacification and to obey him.[1]

The pope indeed appeared on the whole to favour the restoration of the Holy Roman Empire; he had realised that nothing would deter Henry VII from crossing the Alps. He even seems to have been afraid that friction might arise between Henry and the Guelphs in Lombardy, and he urged the prince to preserve the *status quo* which was in their favour.[2] In the main, Clement V accepted the inevitable, watched the progress of events, manœuvred for position, took precautions against surprise and strengthened his ties of friendship with the king of Naples, who had paid homage in the traditional manner [3] and whom the Guelph league, reformed in 1310,[4] regarded as their leader. A Bull of 19 August 1310 appointed Robert of Anjou as rector of Romagna, as though this province, recently ceded to the Church by the Empire, were in some danger of reverting to its former masters.[5] When Henry VII proposed that the date of his coronation should be put forward to 30 May 1311, Clement raised difficulties: the time was too short for him to make adequate preparations for such a magnificent ceremony; the choice of consecrators demanded mature consideration and consultation with the College of Cardinals.[6] To gain time, he sent two nuncios to Italy, to negotiate an agreement; they accepted the date of 15 August 1311.[7]

Clement V's uneasiness is clearly to be seen in the oaths [8] Henry was obliged to swear on 11 October 1310 in Lausanne, just before he entered Italy. The prince undertook all obligations incumbent upon a sincere defender of the Roman Church; he swore to root out heresy, to help the Church against her enemies and not to oppress her 'faithful'—that is, the Guelphs. These conditions were thought at the time to be too harsh, and it was alleged that they created 'a grave peril for the king of the Romans, or at least constituted innovations which he might find prejudicial. The papal court, realising that their intentions were revealed, vigorously countered these objections, and described them as 'mischievous and insidious.' They considered that the Lausanne agreement removed all cause for conflict between Church and Empire, and gave Henry some security against a rebellion on the part of the Guelphs in Lombardy and Tuscany who, appalled at the news of his arrival, were holding themselves on the alert.[9]

[1] Schwalm, *op. cit.* VOL. IV, no. 435.   [2] *Ibid.* no. 441 (8 October 1310).
[3] *Regestum Clementis papae V*, Rome 1884–92, no. 4782 (27 August 1309).
[4] Caggese, *op. cit.* VOL. I, p. 117.
[5] *Regestum Clementis papae V*, no. 10347.
[6] Schwalm, *op. cit.* VOL. IV, no. 586 (28 February 1311).
[7] *Ibid.* nos. 587, 604–08.
[8] *Ibid.* no. 454.   [9] *Ibid.* no. 455 (end of October 1310).

The other articles to which Henry VII subscribed gave rise to no suspicion, being simply the traditional 'ratification, confirmation and renewal' of all privileges granted to the Roman Church by his predecessors and a promise to respect the integrity of the Papal States—to avoid ambiguity they were enumerated in detail—and to exercise no jurisdiction over them.

The actual presence of a legate in the imperial army was not without an ulterior motive, and served to conceal the manœuvres of the papal court, for Arnaud de Faugères had a double mission: to ensure the good offices of the pope as a peace-maker, and to keep an eye on the activities of Henry VII. The instructions he received from Le Groseau give clear proof of this, for they counselled him to practise 'prudence.'[1] Arnaud de Faugères followed these instructions so well that in 1313 the emperor asked to have him recalled.[2]

If Clement V had really been concerned to further the interests of Henry VII, he would have given greater support to a plan suggested in 1309 by Cardinal Giacomo Caetani Stefaneschi for a marriage between the emperor's daughter, Beatrice, and Robert of Anjou's son, the duke of Calabria, in the hope of eliminating all cause of conflict between Guelphs and Ghibellines. Clement V, more aware of the realities, thought agreement between them somewhat unlikely and took only a discreet part in the negotiations which began at Avignon in 1310. For the sake of appearances, however, he declared: 'I should believe it a mortal sin to oppose the marriage that is planned.'[3]

But the demands of the Neapolitan ambassadors proved excessive; they insisted on an enormous dowry which Henry VII was quite incapable of paying and demanded that the kingdom of Arles should be ceded to the house of Anjou. Philip the Fair, who coveted this fine heritage, sounded Clement V. He received a highly reassuring reply from Avignon: the pope, fearing that war might break out between France and Germany, affirmed on 1 May 1311 his 'intention' of giving his consent to no kind of transfer save to the Roman Church.'[4] It would in any case have been rash for him to further the over-bold plans of the Angevins, and contrary to the terms of the homage they had paid to the Holy See. His predecessors had always been careful to curb the ambition of their vassals. Robert of Naples himself had promised in August 1309 to ask for no territorial compensation if he came to the help of the Church, and never to accept

[1] *Ibid.* no. 645 (19 June 1311).
[2] *Primo quod legatus concedatur petitus a domino imperatore, qui verisimiliter habeat majorem voluntatem deducendi ad effectum negotia domini, quam ille qui ibi est ad presens, ibid.* no. 1006, p. 1051.   [3] *Ibid.* no. 514, p. 473.   [4] *Ibid.* no. 612.

an imperial or royal crown, or any lordship in Lombardy or Tuscany, or any office, whether of senator or any other, in the Papal States, without the express consent of the Holy Father.[1] Had he acceded to Neapolitan demands, Clement V would have appeared to be contradicting himself.

The first expedition of the little imperial army [2]—it had about five thousand men—promised to be glorious and profitable. Guelphs and Ghibellines, in a sudden rush of enthusiasm, forgot their old quarrels and came with all haste to pay homage to Henry; at Milan the Visconti and the della Torre were reconciled and embraced one another.[3] Within a month, Pavia, Cremona, Reggio, Piacenza, Lodi, Crema and many other towns welcomed back the exiles that they had long since driven forth from their walls.[4]

But this happy state of concord was short-lived. Whatever might be the personal desires of the king of the Romans, as soon as he set foot on Italian soil he became the leader of the Ghibelline party, and as such inevitably identified himself with their disputes. By 12 February 1311, blood was flowing in the streets of Milan and cries of 'Death to the Teutons!' rang out.[5]

The downfall of the powerful family of the della Torre, which had been deprived of the seignory, sufficed to put the whole of Italy in a state of revolution: Cremona, Crema, Brescia and Lodi shut their gates in the Emperor's face.[6] From an 'angel of peace,' Henry was changed by the force of circumstances into a conqueror whom the excited Guelphs likened to Barbarossa or Frederick II. The Priors of the Arts of Florence [7] wrote that the Tuscan communes 'despair of their safety,' and fear to suffer the same fate as Milan, which is reduced 'to slavery and death,' and they added: 'Wherever the imperial forces set up their headquarters, they have no thought but of booty and pillage, bloodshed and murder and the extermination of the Guelphs.' And so on 1 April 1311 their ambassadors at the papal court were begged to do all they could to prevent Henry VII from entering Tuscany.

The taking of Cremona in May 1311 caused much dismay. The rebels, who had had no hesitation in giving sanctuary to Guido della

---

[1] *Regestum Clementis papae V*, no. 4782.

[2] An account of the expedition was given some time between 24 August 1313 and 20 April 1314, by Nicolas de Ligny, bishop of Bitonto. The text will be found in Baluze, *Vitae*, VOL. III, pp. 491–561.

[3] The act of agreement is dated 27 December 1310. See Schwalm, *op. cit.* VOL. IV, no. 509; Baluze, *op. cit.* VOL. III, p. 501.

[4] Schwalm, *op. cit.* VOL. IV, nos. 526–34, 542–7, 554–8; Baluze, *op. cit.* VOL. III, p. 503.   [5] Baluze, *op. cit.* VOL. III, pp. 505–06.

[6] Schwalm, *op. cit.* VOL. IV, nos. 582–5; Baluze, *op. cit.* VOL. III, pp. 506–07.

[7] Schwalm, *op. cit.* VOL. IV, no. 597.

Torre, surrendered unconditionally and appeared before the imperial forces clad in shirts, their girdles about their necks; despite their humble posture, they were cast into prison, where some of them died. In vain did their wives, with their young children, cry, 'Mercy, Mercy!' and beg for the deliverance of their husbands, brothers or sons and implore the cardinals to intercede on their behalf: the emperor would not forgive them, but pronounced rigorous sanctions against them.[1]

The fall of Brescia on 18 September 1311 had still greater repercussions throughout Italy. This city had welcomed those banished from Milan, Cremona and Tuscany; its garrison, which according to Villani[2] numbered six thousand gallant men, was in active communication with other Guelph cities and incited them to rebel against the king of the Romans. For more than four months—the siege began on 19 May[3]—the inhabitants, full of confidence in the thickness of the city walls and the depth of the moat at their base, repelled all the Germans' attacks and inflicted considerable losses upon them. Unfortunate the man who was taken prisoner, for he was hanged or burned. Ballistas and other engines of war hurled projectiles upon the house where Henry and his wife were living. On 25 July his brother Walram died of the consequences of a wound from an arrow. The royal council suggested that the legate Arnaud de Faugères should excommunicate those of the rebels who continued to resist. But the cardinal got out of this situation with some skill: under the seal of secrecy, he asked the bishop of Bitonto to inform Henry VII that the Italians paid no heed to the 'spiritual sword'—witness the Bolognese and the Florentines, at the time of Napoleone Orsini's legation;[4] and moreover, that before making use of it, he would have to consult the Holy See.

In the end famine overcame the besieged. On 1 October 1311, out of respect for Clement V who had preached mercy[5] and for the cardinals who were in the camp, Henry VII granted them their lives, but exiled those most deeply involved and imposed a heavy fine— 70,000 gold florins—on the rest of the population, and compelled them to fill in the moats that guarded the approaches to the city and to destroy completely all towers, gates and walls.[6]

But the song of triumph so enthusiastically intoned by Henry VII

[1] *Ibid.* no. 631; Baluze, *op. cit.* VOL. III, pp. 509, 515, 516.
[2] Villani, *Istorie fiorentine*, Bk IX, ch. xv.
[3] F. Böhmer, *Regesta Imperii, 1273–1313*, Stuttgart 1844, VOL. VII, p. 290.
[4] See above, p. 69.
[5] Schwalm, *op. cit.* VOL. IV, no. 648 (1 July 1311).
[6] For the siege of Brescia, see Baluze, *op. cit.* VOL. III, pp. 510-17; Villani, *op. cit.* Bk IX, chs. xv, xix; Schwalm, *op. cit.* VOL. IV, nos. 688, 689.

on the occasion of his initial victory [1] was now a little out of tune. It would have been wiser not to have besieged Brescia, but either to have marched on Rome without delay, as he was advised by the best-informed men of his entourage,[2] or to have descended on Tuscany, which, according to Villani,[3] was poorly supplied with both soldiers and victuals. But Henry VII had listened to his brother Walram, to whom the exiled Ghibellines had promised 20,000 florins and guaranteed to surrender the city within a fortnight.[4] Instead of this, the blockade had been inordinately prolonged, and the imperial army had melted away by reason of the large number of slain, and the ravages of an epidemic. In the meanwhile the Florentines had manned the passes of the Apennines and now forbade their access to the imperial troops.[5] Having made his way through northern Italy, the king of the Romans retired on 21 October 1311 to Genoa, where the cold compelled him to spend the winter. It was impossible to advance further: the Ghibellines, tired of the war, had gone home, and even the Germans had done the same; so greatly reduced were the troops escorting the emperor that the bishop of Bitonto feared for his sovereign's safety.[6]

These events in northern Italy put the king of Naples in an embarrassing situation. As protector of the Guelphs, he ought to have intervened on their behalf. But, thinking only of his own interests, Robert did not entirely give up hope of coming to an agreement with Henry VII, and so of avoiding war. All his efforts tended towards a single end: to protect himself at any price from an attack by the king of Sicily, an attack which would almost certainly have taken place had Robert come in on the Guelph side. He thought to achieve this end by playing a dangerous and perfidious game. The two hundred Catalans in his pay, who, to begin with, were concentrated in Romagna, never joined battle with the imperial forces who were fighting in northern Italy, but for a long time remained inactive despite protests from Florence and only very belatedly marched into Tuscany. What is more, outside the very walls of the Guelph city of Brescia, besieged as it was by German troops, two ambassadors from Naples had the effrontery to resume the abortive negotiations concerning a marriage between Beatrice of Luxemburg and the duke of Calabria.[7]

Henry VII was not deceived, and he called upon Robert to withdraw his mercenaries from Tuscany, to pay him homage in person

---

[1] Schwalm, *op. cit.* VOL. IV, no. 688. [2] Baluze, *op. cit.* VOL. IV, p. 510.
[3] Villani, *op. cit.* Bk IX, ch. xv. [4] Baluze, *op. cit.* VOL. III, p. 510.
[5] *Ibid.* p. 522. [6] *Ibid.* pp. 518–19. [7] *Ibid.* p. 511.

for the counties of Provence and Forcalquier, and to be present at his coronation.[1] To fulfil the humiliating conditions of vassalage would have made the king of Naples lose all his prestige and have brought upon him the justifiable anger of the Guelphs, who would have been perfectly warranted in crying treason. Help reached him from the papal court at the right moment, and Clement V pleaded eloquently on Robert's behalf. He pointed out that if Robert were in Rome for the forthcoming coronation of Henry VII disorders would inevitably ensue; Guelphs and Ghibellines would surely fight. On 8 January 1312, he begged the emperor not to break Robert's heart with 'pain and sorrow' but to consent to receive homage by proxy.[2]

Instead of uniting the Guelphs and deceiving Henry VII, the king of Naples had recourse once again to diplomatic intrigue. His excuse was his well-founded fear of warlike intervention by Frederick II, who had, indeed, been seeking the hand of Beatrice of Luxemburg for his own son Peter.[3] Clement V, aware of the danger which was threatening, begged James II of Aragon to do his utmost to prevent open conflict between the courts of Naples and Palermo.[4] In a letter dated 1 April 1312 he suggested to Henry VII that he should turn a deaf ear to the perverse suggestions of advisers who neither loved him nor sought either his well-being or his honour: he ought rather to listen to the fatherly voice of one who had always felt a ' tender ' affection for him and who had supported his elevation to the dignities of Empire. He should not overthrow the kingdom of Sicily, a possession of the Church, and 'an orchard wherein is her delight.'[5]

The papal manœuvres were useless. Henry VII had seen through Robert's subterfuges and considered them a mark of weakness. The alliance with Aragon came into being in March–April 1312, and created a serious danger for the house of Anjou. Frederick II was to supply for the space of one year, seven hundred horsemen and thirty galleys, to help Henry VII 'to acquire, recover, maintain and defend the rights of the Empire against all comers.' In return, he was to be given help 'against any attacker, save Clement V and his successors, the Roman Church and the king of France.'[6]

Robert continued to hope for the best, and still persisted in his temporising methods. In this Henry VII seemed to encourage him for he sought to allay Robert's suspicions by raising once again on 10 March 1312, the question of Beatrice's marriage, which was still

[1] *Ibid.* p. 520; Caggese, *op. cit.* p. 139.
[2] Schwalm, *op. cit.* VOL. IV, no. 726.
[3] H. Finke, *Acta Aragonensia*, Münster-Berlin 1908–23, VOL. I, no. 195.
[4] *Ibid.* no. 196.
[5] Schwalm, *op. cit.* VOL. IV, no. 752.   [6] *Ibid.* nos. 765–6.

unsettled.[1] With an amazing disregard for the true state of affairs, the Angevin prince made exorbitant conditions on 12–18 May 1312: the duke of Calabria was to have the title of vicar of Tuscany for life; Florence, Lucca, Siena and other places were to pay an annual tribute to the emperor, and supply him with soldiers, in return for a guarantee of security; at Rome, Henry was to help in the reconciliation of the Colonna with the Orsini, and he was not to remain there for more than four days after his coronation; in Lombardy, a vicar was to be appointed for a period of ten years, who should be 'non suspect' at the court of Naples; an admiral was to assume command of the combined fleets.[2]

Florence, realising what was being secretly plotted, protested indignantly on 17 June 1312 against a plan that she declared to be 'abhorrent', since it was likely to bring about her ruin and that of the Guelph party.[3]

Meanwhile, the imperial army set sail from Genoa on 16 February 1312 in thirty galleys, landed at Pisa on 6 March, and there awaited the arrival of reinforcements from Germany. They set out for Rome on 23 April, three thousand horsemen strong, according to Cristiano Spinola,[4] or, if we are to believe Villani, with two thousand soldiers.[5] One section followed the Mediterranean coastline, while the remainder proceeded without delay via Siena and Orvieto; they joined forces at Viterbo.

A Neapolitan army under the command of Jean, count of Gravina, King Robert's brother, had been encamped before Rome since 16 April. Troops barred the approaches of the Ponte Molle and, from the top of a tower fortified with ballistas, threatened to deal death to any who attempted to cross the Tiber.

The Colonna and Senator Louis of Savoy had warned Henry VII of the warlike preparations taking place in Rome, and he resolved to negotiate. Two ambassadors made it clear that he wished to receive the imperial crown without any untoward incidents; that the two warring families of the Orsini and the Colonna should be reconciled, or at the worst be compelled to observe a truce; that the soldiers guarding the Ponte Molle should be withdrawn, or how could the king of the Romans and the cardinals cross the river?

On 4 May, Jean, count of Gravina, replied: 'My brother did indeed charge me to receive honourably him who sent you. But later instructions commanded me to forbid him to enter Rome and to do

---

[1] Schwalm, *op. cit.* VOL. IV, no. 751; Baluze, *op. cit.* VOL. III, pp. 530–1.
[2] Schwalm, *op. cit.* VOL. IV, nos. 781–3; Baluze, *op. cit.* VOL. III, p. 536.
[3] Schwalm, *op. cit.* VOL. IV, no. 784.
[4] *Ibid.* no. 1290, p. 1428.   [5] Villani, *op. cit.* Bk IX, ch. xxxix.

my utmost to prevent him from receiving the crown at St Peter's. Therefore I defy your king, all his servants and yourselves. Know that I will not allow him to enter Rome, but I will attack him wherever I may. The Colonna are my enemies; I will make neither peace nor truce between them and the Orsini; wherever I find them I will fight them.'[1]

On 6 May the imperial army crossed the Ponte Molle without much damage despite the many shots fired by the enemy arbalisters. When Henry was venturing across, the count of Savoy called to him, 'Sire, cover your armour, for the gold and precious stones in it mark you out. In the tower there may well be engines able to shoot arrows that will pierce it.' 'My lord count,' was the reply, 'of the two thousand men who have crossed this bridge, have you heard that a single one was killed or mortally wounded?' 'No,' said the Count. 'Very well. God had them in his keeping; he will preserve me too.' Thereupon, the whole escort went across. Some were wounded, but not one was killed; only some horses died.[2]

But once he was inside Rome, Henry VII was to suffer the bitterest disappointment. Neapolitan troops, reinforced by help from Florence, Lucca, Siena and other districts of Tuscany [3] had occupied more than half the city of Rome, including the most densely populated part, the Borgo, Castello Sant' Angelo, Trastevere, all the bridges over the Tiber, Monte Giordano, the Campo di Fiore and Minerva's temple. Barricades were set up in the streets and barred the way to St Peter's, where the emperor's coronation had necessarily to take place. The imperial army, confined to the Lateran, Santa Maria Maggiore, the Colosseum, the Pantheon, the Torre delle Milizie and Santa Sabina, was forced to fight for every inch of ground.

On 26 May a fierce battle took place near the Ponte Sant' Angelo. More than two hundred and fifty Germans were killed or taken prisoner, and Thibaud de Bar, bishop of Liège, died of a treacherous sword-thrust in the back.[4] The imperial forces, discouraged by their failure to dislodge the enemy from the strong-points they were occupying, had to abandon all hope of forcing their way to St Peter's, and Henry VII decided that he could only get there by making a formal approach to the legate. On 10 May 1312 he promised upon oath and under surety, the amount of which was to be settled by the cardinals and other men of worth, not to attack his enemies, provided that they allowed him free passage to the basilica of the

---

[1] Baluze, *op. cit.* VOL. III, pp. 530–3. [2] *Ibid.* p. 535.
[3] The Guelph army included at least nine hundred Catalans and Apulians, seven hundred horsemen and two thousand six hundred foot-soldiers. See Villani, Bk IX, ch. xxxviii. [4] *Ibid.* ch. xlii.

Vatican. If the difficulties proved insurmountable, there was nothing in canon or civil law, nor any statute or privilege to prevent his being crowned at St John Lateran.[1] If the cardinals refused his request, all responsibility for any subsequent 'violence, mischief or damage' must be laid at their door.[2] To persuade them to his point of view, Henry gave into their hands a written legal opinion, full of arguments more or less relevant.[3] But Arnaud de Faugères, Niccolò Albertini and Luca Fieschi hesitated; the orders they had received from the pope were formal, and their letters of appointment gave them no authority to make arrangements for the coronation except in the basilica of the Vatican, as prescribed in the *Pontifical*.[4] In order to compel the cardinals to agree, Henry promised under surety, at the end of May 1312, to sign the contract of marriage between his daughter and the duke of Calabria immediately after his coronation, if Clement V so desired.[5]

The cardinals tried to persuade the Orsini and the count of Gravina to free St Peter's. They warned them on 31 May 1312 that the Romans, weary of hostilities that threatened to destroy the city, were resolved to sound the tocsin and to attack them.[6] The count of Gravina merely replied once again that in accordance with his brother's instructions, he would not permit the imperial coronation to take place at St Peter's and would do all he could to prevent it.

The cardinals' obstinate determination to conform to papal instructions at last gave way before the shouts and threats of the countryfolk who were besieging the Torre delle Milizie, where conversations were going on with the king of the Romans.[7] Unless they received orders to the contrary from the pope before a stated date, the cardinals declared that they would hold the coronation at St John Lateran. Having received no instructions, on 29 June 1312 Niccolò Albertini, bishop of Ostia, anointed Henry VII with holy oil, before a great assembly of archbishops, bishops, abbots, clergy, nobles and citizens of Rome, and after the singing of the Epistle, with the assistance of Arnaud de Faugères and Luca Fieschi, invested him with the mitre, diadem, orb, sceptre and sword, according to the modified rite of the *Pontifical*,[8] necessitated by the absence of the supreme pontiff. In the written account of the ceremony drawn up at their request,

---

[1] Schwalm, *op. cit.* VOL. IV, no. 777.   [2] *Ibid.* no. 780.   [3] *Ibid.* no. 778.
[4] The cardinals' letters of appointment were despatched on 19 June 1311; *ibid.* nos. 644–5.   [5] *Ibid.* no. 779; Baluze, *op. cit.* VOL. III, p. 536.
[6] Schwalm, *op. cit.* VOL. IV, no. 780.
[7] Baluze, *op. cit.* VOL. III, p. 539.
[8] Schwalm, *op. cit.* VOL. IV, no. 644, pp. 609–13.

however, the cardinals state that they acted under pressure of the dangers threatening Rome, and that not one of the canons of St Peter's had been able or willing to receive Henry VII.[1]

Clement V gave no outward sign of displeasure. But when he wrote to Henry VII that 'his heart rejoiced in the Lord,' he was being ironical. The rest of the letter reveals his true sentiments: it is simply a complaint that the imperial messengers bringing news of the coronation have breathed no word of the desirability of peace negotiations with the king of Naples, nor of the marriage of Beatrice.[2] Their silence was deliberate. The emperor wished to take his revenge on Robert and the Guelphs, who had been responsible for the incidents in Rome which had greatly wounded his pride: on 4 July 1312, he appointed representatives who were empowered to sign an alliance with the king of Trinacria and the contract of betrothal between Beatrice and Peter of Aragon.[3] At the same time he announced his intention of declaring war on the Angevin sovereign, whom he accused of treason, and on the Tuscans.[4]

Robert was not unduly dismayed, and patiently waited to be attacked. The truce that Clement V had promulgated on his own initiative on 19 June 1312 [5] provided Robert with a pretext for not going to the aid of Florence. The most he did was to make the empty gesture of begging the pope on 14 August 1312 to include his Guelph allies in the truce.[6] The Florentines would have rejected such an offer, for they had deplored the pope's initiative, taken, as they considered, under pressure from the Ghibellines, who would thus gain the necessary time to prepare to crush the Florentines.[7] Henry VII, for his part, deeply involved in his war-like schemes, made a solemn protest against the truce on 1 August 1312, declaring it to be derogatory to his sovereign rights.[8]

As a result of the summer's heat, the increasing unrest in Rome and his lack of resources,[9] the emperor retired to Tivoli on 20 July and there he suffered a serious disappointment: the legates notified him of the conditions which the pope had imposed upon his coronation. The papal messengers bringing these conditions had travelled too slowly. Certain of these conditions gave rise to no difficulties: for instance, the obligation to leave Rome and ecclesiastical territory on the day of his coronation, and never return there without permission from the Apostolic See; the declaration by letters patent

[1] *Ibid.* no. 797.   [2] *Ibid.* no. 810.
[3] *Ibid.* nos. 815–20.   [4] *Ibid.* nos. 821–2.
[5] F. Kern, *Acta Imperii*, Tübingen 1911, p. 150, no. 227.
[6] Schwalm, *op. cit.* VOL. IV, no. 843.   [7] Caggese, *op. cit.* p. 172.
[8] Schwalm, *op. cit.* VOL. IV, no. 839.   [9] Baluze, *op. cit.* VOL. III, pp. 540–1.

that no act performed by the emperor while in the Eternal City was to create a precedent nor constitute an infringement of the rights of the Church or of the Romans; the liberation of prisoners, the evacuation of fortresses, dwellings and palaces occupied by the Germans and their restoration to their respective owners. By 10 September 1312, these wishes of Clement V had been satisfactorily fulfilled.[1] But to promise not to make any attack, direct or indirect, on the kingdom of Naples or any part of its territory; not to give aid, help or assistance to any invader or belligerent, on pain of excommunication and interdict; not to punish any who had opposed the coronation at St Peter's, including Jean, count of Gravina; and to respect the truce of 19 June 1312,[2] these conditions the emperor's policy forbade him to keep since the conclusion of the alliance he had made with Frederick II king of Trinacria.

Henry VII, without revealing the secret motives behind it, legalised his refusal by a lawyer's arguments. Between 1 and 6 August 1312, he pointed out that a truce implied a state of war; yet no military action had been taken against the king of Naples. The pope's initiative in making the truce had been taken without the emperor's knowledge and was unwarrantable, for the emperor was not a vassal of the Roman Church. Take an oath of loyalty, as the legates had begged him to do, never: like his predecessors before him, no thraldom of this kind bound him to the supreme pontiff. But, none the less, it was his firm intention always to act as 'defender and guardian of the Church's rights.'[3]

Persisting in his plans of vengeance, Henry VII developed an exaggerated idea of his own strength; he determined to punish Florence, and began to besiege the city on 19 September 1312. But it was well enough fortified to withstand all assaults, and, quite downcast, the emperor ordered the army to retreat towards Pisa. There, he brought to an end the proceedings begun against the king of Naples on 12 September 1312 and 12 February 1313[4] by an Act of exceptional severity. The Constitution of 26 April 1313[5] declared him deprived off all 'diplomas, honours, liberties, immunities, privileges, provinces, countries, cities, castles, lands, towns, fiefs, goods, possessions, rights of vassalage and other rights and jurisdictions both perpetual and temporary,' put him under the ban of the empire and condemned him to death. In May, Henry, who was making active preparations for war, 'required' the king of Sicily to begin the

[1] Schwalm, *op. cit.* VOL. IV, no. 847.　　　　[2] *Ibid.* nos. 839–44.
[3] *Ibid.* nos. 839–40; see also the long memorandum, no. 1248.
[4] *Ibid.* nos. 848, 913.　　　　[5] *Ibid.* no. 946.

campaign forthwith by invading the kingdom of Naples and supplying him with men and galleys.[1]

Philip the Fair was much dismayed at the news of the danger threatening a prince of his own blood. In a letter dated 12 May 1313, the king expressed his surprise that, despite his repeated requests, Clement V had as yet done nothing to remedy the critical situation, and begged him to act with all speed.[2] A Bull dated 12 June declared that any person, even though he possessed 'the brilliance of imperial and royal dignity,' would be excommunicate if he dared to 'invade and attack' the king of Naples, vassal of the Church, or supported in any manner whatsoever, but especially by supplying galleys, ships or oarsmen, the equipping of a fleet sailing against his states.[3] Henry VII said in reply to the two nuncios who brought this document from the pope that their master had been misinformed: he had no intention of committing any act derogatory or prejudicial to the rights of the Church of Rome; he was simply making use of his powers to punish a vassal who had failed in his duty.[4] The chancellor, Henry, bishop of Trent, Nicolas de Ligny, bishop of Bitonto, and the count of Savoy were instructed to go to the papal court and there to protest, 'a smile on their lips,' at the conduct of the Holy Father and to demand reparation. Arnaud de Faugères, who was accused of having been uncooperative in putting forward the imperial point of view, was to be replaced by another legate, who would invite all subjects of the empire to submit, on pain of excommunication, and judicial proceedings. Prelates who proved on enquiry to be intractable were to be deprived of their benefices and replaced by others; the faithful of the Church were exhorted not to take any action against the emperor; compensation was to be paid by those who had in any way harmed either the emperor himself or his followers; and Robert, king of Naples, was to be deprived of his office as rector of Romagna. The annulment of the papal decree of 12 June 1313 was, of course, a necessity.[5]

Clement V would not consent to the strange concessions demanded by the imperial ambassadors. Consequently, Henry VII defied the prohibition to attack the king of Naples. But, as he was moving south with a considerable army, a fever attacked and overcame him at Buonconvento in Sienese territory. On 24 August 1313, the emperor died.

This unexpected disaster bewildered Frederick II of Trinacria, who had crossed the straits of Messina and landed on the Calabrian coast and at Piombino on 1 August. Instead of fighting the Guelphs

[1] *Ibid.* nos. 979, 980.　　[2] *Ibid.* no. 948.　　[3] *Ibid.* no. 1003.
[4] *Ibid.* no. 1005.　　[5] *Ibid.* no. 1006.

he returned to Sicily, having refused the Pisans' offer to become their overlord. He acted wisely, for the sentence of excommunication which Clement V reiterated on 7 September 1313 against those who had falsely interpreted the earlier Bull of 12 June was no doubt directed against him.[1]

The sudden death of Henry VII caused great rejoicing among the Guelphs:[2] it was with transports of joy that the Florentines announced the 'very happy news' of the departure from this world of 'that most cruel tyrant.'[3] But though the Italian expedition attempted by the late emperor had proved abortive, was there not every reason to fear that another emperor would renew the attempt? The Guelphs decided to guard against this danger by inaugurating a very bold and novel policy. On their recommendation, the Neapolitan court drew up a memorandum intended for the pope's eye, obviously tendentious in tone and containing the suggestion that from thereon no imperial election should be celebrated, for history proved abundantly that the king of the Romans was the natural enemy of the Church and Italy, of the kingdoms of Naples and France. 'The Germanic race, to which he commonly and generally belonged, usually produced only a nation cruel, intractable, imbued rather with barbarous ferocity than with the Christian spirit, and considering theft to be no crime.' Between this nation and the French and Italian, there could be no sympathy, but only hatred; as for 'sweet' Italy, 'Germanic barbarism was threatening to plunge her into bitterness.' If the German electors did elect a king, there was no need to recognise him, anoint or crown him, and he must be forbidden all access to Italian soil.[4]

It is impossible to know whether this violent diatribe of the Neapolitans influenced Clement V and was the cause of the peremptory decisions, prepared with great expense of time and learning by skilful lawyers[5] and promulgated, first on 14 March 1312 in the Decretal *Romani principes* and later in the Constitution *Pastoralis cura*. In any case, the pope made good use of the interregnum, to make regulations, to his own satisfaction and to his best advantage, for the future relations between Church and Empire. The Decretal *Romani principes*[6] set out the various phases of the controversy provoked by Henry VII concerning the nature of the oath which he

[1] Schwalm, *op. cit.* VOL. IV, no. 1163. See also Villani, *op. cit.* Bk IX, ch. liii.
[2] Caggese, *op. cit.* p. 197.
[3] Schwalm, *op. cit.* VOL. IV, no. 1240 (letter dated 27 August 1313).
[4] *Ibid.* no. 1253.
[5] *Ibid.* nos. 1249–51, 1254–5. See also G. Lizerand, 'Les Constitutions "Romani principes" et "Pastoralis cura" et leurs sources,' *Nouvelle Revue historique de droit français et étranger*, VOL. XXXVII, 1913, pp. 725–57.
[6] *Corpus juris canonici*, Bk II, tit. ix, *in Clem.*

had sworn. This oath, Henry declared, contained no indication of vassalage. Clement V accused the emperor of bad faith. Had not the emperor's ambassadors appeared at Avignon in public consistory and there, in the presence of both clergy and laity, offered and taken oaths of fealty? These facts were not to be disputed, as was proved by the Decretal which was read at Rome before the legates and which contained the complete text of the earlier *Pontifical*. The verdict was unequivocal: 'By virtue of our apostolic authority and having consulted our brethren, we declare that these are oaths of fealty and must be considered as such.'

The Constitution *Pastoralis cura* [1] proclaimed the superiority of the Holy See over the Empire. Having given an account of the procedure followed by Henry VII against King Robert, it gave legal proof of the nullity of this procedure. The summons of King Robert to appear before the emperor, made public at Pisa on 12 September 1312, was invalid, because it had been given outside imperial territory, in the kingdom of Sicily, where it was well known that the king always resided. As judge in ordinary of its vassal, the Holy See should have been required to summon the king. Consequently the imperial sentence against him was illegal. The pope quashed it in the following terms: 'We annul it by virtue of the incontestable supremacy of the Holy See over the Empire and of the right of the Head of the Church to administer that Empire during a vacancy, and by that fulness of power that Peter received from Jesus Christ, King of kings and Lord of lords.' Even before his outspoken Decretal had been made public, Clement had applied the theoretical principles contained in it by appointing Robert on 14 March 1314 to be vicar-general of the Empire in all its Italian dependencies, except in Genoa and the territory belonging to that city.[2] However, the pope's death prevented his seal from being affixed to the fair copy, with the result that the king of Naples could not exercise his office until John XXII rectified the situation on 16 July 1317.[3]

2

Louis of Bavaria and His Conflict with the Papacy

The theories set out in the Constitutions *Romani principes* and *Pastoralis cura* [4] were immediately applied by John XXII. On the

[1] *Ibid.* tit. xi, ch. 2, *in Clem.*
[2] Schwalm, *op. cit.* VOL. IV, no. 1164.   [3] *Ibid.* VOL. V, no. 443.
[4] *Ibid.* VOL. IV, nos. 1165, 1166, 1249–51, 1254–5.

death of Henry VII, the House of Luxembourg ceased to support the
candidature of John of Bohemia, and went over to the side of Duke
Louis of Bavaria. In this way they hoped to counterbalance the excessive influence of the Hapsburgs, whose choice had fallen on a
prince of their own family, Frederick of Austria. The result was a
double election. On 19 October 1314, the archbishop of Cologne and
Rudolf, count palatine of the Rhine, elected Frederick. On the next
day the majority of the prince electors and the archbishops of Mainz
and Trier, King John of Bohemia, Duke John of Saxony and the
margrave of Brandenburg cast their votes in favour of Louis. There
were also two coronations, both on the same day, 25 November,
celebrated in both instances with innovations which gave rise to some
objections. Louis of Bavaria was crowned in the traditional place, at
Aachen, but by the archbishop of Mainz, a prelate to whom, in the
ordinary way this prerogative did not belong. As for Frederick he
was indeed properly anointed by the archbishop of Cologne, but at
Bonn.

The court of Naples hoped to profit by this double election to the
Empire. They submitted to John XXII the draft of a Bull which
would have had the effect of removing Italy from the Empire completely, and of giving the supreme pontiff the right to define the
frontiers both of Germany and Italy, in effect to dispose of the
kingdom of Arles.

But John XXII was too astute a politician to lend himself to such
plans as these. Faithful to the programme followed by his predecessor, he was not anxious to give the kingdom of Arles which surrounded the Comtat-Venaissin to too powerful a master, nor to
assure to the over-ambitious Robert of Anjou the hegemony in Italy.
He temporised until, after the battle of Mühldorf, Louis of Bavaria's
policy came into conflict with his own.[1]

The balance of power in Italy was suddenly threatened in 1327.
On 13 March, Louis of Bavaria left Trent. Passing through Bergamo
and Como, he entered Milan, with a ludicrously small escort of only
six hundred men. On 31 May the iron crown was set upon his brow
by the excommunicate Guido de' Tarlati di Pietramala, the deposed
bishop of Arezzo, instead of by the archbishop of Milan who had
slipped away to avoid officiating at the coronation. The affronts to
the papacy had begun.[2]

Louis, who was 'hard up' according to Villani who always speaks

---

[1] P. Fournier, *Le Royaume d'Arles et de Vienne. Étude sur la formation territoriale de
la France dans l'Est et le Sud-Est*, Paris 1891, pp. 527–39.
[2] Villani, *op. cit.* Bk IX, chs. xv, xviii.

of him in disdainful and contemptuous tones, lingered at Milan until 12 August, to collect money and troops. Being asked to supply him with these commodities the haughty Galeazzo Visconti arrogantly replied: 'You will get them when and where I choose.' Such an impertinent answer called for punishment. On 6 July Galeazzo, together with his son Azzo and his brothers Marco and Luchino, was in all innocence attending a general council when the imperial marshal arrested him and his family.

The seizure of so eminent a person caused general amazement: how could it happen that the instigator of the Italian expedition was in prison? At the castle of Orzi, Louis of Bavaria justified himself by showing letters, most probably forged, in which Galeazzo had proposed an alliance with Bertrand du Poujet, and had gone so far as to appoint three bishops, to Cremona, Como and Città di Castello.

Louis, now supplied by the Ghibellines with 200,000 gold florins and reinforcements, crossed the Po near Cremona and advanced as far as Borgo San Donnino. Bertrand du Poujet, whose forces were numerically superior, could well have prevented him from crossing the passes of the Apennines; but he made no attempt to do so, and thus roused the wrath of the Tuscans, who regarded him as a traitor, unjustly as it would seem, for it was lack of cash which prevented him from ordering his mercenaries, many of whom were German, to advance.[1]

The Ghibelline city of Pisa gave Louis of Bavaria an unpleasant welcome. Although when they learned of the coronation of 31 May, the common people had cried, 'Death to the pope! Death to King Robert! Death to the Florentines! Long live the Emperor!'—the richer citizens were by no means anxious to have an excommunicate within their walls, and had no desire to break off their negotiations with the Guelphs. Ambassadors offered Louis 70,000 florins not to enter Pisa. Their unlawful arrest drove the city to resist. The siege lasted from 6 September until 8 October. Victorious, Louis extorted the 70,000 florins and, furnished with this viaticum, went on his way to Rome.[2]

Entry to Rome was easy but not because of any sympathy of its inhabitants for the invader. Cardinal Napoleone Orsini describes their mentality with some humour in a letter to Ferrer d' Abella, the agent of the king of Aragon. 'It is true that the Romans have friends and enemies; they accept help from their friends, be they Guelph or Ghibelline; they do even give help to their friends, and love them, whoever they be; but you will not find a single Roman who is at heart

[1] *Ibid*. chs. xxx, xxxi.   [2] *Ibid*. chs. xxiii, xxxii, xxxiii, xlvii.

either Guelph or Ghibelline.'¹ The one great wish of the people was
to compel John XXII to bring the papacy back to the banks of the
Tiber. Their ambassadors pointed out to him that, if he did not take
their wishes into account, Rome would welcome Louis of Bavaria as
Emperor. The pope promised to come as soon as he could, when the
time was ripe, but exhorted them not to receive one who was an
excommunicate, a heretic and an enemy of Holy Church.

The Romans remembered how their peace had been disturbed by
street-fighting at the time of Henry VII's Italian expedition. So they
drove out those nobles who might have offered the lordship to
Robert of Anjou, and appointed Sciarra Colonna as captain, together
with fifty-two counsellors, four from each district.

The king of Naples was, in fact, thinking of making use once more
of the tactics that had been so successful in 1312. His brother John,
prince of Morea, arrived at Rome, but the people refused him entry
to the city. The blockade of the mouth of the Tiber by a Genoese
fleet from 5 August 1327 deprived the city of corn and victuals, but
failed to break down its resistance. The city militia were sent out
against the sailors, who had landed at Ostia, but fell back before the
heavy fire of the enemy's crossbows. The Genoese attack exasperated
the populace and drove them to break with Robert of Anjou, who had
been its contriver.

The legate Giovanni Orsini and the prince of Morea now tried a
surprise attack: during the night of 27–28 September, five hundred
horsemen and some footsoldiers entered the city through a breach in
the walls of the garden of St Peter's, invaded both the Vatican
basilica and the adjacent square and the Borgo, killed the sentinels
and erected barricades. The Romans, roused by the tocsin, ran to
take up arms, rushed the barriers, and put the Guelphs to flight: the
latter, to cover their retreat, set fire to the Borgo. A second attack
made on St Sebastian's gate on 29 September was unsuccessful.²

Louis of Bavaria entered Rome on 7 January 1328, bringing in his
train large numbers of clerics, prelates, and religious of various
orders, especially Franciscans whom the Church had condemned as
heretics. As the city had been placed under an interdict, there were
only these excommunicates to celebrate divine office and ring the
bells; the clergy faithful to the pope refused to violate the interdict
and hid the vernicle.

As the Holy See refused to invest Louis as king of the Romans,
he had to have recourse to laymen. The exigencies of the moment

¹ H. Finke, *Acta Aragonensia*, VOL. I, no. 391 (quoted by E. Berger, in *Journal des
Savants*, 1908, p. 289). ² Villani, *op. cit.* Bk X, chs. xix, xx.

compelled him to put into practice ideas which contained a threat to the imperial power, and to apply the principle of popular sovereignty put forward, not without certain specious reservations, by Jean de Jandun and Marsiglio of Padua. By some strange lack of insight, Louis of Bavaria did not realise the full implications of his gesture; for by accepting revolutionary theories, renouncing theocratic prerogatives and reducing his office to the level of a power of democratic origin, he was irrevocably lowering the status of the ancient Empire. On 11 January those Romans who supported Louis of Bavaria met at the Capitol, where the schismatic bishop of Aleria, in Corsica, addressed them in flattering terms, promising them wonders of every description, and asked them to grant Louis the imperial crown. The crowd greeted his words with cries of 'Long live our lord! Long live the king of the Romans!' and elected four syndics who were to proceed to crown him.

On the morning of 17 January 1328, a solemn procession went to escort the future emperor from Santa Maria Maggiore, where he was living. Clad in white silk and mounted on a white charger, he rode through the streets of Rome, whose houses were richly decorated, and reached St Peter's. There the bishops of Aleria and Castello anointed him according to the traditional rite; and then Sciarra Colonna, captain of the people, clothed in cloth of gold, in the name of that same people, placed the diadem on the head of 'the anointed of the Lord.'[1]

Louis of Bavaria's relations with the Romans soon became strained. On 4 March, a revolt broke out when the occupying troops requisitioned victuals without making any attempt at payment. Arms were taken up, barricades erected, Germans killed. The severity of the punishment meted out to the rebels caused some indignation[2] and public discontent was rapidly increased when the emperor, finding himself short of money, levied a financial contribution of 30,000 gold florins. The Romans were willing enough to benefit by his presence, but they had no wish to suffer from it.[3] In any case, many of them had disapproved of his coming from the beginning, and feared that the Church would make reprisals.[4]

John XXII was not disheartened by the success of the German expedition to northern Italy; on the contrary, he put new vigour into his conflict with Louis of Bavaria. A Bull dated 3 April 1328 had deprived Louis of the duchy of Bavaria, and of all his fiefs, both imperial and ecclesiastical, and summoned him to come and hear

[1] *Ibid.* chs. liii, liv.
[2] *Ibid.* ch. lxiv.
[3] *Ibid.* ch. lxvi.
[4] *Ibid.* ch. liii.

read his sentence of condemnation.[1] A second Bull [2] of 23 October had declared him to be a heretic, since he had defended the doctrines of the Spirituals and encouraged the pernicious work of Marsiglio of Padua and Jean de Jandun; on the same day the *Defensor pacis* was censured,[3] and the duke's vassals were freed from their oath of loyalty. In Italy, a league [4] formed on 2 March 1328, with Robert of Anjou and the inhabitants of Bologna, Florence, Siena and Perugia, raised an army of about five thousand men ready to cut off Louis of Bavaria's retreat, or at least prevent him from invading the kingdom of Naples. The crusade preached against him was producing results. As for his coronation,[5] on 31 March it was pronounced null and void.

Meanwhile other dangers threatened the emperor: in Germany, the Austrian faction were negotiating for the recognition of Frederick the Fair. John XXII might perhaps have agreed to this, but as the report of the election of 1314 was not submitted to him the negotia tions came to nothing.[6] Those with the German princes almost suc ceeded: being invited by the pope in April–May 1328 to proceed to a new election, the electors seemed willing to do so, but could not agree among themselves. Everything was a topic for misunder standing, the choice of the place to hold the election, its date and the name of the final candidate.[7]

John XXII's vigorous action redoubled the antagonism of his enemies, who were determined to see things through to the end. Marsiglio of Padua took his revenge for the condemnation of his writings by persecuting the few clerics who had remained in Rome and who had been guilty of observing the interdict placed upon the city. Upon his orders, the prior of the Augustinians at San Trifone was delivered to be eaten by lions in the Capitol. Meanwhile, Jean de Jandun, Ubertino da Casale and Fra Bonagrazia roused the Roman populace. On 14 April, when they thought public feeling had been sufficiently excited, Louis of Bavaria summoned a parliament in the forecourt of St Peter's. The meeting, consisting of a small number of clerics and many laymen, questioned the orthodoxy of John XXII and begged the emperor, in virtue of his office as supreme judge, to bring a case against him.[8]

A second parliament met in the forecourt of St Peter's on 18 April.

---

[1] Schwalm, *op. cit.* VOL. VI, nos. 273, 274.   [2] *Ibid.* no. 361.
[3] Five statements from the *Defensor pacis* were condemned. See Rinaldi, *ad annum* 1327, §27–36.
[4] F. Gregorovius, *Storia della città di Roma nel medio evo*, VOL. III, Rome 1901, p. 307, *n.* 50.
[5] Schwalm, *op. cit.* VOL. VI, nos. 427, 428.   [6] *Ibid.* no. 409.
[7] K. Müller, *Der Kampf Ludwig des Baiern mit der römischen Kurie*, VOL. I, pp. 230–4.
[8] N. Valois, in *Histoire littéraire de la France*, VOL. XXXIII, pp. 595–6.

The dais was erected on the steps of the basilica: there sat Louis of Bavaria, dressed in purple, a crown on his head, in his right hand the sceptre, in his left the golden orb, around him prelates, barons and knights-in-armour. Three times the Augustinian Niccolò da Fabriano cried out: 'Is there any counsel willing to defend the priest Jacques de Cahors, styled John XXII?' There was no reply. Then a German abbot made a long speech beginning with the words, '*Haec est dies boni nuntii.* . . .' First he flattered public opinion in Rome. Louis, their master, had left behind him his kingdom and his young children, and had come in haste to the capital of the whole world of Christendom, to set it up again in vigour and to make it once more the spiritual and temporal seat of the papacy. John XXII, still in Avignon, had preached a crusade against the Romans. And so it was by the express desire of the syndics of the clergy and people, that an action was being brought against him. 'A holy pastor and a faithful Christian' must be set in his place following the example given in times past by Otto III.

Then the German monk added argument to argument to support the accusation of heresy levelled against Jacques de Cahors. He reproached him for his sympathetic attitude to the Saracens, for holding doctrines that ran counter to the poverty of Christ, and for despising the teaching of the Gospels concerning the distinction between spiritual and temporal. The chief article of his indictment was treason committed against the imperial authority by the revocation of the election of 1314. As a result the final sentence,[1] which was in effect dictated by Marsiglio of Padua, deposed from his office the heretic pope. Villani tells us that though the common people heard this sentence with pleasure, persons of judgment were somewhat uneasy.[2]

John XXII's supporters boldly disturbed the public rejoicings. Jacopo Colonna summoned more than a thousand citizens to the Piazza San Marcello, and made public the proceedings instituted by the Holy See against Louis of Bavaria, a convicted heretic and excommunicate. The fifty-two syndics from the districts of Rome and those representing the clergy were excommunicated, as were all those who had given aid or assistance to the emperor. Thereupon, Jacopo nailed the papal document to the door of the church of San Marcello, and, mounting a horse, was soon far from Rome.[3]

Louis of Bavaria thought to regain popular favour by publishing on 23 April a proclamation which he considered likely to give

[1] Schwalm, *op. cit.* VOL. VI, nos. 436, 437.
[2] Villani, *op. cit.* Bk X, ch. lxviii.   [3] *Ibid.* ch. lxix.

complete satisfaction. 'The supreme pontiff should be compelled to reside permanently in Rome, and go no further away than a two-days' journey without asking and obtaining the permission of the clergy and people.' If he did not return to his post after three requests, he should be liable to forfeiture.[1]

The aftermath of the struggle against John XXII came but slowly. The question of his replacement posed problems difficult to resolve, for instance, of whom was the College of Electors to be composed? There were no cardinals living in Rome. Not one of them had deserted the pope, not even Napoleone Orsini, who had little liking for him, or rather who detested his policy. Sciarra's son, Giovanni Colonna, and Marsiglio of Padua induced the clergy of Rome to set up by means of election a college of thirteen electors, who in their turn voted for the friar minor Pietro Rainallucci, a native of Corbara. The antipope was therefore elected according to a mode of election well known in canon law and frequently used in the Middle Ages: that of ballot by arrangement.[2]

On 12 May 1328, the populace was once more summoned to assemble in the forecourt of St Peter's. The ceremony which there took place was the solemn ratification by the people and the emperor of the choice of the Roman clergy, followed by the enthronement of their nominee. The Augustinian, Niccolò da Fabriano, opened the session with a discourse on the following theme: *Reversus Petrus ad se dixit: Venit angelus Domini, et liberavit nos de manu Herodis, et de omnibus factionibus Judaeorum*, in which he compared Louis of Bavaria with the angel of the Lord, and John XXII with Herod! After this violent harangue, the bishop of Castello rose to his feet and cried three times to the people: 'Do you wish to have Fra Pietro da Corbara for pope?' The people were already disillusioned by the unprepossessing appearance of the friar minor, as he stood beneath the canopy sheltering the emperor, and had in any case hoped that a Roman would be chosen, but they dared not voice their opinion, and replied: 'We wish it.'

The vote of the populace was immediately ratified by an imperial decree, read out by the bishop of Castello. Louis of Bavaria rose from his throne, gave the newly elected pope the name of Nicholas V, placed the fisherman's ring on his finger, delivered to him the temporal power of the Church, and led him into the basilica of the Vatican, where he was enthroned. On 22 May a twofold coronation took place: that of the antipope, and a repetition of that of Louis of

[1] Schwalm, *op. cit.* VOL. VI, p. 362 (23 April 1328).
[2] G. Mollat, 'Miscellanea Avenionensia,' in *Mélanges*, VOL. XLIV, 1927, pp. 5–

Bavaria, since the first had taken place in such unusual conditions that its validity was in question. In order to emphasise the abolition of all the claims made against the Empire by Popes Clement V and John XXII, the emperor confirmed the earlier sentences pronounced by Henry VII against Robert of Anjou, the Florentines and certain Guelph cities.[1]

3

The Schism of Pietro Da Corbara

Louis of Bavaria had had no difficulty in creating a schism: but now he had to persuade Christendom to accept the pope he had made. This task was rendered the more thankless by the fact that he had chosen a man of negative personality, about whom his contemporaries expressed diametrically opposed opinions. Albertino Mussato praises his learning and his gifts as an administrator; others relate that after five years of married life, he left his wife against her will to enter the order of the Friars Minor. An anonymous Franciscan writer describes him as 'a great preacher, confessor and director of souls,' who had laboured for more than fifty years for the conversion of sinners, an ascetic, a lover of holy poverty and a model of obedience. Even Villani, who did not like him, admits that his reputation was good and his life holy. But Alvarez Pelayo, the author of *De planctu Ecclesiae*, who had known him in the convent of Ara Coeli at Rome, and seen him at work, has painted a very unflattering portrait of him. Unless this writer is disparaging him, which he probably was, Pietro da Corbara was an egregious hypocrite, who made a show of asceticism while he secretly amassed ill-gotten gains, tirelessly frequented women of doubtful reputation and ran after honours.[2]

Whatever may be the value of this collected evidence in forming an opinion about him, Pietro da Corbara himself revealed what feelings governed his conduct towards the emperor. Instead of obeying the orders of the provincial, Giovanni da Magliano, and the legate, Giovanni Orsini, he had not left Rome when the emperor arrived, and had celebrated Mass in spite of the proclamation of the interdict. For this the chapter, meeting at Anagni, condemned him to life imprisonment. In accepting the papal crown, he was acting, according to his own account, out of consideration for Louis of Bavaria and Michael of

---

[1] Villani, *op. cit.* Bk X, chs. lxxi, lxxiv.
[2] See the evidence collected in Baluze, *Vitae* (ed. Mollat), VOL. II, pp. 196–200.

Cesena, the Minister-General of his order, whom John XXII had deposed.[1]

We may think of him as an honest friar, devoted to absolute poverty, grateful to Louis of Bavaria for the protection he had afforded to members of the order persecuted by the Holy See, but spineless to a degree and always ready to carry out slavishly the emperor's wishes.

According to the theory set out in the *Defensor pacis*, the antipope should have set the example of complete poverty. But how could he rule Christendom without some outward show of temporal power, without a court modelled on the one at Avignon? So a Chancery, an Apostolic Camera, and a Penitentiary, with all their complicated machinery came into being. In the Chancery alone there were six abbreviators, a corrector, eleven scribes, a protonotary, five notaries, a registrar and an *auditor litterarum contradictarum*. Pietro da Corbara was soon to be surrounded by chaplains, household staff, an auditor of the Rota and a lay staff consisting of a marshal, squires, sergeants, mace-bearers, janitors and two treasurers.[2]

The Sacred College was recruited only with very great difficulty. Any Roman who had any forebodings declined the offer of the red hat.[3] By 15 May 1328, Nicholas V had only succeeded in collecting six cardinals who had broken with the official church or were already involved in schism. These were Giacomo Alberti, the deposed bishop of Castello; the German abbot who had read the sentence deposing John XXII; the Augustinian monk Niccolò da Fabriano; the Pisan Bonifazio di Donoratico; and two Romans, Pietro Oringa and Giovanni Arlotti. Later promotions included a friar minor, Paolo di Viterbo, Pandolfo Capocci, the pseudo-bishop of Viterbo, and Giovanni Visconti who accepted the purple with an ill grace and shortly after resigned it.[4]

The newly constituted court was lacking in universality; it was chiefly distinguished for its Italian, and more especially Roman element.

The antipope inevitably betrayed the ideal of holy poverty, and lived in the very luxury so condemned by the Spirituals. Inevitably he and his cardinals had at their disposal horses, liveried household servants, knights and well-equipped squires; inevitably, their tables were lavishly served.[5]

The upkeep of a court was expensive and necessitated more

[1] C. Eubel, *Bullarii franciscani epitome*, 1908, pp. 311–13.
[2] G. Mollat, 'Miscellanea Avenionensia,' *Mélanges*, VOL. XLIV, pp. 7–10.
[3] Villani, *op. cit.* Bk X, ch. lxxiii. See also J. Schwalm, *op. cit.* VOL. VI, no. 454.
[4] Baluze, *op. cit.* VOL. II, pp. 202–03.　　[5] Villani, *op. cit.* Bk X, ch. lxxiii.

financial resources than the needy Louis of Bavaria could supply. He was consequently compelled to remove from their benefices those incumbents who had remained faithful to John XXII, and to re-distribute these benefices generously among the schismatics; the strongly criticised practice of pluralism inevitably flourished.[1]

Despite all the ridicule he brought upon himself, Nicholas V had many supporters in Rome, as we may learn from the papal registers. One Bull shows, for example, that 'almost all the canons of St John Lateran' had embraced his cause.[2] In the rest of Italy he had a fairly closely defined zone of influence, having adherents at Milan, Cremona, Como, Ferrara, Savona, Albenga, Genoa, Pisa, Lucca, Pistoia, Volterra, Chieti, Arezzo, Borgo San Sepolcro, Città di Castello, Viterbo, Todi, Bagnorea and Camerino. In the Marches, the procurators of the towns of Fermo, Osimo, Urbino, Jesi, Fabriano, Matelica, Sant' Elpidio and Serra de' Conti alleged in 1331 and 1333 that their allegiance to Nicholas V was simulated and occasioned by fear.[3] The whole episcopal hierarchy consisted of only sixteen bishops, recruited for preference from the hermits of St Augustine and the friars minor. While, of the various prelates who had been promoted, there were only about four who took possession of their sees.[4]

The schismatic party's most enthusiastic supporters were to be found among the Augustinians and Franciscans. The Dominicans supplied fewer recruits, and those were placed under the direction of Cardinal Bonifazio di Donoratico.[5] All these friars displayed a fanatical zeal in rousing world opinion in support of Nicholas V. Michael of Cesena and William of Ockham were to collect innumerable defamatory tracts against John XXII. At Milan, friars frequently preached in public places, denouncing the pope as a heretic and excommunicate, one who was 'deposed' and 'the worst of murderers.' On the other hand, they were loud in their praises of the antipope. Galvano della Fiamma remarked sadly that Milan, formerly noted for the wisdom of its inhabitants, had become 'a spring of impiety and a nest of heretics.'[6] At Amelia, the people set fire to a sack of straw representing John XXII; they also chased a dog named after him, threw it in the water and drowned it.[7]

[1] See the register of Bulls issued by Nicolas V, published in Mollat VOLS. VII and VIII.
[2] Mollat, VOL. XIII, no. 63389.
[3] *Ibid.* VOL. IX, no. 54855; VOL. XII, no. 61291.
[4] K. Eubel, 'Der Gegenpapst Nikolaus V. und seine Hierarchie,' *Historisches Jahrbuch*, VOL. XII, 1891, pp. 277–308.   [5] Mollat, VOL. VII, no. 42499.
[6] Galvano della Fiamma, *Opusculum de rebus gestis ab Azone, Luchino et Johanne Vice-comitibus*, ed. C. Castiglioni, Bologna 1938, p. 6. See also *Annales Mediolanenses* in Muratori, VOL. XVI, ch. ci.   [7] *Histoire littéraire de la France*, VOL. XXXIII, p. 477.

In Sicily, Nicholas V put the metropolitan see of Monreale in charge of Jacopo Alberti, a cardinal of his faction, on 18 May 1328.[1] There the regular and secular clergy, weary of the interdict which had long lain heavy on the churches and disorganised their services, publicly preached adherence to Nicholas V. According to the correspondents of the king of Aragon, the whole island would have gone over to the antipope, but for the opposition of Frederick II: he published a decree forbidding on pain of death the making of any speech against John XXII.

Frederick's attitude is somewhat surprising. He had plenty of grievances against the pope in Avignon, who had always supported Robert of Anjou. Moreover, he was already allied to Louis of Bavaria. Of this the emperor was careful to remind him, and he added his threats to the tempting offers of Nicholas V. Frederick's answer was that their alliance was only temporal and not spiritual, and that, although John XXII might be his mortal enemy, he still regarded him as the true Shepherd of the Church.[2]

Despite this, the rumour that Frederick had joined the schism was so current that Alfonso IV, as head of the house of Aragon, informed Frederick of his firm intention of breaking off relations with him, if he persisted in the plans attributed to him.[3]

The influence which Nicholas V had acquired in Italy, through the active propaganda of those Franciscans who had rebelled against the Church was chiefly dependent for its continuance on the support of the Emperor, and it declined rapidly as soon as the latter was obliged to leave Rome. The growing hostility of the inhabitants, the discord in the ranks of the German mercenaries and the lack of both victuals and money, made his departure imperative. Louis of Bavaria and his 'idol'—as contemporaries called the antipope—left Rome amid the jeers of the populace on 4 August 1328. The fickle crowd gave an enthusiastic reception to Bertoldo Orsini and Stefano Colonna and to the legate Giovanni Orsini. A bonfire was lighted before the Capitol, and piled high with imperial privileges; the bodies of Germans were dug up, dragged through the streets and thrown into the Tiber. On 23 August eight hundred Neapolitan horsemen entered the city and restored order.[4]

After its ignominious departure from Rome, the imperial army ravaged the duchy of Spoleto, and exacted forced contributions from

[1] Mollat, VOL. VII, no. 42500.
[2] Nicola Speciale, *Historia Sicula*, in Muratori, VOL. X, col. 1075.
[3] Schwalm, *op. cit.* VOL. VI, pp. 423–4, 438–44.
[4] Villani, *op. cit.* Bk X, ch. cxvi. See also Schwalm, *op. cit.* VOL. VI, pp. 396–7, 399–400, 405–06.

Todi. It might perhaps have marched as far as Florence, if Castruccio Castracani had lived; but the death of this powerful ally brought to nothing the plans for an expedition to Tuscany, and compelled Louis of Bavaria to make his way to Pisa on 21 September 1328 in order to deprive the dead man's sons of their rights of lordship.[1]

Nicholas V, having passed through the Patrimony of St Peter and having robbed the treasure of the church of San Fortunato at Todi of all its jewels and silver lamps of great value—a curious action for a believer in holy poverty—joined the emperor at Pisa on 2 or 3 January 1329. His reception was on a grand scale and a magnificent procession came to meet him. On 8 January he preached and granted forgiveness to all who had repudiated John XXII, and confirmed the sentence of deposition proclaimed with much commotion by Louis of Bavaria on the previous 13 December, following the indictment drawn up by Michael of Cesena.[2] On 20 January he conferred the purple on Giovanni Visconti, canon of Milan, and made him legate in Lombardy, while the emperor confirmed the granting of the lordship of Milan to Azzo Visconti in return for a promise of 125,000 florins.[3] On 19 February a farcical ceremony took place in the cathedral where, according to the chronicler Heinrich von Erfurt, the antipope condemned as a heretic a dummy dressed in pontifical vestments to represent John XXII, deprived it of its dignities and handed it over to the secular arm.[4] The Pisans showed little enthusiasm for attending this travesty; those who did come were brought by force of arms.[5]

Policies in Italy were so inconstant that a sudden change in them brought about an entirely new situation. Azzo Visconti, to everyone's surprise, had an interview with the legate, Bertrand du Poujet. This defection determined Louis of Bavaria on 11 April 1329 to leave Pisa, and to come to an agreement on 21 April with the Ghibellines of Mantua, Como and Cremona, in order to attack the traitor.[6]

The sudden departure of the emperor was the signal for the general melting-away of the supporters of the antipope. Did he himself make a break with his protector of his own accord, as his act of recantation declares? It seems likely that he did since Michael of Cesena, William of Ockham and the cardinals, with the exception of Paolo di Viterbo, all abandoned him. As a final blow, Pisa drove him out. He was obliged to seek refuge at the castle of Burgaro where he lived shut up for three months. The secret of his hiding-place was

---

[1] *Ibid.* chs. xcvii–xcviii, cii.   [2] *Ibid.* chs. xcvii, cxiii, cxiv.
[3] *Ibid.* ch. cxvii. See also Schwalm, *op. cit.* VOL. VI, p. 451.
[4] *Histoire littéraire de la France*, VOL. XXXIII, p. 477.
[5] Villani, *op. cit.* Bk X, ch. cxxi.   [6] *Ibid.* ch. cxxviii.

so well kept that no one knew where to lay hands on him. His host, Count Bonifazio di Donoratico, took fright at the approach of an army from Florence, and had him secretly transferred to his own house in Pisa, where his presence soon became known. Informed of this, John XXII immediately requested the count to hand over the antipope (10 May 1330). Negotiations were begun. In July John guaranteed the pretender's life and absolution from his crimes, provided that he made formal abjuration, and at the same time assured him of an annual pension of 3,000 florins and exemption from all lesser authority than that of the Holy See. The terms of the agreement were accepted. Pietro da Corbara wrote a very humble letter to the supreme pontiff, offering to renounce his errors in public, wherever it should be convenient.[1]

On 25 July, the archbishop of Pisa and the bishop of Lucca received the solemn recantation of the antipope. On 4 August a galley in charter to a private owner from Marseilles took him aboard. A favourable wind brought him to Nice in two days. On 24 August Pietro da Corbara entered Avignon, and the following day, with a rope about his neck and dressed in his Franciscan habit, he appeared in Consistory where he renewed his act of recantation and received pardon. The pope treated him generously: his prison was the papal palace. After three years' detention, far from harsh, Pietro died quite forgotten on 16 October 1333.[2]

Thus the schism into which Louis of Bavaria had so irresponsibly plunged Christendom petered out miserably. Instead of furthering his cause, the schism had compromised it even in the eyes of the Ghibellines who everywhere in Lombardy, except at Vercelli, shut the gates of their cities against him. The sentinels on guard on the walls of Milan shouted abuse at the emperor: 'Drunken sot! fathead!' they cried, 'Drink, baby, drink! *babo!*'[3] Unable to chastise their abuses, the German army went off to Pavia and thence to Reggio Emilia and Parma; there a plot was hatched which, had it been successful, would have been disastrous for the Church. It was decided that Louis of Bavaria should go to Modena and then lead his cavalry against Faenza which, he was assured, would not resist. Bertrand du Poujet would be sure to send his troops against the enemy, thus withdrawing them from the defence of Bologna, where he was in residence. At this precise moment a riot was to break out, while considerable forces of foot-soldiers were to come down from the mountains; they would seize Bologna, and then drive out the

[1] Eubel, *Bullarium franciscanum*, VOL. V, Rome 1898, p. 472.
[2] *Ibid.* pp. 470–9, 510–11.   [3] Galvano della Fiamma, *op. cit.* p. 6.

legate and hand the city over to the emperor. But Bertrand du Poujet, who had been secretly informed of the conspiracy, had its ringleaders arrested and summoned the Florentines to his aid. With the three hundred cavalry and the four hundred cross-bowmen that they sent him he was able to put down the conspiracy with severity; all the chief culprits were beheaded in the main square, except the archbishop, who escaped capital punishment by virtue of his sacerdotal office; but his fate was not much better, for he died in prison from the consequences of his detention, in November 1329.[1]

In chagrin, Louis of Bavaria retreated to Trent and planned revenge. A meeting was held, at which it was decided, in agreement with the Ghibellines in Lombardy, that Bologna should be invested and captured, and Romagna invaded. But, learning on 13 January 1330 that his rival, Frederick of Austria, had died, the emperor determined to cross the Alps.

4

Louis of Bavaria and John XXII, from 1330–34

The death of Frederick of Austria gave new hope to the supporters of the duke of Bavaria. One after the other, the king of Denmark, Count William of Holland, King John of Bohemia, Duke Otto of Austria and the archbishop of Trier, each thought to appease the wrath of John XXII. The pope, however, remained adamant. Before any reconciliation could take place he insisted that Louis must resign the imperial title, of which he had been deprived by papal decree. Now, in the very petition in which he begged for pardon, Louis had made the express condition that he was to be continued in his existing status and dignities. In any case, his approaches did not appear particularly sincere, for heretics like William of Ockham, Michael of Cesena and Fra Bonagrazia frequented his court as assiduously as ever.[2]

John XXII's plan was clear-cut: to compel the emperor to abdicate and so bring about a new election.

From 1331, France and Bohemia came over to his point of view. By the Treaty of Fontainebleau of January 1332, the king of Bohemia promised to ratify Philip VI's encroachments upon imperial territory and to cede to him the kingdom of Arles, if he himself were allowed complete freedom of action to cause the imperial crown to fall to a

---

[1] Villani, *op. cit.* Bk X, chs. cxlvi, cxlvii.
[2] *Thesaurus novus anecdotorum,* VOL. II, cols. 800–06.

member of his own family. In November 1332, the pope joined in their schemes, and, in addition, allowed the king of Bohemia to create a kingdom for himself in northern Italy.

Louis of Bavaria, dismayed at the coalition formed against him, abdicated in favour of Henry of Bavaria, on condition that the Holy See promised him absolution from the censures imposed upon him. By this means he was able at least to keep for himself the duchy of Bavaria, of which he had been dispossessed by the Bull of 3 April 1327.

The Bavarian plan was acceptable to Philip of Valois, and at Frankfurt, on 17 December 1333, he guaranteed to supply Henry of Bavaria with the money he required for his election, namely 300,000 marks of pure silver; he felt sure that he would never have to give back the kingdom of Arles, which was handed over as a pledge for this loan.

The Treaty of Frankfurt, signed by the pope and the king of Bohemia, was so favourable to France that it was bound to cause some opposition. Rather than have any hand in ceding the kingdom of Arles to Philip VI, Robert of Anjou[1] changed his tactics completely and, abandoning all the traditions of the Guelphs, whose leader he was in Italy, he joined forces with a thoroughbred Ghibelline, Cardinal Napoleone Orsini, in order to foil France's intentions. Orsini advised Louis of Bavaria to bring his case before a general council, at the same time suggesting that he should not abdicate, and putting him on his guard against Henry of Bavaria and John of Bohemia.[2]

Louis of Bavaria, a man 'of wavering character, easily influenced in any direction, and so quickly moved that he could shift suddenly from one extreme to the other,' allowed himself to be persuaded, and on 24 July 1334 a circular letter announced to the cities of the Empire that it had never been the emperor's intention to abdicate.[3] Orsini's advice, supported by that of the Franciscans who had taken refuge at the Bavarian court, had ruined a scheme which had the advantage of dealing tactfully with the susceptibilities of both emperor and pope, and of making possible the reconciliation of these two enemies.

[1] K. Müller (*Der Kampf*, VOL. I, pp. 394–405), has published a violent memorandum against the king of Bohemia issued by the Angevin chancellery.
[2] For the part played by Orsini, see the report made by the friar Gauthier to Michael of Cesena, in Höfler, *Aus Avignon*, p. 11.
[3] P. Fournier, *Le Royaume d'Arles*, pp. 391–405.

5

Louis of Bavaria and Benedict XII

As uncompromising as had been the policy of John XXII towards Louis of Bavaria, so that of his successor, Benedict XII, was from the outset conciliatory. The emperor, determined to take advantage of the pope's favourable attitude, sent four ambassadors, Count Ludwig von Ottingen, Eberhard von Tumnau, Markwart von Randeck and Ulrich von Augsburg, on 20 March 1335, to investigate the real intentions of the Curia and to find out on what conditions he would be pardoned.[1] Discussions, begun on 28 April, continued for a long time. On 5 July, the ambassadors returned, bringing the peace conditions stipulated by the pope.[2] Although harsh, Louis accepted them and sent a second embassy, which reached Avignon about 8 September. In addition to the previous ambassadors, it consisted of Count Ludwig von Ottingen the elder and Heinrich von Zipplingen, commander of the order of the Teutonic Knights. In a letter addressed to the supreme pontiff, Louis declared himself ready to take the pope's advice as a command, and in particular to be entirely at the pope's discretion concerning the agreement to be concluded with the kings of France and Naples, which agreement was one of the essential conditions of his own reconciliation with the pope.[3]

Markwart von Randeck appeared at a meeting of the Consistory on 9 October, and there read a long speech, full of quotations from legal and scriptural sources, setting forth seven reasons why his master's pardon should no longer be deferred.[4]

At once, Benedict XII declared himself ready to grant it; but this graciousness upset the plans of the kings of France and Naples. Philip VI was opposed to any reconciliation, or, at the least, thought that it should be bought as dearly as possible, and on the condition that the emperor ceded territories on the other side of the Rhône. Robert of Anjou, for his part, after the set-back suffered by John of Bohemia in Italy,[5] had turned against the emperor, and had no wish to see a peace between him and the pope, by which he would himself inevitably lose the advantages he had gained as vicar of the Church

---

[1] J. Schwalm, 'Reise nach Italien . . . ,' *Neues Archiv*, VOL. XXVI, 1901, pp. 709–13.
[2] K. Rümler, ' Die Akten der Gesandschaften Ludwigs des Baiern an Benedikt XII. und Klemens VI.,' *Quellen-Studien aus dem historischen Seminar der Universität Innsbruck*, VOL. II, 1910, pp. 112–20.
[3] S. Riezler, *Vatikanische Akten*, p. 592, no. 1748.
[4] *Ibid.* pp. 597–600, no. 1759.   [5] See above, p. 212.

in Italy. The two monarchs had therefore combined their efforts to prevent any understanding, and were constantly creating fresh impediments. In full Consistory, their emissaries made clear to Benedict how very unseemly it would be for the Holy See to resume relations with Louis of Bavaria, and thus to favour a prince who was a notorious heretic, at the expense of Catholic sovereigns like themselves.[1] In short, the French and Neapolitan requirements were so severe that the German ambassadors had to depart at the beginning of 1336, to arm themselves with fresh authority.[2]

Supplied with letters containing more extensive powers of attorney and dated 5 March 1336,[3] the ambassadors soon returned to the Curia. Negotiations were proceeding normally when suddenly, in May, the pope learned that Louis of Bavaria was making ready to join a league formed by the nobles of Germany against France. This was an act of treachery, for on 4 August of the previous year,[4] Louis had left to Benedict XII the task of contracting an alliance with France. When the Bavarian ambassadors were summoned before the pope on 15 May 1336, they could not conceal their embarrassment, and begged leave to withdraw.[5]

But Louis of Bavaria wrote to Benedict protesting that he was not to blame, and that the pope had been misinformed, and indeed a third embassy, accredited on 28 October 1336,[6] reached Avignon on 31 January of the following year, having first gone to Paris where an alliance with France had been discussed. Philip VI had promised to send his delegates to the Curia without delay, so that they could state the basis of agreement in the presence of the supreme pontiff. Having been long awaited the ambassadors finally arrived about 3 April 1337 but only to ask the pope to allow the affair to drag on, and even to hinder its progress.[7] Benedict XII consented unwillingly, for he considered that at a time when Edward III of England was seeking allies against France, it was a mistake not to fall in with the overtures of Louis of Bavaria. 'In the end,' he said, 'the Germans will learn the reason for all these delays, and will make an alliance with England.'

The pope's forecast proved correct. On 26 August, the emperor, realising that France was playing with him entered into an alliance, both defensive and offensive, with Edward III. From this time, there were no further negotiations with the Avignon court.[8]

[1] Böhmer, *Fontes rerum germanicarum*, VOL. IV, pp. 206–08.
[2] Rümler, *op. cit.* pp. 120–5.
[3] J. Schwalm, in *Neues Archiv*, VOL. XXVI, pp. 713–24.
[4] Riezler, *op. cit.* p. 592, no. 1748.   [5] Rümler, *op. cit.* pp. 125–32.
[6] J. Schwalm in *Neues Archiv*, VOL. XXVI, pp. 724–6. See also Riezler, *op. cit.* pp. 637–654, nos. 1841, 1842.
[7] Riezler, *op. cit.* p. 668, no. 1876.   [8] Rümler, *op. cit.* pp. 132–42.

The interdict under which Germany lay was annoying the populace; by fair means or foul, the clergy defied it. The archbishop of Mainz had rebelled, and unfortunate disagreements split the religious orders into two rival camps: the Hospitallers of St John of Jerusalem, the Teutonic Knights and the Franciscans were rent by schism. The German bishops, anxious to improve this unhappy state of affairs, summoned Louis of Bavaria to Speyer. They begged him to be reconciled with the Curia, and on 27 March 1338 themselves sent a message to the pope to this effect, carried by Count Gerlach von Nassau and Ulrich, bishop of Chur. The Estates of the Empire added their requests to those of the bishops.[1] When Benedict XII failed to respond to the wishes of the German people, popular indignation was aroused. At Rense, on 16 July,[2] all the prince Electors except the king of Bohemia swore to defend the liberties, rights and customs of the Empire. They proclaimed that the dignity of the emperor came direct from God and that he who had been elected by a majority vote was the legitimate king. Consequently, from the time of his coronation at Aachen, the emperor could govern without the approval, confirmation or consent of the pope or of any person whatsoever. The threatening decrees formerly issued by John XXII against Louis of Bavaria were declared illegal. Foreseeing that the Holy See might persist in upholding these decrees the ecclesiastical Electors wrote, somewhat insolently, to Benedict: 'We shall be reluctantly compelled to seek and find suitable remedies against the said proceedings and decrees.'[3] On 6 August, in the edict *Licet juris*[4] Louis of Bavaria gave his sanction to the Rense decision, and even decreed that anyone contesting it would be deprived of his fiefs and considered guilty of treason.

In order to conform with the injunctions of the German clergy, Louis renewed relations with the papal Curia. In August 1338 the abbot of the Cistercian monastery at Ebrach[5] was sent with letters protesting the emperor's feelings of respect and obedience towards the Holy See. When he asked for his master's pardon, it was no longer on the old terms. Although the documents do not reveal the nature of these terms, there can be little doubt that they included the French alliance, which had previously been stipulated. But in

---

[1] J. Schwalm in *Neues Archiv*, VOL. XXVI, pp. 727–33.
[2] K. Zeumer, 'Ludwigs des Bayern, Königswahlgesetz "Licet juris" vom 6 August 1338. Mit einer Beilage: Das Renser Weisthum vom 16 Juli 1338,' in *Neues Archiv*, VOL. XXX, 1905, pp. 110–12.   [3] J. Schwalm in *Neues Archiv*, VOL. XXVI, pp. 734–7.
[4] K. Zeumer in *Neues Archiv*, VOL. XXX, pp. 100–02.
[5] According to Friedrich Bock, the abbot of Ebrach was given this mission during the pontificate of John XXII. See his 'Die Prokurationen Kaiser Ludwigs IV. und der Papst Benedikt XII.,' *Quellen*, 1933–4, pp. 251–91.

1338, this was no longer to be talked of. At the meeting at Coblenz on 5 September, Edward III had received the golden rods, the insignia of the imperial vicariate in southern Germany. Benedict XII, embarrassed, sent his chaplain, Arnaud de Verdale, to Louis of Bavaria on 13 September 1338, to find out what were his real intentions.[1] The nuncio had an easy interview with the emperor, who, together with the prince Electors, promised to send ambassadors to Avignon. However, not one put in an appearance. Only on 15 March 1341 did the agreement between the Empire and France, which had superseded that between the Empire and England, bring about a reconciliation with the Curia. But Louis of Bavaria, who seems to have been incapable of acting consistently, alienated the Church and made all efforts at reconciliation useless; for, in order to make sure that his son Louis, the margrave of Brandenburg, would have the Tyrol, he married him on 10 February 1342 to Countess Margaret Maultasch. Her earlier marriage to John, son of the king of Bohemia, he annulled, on his own authority, on grounds of impotence[2] and had even granted to the two parties the necessary dispensations for consanguinity.

6

The End of the Struggle between the Church and the Empire

France's constant intervention had made all Benedict XII's well-meaning plans for Louis of Bavaria come to nothing. Clement VI adopted different tactics, and reverted to the harsh policy pursued by John XXII. It is true that Louis first took the offensive by announcing his intention of going to the assistance of the Ghibellines in Italy. The pope's retort to this act of provocation was to appoint a legate on 19 July 1342, whose special mission was to prevent the emperor from having access to Lombardy.[3]

In spite of that, Louis of Bavaria, confident of the support guaranteed him by France at the Treaty of Vincennes on 15 March 1341, once more made overtures for a reconciliation with the Church. Discussions took place between October 1342 and January 1343, but Philip VI of Valois by betraying his promises contributed to the failure of these negotiations.[4]

---

[1] Riezler, *op. cit.* pp. 714–16, nos. 1974, 1975.
[2] On this occasion Marsiglio of Padua composed an apology for the emperor's conduct, see N. Valois in *Histoire littéraire de la France*, VOL. XXXIII, pp. 617–18.
[3] Rinaldi, *ad annum* 1342, §17.   [4] Rümler, *Die Akten*, pp. 142–52.

On 12 April 1343, the pope published the Bull *Prolixa retro*, in which, after setting forth the lengthy catalogue of the misdeeds of Louis of Bavaria, he called upon him to resign the imperial authority within the next three months.[1] When this length of time had expired, on 11 July, the emperor was declared contumacious, and Clement VI wrote to the archbishop of Trier, asking him to place on the throne of Germany some prince who was a devoted son of the Church.[2]

The pope's uncompromising attitude alarmed Louis, especially as the ranks of his supporters were growing disquietingly thin. The marriage between his son Louis and the heiress of the Tyrol had alienated the house of Luxembourg. Moreover, the persecution of such of the clergy as had remained faithful to the Holy See had roused popular discontent: the Dominicans, for instance, had been driven from seventeen of their convents.[3] In these menacing circumstances, Louis instructed a second solemn embassy, led by the dauphin of Vienne, to offer his submission to the court at Avignon in the humblest terms. In the procuration drawn up for the occasion on 18 September 1343, he admitted his former misdeeds, retracted his heretical opinions, accepted in advance any penance that the Holy See cared to impose upon him, and abdicated.[4]

This act of respect gave Clement VI pause; but the pressure brought to bear by the kings of France, Bohemia and Naples, and also by such Italian cities as Florence,[5] got the better of his hesitation. Lest he should incur the odium of causing a rupture, the pope insisted on such harsh terms for peace that the Estates, when they met at Frankfurt on 8 September 1344, refused to agree to them. The princes held an assembly a few days later at Rense, and expressed the view that a new election should be held, putting forward the name of Charles of Moravia, the son of King John of Bohemia. When Louis of Bavaria pleaded on behalf of his son, Louis of Brandenburg, he was told bluntly: 'As for you, Bavarian, you have brought the Empire to ruin; we want no more Bavarians on the throne!'[6]

From this time, the Luxemburg faction worked actively to further the cause of Prince Charles. Without paying any heed to the protests of Philip of Valois, who, after the announcement of the Bohemian candidature, had begged his pardon of Louis of Bavaria, Clement VI patiently pursued his ends. On 7 April 1346 Heinrich von Wirnemburg, a warm supporter of the emperor, was canonically deposed and

---

[1] Rinaldi, *ad annum* 1343, §43–58.
[2] Riezler, *Vatikanische Akten*, p. 775, no. 2151.
[3] *Neues Archiv*, VOL. XXX, p. 447.   [4] Riezler, *op. cit.* pp. 780–5, no. 2167.
[5] *Archivio storico italiano*, ser. 3, VOL. II, 1865, pt I, p. 184.
[6] Böhmer, *Fontes rerum germanicarum*, VOL. IV, pp. 229–30, 526.

replaced as archbishop of Mainz by Count Gerlach von Nassau.[1] Six days later, a Bull proclaimed the complete downfall of Louis of Bavaria and deprived him of the Empire; while another, dated 28 April, urged the Electors to make a fresh election.[2] On 22 April, Charles of Moravia solemnly swore at Avignon that, should he be elected king of the Romans, he would annul all proceedings instituted against Robert of Anjou, Rome and Florence by Henry VII; revoke all the acts of Louis of Bavaria and respect the Church's domains in Italy; never enter any territory belonging to the Church without formal permission from the Holy See; not enter Rome before the day appointed for his coronation, and leave it on the evening of the same day; remove from their sees all bishops improperly appointed and replace them by prelates nominated by the Roman Curia etc.[3] Finally, on 11 July, the king of Bohemia, Duke Rudolf of Saxony and the archbishops of Trier, Mainz and Cologne, gathered at Rense, declared that they were putting an end to the vacancy of the Empire by voting unanimously for Prince Charles.

The Rense election was received with a marked lack of enthusiasm, especially in northern Germany. The malcontents mocked the newly elected prince, calling him 'the priests' emperor.' The gates of Aachen were shut against him, and by an apostolic dispensation the coronation took place at Bonn on 26 November. Louis of Bavaria was even preparing to invade Bohemia, when he died suddenly of an apoplectic attack while on a bear hunt, 11 October 1347. His followers elected Count Gunther von Schwarzenburg king, but death was still on Charles's side, and rid him of this second rival on 14 June 1349, thus ensuring that he would possess the Empire in peace.

But the Holy See's triumph was more apparent than real, for Charles IV paid no heed to the oaths he had sworn in 1346. Though he had promised to enter Italy only after the Curia had confirmed his election, he made no formal request for approval, but was content to beg for favours, notably that of being crowned emperor. Charles had also undertaken to oppose those bishops who had been put into German sees by Louis of Bavaria against the wishes of the pope; but as soon as Heinrich von Wirnemburg, who had been deprived by Clement VI of the archbishopric of Mainz, recognised Charles as his legitimate sovereign, Charles ceased to support the Curia's candidate Gerlach von Nassau, and took refuge in strict neutrality.

Nor were these the only disappointments in store for the papacy. It was with bitterness that Clement VI saw his former pupil turn a

---

[1] K. Zeumer and R. Salomon, *Constitutiones*, VOL. VIII, pt 1, no. 4. (*Monumenta Germaniae Historica.*) [2] *Ibid.* nos. 7, 16–49. [3] *Ibid.* nos. 9–13.

deaf ear to his advice, by refusing the hand of a daughter of France and marrying the Princess Palatine Anna, thus becoming reconciled with the house of Wittelsbach. The pope took his revenge by once more excommunicating the Margrave Louis the Old and his adherents. He distrusted Charles's independent policy and opposed any suggestion of an expedition to Rome, no doubt fearing that the German king might encroach upon the Holy See's rights in Italy.[1] His successor, Innocent VI, was more conciliatory: he permitted Charles IV to cross the Alps in 1354 and had him crowned emperor at Rome on 5 April 1355 by Cardinal Pierre Bertrand de Colombiers.[2]

Innocent VI received a poor return for his friendliness. Charles IV had realised that Germany was weary of the quarrels caused by the popes' intervention in the election and confirmation of German kings. He broke the bonds that had for so long held Church and Empire together. This was the purpose of the Golden Bull[3] published on 13 January 1356. This celebrated edict, amongst other things, reserved to the seven Electors the right to elect to the throne of Germany and, in time of a vacancy, decreed that the prince of Saxony should be Vicar for the North and the Count Palatine of the Rhine Vicar for the South. It completely ignored the Curia's claims both to approve and confirm the election of the king of the Germans, and to assume imperial authority in Italy during an interregnum.[4]

So came about the final separation of spiritual from temporal power, the assertion of the independence of rulers and nations with regard to the papacy, the overthrow of the universal monarchy which the Holy See had exercised throughout the Middle Ages, the first manifestation of what has been called the spirit of the modern age.

Charles IV had put an end to the Roman Curia's pretensions, by the simple method of disregarding them. His object in so doing was to avoid a conflict with Innocent VI. The pope made no protest.[5] After the Diet of Metz, in 1355, when the Golden Bull was first issued in the presence of the papal delegate Androin de la Roche, Innocent sent the emperor a very friendly letter. If he felt slighted,

[1] W. Scheffler, *Karl IV. und Innocenz VI. Beiträge zur Geschichte ihrer Beziehungen, 1355–1360*, Berlin 1912, pp. 17–22.
[2] E. Werunsky, *Der erste Römerzug Kaiser Karls IV. 1354–1355*, Innsbruck 1878. *Johannis Porta de Annoniaco liber de coronatione Karoli IV. imperatoris*, ed. R. Salomon, Hanover 1913.
[3] K. Zeumer, *Die goldene Bulle Kaiser Karls IV.*, Weimar 1908 (text of the Golden Bull).
[4] Contrary to the generally accepted view, K. Zeumer, *op. cit.* pp. 192–4, alleges that Charles IV did not mention the claims of the Curia, in order to leave the difficulty unresolved.
[5] Many historians have wrongly alleged that the opposite was true. M. Scheffler has proved that there is no evidence whatever of a protest by Innocent VI (*op. cit.* pp. 101–104).

he at least concealed his resentment. There is no reason to be surprised at this attitude. The Golden Bull 'legalised, once and for all, Germany's constitutional anarchy, and made the country into one huge confederate state.' As a result, it weakened imperial authority, and so indirectly furthered papal claims in Italy: in effect it separated the peninsula from the Empire. Moreover, Innocent VI had no interest in quarrelling with Charles IV in 1356; he was counting on his support to further his Italian policy, to gain financial assistance from the German clergy and to repel the incursions of the Great Companies into the Comtat-Venaissin. For the rest, the supreme pontiff's real feelings emerge in the decision he took concerning the two Constitutions *Romani principes* and *Pastoralis cura* promulgated by Clement V.[1]

When he felt that his end was near, Charles IV wanted to secure the imperial throne for his son Wenceslas. Gregory XI announced his intention of publishing a decree with reference to the election of the king of the Germans. Charles pointed out to the pope that he could pass as many laws as he pleased, but that they would be completely worthless, since neither he nor the prince Electors would give them any authority. In practice, however, the emperor realised that he must respect the pope's feelings in this matter. He sent him the decree electing Wenceslas without expressly asking for papal approval. As Gregory XI did not at once recognise the validity of the election, Charles made promises on his own behalf, without the sanction of the electoral college, and drew up a request, under a false date, for the Holy See's approval of the election. Moreover, he conceded that, so long as the emperor remained alive, the Curia had the right to intervene in the election of the king of the Germans. But this concession should not be regarded as a negation of the Golden Bull. It was nothing more than a diplomatic expedient, quite worthless legally, and without consequence for the future, but necessary in order to avoid a conflict with Gregory XI. But Charles IV did not deceive the pope, who died without recognising the election of Wenceslas.[2]

[1] See above, pp. 204-05.
[2] Scheffler, *op. cit.* p. 93. See also J. Weizsäcker, *Deutsche Reichstagsakten unter König Wenzel*, VOL. I, Munich 1867, for many documents concerning the relations between Charles IV and Gregory XI.

CHAPTER III

The Papacy and France

1

The Trial of the Templars

FOR six hundred years, Christendom has been moved and troubled by the story of the trial of the Templars; men's minds have never ceased to find in it the fascination inherent in every famous unsolved mystery. Popular imagination and that of informed and thoughtful persons are alike stirred by the question of the order's innocence or guilt. We are more fortunate than the people of the fourteenth century, whose judgment was systematically warped by conflicting rumours purposely let slip from prisons and torture-chambers by judges and gaolers; at the present time we can give a more reasonable appraisal to the facts in the light of documents recently made available in the archives. We now have so complete a dossier on the trial that the parts played by Clement V and Philip the Fair can be exactly defined. It seems unlikely that any further discoveries will do more than throw light on minor problems.

About the year 1119, on the site of Solomon's Temple at Jerusalem, there settled a number of knights who had come from Champagne and Burgundy under the leadership of Hugues de Payens. They proposed to set up a society at once military and religious, for the defence of the Holy Places. They added a fourth vow to the three usually governing the religious life: to protect pilgrims and guard the routes to Palestine. The Council of Troyes (1128) sanctioned their existence and gave them a rule that was short, hard and war-like, drawn up under the inspiration of St Bernard.[1]

At first the order distinguished itself by real feats of arms, such as the defence of Gaza (1171), the battle of Tiberias (1187), the conquest of Damietta (1219) and the expedition to Egypt (1250). But the exploits of the knights could not prevent the decadence of the little kingdom of Jerusalem and the return of the Saracens to the offensive. In 1291, the recapture of St John of Acre by the Infidels

[1] L. Bréhier, *L'Église et l'Orient au moyen âge. Les croisades*, Paris 1928, pp. 96–7.

completed the loss of the Holy Land.[1] The knights, having failed to settle on the island of Cyprus, were driven back to Europe, where they possessed considerable domains and strongholds. Far from their sphere of action, they were now in the position of a permanent army receiving news of universal peace. There was no longer any reason for their existence unless they made a new one for themselves, by finding a different but useful way to serve Christendom. If the order did not reorganise itself, it would have to disband.

By the beginning of the fourteenth century, the Templars could plead little to justify their existence except the general services they rendered as skilled financiers. Unrivalled in handling money, judicious, positive and practical in matters of administration, they had rapidly gained the confidence of the whole world. As bankers their credit exceeded that of the Jews and Lombards, who were usurers rather than financiers. Their houses, being at once impregnable fortresses and inviolable religious buildings, were thought to be the safest possible trustee banks. The Templars, far from freezing the capital entrusted to them, knew how to make intelligent use of it: they opened current accounts for the solvent, made themselves into brokers and arranged payment anywhere, either by transporting from one country to another considerable sums of money under strong escort, or by transfer of credits and a system of accounts. Their book-keeping had so high a reputation that popes, kings and princes made them responsible for their treasury transactions. The Templars had to bank the income from taxes, pay dues, reimburse sums borrowed by the French royal house. From Philip Augustus to Philip the Fair, the history of the royal treasury is that of the treasury of the Templars.[2] It is true that in 1295 the management of state funds was withdrawn from the knights. This, however, was not the result of any disgrace, but an attempt at direct royal administration. It appears that the attempt was unsuccessful, for in the spring of 1303, the brother treasurer resumed his duties under the control of royal officials.[3]

A religious order, however, cannot become a financial power and the creditor of kings and popes without arousing jealousy. Temporal prosperity almost inevitably produces a slackening of discipline, excites pride and favours the deterioration of moral standards. By the

[1] L. Bréhier, *op. cit.* pp. 114–15, 222–9, 245–6.
[2] L. Delisle, 'Mémoire sur les opérations financières des Templiers,' *Mémoires de l'Académie des inscriptions et belles-lettres,* VOL. XXXIII, Paris 1889, pt 2, *passim.*
[3] Borrelli de Serres, *Recherches sur divers services publics du XIIIe au XVIIe siècle,* VOL. III, Paris 1909, pp. 1–45. See also Ch. V. Langlois, 'Études sur l'administration royale du XIIIe au XVIe siècle,' *Journal des Savants,* 1910, pp. 489–98.

end of the thirteenth century public opinion had turned against the Templars. They were said to be backward in almsgiving. They were reproached with having forsaken the cause of the Crusades, and secretly accused of having made a pact with the Infidel. The secular clergy protested vigorously against their immunities and exemptive privileges, while the mendicant orders complained of competition from lay collectors employed by the Templars. Vague rumours circulated among the common people. There was talk of the knights' greed and unscrupulousness, of their passion for self-aggrandisement and their rapacity. Their insolent bearing was a byword. They were said to be given to drunkenness; the saying 'to drink like a Templar' was already in use. The Old German word *Tempelhaus* meant a house of ill-fame. Guardroom gossip was repeated, such as the story of the knight who bragged: 'It is of no consequence to deny Jesus. In my country he is denied a hundred times for the sake of one flea.'[1] Such talk as this roused all kind of suspicion against the orthodoxy of the order.

The secrecy with which the chapter meetings were surrounded in accordance with the rule of the order, gave credence to all kinds of rumours. The ceremony for receiving novices took place at night. Sentinels guarded the closed doors of the rooms where meetings were held. Only a few of the dignitaries of the order knew the whole content of the rule; ordinary brethren practised it without ever having seen it or read it. What could the common people think when they heard a Templar say, 'We have articles that are known only to God and the devil and to us brethren'?[2] They were driven to the conclusion that the rule must contain some dreadful secrets, if indeed it did not actually prescribe abominable practices. At every period of history *monita secreta* have been a bogy to scare simple people.

Undue weight should not be given to the accusations that popular spite levelled against the Templars. The Knights of St John and other orders were equally decried. Rightly or wrongly, the literature of the Middle Ages condemns monastic morals crudely and indiscriminately. The wealth of the Templars in landed property was far less than that of the Hospitallers, and only a half or two-thirds that of the Cistercians.[3] One fact is especially worthy of attention and shows how far public opinion had gone astray: in the famous memorandum *De recuperatione Terrae Sanctae* (1305–07), in which he recommends

[1] Ch. V. Langlois, 'Le Procès des Templiers,' *Revue des deux mondes*, VOL. CIII, 1891, p. 389. [2] *Ibid.* p. 390.
[3] H. Finke, *Papsttum und Untergang der Templerordens*, VOL. I, Münster 1907, pp. 70, 85. See also Ch. V. Langlois, 'L'Affaire des Templiers,' *Journal des Savants*, 1908, pp. 420 ff.

the suppression of the order, Pierre Dubois does not make any complaint against the orthodoxy of the morality of its members; he is only questioning its usefulness as an institution.[1] He accepted in principle the opinion of the popes and councils, who had already thought of uniting the Hospitallers and the Templars.

It is rather difficult to say what were Philip the Fair's motives in doing all he could to destroy the Templars. Before 1307 there had never been any misunderstanding between the king and the order. During the conflict with Boniface VIII, indeed, the Templars had supported the king, who, in token of his gratitude, had confirmed its privileges in 1304. On 12 October 1307, at the funeral of the wife of Charles of Valois, the Grand Master, Jacques de Molai, had held one of the cords of the pall. The Templars' European policy had never been anti-French. Their strength could never be a cause for alarm, for a document dated 1308 puts the number of their knights in France at no more than two thousand.[2] There had never been any criticism of their handling of the royal finances.

It is perhaps possible that Philip the Fair's greed was excited by the wealth of the Templars. Contemporaries certainly thought so,[3] and there was strong evidence to support them in this belief. They had seen the king, who was for ever in urgent need of money, driven to debase the coinage, and then, in 1291, to despoil the Lombard bankers and, in 1306, the Jews. No doubt they noticed how, as soon as the Templars were arrested, the king began to assign the rents from the sequestrated property, as if he were certain to keep it for the future.[4] They concluded that Philip's motives were not disinterested. Their guess, indeed, still seems a plausible one; but, in the absence of documentary proof, we cannot make any categoric statement on the reasons for the attitude taken up by the French king. One thing alone remains quite certain: it was Philip who was the chief author of the downfall of the Templars.[5]

At the beginning of 1305, some denunciations of the order had already been made. A certain Esquieu de Floyran, a native of Béziers, came to Lérida and confided to James II of Aragon the revelations that had been made to him, while in prison, by a Templar who was incarcerated at the same time. Having failed to impress the Aragonese king, he went to Philip the Fair whom he found easy to

[1] Pierre Dubois, De recuperatione Terrae Sanctae, ed. Ch. V. Langlois, Paris 1891, pp. 13–15. [2] Finke, op. cit. VOL. II, p. 114.
[3] Gestes des Chiprois, in Recueil des historiens des croisades, Documents arméniens, VOL. II, Paris 1906, pp. 869–70.
[4] Borrelli de Serres, op. cit. p. 41. Regestum, no. 4404.
[5] Finke, op. cit. VOL. I, pp. 54–61. See also Langlois, in Journal des Savants, 1910, pp. 489–98; Borrelli de Serres, op. cit. p. 39.

convince.[1] At about the same time further accusations joined those of Esquieu; they were made by Bernard Pelet, a clerk from Languedoc, and by a Gascon Templar, Géraud Lavernha.[2] These various depositions were made known to Clement V, before and during the celebrations of his coronation. But whereas the pope attached no importance to these moves, Philip the Fair was already at work, in the strictest secrecy, collecting evidence against the order. Twelve spies were infiltrated into the Templars' ranks to find out their alleged misdeeds. Some renegade Templars, who had come forward as informers, found themselves inside the royal prisons.[3]

After two years, enough charges against the order had been accumulated. But Clement V had still to be convinced. The overtures made to him at Poitiers, in April–May 1307, had come to nothing. Then the king began to assail the pope with letters. His ambassadors urged him to take action. Finally, on 24 August, at the request of Jacques de Molai, Clement ordered an enquiry in accordance with strict legal procedure.[4]

Philip was well aware of the slow machinery of proceedings in canon law, and had no wish to be subjected to them. After lengthy discussions with his council, he played a master-stroke: on the morning of Friday, 13 October, all the Templars in France were arrested. On the 14th and 15th, Guillaume de Nogaret,[5] the instigator of this action, made it his business to legalise the king's conduct. By means of proclamations and speeches, he made clear to the clergy and people of Paris that the king had acted upon a request from the Inquisitor-General of France, Friar Guillaume Imbert, after consultation with the pope and on the advice of the barons. He enumerated the infamous crimes of which the Templars were guilty: on the day they were received into the order, the knights denied Christ three times, and spat thrice on the crucifix; they were encouraged to practise sodomy; they worshipped an idol; at Mass, when priests of the order officiated, they left out the words of consecration.

The sudden arrest on 13 October was, strictly speaking, legal; but, whatever the king's followers might allege, it had not been carried out with the pope's consent. Clement wrote to Philip on 27 October:

[1] Finke, op. cit. VOL. II, pp. 83–5.

[2] J. Michelet, Procès des Templiers, VOL. I, Paris 1841, p. 37. Finke, op. cit. VOL. II, p. 319. Langlois in Journal des Savants, 1908, p. 425, suggested that these three persons were perhaps acting on behalf of Guillaume de Nogaret. Esquieu de Floyran was in fact rewarded for his denunciation by being given the spoils of the temple of Montricoux (Tarn-et-Garonne). See Mémoires de la Société archéologique du midi de la France, VOL. V, p. 193, and Mémoires de l'Académie de Toulouse, VOL. II, 1864, p. 122.

[3] Finke, op. cit. VOL. II, p. 145. [4] Baluze, Vitae, VOL. III, p. 60.

[5] Boutaric, 'Clement V, Philippe le Bel et les Templiers,' R.Q.H. VOL. X, 1871, pp. 327–9.

'Most dear son, we declare with sorrow that, in defiance of all rules, while we were far from you, you stretched forth your hand against the persons and goods of the Templars; you have gone so far as to cast them in prison, and have not released them—the which causes us the greatest sorrow. It is even said that you have added to the affliction of captivity a further affliction which, for the Church's modesty and our own, we think best to pass over at present in silence. . . . We have told your Serene Highness, in our letters, that we have taken this affair in hand, and that we wished diligently to seek out the truth. In the same letter, we begged you to take care to inform us of what you had discovered concerning this, promising that we would tell you what we ourselves discovered. Despite this, you have committed these outrages against the persons and goods of men who are immediately subject to us and to the Roman Church. In this hasty action all men see, and not without reasonable cause, an insulting scorn of us and of the Roman Church.'[1] The pope ended his letter of protest by requesting Philip to transfer the persons and goods of the Templars to the Cardinals Bérenger Frédol and Étienne de Suisy. Nevertheless—and this is not without importance—he had nothing to say about the innocence of the knights, and was only protesting against the lack of respect that had been shown to himself.

Clement's wrath was soon appeased. After the dramatic events of 13 October, the king's officers, anticipating in almost every case the action of the Inquisition, had obtained damning confessions, by applying every possible method of intimidation. Most cruel torture had overcome all resistance. The prisoners had no choice but to confess the crimes attributed to them, or to go to certain death. The king's orders were formal and explicit: 'And let them [the Templars] be promised pardon if they confess the truth and return to the faith of Holy Church; otherwise let them be condemned to death.'[2] Those unfortunates who were arraigned before tribunals of the Inquisition had no such chance of recantation. According to the corrupt practice then current, the king's men were present at the interrogation, and made sure that they adhered to their original declarations.

Of the one hundred and forty accused who were brought before the Inquisitor-General, Guillaume Imbert, only four declared that they were innocent. All the others, including the high dignitaries of the order, confessed to blasphemies; about three-quarters of them admitted to using obscene gestures at the time of their initiation, and almost one-quarter to having incited others to sodomy. Almost all of

[1] E. Renan, *Études sur la politique religieuse de Philippe le Bel*, Paris 1899, pp. 417–19.
[2] Boutaric, *op. cit.* p. 331.

them rejected with horror the suggestion that they had ever practised this degrading vice. Twice, on 24 and 25 October, the Grand Master acknowledged his own shame and that of his subordinates. He humbly begged pardon of the king and absolution of the pope and declared that he was ready to accept whatever penance was given him. Moreover, a note, sealed with his own seal, directed the Templars, by virtue of holy obedience, to confess before the Inquisition or the episcopal authority the crimes with which they were charged.

On 22 November 1307, when Clement V had been fully informed of events and the whole collection of confessions had been placed before him, he urged all Christian princes to seize the Templars and to sequester their property in his name.[1] He hoped in this way to prevent other monarchs from imitating the violent measures of Philip the Fair.

Pleased with this gesture which to a certain extent justified his own action, the king of France reserved to himself the right to administer the lands and goods of the Templars, and handed over their persons to the Cardinals Bérenger Frédol and Étienne de Suisy. But suddenly his good humour vanished, for instead of adhering to their confessions, the Templars, even Jacques de Molai, solemnly withdrew them in the presence of the Holy See's representatives. This news dismayed the pope, and in February 1308 he suspended the judicial activity of the inquisitors and bishops, declaring that he alone would now deal with the matter.

The pontiff's change of attitude quite thwarted Philip's plans. Alarmed at the turn events had taken, the king decided to keep hold of both the property and the persons of the Templars; then he launched a furious campaign of blackmail against this order that he was determined to destroy, and against Clement V. Vile pamphlets from the learned and venomous pens of Guillaume de Nogaret and Pierre Dubois[2] held the pope up for public execration. Everything that had formerly been said about Boniface VIII was now repeated against the new pope. Everything provided material for adverse criticism: Clement's nepotism, and his extortion of the clergy's goods. Since the pope, it was alleged, neglected the duties of his pastoral charge, it was for the king, that zealous upholder of divine law, to take immediate action. Straightway an Assembly of Notables meeting at Tours from 5 to 15 May 1308, approved the king's conduct and declared the Templars worthy of death for their crimes.

[1] P. Dupuy, *Histoire de la condamnation des Templiers*, Brussels 1713, p. 227.
[2] Boutaric, in *Not. et extr. des mss.* VOL. XX, pt 2, pp. 166–86.

Armed with the approval of his Estates, the king went boldly to Poitiers, there to have a further interview with the pope. He appeared in great pomp at the meetings of the Consistory, surrounded by the princes of the blood, barons, bishops and delegates from the Estates meeting at Tours, and there launched a formidable attack against Clement V. 'Holy Father, Holy Father,' said Plaisians, 'act quickly, otherwise the king will not be able to forbear, and if he could, the barons will not be able to forbear, and if the barons could, the very people of this glorious realm will not be able to forbear to avenge the insult to Christ. . . . Rouse yourself, therefore, to action! Or we will have to use other words to you!' Gilles Aycelin whispered slyly in his ear: 'When a prelate fails to stamp out terror, it is as if he made himself guilty of it.'[1] But Clement remained equally undismayed by the insolent speeches of Guillaume de Plaisians and the threatening tones of Gilles Aycelin; despite all their efforts, he still refused to believe in the Templars' guilt, and to condemn them.[2]

Faced with the pope's courageous resistance, Philip realised that he must change his tactics. On 27 June 1308 he officially handed over the persons of the Templars to the Church; but, alleging that Molai was ill, he took care to keep him in the dungeons at Chinon, and did not relinquish his hold on any of the great dignitaries of the order.[3] On the other hand, he sent seventy-two Templars to Poitiers: heads of houses, lay brethren, renegades and members of the rank and file, all carefully sorted out and duly catalogued by Guillaume de Nogaret's minions. The pope may have been unaware of the quality of these witnesses; in any case, their depositions, all unfavourable to the order, made such a vivid impression upon him that, in a series of solemn pronouncements, he gave up his objections one by one. Doubtless Philip the Fair did not obtain full satisfaction, but the Inquisition was reorganised so that the trial might begin again on a different basis. Two enquiries were to be set up simultaneously: the first, or episcopal enquiry, was to take place in the dioceses; it was to be directed against the persons of the Templars and carried out under the auspices of the Ordinary, assisted by two delegates from the cathedral chapter, two Dominicans and two Franciscans; the other was the papal enquiry, directed against the order itself and carried out by commissioners appointed by the pope. Provincial councils were to judge individuals in accordance with the results of

---

[1] Langlois, in *Journal des Savants*, 1908, p. 429.
[2] Finke, *op. cit.* VOL. II, pp. 140–50.
[3] In August 1308, they appeared before the Cardinals Bérenger Frédol, Étienne de Suisy and Landolfo Brancacci, and confessed their guilt. See Finke, *op. cit.* VOL. II, pp. 324–8.

the diocesan enquiries; while an œcumenical council would decide the fate of the order after the investigation made by the papal commissioners. The first session of the General Council was to take place at Vienne, on imperial soil, on 1 October 1310. Meanwhile, the Templars' property was in theory to be held in trust by four persons in each diocese, two designated by the bishops and two by the king; in actual fact the king disposed of this property as he pleased, since he had been skilful enough to compel the bishops to accept men devoted to himself. Clement V made one last mistake—though indeed he could scarcely have acted otherwise: he made Philip responsible for the custody of the Templars, and thus gave him the opportunity to impede the subsequent progress of the trial.

The tribunals of the Inquisition instituted in July and August 1308 were slow to begin the work. The papal commission met for the first time on 8 August 1309 and did not actually function until the following November, when it met at the Benedictine monastery of Sainte-Geneviève in Paris. It can hardly be regarded as having enjoyed any real independence of the French king, for the pope had acted weakly in having it composed of prelates who had Philip's interests at heart. The president was Gilles Aycelin, that same archbishop of Narbonne who, at Poitiers in 1308, had made a violent speech in condemnation of the order and called for its suppression. The assessors were Guillaume Durant, bishop of Mende; Guillaume Bonnet, bishop of Bayeux; Renaud de la Porte, bishop of Limoges; Mathieu de Naples, an apostolic notary; Giovanni of Mantua, auditor of cardinal Pietro Colonna; Jean de Montlaur, archdeacon of Maguelonne; Jean Agarvi, provost of Aix-en-Provence. All these churchmen failed in their duty, at least in this that they allowed officers of the king to be present at interrogations and did not respect the secrecy of depositions made to them.[1]

As had already happened during the winter of 1307–08, many of the Templars, confident of the impartiality of the papal commission, recanted their confessions, and explained that their earlier admissions had been extracted under torture. Brother Ponsard di Gisi described the appalling suffering that was inflicted upon them: 'Three months before my confession,' he recounts, 'I had my hands bound behind my back, so tightly that the blood gushed from my nails, and I was put into a pit and tied by a tether. If I am made to suffer such torture again, I will deny all that I am now saying, and tell you anything you wish. I am prepared to suffer torture, so long as it does not last long; they can cut off my head, or boil me alive for the honour of the

[1] G. Lizerand, *Clément V et Philippe IV le Bel*, Paris 1910, pp. 128–32, 139–50.

order; but I cannot bear slow tortures such as have been inflicted on me for more than two years in prison.'[1] Many others said the same.

Jacques de Molai's attitude was less noble. Terrorised, ill-advised, deprived of legal aid, the plaything of Guillaume de Plaisians, he did worse than fail to defend his order; he deserted it. The other holders of high office were equally pusillanimous: reading their depositions, it is impossible to avoid the impression that their dominant emotion was the fear of death. They were frightened of their judges, and cast about for any subterfuge to avoid being compromised. When they were confronted with the crimes confessed by their brethren, they pled ignorance, or prevaricated. Yet, everything considered, if they did not defend their order, neither did they condemn it, nor supply any weapons to attack it.[2]

The cause of the Templars, then, did not appear to be going too badly about May 1310. Those who, braver than their leaders or perhaps merely more ingenuous, came forward to defend their order, reached the number of five hundred and seventy-three. The witnesses for the prosecution were a few laymen, brought forward by the king's men, and their allegations were vague and incoherent. It seemed likely that the trial would turn out badly for Philip the Fair. Once again, however, he did not hesitate to try one of those strokes of violence that had been so successful in the past. At his instigation Philippe de Marigny, the brother of the minister Enguerrand and recently made archbishop of Sens, convoked to Paris a provincial council which, according to the law, had the right to judge the Templars. The members of the papal commission made no serious attempt to prevent this council from opening proceedings before their own enquiry was complete. When the Templars, feeling that they were lost, implored Gilles Aycelin to intervene on their behalf, that prelate replied with various excuses, either that he had to hear a Mass or celebrate one. His assessors declared themselves powerless to curb the action of Philippe de Marigny, action which was more-over strictly legal. On 11 May 1310, without having given any further hearing to the accused, the provincial council of Sens condemned as relapsed heretics fifty-four Templars who had recanted their earlier confessions. The next day these unfortunate men died at the stake outside the walls of Paris, between St Antoine and the windmill. To the very last they protested their innocence.[3] In like manner nine were burned at the stake at Senlis on 16 May. The surviving

---

[1] Langlois, in *Revue des deux mondes*, VOL. CIII, 1891, p. 408.
[2] *Ibid.* p. 406–08.   [3] Lizerand, *op. cit.* pp. 155–7.

Templars were horror-stricken. The knight Aimery de Villiers-le-Duc, pale and dispirited, cried out before the papal commissioners on 13 May: 'I confessed to some things because of the tortures inflicted on me by Guillaume de Marcilly and Hugues de la Celle, knights of the King; but they were not true. Yesterday, when I saw fifty-four of my brethren going in carts to the stake because they would not confess to the sins imputed to us, I thought that I should never be able to withstand the fear of the fire. I know in my heart that I would confess to anything; I would confess that I had killed God, if they asked me.'[1]

The fear of the stake had its effect. The defenders of the Temple faded away. Only confessions were now heard, about two hundred as against twelve denials. The papal commission, being as it were in a state of paralysis, saw no point in summoning three-quarters of those who had undertaken to defend the order. With the consent of the pope who had declared himself satisfied, the commission brought its proceedings to an end on 5 June 1311.[2]

On the whole the papal enquiry in France had been unfavourable to the Templars. The same cannot be said of the enquiries set on foot in the rest of Europe.

Immediately after the rounding up of the Templars on 13 October 1307, Philip the Fair had warmly encouraged other sovereigns to follow his example: he met with resistance on every hand. Writs for arrest were issued only after Clement V's order of 22 November. In England, Edward II allowed the Templars to continue in provisional liberty for some considerable time. The Council of London, which met on 20 October 1309, put them into close confinement and had them interrogated to no purpose; it broke up without having found any conclusive evidence against the order. It was the same at the councils held at York, on 30 July 1311, and in Ireland and Scotland. As for the members of the papal committee of enquiry, in order to achieve even a trumped-up charge, they were reduced to listening to a large number of witnesses not themselves members of the Temple.[3]

The attempts made to brand the Templars in Spain with heresy and idolatry failed completely. A verdict of not guilty was pronounced by the councils of Tarragona (October 1310–4 November 1312) and Salamanca (October 1310). In the same way, the papal enquiry resulted in a declaration of the order's innocence.[4]

[1] Langlois, in *Revue des deux mondes*, VOL. CIII, 1891, p. 411.
[2] Michelet, *op. cit.* VOL. II, pp. 270–3.
[3] Delaville le Roulx, 'La Suppression des Templiers,' *R.Q.H.* VOL. XLVIII, 1890, pp. 40–2; see also Finke, *op. cit.* VOL. I, pp. 312–17.
[4] Finke, *op. cit.* VOL. I, pp. 282–312.

In Germany, despite the use of torture, the commission appointed
by Clement V could collect only evidence in favour of the Templars,
and honourably paid them a public tribute.[1]

Provence, the kingdom of Naples and the Papal States, all subject
to influence by the king of France, were the only countries where
certain depositions laid before the provincial synods tended to prove
the existence of the crimes with which the French Templars were
charged. And it must be said that such depositions were extremely
few and came from persons of secondary importance, who, on the
rack, said anything their torturers wanted.[2]

In Cyprus, the order was at first acquitted; but the accession of
Henry of Lusignan to the throne proved disastrous for it. At the
pope's instigation, a fresh enquiry was instituted; but before any
legal judgment could be made, the Templars were put to death by
drowning or burning. Their appalling death was a political crime:
Henry of Lusignan was taking his vengeance on those who had given
powerful assistance to his brother Amaury de Tyre in his attempt to
gain the throne.[3]

To sum up, the twofold enquiry set up by Clement V resulted in
conclusions that were somewhat contradictory, but for the most part
favourable to the Templars. As a result, the General Council which
met at last on 16 October 1311 at Vienne was, on the whole, well disposed towards them. To the pope's deep disappointment, the high
commission, which had been set up to review the trial, in December
expressed the view, held by a large majority, that the Templars
should be permitted to appear and put forward their defence.
Clement, who was determined to ruin them, tried the effect of a
diversion, and encouraged the discussion of reforms to be introduced
in the Church, and plans for a crusade. Meanwhile Philip the Fair,
careful not to lose the game to which he was pledged, consulted the
Estates at Lyons, revived the trial of Boniface VIII which had
momentarily been forgotten, and worked on public opinion. When
he thought the time was ripe, he went to Vienne, intimidated the
opposition and coerced the waverers by threats or promises. On
22 March 1312, in a secret consistory, the members of the commission voted for the suppression of the Templars by a four-fifths'
majority. The Fathers of the council would perhaps not have ratified
this decision, but, at the second session on 3 April, they learned that
silence was to be imposed upon them on pain of excommunication,
and they had to listen to the reading of the papal sentence. Clement V

---

[1] Finke, *op. cit.* VOL. I, pp. 317–20.   [2] *Ibid.* pp. 320–2.
[3] *Ibid.* pp. 322–3. See also Delaville le Roulx, *op. cit.* pp. 47–9.

abolished the order by virtue of his apostolic authority, and by way of precaution rather than of condemnation. After overcoming much resistance from Philip the Fair and the Fathers, the pope decreed at the third session of the Council on 3 May, that the property of the Templars should be handed over to the Hospitallers of St John of Jerusalem, except in the kingdoms of Aragon, Castile, Portugal and Majorca, where it should fall to the national orders then engaged in fighting the Saracens. Finally, on 6 May, he allowed the provincial councils to settle the fate of individual Templars, leaving for himself the sentences to be imposed on the Grand Master, the Visitor for France, on Olivier de Penne, and on the overseas preceptors of Normandy, Aquitaine, Poitou and Provence. On the same day the Council of Vienne came to an end. It had really been nothing more than an expedient designed under pressure from Philip the Fair to give an appearance of legality to the speedy winding up of the trial of the Templars. The other business on the agenda of the Council, such as Church reform and the crusade, had been despatched in all haste.[1]

The great wealth of the Templars aroused everyone's greed. Lesser princes as well as the great sovereigns hoped that they would have their share of the booty. Clement V's decision disappointed them all. If Philip the Fair had really worked to destroy the order, with a view to growing rich on its spoils, then the issue must have proved a cruel disappointment. His financial difficulties were not lessened, even while he was receiving the revenues from the confiscated property,[2] though he received at least 200,000 pounds *tournois* as compensation from the Hospitallers.

In other countries, the knights of St John had to agree to tiresome compromises. But despite the difficulties they encountered from those whose hopes had been dashed, within ten years they had taken possession of the greater part of the landed property of the Temple all over Europe.[3]

---

[1] Lizerand, *op. cit.* pp. 250–340. See also Finke, *op. cit.* VOL. I, pp. 345–69. The Council ordered a sexennial tenth to be levied for the organisation of the crusade that Philip the Fair promised to undertake. It also dealt with the question of the Spirituals (see F. Ehrle, 'Zur Vorgeschichte des Concils von Vienne,' *Archiv*, VOL. II, 1886, pp. 353–416; VOL. III, 1887, pp. 1–95, 409–552), issued certain edicts concerning the reform of the Church and morals (see J. Haller, *Papsttum und Kirchenreform*, Berlin 1903, pp. 52–73), and after hearing the complaints of the whole episcopate, did nothing more than declare that those who threatened the liberties of the Church would be excommunicated (see M. Heber, *Gutachten und Reformschläge für das Vienner General-concil (1311–1312)*, Leipzig 1896; J. Duffour, 'Doléances des évêques gascons au Concile de Vienne (1311),' *Revue de Gascogne*, 1905, pp. 244–59; G. Lizerand, *op. cit.* pp. 309–36). On the Council, see M. Debièvre, 'La Définition du Concile de Vienne sur l'âme (6 mai 1312),' *Recherches de science religieuse*, VOL. III, 1912, pp. 321–44; Cl. Bouvier, *Vienne au temps du Concile (1311–1312)*, Paris 1912.
[2] Borrelli de Serres, *op. cit.* VOL. III, p. 39.
[3] Delaville le Roulx, *Les Hospitaliers à Rhodes*, Paris 1913, pp. 28–50.

The fate of the dignitaries of the order had not been settled at the Council of Vienne. At long last, on 22 December 1313[1] Clement V delegated to the three cardinals, Nicolas de Fréauville, Arnaud d'Aux and Arnaud Nouvel, the authority to pronounce final judgment upon them. Their sentence was read out to the crowd that had gathered before Notre-Dame on 18 March 1314. The leaders of the order were sentenced to life imprisonment. In a burst of sincerity and courage, Jacques de Molai and Geoffroi de Charnay cried out, 'We are not guilty of those things of which we are accused, but we are guilty of having basely betrayed the order to save our lives. The order is pure; it is holy; the accusations are absurd and the confessions false.'[2] Taken aback at this unexpected incident, the cardinals put off their decision until the following day, and contented themselves for the time being with handing Molai and Charnay over to the Provost of Paris. That very day, the king's council decided that the two renegades should be put to death without delay. As it grew toward dusk, the fire was built up on the Ile des Javiaux and its flames cast their gloomy light on the walls of the royal palace. Molai and Charnay died heroically with their eyes turned towards Notre-Dame, still proclaiming their innocence.[3]

Certain facts emerge from the foregoing account which make it possible to come to a definite conclusion concerning the extremely perplexing question of the guilt of the Templars. Earlier historians have resolved this question in various ways according to their personal prejudices, because they lacked the necessary material for forming a final judgment. The question of the Templars' guilt does not arise except for the French section of the order: in all European countries not under French influence, the Templars' innocence was abundantly evident. Even in France, the problem is reduced to a few points of detail: were the denial of Christ, the spitting on the crucifix, the encouragement of sodomy, the obscene kisses, the adoration of the idol Baphomet[4] prescribed by the rule? Did they form part of the

---

[1] *Regestum Clementis Papae V*, no. 10337.

[2] Langlois, in *Revue des deux mondes*, VOL. CIII, 1891, p. 419.

[3] Molai's attitude is surprising. On 24 and 25 October 1307, he confessed to the crimes of which the order was accused; the following spring he withdrew this confession in the presence of the papal commissioners; in August 1308, at Chinon, he again confessed; in November 1309, though he did not repeat this confession, he did nothing to defend the order; he protested his innocence on 18 March 1314. Viollet has put forward the suggestion that Cardinal Bérenger Frédol falsified the depositions made at Chinon in the hope of saving Molai's life. This would explain why he was so amazed to hear his alleged deposition read out in 1309. See *Les Interrogatoires de Jacques de Molai*, Paris 1909. Lizerand has rejected this hypothesis, giving substantial reasons for his objection. See 'Les Dépositions du grand maître Jacques de Molay au procès des Templiers (1307–1308),' *Le Moyen Age*, VOL. XXVI, 1913, pp. 81–106.

[4] Following a paper read by M. Salomon Reinach to the Académie des Inscriptions et Belles-lettres on 26 August 1910, on the origins of the legend that the Templars had

ceremony of initiation? Were they customary at chapter-meetings?

It should be noted in the first place that the surprise perquisitions made by the royal sergeants in the autumn of 1307 yielded no material evidence. They found no idols, no heretical books, no copy of a secret rule extolling an immoral way of life. All they could seize were copies of the pure and noble rule of St Bernard, translations of the Bible into the vulgar tongue and a large number of account books. A head made of silver-gilt was exhibited in Paris, containing female bones and bearing the inscription *Caput LVIII*; it was a reliquary such as is still frequently used by popular devotion to deck altars on feast days.[1] In 1789 a chest of carved stone, on which Arabic characters were engraved, was dug up at Essenois, a few miles from the site of the Voulaine commandery. One archaeologist tried to identify this with the Ark where the mysterious idol Baphomet was kept;[2] but he was unable to produce any evidence in support of this theory, which existed only in his own imagination. There are a number of small bronze statuettes in the Louvre, with the word *Baphomet* engraved on the base. One of them is even dated 1156. Monsieur Héron de Villefosse has submitted these to a searching investigation, and concluded that they are clumsy fakes. 'It is likely,' he wrote, 'that the date for the manufacture [of these fakes] cannot be put much earlier than 1819: a year in which there was much discussion concerning the practices of magic and sorcery attributed to the Templars.'[3] There is, therefore, no material proof whatever of the infamy of the knights.

We must now consider whether the verbal evidence provides acceptable proof of their guilt. At first sight, the confessions obtained in France seem so multifarious and so precise in detail that they baffle all attempts to form an opinion. A critical examination of this evidence, however, can do much to dispel the first unfortunate impression. Heinrich Finke [4] has performed the service of proving categorically that the reports of the French trials cannot be used as historical proof of the guilt of the order.

Whatever the outcome, it is extremely unlikely that the admission ceremonies could have been tainted for a long time by any blasphemous or ignoble rites without any hint of them being noised abroad.

worshipped Baphomet, it was stated that there is no idol at present existing that was once thought to be a 'Baphomet.'   [1] Michelet, *op. cit.* VOL. II, p. 218.
  [2] A mould of this casket is in the Dijon museum, and there is a reproduction of it in Loiseleur, *La Doctrine secrète des Templiers*, Paris 1872. See also E. Pfeiffer, 'Zwei vermeintliche Templerdenkmale,' *Zeitschrift für Kulturgeschichte*, VOL. IV, 1897, pp. 385–419; Mignard, *Monographie du coffret du duc de Blacas*, Paris 1852; S. Reinach, 'La Tête magique des Templiers,' *Revue de l'histoire des religions*, VOL. LXIII, 1911, pp. 25–39.
  [3] *Bulletin de la Société nationale des antiquaires de France*, 1900, pp. 305–12.
  [4] Finke, *op. cit.* VOL. I, pp. 326–44.

How could it be that there was none to protest among men so famed for their piety as were the Templars? How could an order to which so many honourable men belonged have based its principles of belief and its rule on such wickedness? Truth, however, can sometimes be improbable. But if we do for one moment suppose that the Templars did indulge in shameful practices and detestable error, we are confronted by a further improbability, namely that not one among them died for this alleged heresy. Not one Templar persisted in the errors he confessed; all abjured them without a moment's hesitation. Not one deluded soul died to defend his belief or to uphold the honour of his practices. The fire consumed only those who refused to admit their guilt, or withdrew confessions extorted by violence or the fear of torture.

If we consider one by one the statements of the Templars who pleaded guilty, new difficulties arise. Why do these supposedly true statements not agree with each other? When the Templars were asked to describe the idol, in the form of a head, which they confessed they had worshipped, the judges received completely contradictory answers. 'For one this head was white, for another black, gilded for a third, a fourth had seen its eyes blazing like carbuncles, a fifth had seen two faces, a sixth three faces, another gave it two pairs of legs, and yet another three heads. One said it was "a statue," another "a painting on a plaque." One said, "We believed it to be our Saviour," another "It is Baphomet or Mahomet." For some it was the Creator, who makes the trees blossom and ripens the harvest; for others, a friend of God, a powerful intercessor. Some had heard it speak; others had seen it suddenly turn into a black cat, or a crow, or a demon in the guise of a woman.'[1]

The use of torture is sufficient explanation and excuse for the large number of confessions, but at the same time it invalidates them. How could a man withstand such torments as are described by Bernard de Vado? 'So greatly was I tortured, so long was I held before a burning fire, that the flesh of my heels was burned away: and these two bones, which I now show to you, these came away from my feet. Look and see,' he added, turning to the papal commissioners, 'if they be not missing from my body.'[2] In Paris thirty-six prisoners died as a result of the tortures inflicted on them by the bishop's executioners.[3]

The methods used in the enquiry allowed of only one way of escaping the stake: confession. This was the sensible course followed

---

[1] Langlois, in *Revue des deux mondes*, VOL. CIII, 1891, p. 415.
[2] Raynouard, *Monuments historiques relatifs à la condamnation des Templiers*, Paris 1813, p. 73.   [3] Raynouard, *op. cit.* p. 63.

by ignorant men, depressed after lengthy confinement, terrified by the threats of their gaolers or intimidated by the legal experts who had charge of the interrogations. Philip the Fair was so well aware of the insincerity of his prisoners' confessions that he would not allow either Molai or any of the other dignitaries of the order to appear before the pope in 1308. At the Council of Vienne, when seven knights came forward to defend their order, Clement V had them put in irons, to get rid of awkward witnesses whose revelations might perhaps influence the Fathers.[1] Nor was this all: though Clement suppressed the Templars, he did not condemn them; he proceeded cautiously, and to support his decision—which was not to be disputed—he invoked the unprecedented scandal that the trial had caused in the Christian world. The order was too notorious and had lost its reputation too thoroughly to continue in existence.

The unanimity of the confessions is largely counterbalanced by the solemn affirmations made in support of the order's innocence. As we have seen, in 1310 nearly six hundred knights rose in its defence. Their declarations are all the more worthy of belief because exceptional courage was needed to proclaim the truth. If a man recanted he was considered perjured and a relapsed heretic, and this was tantamount to condemning himself to the stake.

The absence of material proof, the improbability of the charges, the contradictory nature of the statements, the brutal methods used at the enquiry, the number of recantations, the courage of those who defended the order—all go to prove the Templars' innocence.[2] Their trial was a trumped-up affair, and bears the unmistakable mark of Guillaume de Nogaret. The relentless pursuit of the Templars shows the same tactics as those employed against Boniface VIII and Guichard de Troyes: a war of propaganda, the summoning of the Estates, speeches to the common people, violence, charges of heresy and grotesque accusations of dealings with succubi and incubi.[3] The whole course of the trial reveals the undisguised hand of Nogaret. The arrest of the Templars, like that of the Jews in 1306 and the Lombard bankers in 1291, came suddenly. The technique seems to have been Nogaret's own invention, for it was he who had taken charge of the great seal on the previous 22 September. It was he who arrested the Templars living in Paris, drew up the writ of accusation

---

[1] Lizerand, op. cit. p. 259.

[2] It cannot be denied that some Templars committed acts contrary to faith and morals. But these are only individual cases, which in no way impugn the reputation of the order as a whole.

[3] A. Rigaud, Le Procès de Guichard, évêque de Troyes, Paris 1896. See also Ch. V. Langlois, in Histoire de France (ed. Lavisse), VOL. III, pt 2, pp. 201–21.

against the order, and, in defiance of all principles of law, was present at the interrogation of the accused either in person or through the intermediary of his kindred spirit, Guillaume de Plaisians. In the Estates of Tours Nogaret played a major part, for he had been authorised to represent several of the great lords of Languedoc.

It is impossible to know for certain whether Nogaret inspired the king's policy, or was simply carrying out the orders of Philip the Fair. In any case, the king and his minister together contrived the suppression of the Templars. To achieve their ends, they exerted overbearing pressure on a pope poor in health and weak and conciliatory in character. They blackmailed Clement V by constantly threatening him with the resumption of the trial of Boniface VIII. In this way they succeeded in overcoming the pontiff's distaste for the task, and forced him to make the most regrettable concessions.

2

The Trial of Boniface VIII

The trial of the Templars is very closely linked with that of Boniface VIII: the one cannot be understood without the other.

In the course of the struggle between Philip the Fair and Boniface, Nogaret, in order to counter the attack on the king, had accused that pontiff of serious crimes—sodomy, heresy and simony—and had demanded that he should be severely punished. Once begun the trial did not end with the pope's death, for Nogaret pursued the memory of the dead man with extraordinary bitterness and did everything in his power to procure his final condemnation. Benedict XI was skilful enough to avoid calling a council, and to consider Philip's case separately from that of his minister, Nogaret. He annulled the measures taken against the kingdom of France, conferred favours on the king and granted a general absolution to the guilty parties. Only the instigators of the outrage at Anagni failed to receive a pardon; on 8 June 1304 they were summoned to appear at Perugia on the 28th of the same month.[1]

The outlook for Nogaret seemed black; but the death of Benedict calmed his fears. Clement V was a much less formidable opponent. With great skill, Nogaret saw to it that his own interests were closely interwoven with those of the king, and played in masterly fashion

[1] Ch. Grandjean, *Les Registres de Benoît XI*, Paris 1885, nos. 1254, 1255, 1257, 1258, 1260, 1261, 1263, 1276.

upon the fear that the resumption of the trial of Boniface VIII roused at the papal court. Each time that Clement hazarded some resistance to the king's wishes, he saw the trial revived; he saw it as lightly adjourned whenever he had weakly consented to the demands made upon him.

From the beginning of his reign, although he kept up an appearance of respect for his predecessor and made certain reservations, Clement lost no time in annulling, on 1 February 1306, the two notorious Bulls of Boniface VIII, *Clericis laicos* and *Unam sanctam,* which had exasperated Philip the Fair.'[1] The king seemed satisfied, and did not then insist on the resumption of the proceedings; he bided his time, and made the demand at Poitiers in 1307. The committee of cardinals which had assembled for this purpose arranged a compromise: the pope should annul the measures taken against France by Boniface and Philip should leave the task of ending the proceedings against the late pope's memory entirely in Clement's hands. But—either because the conditions under which Nogaret was to be released from excommunication seemed too harsh, or else because the intrigues of the Cardinals Colonna, who had hated Boniface, prevailed—the king refused to accept the Curia's offer of conciliation.[2]

At the time of the second meeting at Poitiers, on 6 July 1308, the case of the Templars was uppermost in the king's mind. Moreover, Philip now started making excessive demands: he asked for the canonisation of Celestine V, the alleged victim of Boniface, and wanted the pope's bones exhumed so that they could be burned. In vain Clement V tried to make him change his attitude; he had reluctantly to resign himself to granting permission, in the Consistory of 12 August, for the proceedings to be re-opened after Candlemas 1309.[3] This was one way of gaining time, and the expedient proved successful. The accusers of Boniface VIII did not come to Avignon until 16 March 1310: they were Nogaret, Guillaume de Plaisians, Pierre de Galard, the seneschal of Beaucaire, Pierre de Broc and the archdeacon of St Brieuc, Alain de Lamballe. The king had at first been included in the list, in the Bull of citation of 13 September 1309, but had prudently declined to give evidence, and Clement approved of his action. Among the defenders of Boniface were Cardinals Francesco Caetani and Giacomo Stefaneschi, together with some renowned Italian legal experts.

A fierce battle began between the two opposing camps. The

---

[1] *Corpus juris canonici,* Bk III, tit. xvii, *in Clem.; Extravagantes communes,* Bk V, tit. vii, ch. 2; *Regestum Clementis V,* no. 906.
[2] Lizerand, *Clément V et Philippe le Bel,* pp. 71–5.   [3] *Ibid.* pp. 134–7.

defenders and accusers of Boniface in turn made violent attacks upon each other, each pleading that the arguments of their opponents were inadmissible. Meanwhile Clement was using all his ingenuity to slow up the normal course of the proceedings as much as possible, by frequent adjournments of the hearing. Even an attack of nose-bleeding gave him an excuse to put off the appearance of the claimants until the following day. As summer approached he invented a new delaying tactic; he insisted that verbal proceedings should be given up, and that henceforward the opposing parties should make their depositions in writing. At that time no decision at all had been made about the admissibility of the evidence for either side. The pope's object was to persuade the king to waive his interest, and he offered to finish the business on his own. But this solution did not fit in with Philip's private ideas, and he bitterly reproached Clement for the slowness of the trial, and so in the heat of the summer of 1310, the witnesses for the prosecution were examined at Le Groseau, where the pope was staying.

In November, when the court returned to Avignon and the trial began again, Clement continued to prevaricate, this time with better prospects of success. He tried to create a diversion, and, in order to overcome Philip's obstinate attitude, refused to intervene on his behalf against the Flemings, while the supporters of Boniface made an alliance with the emperor of Germany and King Robert of Naples, by which the kingdom of Arles was restored to the house of Anjou. Philip the Fair took fright and sent an embassy to Avignon, where it was coldly received by Clement. The cardinals, who had the true interests of France at heart, advised the king to leave the trial of Boniface VIII to the pope. Philip was disturbed by their advice and in the end agreed to act on it. By February 1311 all difficulties had been smoothed out. Although the condition was not expressly stated in the king's letters, it was agreed that the fate of the Templars should be decided at the Council of Vienne. In return for this, the accusers of Boniface withdrew. A similar withdrawal had already been agreed to by his defenders.[1] A number of Bulls, dated 27 April, clarified the situation. Clement acquitted Philip, praised his zeal and solemnly declared his own good intentions. He annulled all acts made by Boniface VIII and Benedict XI after 1 November 1300 which were contrary to the interests of the king or his kindred; these acts were indeed to be erased from the papal registers within four months. Nogaret was provisionally released from excommunication—a grace for which he had been continually begging, but unsuccessfully—

[1] Lizerand, *op. cit.* pp. 190–243.

provided that he made certain pilgrimages, went to the Holy Land with the next crusade and stayed there, unless he were subsequently dispensed by the Holy See. Absolution was also granted to Sciarra Colonna, Rinaldo da Supino and the inhabitants of Anagni; but it was withheld from those who were still keeping the papal treasures that had been pillaged at the time of the attempt on the person of Boniface.[1]

It is true that the decisions made by Clement V were humiliating for the papacy and cast a slur on the conduct of his immediate predecessors; but they had the enormous advantage of imposing silence on the most bitter accusers of Boniface VIII, and of interrupting a trial which had shocked the whole of Christendom. But to prolong the agony, Philip would not allow the proceedings to be definitely closed. Witnesses for the prosecution and the defence were still free to give evidence. The king would not abandon a weapon of intimidation which had proved highly effective in his dealings with Clement, and indeed, at the Council of Vienne, Philip threatened to resume the trial of Boniface VIII as soon as the Fathers showed themselves unwilling to condemn the Templars. Later, on 5 May 1313, to humour the monarch, Clement canonised Celestine V.[2] But in order to bear witness to the legality of the election of Boniface and the validity of Celestine's renunciation, he was careful to canonise the latter under the name of Pietro da Morrone.[3]

3

The Papacy and France from John XXII to Gregory XI

Although Clement V did from time to time suffer the constraint of Philip the Fair to an unwarranted degree, he none the less eluded his importunities on many occasions, notably in the question of the election to the throne of Germany.[4] The policy of his successors was consistently favourable to France, but without servility; on occasion, they proved quite independent.

The Avignon popes showed their favour especially by giving financial assistance to the kings of France. They advanced them considerable sums of money during the monetary crises caused by the

---

[1] *Regestum Clementis V*, nos. 7501, 7503, 7504, 7507.
[2] Rinaldi, *ad annum* 1313, §40–2. See also Cocquelines, *Bullarum*, VOL. III, pt 2, pp. 140–3.
[3] C. Borromeo, *Avignone e la politica di Filippo il Bello nella canonizzazione di Pietro da Morrone*, Modena 1894. [4] See above, pp. 190–1.

misfortunes of the Hundred Years' War,[1] and allowed them to benefit from certain taxes levied on ecclesiastical benefices, such as tenths, annates and caritative subsidies.[2]

The profits from the sexennial tenths, decreed in 1312 and 1333 for the purpose of the crusade, were to be handed over to the kings of France, who had been appointed captains-general of the proposed expedition. But neither Philip the Fair, Louis X nor Philip VI of Valois had any desire to go to the Holy Land and the money collected for this expedition was used for the war in Flanders and the general needs of the kingdom. John XXII and Clement VI dispensed the kings from any obligation to make good the money thus misappropriated.

In addition to these tenths, the popes granted many others. The amount received was sometimes considerable. In 1330, the net revenue from taxes that found its way into the royal coffers amounted to 265,990 livres *tournois*, 14 shillings and 8 pence, or, in gold, 4,872,936·80 francs.

Philip the Tall had the unprecedented privilege of collecting the annates in France, Navarre and the county of Burgundy for a space of four years beginning on 14 September 1316. Such a favour was never again granted, despite the urgent entreaties of the kings.

Philip the Tall also received some caritative subsidies at the beginning of the reign of John XXII. But later neither he nor his successors were able to overcome the unwillingness of the pope who pleaded that the Gallican church had already been drained dry. Benedict XII, Clement VI and Innocent VI also refused to listen to the repeated demands they received. Urban V, however, allowed himself to be persuaded, and on 17 July 1364 permitted Charles V to levy a subsidy; but this favour was withdrawn, since the conditions he imposed were not fulfilled. On 21 July 1369 Charles at last received authority to levy a subsidy of two years' duration on the whole kingdom with the exception of the Languedoc. Gregory XI was more gracious to him and the last subsidy he granted to the king continued until 18 September 1377.[3]

Such advantages were not exclusively reserved to the kings of France. The Emperor Charles IV and the kings of Aragon, Castile, Majorca, Naples, Hungary, Norway and England all enjoyed some tenths.[4] Nevertheless, it appears that the financial aid given to the

---

[1] See above, p. 38–9.   [2] On the question of these taxes, see below, Bk III, ch. 11.
[3] Samaran and Mollat, *La Fiscalité pontificale en France au XIVᵉ siècle*, Paris 1905, pp. 14–20, 24, 59.
[4] E. Hennig, *Die päpstlichen Zehnten*. See also L. Möller, *Die Einnahmen*, pp. 98*–99*.

French royal house surpassed in both variety and value that granted to sovereigns of other nations. It should be noted, however, that Clement VI's only reason for allowing John the Good to levy an extraordinary tax, a thirtieth, on the clergy was to facilitate the repayment of the sums he had lent to the Crown, and that certain tenths were used to drive out the Great Companies, which were as great a threat to the Church as they were to France itself.

Not content with promising the kings of France substantial financial aid, the Avignon popes also gave vigorous support to their foreign policy. If, for example, Philip the Tall conquered the Flemings, was it not due to the use of what a chronicler has picturesquely called the 'papal arms'—*armis papalibus*—in other words, to the use of sentences of excommunication and interdict pronounced against the rebels.[1] Some fifteen years later, Benedict XII used all his ingenuity to prevent the Flemish towns from becoming the allies of England: he excommunicated Count William of Hainault, who had dared to revolt against his sovereign lord Philip VI and make an alliance with Edward III of England. When, due to French pressure, Count Henry IV, of Bar, was betrothed to Yolande, the daughter of Robert of Cassel, who had earlier been promised to Louis de Maele the pope feared that hostilities might break out between the houses of Flanders and Bar, and, to avoid any such danger, sent Queen Jeanne of France a marriage dispensation to use as she thought fit.[2] When Edward III sought the hand of Margaret, heiress of Flanders, for his fourth son, Edmund, earl of Cambridge, he found himself in conflict with Urban V, who refused to grant him 'a general dispensation so that his children might contract marriages with their kinsfolk to the third or fourth degree' (18 December 1364). On 30 October 1365, the pope revoked all marriage dispensations granted in general terms to the English sovereign by Clement VI and Innocent VI and, on 3 November 1367, all reciprocal undertakings made by Edmund and Margaret. On the other hand, he removed all obstacles to the marriage of that princess with Duke Philip of Burgundy. Urban did not want Margaret's inheritance, which included Flanders, Artois and the Nivernais, to fall into English hands; and indeed, this would have been an unprecedented disaster for the French.[3] In a word, it is obvious that the papacy was on the side of France rather than of England during the Hundred Years' War.

[1] P. Lehugeur, *Histoire de Philippe le Long, roi de France (1316–1322)*, Paris 1897, pp. 120–50. [2] A. Fierens, *Lettres de Benoît XII*, pp. xiv–xxviii.
[3] M. Prou, *Étude sur les relations politiques du pape Urbain V avec les rois de France, Jean II et Charles V (1362–1370)*, Paris 1888, pp. 74–6. See also R. Delachenal, *Histoire de Charles V*, Paris 1909–28, VOL. III, pp. 499–510.

Despite certain appearances to the contrary, the relationship of the Avignon popes with France was in no way tainted with servility. They supported French diplomacy to the utmost, because to do so was in their own interests. John XXII, it is true, flattered Philip the Tall, Charles the Fair and Philip of Valois; but this was done so that they would adopt his Italian policy and support him against Louis of Bavaria. In turn, Clement VI, Innocent VI, Urban V and Gregory XI, who had no reason to fear anything from the Empire, set themselves to restore peace between France and England. Their legates were constantly being sent out into the highways and byways, scouring battlefields, forcing truces or armistices on the belligerents. Sometimes peace talks took place at Avignon, although the negotiations never in fact had any definite result. For this the English blamed the Holy See, which they accused—not without some apparent reason—of favouring their enemies. Yet the attitude of the French popes was dictated not so much by patriotism as by their desire to carry out their cherished plans for a crusade; for the journey to the Holy Land could never take place until the kings of France and England, the eventual leaders of such an expedition, were reconciled.

Benedict XII, far from being influenced by Philip VI of Valois, as has been generally supposed, had interests totally opposed to those of the king. A man of 'imperious temperament,' he had determined to compel Louis of Bavaria to bow to his authority, by isolating him and grouping the other Christian princes round the Holy See. To succeed in such a plan he had to impose peace on Europe, an arduous task at a time when France and England were preparing for battle; but the pope did not hesitate to undertake it. Philip VI sought to make an alliance with Louis of Bavaria; Benedict forbade it. The king wanted to intervene between Scotland and England; the pope 'dissuaded him and turned him aside.' Philip announced the confiscation of Guyenne; Benedict requested him to revoke it. Most important of all, from 1337 until 1341, the supreme pontiff prevented the king of France from taking the offensive, at a time when, deprived of the help promised him by his allies, Edward III could easily have been crushed by his adversary. The king of England took advantage of Philip's mistake, made an alliance with Louis of Bavaria even though the pope forbade it, and secretly prepared for war.[1] Thus, though France and the papacy were often pursuing a common foreign policy, neither power was really concerned with anything except its own interests.

[1] E. Déprez, *Les Préliminaires de la guerre de Cent Ans*, Paris 1902, pp. 400–06 and *passim*.

Private relations between the kings of France and the popes of Avignon were often friendly and trusting, but they were not marked by excessive partiality or favour on the part of the popes in matters concerning the domestic affairs of the kingdom. There was a real friendship between John XXII and Philip the Tall. The pope had a deep affection for the king, whose attitude towards him was one of filial respect. John frequently gave him good advice and sometimes even rebuked him with a solicitude that is surprising. He urged him to be attentive at Mass and during the sermon, not to be shaved on Sunday, to avoid making unseemly gestures, to dress like a king and to reduce his household expenditure. If the king fell ill, the pope was anxious about his health. When he recovered, he rebuked him for not following the advice of his doctors, who had recommended a moderate diet, and, fearing that his advice would not be heeded, he asked Henri de Sully, the royal cellarer, to do his best to prevent Philip from indulging his convalescent greed.[1]

Philip the Tall made no secret of his gratitude to the pope. He was grateful to him for having dissolved the feudal leagues formed against him at the beginning of his reign, and for having prevented Queen Clementia, the widow of Louis X, from joining the party of the malcontents. Royal couriers were constantly coming to Avignon bearing gifts—joints of venison, cheeses, fish, precious jewels. Philip also lavished favours on the pope's relatives and the dignitaries of his court.[2]

Passing disagreements occasionally estranged the two friends. From time to time John XXII would interfere directly in the affairs of the kingdom. He had imposed a truce on Amanieu d'Albret and Sans-Aner de Pins, on Béraud de Mercœur and Hugues de Chalon, and on certain nobles from the Mâcon.[3] On two separate occasions, on 11 May and 17 August 1318, he had commissioned the bishops of Bayonne, Dax and Aire to give notice of a truce to Mathe and Bernard d'Armagnac and Marguerite de Foix.[4] Philip expressed his displeasure to the pope, and questioned his right to interfere in the affairs of the king's own vassals. Instead of giving him any satisfaction on this point, John XXII replied tersely: 'Surely, my son, if you think carefully about events that the future may hold in store, you cannot disapprove of the Holy See's exercising its right to impose truces, or find it prejudicial to yourself or your kingdom.'[5]

On other occasions, too, the supreme pontiff uncompromisingly

[1] Coulon, nos. 116, 1309, 1343, 1347, 1348, 1351, 1367, 1369. Lehugeur, *op. cit.* pp. 199–211.　　　　　　　　　　　　　　[2] Coulon, nos. 280, 966.
[3] *Ibid.* nos. 32–6, 583–7.　　　　　　　　[4] *Ibid.* nos. 588–678.
[5] *Ibid.* no. 704. See also *Bulletin critique*, VOL. VIII, ser. 2, p. 87.

upheld the old-established doctrine of the superiority of spiritual over temporal power. When the king complained that clerks supplied with apostolic letters received preference in obtaining benefices which he was keeping for his favourites, the pope politely refused to listen. When Philip V demanded the breaking off of proceedings against a member of his council, Bishop Guillaume Durant of Mende, accused of holding schismatical views, the pope overruled him. Furthermore, the parcelling out of the ecclesiastical province of Toulouse into several bishoprics took place without any warning or consultation of the king.[1]

These few examples, selected from among many others, indicate how great was John XXII's independence of Philip V. During the reigns of Charles the Fair, Philip VI, John II and Charles V, the pope and his successors were again to meddle in the kingdom's affairs, the only difference being that they were less heeded. The court of Avignon exercised in France a jurisdiction which was but little restricted, a jurisdiction which might even be described as sovereign. Some difficulties were to arise over the question of rights to the goods of deceased clergy, and the heirs of deceased bishops demanded justice of the King. In every known case, the papal treasury had the last word, and as a rule the king's officers confined their activities to delaying the settlement of the disputed inheritance. The papal tax-collectors did their work without encountering any serious obstacles; but the French kings would have been ungracious indeed had they impeded them, since they themselves had the privilege of levying subsidies on the clergy. Because they drew substantial profits from them, these monarchs were careful not to protest against papal reservations as did the English sovereigns. On the contrary, they even went so far as to beg the pope to extend them still further.[2]

The question of ecclesiastical jurisdiction gave rise to serious and prolonged disagreements between the papacy and the French royal house. The fourteenth century saw an extension of the influence of royal justice by means of a systematic encroachment on all other forms of justice in the kingdom, both in the seignorial courts and in those of the Church. Because the latter were better organised, more powerful and more respected, they were more bitterly opposed. It is true that in two ordinances, dated 1315 and 1316 respectively, both Louis X and Philip V had guaranteed ecclesiastical liberty and ordered their bailiffs to respect the rights of ecclesiastical courts;[3] but in practice there were a large number of petty conflicts. These grew to such

[1] Coulon, nos. 967, 775, 849, 374, 410, 516, 330.   [2] *Ibid.* no. 667.
[3] O. Martin, *L'Assemblée de Vincennes de 1329 et ses conséquences*, Paris 1909, pp. 44–6.

a pitch that an assembly of prelates and barons met in 1329 at Vincennes, or, to be more precise, in Paris, under the presidency of Philip V. The legal expert, Pierre de Cugnières, developed the thesis of the absolute distinction between the two jurisdictions, temporal and spiritual, and accordingly concluded that they could not both be in the hands of the same person.

The clergy's spokesmen, the bishop of Autun, Pierre Bertrand and Pierre Roger, the future Clement VI, instead of agreeing to concessions, boldly upheld the argument of possession, and the theory that temporal must be subordinate to spiritual justice; they undertook only to put down specified abuses. The king, for his part, invited the bishops, in very vague terms, to correct these abuses, and assured them that the Church in France would have nothing to fear in the future; indeed, no ordinance was promulgated. Yet the assembly of Vincennes, while not the starting-point of immediate action against ecclesiastical jurisdiction, did mark a significant stage in the slow and crafty war waged against it by the Parlement in Paris and by the secular courts. From this time onwards, there were continual conflicts. The officers of the king had no respect for the benefit of clergy: they arrested clerks, imprisoned them, judged them and even hanged them without any scruple. Benedict XII and his successors were often obliged to instruct the kings, either by letter or through legates, to safeguard the freedom of the Church.[1] For the most part their protests were fruitless. In 1372 there was great dismay at the Court of Avignon. A royal ordinance, dated 8 March, forbade French prelates to deal with actions of real estate which had up till then been submitted to their courts: 'Actions for recovery of property, suits of succession, possessory injunctions, suits for redemption in tail, actions concerning annual rents assessed on heritable property,' etc. Any trial in the ecclesiastical courts resulting in a decision adverse to the defendant was to be revoked. If they encountered opposition, the royal bailiffs were to proceed to constrain the offenders by seizure of their property and by other means. Gregory XI made a vigorous protest. Bulls were sent to the powerful nobles of the kingdom, urging them to dissuade Charles V from his plan.[2] Two nuncios came to the court. The king apparently withdrew his edict, but in 1377 new difficulties arose concerning a sentence of excommunication pronounced by the chapter at Lyons against judges in commercial actions.

Following the example of the king of England, Philip VI of Valois decreed that all goods, tithes and ecclesiastical revenues of

[1] *Ibid.* pp. 249–51, 254–6.   [2] *Ibid.* pp. 342–7, 404–07.

prelates and clergy not residing within the kingdom on 13 February 1347 should be seized. The cardinals who were affected by this ordinance quickly protested. Two internuncios, Guillaume Lamy (*Amici*) and Pasteur de Sarrats, brought the protests to Paris. Thanks to the queen's intervention, the king agreed to make a partial withdrawal of his edict, in so far as it affected cardinals, employees of the court at Avignon and his own entourage. But this was not enough for Clement VI. He gave notice of his intention, however reluctantly, to make use of 'opportune and proper remedies' if the king did not revoke his ordinance completely. Philip was not to be moved. The sequestrated benefices were not restored until October 1360, after the Treaty of Brétigny had been signed.

CHAPTER IV

The Papacy and England

1

The Reigns of Edward I and Edward II

A STATE of almost perfect understanding existed between Clement V and Edward I; doubtless the pope remembered how, as archbishop of Bordeaux, he had been the king's vassal. His goodwill towards Edward even led the pope to take his side against the English people: on 29 December 1305 he freed the king from all concessions previously granted to the great nobles, the barons and 'other persons,' concerning certain forest rights and royal prerogatives. Archbishop Winchelsey, the primate of the Church in England and one of the king's bitterest opponents, was summoned on 12 February 1306 to appear at the papal court, and, on 6 April, was suspended from his duties. The Apostolic Camera seized his revenues. In August 1306 Clement helped Edward by granting him a tenth; later, he helped to strengthen the peace between France and England by encouraging the marriage between the prince of Wales and Isabella, daughter of Philip the Fair; and he solemnly excommunicated Robert Bruce, who was stirring up trouble in Scotland.[1]

The English barons by no means approved of Clement V's interference in their country's affairs. At the Parliament of Carlisle, in January 1307, a pamphlet was read violently attacking him. He was accused of systematically excluding 'native Englishmen and learned clerks' from holding episcopal office, and consequently of depriving the king of the counsel of wise men who were concerned with the interests of the nation, and in this way of causing harm to the just government both of the Church in England and of the kingdom. 'The unbridled multitude of apostolic provisions' to strangers, especially to cardinals, had had, they alleged, disastrous consequences, such as the absenteeism of incumbents who nevertheless continued to draw the income from their benefices, the sending of capital

---

[1] Rymer, *Foedera*, VOL. I, pt 2, pp. 45, 49, 52, 53, 56, 61, 66. See also Stubbs, *Chronicles of the reigns of Edward I and Edward II* (Rolls Series), London 1882, VOL. I, p. 145.

outside English territory, the falling off of popular piety, the less frequent celebration of the divine office, the poor upkeep of sacred edifices which were falling into ruin for lack of repair, and the failure to distribute alms or to provide shelter for the needy, contrary to the express intention of the founders of churches.[1]

Although exaggerated and partly unfair, the complaints voiced by the Parliament at Carlisle do none the less express English public opinion in the fourteenth century. Successive parliaments continue to reiterate them and chroniclers and kings to paraphrase them. The truth is that chapters could not forgive the pope for the loss of their privileges of election, while laymen deplored the disappearance of rights that had entitled them to the patronage of religious foundations. Both clergy and laity were to point out with asperity that national usage was opposed to the growing tendency of the papacy to monopolise presentations to benefices: according to English law and custom, did not all ecclesiastical property remain in the possession of the patron? Had not the Constitutions of Clarendon declared that the king was entitled to the revenues from any archbishopric, bishopric, abbey or priory falling vacant within the lands under his jurisdiction? Did not the king invest prelates with their temporalities? To admit the popes' claims to the right to dispose of benefices as they pleased, or to burden them with taxes—England was the first country to pay annates—was tantamount to conspiring 'to disinherit the Crown of its rights and to destroy the English Church.'[2]

Edward I had too great a need of the Holy See's support against his barons to subscribe to the acrimonious declarations of the Parliament at Carlisle. He prudently manœuvred between the malcontents and Clement V.

His son, Edward II (1307–27), was less discreet. He issued ordinances decreeing that all bearers of documents or bulls in any way contrary to the interests of the Crown were to be seized and held. When the pope reserved the see of Worcester, the king wrote haughtily to the cardinals: 'We cannot suffer such unprecedented and unheard-of reservation to take place within our kingdom.' The Parliament of 1309 in its turn sent a letter of protest to the pope, in the name of all England.[3]

Clement V returned like for like. In 1310 the bishop of Poitiers, Arnaud d'Aux, presented the English king with a long list of grievances. He complained of the tiresome measures taken against the

[1] *Rotuli parliamentorum*, VOL. I, pp. 217–23.
[2] J. Haller, *Papsttum und Kirchenreform*, VOL. I, Berlin 1903, pp. 388–92.
[3] Rymer, *op. cit.* VOL. I, pt 2, p. 109.

cardinals to prevent them from enjoying their benefices in England, the impediments which hindered papal provisions from taking effect and which debarred recourse to papal justice, the encroachments of royal officials on ecclesiastical jurisdiction, the maladministration of monasteries and churches during vacancies and the non-payment by the Crown of taxes due to the Holy See.

The English clergy supported the pope's complaints. In the provincial synod of November 1309, Archbishop Winchelsey, the leader of the ultramontanists, who had been restored to favour and reinstated at Canterbury, had already posed as the champion of ecclesiastical liberty against the oppression of the king. Accompanied by several bishops, he read to Edward the remonstrances of Clement V.[1]

The king changed his attitude, apologised and took under his protection the collectors charged with the levying of annates. It was politically inadvisable for him to offend the pope, whose protection he needed more than ever, now that the royal favours lavished on Piers Gaveston had exasperated the barons.

There was a close friendship between Edward and this lord, the son of a gentle family of Guyenne, who had been in turn his childhood's playmate and his boon companion. Gaveston's influence on the young prince had been so pernicious that Edward I had banished him from England.

Immediately after his father's death, Edward recalled Gaveston from exile and loaded him with honours and riches. The disdain and the sarcastic tongue of the haughty favourite soon earned him the hatred of the barons, who shook off his detested yoke and in 1308 insisted on his dismissal.

This was a cruel separation for the king. He persuaded Clement V to annul Gaveston's oath promising not to return to England and, by a skilful distribution of favours, succeeded in breaking the opposition of his barons.

But the reconciliation was short-lived, for Gaveston's extravagant behaviour began again and civil war broke out. In an effort to avert the danger, the pope sent his vice-chancellor Arnaud Nouvel and his camerarius, Arnaud d'Aux to England.[2] The murder of Gaveston on 19 June 1312 made the task of the two nuncios easier, and in 1313 they succeeded in settling the differences between Edward and his nobles.[3]

[1] Stubbs, *op. cit.* VOL. I, pp. 161–7.
[2] *Regestum Clementis V*, no. 8786 (14 May 1312); Appendix, VOL. I, nos. 699–708.
[3] Lingard, *Histoire d'Angleterre*, VOL. I, Paris 1842, pp. 470–7.

But in sending help to Edward II, the pope had every intention of reaping some benefit for himself. Indeed, the annates were now collected without difficulty; the taxes owed by the crown were henceforward regularly paid; papal reservations were extended to include bishoprics and other benefices, both large and small; capitular elections hardly ever took place; after a preliminary agreement with the king, the pope nominated bishops, abbots, canons, priors and parish priests; expectative graces were generously distributed even to ecclesiastics who were not English.

John XXII took advantage of the difficulties of the king's situation to follow exactly the same line of conduct as his predecessor, or rather to increase the number of reservations and papal nominations. Far from protesting, Edward gave pensions to the cardinals and sought their favours. He did indeed owe a debt of gratitude to the supreme pontiff who placed the arms of the Church at the service of his throne.[1]

While England was grieved by civil war, sometimes overt and sometimes concealed, Robert Bruce roused Scotland and made himself its king. His brilliant victory at Bannockburn on 23 June 1314 had ratified his act of usurpation. From that time, following Edward's refusal to recognise the kingship of Bruce, there was a constant state of hostility between the two countries. Drunk with power, the Scots made their way to Ireland, hoping to drive out the English. The campaign, at first successful, ended in a series of bloody defeats, caused by the lack of discipline of the Irish. To make good the disaster, Robert Bruce landed on the Ulster coast with a large army. John XXII opposed him resolutely, and the bishops of Cashel and Dublin and the dean of Dublin were ordered to excommunicate the invaders as well as the Irish clergy who were constantly inciting the people to rebel against England.[2] At about the same time, the pope sent Cardinals Gaucelme de Jean and Luca Fieschi to impose peace on the belligerents.[3]

This papal intervention caused much indignation among the Irish chieftains, who justified their conduct to the nuncios and begged the Holy See to protect them against persecution by the English. The memorandum that they sent to the pope excited his interest. Cardinals de Jean and Fieschi, speaking in the name of John XXII, requested Edward II to see to it that the acts of oppression which his Irish subjects claimed to have suffered were discontinued. The king

[1] Haller, *op. cit.* pp. 400–02.
[2] Rymer, *op. cit.* VOL. II, pt I, p. 118 (29 March 1317), p. 122 (10 April 1317).
[3] Many Bulls were issued, conferring full authority on them. See Mollat, nos. 5148–5223 (16 March 1317), 5208–23 (24 April), 5232–4 (1 May).

promised to heed their protests, and undertook to deal justly and leniently with the rebels. Shortly afterwards, on 5 October 1318, Edward, the brother of Robert Bruce and leader of the Scots army, died on the battlefield of Faughart. With his death, peace returned to Ireland.[1]

In Scotland itself the pope intervened with equal energy. As early as 16 March 1317, Gaucelme de Jean and Luca Fieschi had been empowered to take proceedings against Robert Bruce. The apostolic letters omitted the title of 'King' to which the pretender laid claim. Their superscription bore these significant words: *Nobili viro Roberto de Brus impresentiarum regnum Scotie, ut dicitur, gubernanti.* A Bull of 24 April gave the legates permission to take disciplinary action against Robert if he opposed a peace-settlement, and even to free his subjects from the oath of fealty that they had made to him. On 1 May another Bull invited them to arrange a truce, when the time seemed ripe, to last for two years.[2]

The nuncios' mission was not carried out without incident. Between Rushyford and Ferryhill, six leagues from Darlington, a band of robbers stripped them of their possessions and the pope had to send them in all haste 1,000 gold florins to make good their losses. When they tried to present their credentials to Robert Bruce, he refused to open them, because the address did not give him his title of 'King of Scotland.' In vain did the legates insist, pointing out that the supreme pontiff must not show any prejudice towards either side. Robert only replied: 'I cannot accept letters that are not addressed to me as king, nor reply to your request until I have consulted my parliament. You will hear from me after Michaelmas.'[3]

Gaucelme de Jean and Luca Fieschi went back to London and awaited the promised note for a long time. When at length it reached them, they learned that Robert refused to enter into negotiations before he had been recognised as king of Scotland. Thereupon the legates promulgated a two-year truce. Bruce disregarded this completely, seized Berwick, Wark, Harbottle and Mitford, and set fire to other strongholds. Annoyed at his effrontery, the nuncios declared him and his followers excommunicate, and went back to the court at Avignon, which they reached on 5 November 1318.[4]

Thereupon John XXII started proceedings against Robert and his supporters, the bishops of St Andrews, Dunkeld, Moray and

---

[1] Lingard, *op. cit.* pp. 466–70, 477–83. See also Fordoun, *Scottichronicon*, Bk XII, VOL. II, chaps. xxvi–xxxiii, pp. 259–68.
[2] Mollat, nos. 5155, 5162, 5174, 5216, 5232, 5233.
[3] Rymer, *op. cit.* VOL. II, pt I, p. 134 (letters dated 7 and 10 September 1317).
[4] Lingard, *op. cit.* pp. 485–6; see also Coulon, no. 424.

Glasgow. All were summoned to appear before him on 1 May 1320.[1]

On 6 April, before the expiry of this term, Robert sent a memorandum to Avignon, justifying his conduct and asking to be reconciled to the Church. The pope consented to suspend proceedings for the time being. Robert's plenipotentiaries, in agreement with those of the king of France, were to arrange a final peace settlement with England. But the discussions dragged on, and war broke out afresh in 1322. On 14 October, the English army was routed. Despite this success, the victorious Bruce, worn out by military operations, which had lasted nearly twenty-three years, of his own accord offered to sign a thirteen-year truce; Edward II hastily agreed to this suggestion.[2]

2

The Reign of Edward III 1327–77

The year 1327 was marked by tragic events. Revolution broke out, and Edward II was dethroned and his son put at the head of the government; on 21 September the fallen monarch was murdered in his prison by the order of his wife's lover, Mortimer. In 1330, Edward III overthrew the regency council which was keeping him in subjection, and exiled his mother to Castle Rising. Parliament condemned to death Mortimer and his accomplices in the late king's murder. It was only because John XXII pleaded on her behalf that the queen mother escaped the punishment she deserved. The pope gave the young king some fatherly advice; he wrote: 'As king, you should take care not to entrust the government to the hands of one or two persons, nor permit the rise to power of one or two counsellors; but govern prudently with the collaboration of prelates, lords, gentles and commons alike.'[3]

The relationship between Edward III and John XXII, which now and again was strained, was on the whole a friendly one. The king lavished gifts on the cardinals and the pope's nephews, allowed the collectors to levy ecclesiastical taxes, and promised to preserve entire the freedom of the English church.

But this state of harmony was only superficial: the king, fearing opposition from the queen mother's party at the beginning of his

[1] Mollat, nos. 10674, 10675, 12040, 12041.
[2] Lingard, *op. cit.* pp. 486–7, 492–3. See also G. Mollat, *Études et documents*, pp. 125–129.
[3] Rinaldi, *ad annum* 1331, §35, 36. See also Lingard, *op. cit.* pp. 494–510.

reign, was making a virtue of necessity. Slight differences were constantly arising with John XXII and Benedict XII. The king had no intention of abandoning the right of the Crown—which the papacy refused to recognise—to appropriate the revenues of vacant bishoprics. He created difficulties for those who appealed to the Roman Curia. Once he imprisoned an incumbent for having had recourse to papal jurisdiction.

With Clement VI the conflict, which till then had been latent, became overt and bitter. The pope's generosity in distributing expectative graces and exercising his right of grants *in commendam*, and the well-known anglophobia of his cardinals, especially Talleyrand de Périgord, had been the cause of violent incidents. On the other hand, English opposition to papal pretentions which had been curbed by the agreement that had existed for some time between the king and the Roman Church, now manifested itself anew. There was ample opportunity, now that war between England and France was imminent, to cast some doubt on the impartiality of Clement VI, who had once been chancellor to Philip VI of Valois. The English could not remain blind to the fact that the subsidies levied on incumbents in England passed from the papal coffers to those of the enemy. To continue to pay them was equivalent to supplying France with arms.[1]

In the Parliament of 1343, the nation's grievances were voiced with acrimony. It was expressly forbidden to introduce into the kingdom or to receive or to execute, letters, briefs, suits, reservations, provisions, instruments or other documents contrary to the rights of the king or his subjects. Offenders were to be handed over to the king's justice.[2]

This decree was at once put into operation. The sheriff of London arrested the attorneys of Cardinals Adhémar Robert and Gérard de Garde and banished them from the country.

Clement VI was much annoyed when he learned of this assault, and wrote letters reproaching the king. The pope even used the word 'rebellion' and threatened excommunication. His displeasure increased when, about the middle of October 1343, the jurist John Shoreditch brought him protests from Edward and the Lords and Commons. He decided, however, that it would be more prudent to conceal his resentment, and dismissed the ambassadors with the promise of a reply which was never sent. Knowing full well the power of court intrigues he began secret discussions and hampered

[1] Haller, *op. cit.* pp. 402–11.
[2] *Rotuli parliamentorum*, VOL. II, pp. 135–45, 172.

the execution of the king's will by means of the insidious schemes he fostered among members of the king's entourage.

This cunning policy was remarkably successful. The measures passed by Parliament in 1343 and reinforced by penal sanctions in 1344 were never implemented. In a famous letter, dated 11 July 1344, Clement declared the primacy, derived from God, of the Roman pontiff over all churches in the world and announced that, by virtue of this right, he possessed 'full authority to dispose of all churches and all ecclesiastical dignities, offices and benefices.' [1]

The following spring, two nuncios made Edward promise that he would not give to the decisions of the censorious Parliaments of 1343 and 1344 the status of laws. The collectors carried out their duties as usual and the Holy See made appointments to bishoprics, abbeys and other lesser benefices.

After a very brief lull, hostilities began again in 1346, when the king confiscated all benefices held by foreigners. In 1347, Parliament made many bitter complaints against the papacy. On 9 February 1351 the Statute of Provisors was published. This declared that if the pope, by provision or reservation, opposed an election or the presentation to a benefice in the normal manner, and if the patrons and bishops did not within six months exercise their respective rights, the collation was to revert to the king, or to the nobles who had originally been entitled to nominate the holders of such benefices. Anyone contravening this statute was liable to imprisonment and fines. [2]

This measure did not only abolish papal prerogatives; it also aimed a still more formidable blow at the principle of election and at the freedom of the Church, by giving its blessing to the seizure of Church property by the state.

Oddly enough, Edward III did not put this legislation into effect. He seems to have kept it in reserve, as an effective weapon to use against the papacy. Clement seems to have been unaware of the Statute, or at least he pretended to be. When he threatened to excommunicate the king and to place his lands under an interdict, it was in the vain hope of obtaining the revenues made available by the sequestration of benefices held by cardinals, courtiers and prelates who were not English. [3]

[1] Rinaldi, *ad annum* 1344, §55–9.
[2] *Rotuli parliamentorum*, VOL. II, p. 232. See also *Statutes of the Realm*, VOL. II, p. 316.
[3] Rome, Vatican Archives, *Regesta Vaticana, 138*, epistles 323, 324, 378, 468, 704, 939; *139*, epistles 1177, 1178, 1189; *140*, epistles 1139, 1160; *141*, epistle 596; *142*, epistle 916; *143*, fol. 44ᵛ; *145*, fol. 87ʳ; *146*, fol. 70ʳ; *212*, fol. 354ʳ.

The Holy See continued to be attacked by the English in the time of Innocent VI. In January 1353, the apostolic collectors were informed that they were forbidden to collect the annates in cases where incumbents appointed in defiance of papal reservations had not taken possession. The Statute of *Praemunire*, 23 September 1353, laid down very strict rules: 'Whosoever shall arraign the king's subjects in a foreign court, in matters whose cognizance belongs to the king's courts, or shall seek by the same means to annul the judgments made by these courts, shall have two months to answer for the reasons for his defiance; at the expiry of which term, his procurators, advocates, executors and notaries, and he himself and his abbettors, shall be out of the king's protection, his lands, merchandise and chattels shall be forfeit to the king and if he is seized, he shall be imprisoned until the payment of a ransom fixed by the king.' [1]

This legislation, so prejudicial to the papacy, remained for the time being merely theoretical. Edward III was the first to contravene the regulations that he himself had approved. The queen and her lords continued to beg the Curia to grant expectative graces to their protégés. Elections now scarcely ever took place. Apostolic provisions were sought as eagerly as they had been in the past. In 1365 Parliament vainly renewed the regulations made in 1351 and 1353.

At this juncture Urban V's untimely demand for the realm's quota of taxes now in arrear for some thirty-three years, caused the Parliament of 1366 to pass a very serious measure.[2] The Lords and Commons, after consulting the clergy, freed Edward III from any obligation to pay these taxes to the Roman pontiff, under the pretext that the grant formerly made by King John had been without the people's consent and contrary to the king's oath at his coronation. If the pope instituted canonical proceedings against Edward, the Lords and Commons would oppose them to the utmost. This was tantamount to abolishing the sovereignty of the Roman Church over England.

The promulgation of a caritative subsidy, made necessary by the costly wars in Italy and fixed in 1372 at 100,000 florins, caused renewed conflict between the papacy and Edward III. The king of England forbade his clergy to make any payment at a moment when he himself was about to ask for their financial help. Moreover, an embassy led by the bishop of Bangor went to Avignon and made a violent protest against the way that papal tribunals had treated Englishmen, and against reservation of benefices, expectative graces

---

[1] Rymer, *op. cit.* VOL. III, pt I, p. 81; *Statutes of the Realm*, VOL. I, p. 329.
[2] *Rotuli parliamentorum*, VOL. II, pp. 289–90.

THE POPES AT AVIGNON

and apostolic provisions.[1] On 21 December 1373, Gregory XI granted certain concessions, such as the suspension until the following 24 June of suits pending before the two courts concerning the exercise of the right of provision to benefices, and the adjournment for one year of summonses to appear before his judges. For his part, the king of England agreed to leave in possession the clergy who had been appointed to benefices by the Holy See, and not to dispose of those benefices which were already affected by papal reservation or which already had a titular holder furnished with a Bull to this effect and whose vacancy would raise the question of the right to present. It was at length agreed that discussions should begin either at Bruges or Calais in an attempt to reach a satisfactory agreement on this thorny question of benefices. In order to prove his goodwill, Gregory XI made a verbal undertaking in December 1373, to restrict the number of expectative graces, apostolic provisions and Bulls of reservation; to take more account of the wishes of the chapters and of the king in the choice of bishops, abbots, priors and those elected to office in cathedrals; and to reduce the amount of the taxes levied by the Holy See.[2]

The agreed negotiations proceeded slowly at Bruges during the years 1374–5. The results were made known in six Bulls dated 1 September 1375.[3] Gregory annulled all the reservations and expectative graces not yet utilised by the beneficiaries. He legalised the granting of benefices by the king contrary to apostolic reservations, and annulled legal proceedings on this and other accounts in progress at the Curia. He gave up his claim to the annates which illegal holders of benefices and litigants ought to have paid to the Apostolic Camera. For the next three years, provided that a peace settlement had not meanwhile been made with France, no Englishman was to be summoned to appear at Avignon, and cases were to be heard either at Bruges or in some other safe place. The archbishops of York and Canterbury were to see to it that buildings and religious foundations held *in commendam* were maintained and repaired at the expense of the commendatory cardinals.

All in all, the agreements of 1374–5 were not so much a concordat as a settlement of accounts and an amnesty. Both parties preserved their rights intact, and consequently the causes of conflict were not removed.

---

[1] For the mission of the bishop of Bangor, see E. Perroy, *L'Angleterre et le Grand Schisme d'Occident*, Paris 1933, pp. 32–3.
[2] M. Perroy has put forward good reasons for suggesting 1373 and not 1377, the date which used to be generally accepted. Gregory's verbal promises are not in fact dated, and appear in Rymer's *Foedera* after the royal decrees of 15 February 1377. See Perroy, *op. cit.* pp. 45–6.   [3] Rymer, *op. cit.* VOL. III, pt 2, pp. 34–6.

The English were well aware that they were being deceived, and in 1376 many complaints were made at the Parliament in London. The papacy was considered to be responsible for all the ills that beset England: this was the time of English reverses on French soil. 'What the Curia levies in taxes for vacant benefices,' it was said, 'amounts to a sum five times greater than the king's revenues. In return for financial gain, the courtiers at Avignon thrust ignorant good-for-nothings into high office. English benefices are in the hands of strangers, and even of enemies of the country, who have never even seen their flock. Every year the papal collector sends up to 20,000 marks to the pope. In all Christendom there is not one prince whose riches amount to even one quarter of the sums criminally extorted in this country. The pope levies taxes and subsidies on the English clergy to pay the ransoms of Frenchmen who are prisoners of war in England, or to carry on the war in Lombardy.' [1] But neither Gregory nor Edward would heed such protests, which sounded in their ears like old familiar oft-heard repetitions.

Nevertheless, the king, recalling perhaps the grudging concessions made by the pope on 1 September 1375, did give some satisfaction both to the Curia and to the ordinary patrons. Two decrees, dated 15 February 1377, settled the future of benefices which, since 15 February 1376, had become subject to the royal prerogative of regale and were still without incumbents: the sovereign renounced his right of presentation, annulled all favours granted to those of his candidates who had not taken possession and broke off any proceedings in progress between claimants at English courts.[2]

By a strange irony of fate, the Bruges discussions, which were never put into effect, eventually proved detrimental to the papacy. Public opinion in England was by no means grateful for the papacy's conciliatory attitude: there were attempts to take advantage of even the verbal promises made in 1373, and demands for their implementation *in toto*, whereas Gregory XI had in fact only made a retrospective undertaking. When annates were claimed, when reservations affected certain benefices, when lawsuits began at the Curia between clergy appointed by the king and those provided by an apostolic grace, there were cries that 'the aforementioned treaty' had been violated, though in fact no agreement had been signed. The Holy See was thus placed in a humiliating position: unless the alleged agreements were interpreted 'in the sense most favourable to the temporal power,' there was serious risk that the full force of the 'anticlerical

---

[1] Pastor, *Geschichte der Päpste*, Freiburg 1885–1933, VOL. I, p. vii.
[2] Rymer, *op. cit.* VOL. III, pt 2, pp. 55–6.

THE POPES AT AVIGNON

legislation' symbolised by the Statutes of Provisors and *Praemunire* would be unleashed.[1]

The perpetual complaints of the representatives of the English people were to increase and at length to pervade the mass of the populace and there to give rise to an opposition highly dangerous to the papacy.[2] The unrest of a whole nation cannot be stifled indefinitely. If it is perhaps too much to assert that a national church was already beginning to form, it is at least true that men's minds were ready to listen to Wycliffe's violent attacks on the constitution of the Church of Rome, and that England was gradually becoming ripe for schism.

[1] Perroy, *op. cit.* pp. 48–50.
[2] See especially the *Brocours de bénéfices demorantz en la pecherouse cité d'Avenon*, in *Rotuli parliamentorum*, VOL. III, p. 337, no. 96.

CHAPTER V

The Papacy and Spain

1

The Kingdoms of Aragon and Majorca

OF the various states formed in Spain as the Moslems were gradually driven back, the kingdom of Aragon, by the beginning of the fourteenth century, showed the most signs of increasing in size and strength. One branch of the royal house had been reigning over the island of Sicily, now known as the kingdom of Trinacria, since 1282. The Balearic Islands, Roussillon and Cerdaña had, like Sicily, their own dynasty, and formed the kingdom of Majorca.

The death of King Sancho on 4 September 1324 raised the thorny question of the succession to the throne of Majorca. Sancho, who died without issue, had bequeathed his crown to his own nephew James and had established a regency council, which was to choose a tutor for this child of ten. On 11 September, the people enthusiastically acclaimed the young prince as their rightful sovereign.

But, in defiance of all right, a rival immediately rose in opposition to him: James II of Aragon claimed the kingdom of Majorca. As his claims were coldly received at Roussillon, he commanded the Infante Alfonso to mobilise an army. John XXII determined to support the cause of the little James, and, without wasting words, pointed out to his rival how ill-founded were his claims, and urged him to abandon his projects.

In these circumstances, it was essential that the regency council, laid down in Sancho's will, should shortly provide the young king of Majorca with a tutor well able to defend his interests which were threatened. Their choice fell on Don Philip of Majorca. Unfortunately this choice displeased certain turbulent nobles, and roused considerable discontent in the country. At Perpignan and in the Balearic Islands, Philip was sharply criticised for having lived for many years in France, for his close relations with the court in Paris, and for his sympathies with a country which had given Roussillon cause for complaint. Conditions were imposed upon him, his actions were closely supervised and care was taken that he should not

influence his pupil in favour of France. The king of Aragon had a hand
in these intrigues. His policy was to prevent the alliance of James of
Majorca with France. After isolating the young king, he might hope
to crush him more surely. Meanwhile, he encouraged anarchy in
Majorcan territory and tried to find some pretext for occupying part
of the little kingdom. His principal interest, therefore, was to thwart
the policy of Philip of Majorca and to raise a party in opposition to
him.

On this occasion, John XXII's intervention was sufficient to avert
the danger. He sent letters reproving his subjects in Majorca so
emphatically that they accepted Philip as royal tutor, made an oath of
fealty to him and even paid him liege homage.

But danger threatened again in January 1325. The municipal
officers and people of Majorca, Cerdaña, Conflent, Perpignan and
Collioure renounced their oath of fealty, refused to obey the regent
and set to work to impede his government in every possible way.
Civil war, for which Gaston de Foix and the king of Aragon had been
secretly preparing, was now imminent. John XXII hurriedly sent to
the unhappy kingdom two nuncios, the bishops of Bazas and Agde,
charged with bringing to a speedy end the growing discord between
James's tutor and his subjects. They had powers to put down, if
necessary, any association contrary to the public good, to pronounce
excommunication upon disturbers of the peace and to impose an
interdict on rebellious cities and districts.

These papal threats only served to excite the insurgents still
further. The inhabitants of Perpignan even made their way into the
royal palace of their city, seized hold of the young prince and put his
tutor to flight. Regardless of the pope's warnings, they even had the
effrontery to make a seal, bearing the likeness of the king, now their
prisoner, and affix it to the letters they sent to the regent's counsellors,
telling them to leave the kingdom of Majorca with all speed.

The nuncios from the Holy See took decisive action. Despite the
public excitement, they issued summonses in the normal manner,
and then declared the organisers of the revolt excommunicate, and
Perpignan and the other towns involved under an interdict.

The suspension of all religious offices at Roussillon resulted in a
temporary slackening of tension. At the beginning of May 1325, representatives of the rebel towns went to Avignon to confer with the
regent, whom John XXII had summoned there. But, as agreement
was not reached, the interdict, which had been lifted for a short
while, once again lay on the rebellious country.

Thanks to France, which had been approached through diplomatic channels by Naples and the pope, the conflict was resolved. On 11 July, Charles the Fair told Gaston de Foix that he must cease all intrigue in the town of Perpignan, and ordered the seneschals of Beaucaire, Carcassonne and Toulouse as well as the rector of Montpellier to compel the rebels to recognise Philip of Majorca as James's tutor.

While John XXII was busy on his behalf, the regent was discussing with the representatives of James II of Aragon the question of who should succeed the late King Sancho. The discussions, though they bristled with difficulties, resulted in an agreement on 24 September 1325: James gave up all claims to the kingdom of Majorca, on condition that the little Majorcan prince married Constance, daughter of the Infante Alfonso. This clause eliminated the much-feared contingency of an alliance between the king of Majorca and France, and provided the successors of the king of Aragon with the possibility of seizing a kingdom which for the moment had eluded his jealous grasp.

But Constance and James were closely related, and could not marry without a papal dispensation. John XXII, realising the ultimate intentions of the king of Aragon, refused to grant the indulgence, and resisted all attempts to make him change his mind. At last he did yield, but only after the king of Aragon had, in 1326, brought troops into Perpignan, pacified the town, and handed over the person of the young king to Philip of Majorca.[1]

John XXII's skilful policy had proved brilliantly successful. He had succeeded in thwarting the plans of the house of Aragon, disarmed the insurrection at Perpignan, suggested a wise line of conduct to the regent, taken advantage of the goodwill of the queen of Naples, caused France to intervene tactfully, and, finally, ensured that James of Majorca would keep his throne. Later Avignon Popes were to show equal solicitude in protecting the young king against enemies determined to bring about his downfall.

Unfortunately James II of Majorca, overbold, inexperienced, surrounded by bad advisers, contributed more than anyone else to his own downfall. Instead of strengthening the alliance with France, he made the mistake of quarrelling with her. While Aragon kept a watchful eye on his actions and prepared to engulf his states, he foolishly wasted his resources in extravagant living, and exasperated his cousin, Peter the Ceremonious,[2] by his ill-timed recriminations.

[1] G. Mollat, *Jean XXII et la succession de Sanche, roi de Majorque (1324–1326)*, Paris 1905.
[2] James II of Aragon had been succeeded by Alfonso IV in 1328 and by Peter IV, 'the Ceremonious' in 1336.

The crisis had for long been quietly threatening, and though Benedict XII succeeded by his wise intervention in 1338–9 in averting it for the time, it broke out suddenly in 1342. The king of Aragon instigated proceedings against James II for having struck an illicit coinage in the province of the County of Roussillon. Clement VI, realising what danger the prince was in, sent a nuncio, Armand de Narsès, to the spot, and he persuaded the two rivals to agree to a meeting. In August 1342 James went to Barcelona, suspecting nothing. To his great surprise he was not admitted to his cousin's presence to converse with him, and learned that he was summoned to appear before a court of justice in Aragon. Full of indignation at this trap that had been set for him, and loudly protesting that it was his firm intention to submit only to the arbitration of the pope, he escaped from Barcelona. This act constituted the final rupture.

Armand de Narsès was replaced as nuncio by Cardinal Andrea Ghini di Malpighi, but he was no more successful in securing peace than his predecessor. Then events followed rapidly one on the other: on 23 February 1343, the king of Aragon announced that Majorca, Roussillon and Cerdaña were to be confiscated and made over to him; in the same year the Aragonese army invaded the Balearic Islands.

Andrea Ghini di Malpighi died in office and was succeeded as legate by Cardinal Bernard of Albi, who went to Barcelona on 11 July 1343 in an attempt to make Peter IV relent. The king refused to listen to his advice and hurriedly left to take command of his troops, who were ready to advance on Roussillon. The legate followed him to the walls of Perpignan and with great difficulty succeeded, in August, in making him sign, under those very walls, a truce to last until 1 May 1344. The conditions of the truce were harsh ones for James of Majorca: the king of Aragon was allowed to keep the places his soldiers had captured, and the legal proceedings which had been begun against James II were to take their normal course.

Shortly before the truce was due to expire, Clement VI attempted to have it extended until the following Michaelmas. The archbishop of Aix, who brought the pope's exhortations, was given a cold reception by Peter IV, who had renewed his campaign in Roussillon in May 1344. When Cardinal Bertrand de Déaulx called for the ending of hostilities, the king of Aragon declared that he was bound by no ties of vassalage to the Holy See.

Having exhausted his powers of persuasion, the nuncio was driven to advise James II to submit to Aragon. Scarcely had the prince handed over his person and his lands to Peter IV on 15 July 1344, than it was announced, on 22 July, that Roussillon and Cerdaña were now annexed to Aragon. In October, the Cortes, in session at Barcelona, deprived James of his throne, and, in mockery, allowed him to keep Montpellier and the County of Aumelas and Carlat, which had been in the hands of Philip VI of Valois for the past three years.

Despairing, James II had no alternative but to take refuge at the Avignon court where Clement VI received him kindly. There it was arranged that Montpellier and the port of Lattes should be sold to France for 120,000 gold crowns. This money, together with what the pope and the cardinals lent him, enabled James II to hire mercenaries and charter a fleet. He succeeded in landing on the island of Majorca, but died in battle on 25 October 1349.

His son, James III, had been captured in the thick of battle, and, for thirteen years, despite the repeated demands of Innocent VI for his release, the unfortunate prince was imprisoned in an iron cage. Finally, in May 1362, he escaped and married Queen Joanna of Naples. Being of a very adventurous disposition, he later fought in Castile under the banner of Pedro the Cruel. In 1374 he obtained permission from Gregory XI to prepare an expedition to recapture his father's kingdom. He began to campaign in Roussillon, but died in the following year. He was succeeded by his sister Isabella, who realised that any efforts she might make to win back her ancestral states were doomed to failure. Accordingly, on 30 August 1375, she sold them to Duke Louis of Anjou, who was on the look-out for a throne. The king of Aragon though much displeased dared not make war on Louis, who could count on valuable support from the papal court and the alliance with Castile. He was indeed bold enough to sound Charles V on the subject but Charles, not wishing to be involved, advised recourse to the judgment of the Holy See. The two rivals accepted the compromise. Gregory XI acting with complete impartiality, gave Cardinal Gilles Aycelin full authority, in 1376, to draw up an agreement on a friendly basis, without legal formalities. The arbitrator went to Catalonia, but Peter IV would have nothing to do with any idea of appeasement. He tried every method of evasion, and finally refused to accept the arbitration of the Holy See, which he accused of prejudice. He demanded a tribunal of guaranteed impartiality, and suggested as such his own court of justice! Cardinal Aycelin did not despair even at this evidence of bad faith. He went tirelessly to and fro between Perpignan and Narbonne, doing his utmost to wring concessions now from the king of Aragon's representative, the duke of Gerona, and now from Louis of Anjou. But his efforts were not crowned with success; Gregory XI died without having reconciled the two opponents.[1]

2

Castile

Throughout the fourteenth century the policy of the Holy See towards Castile remained consistent: it combated English influence and promoted that of France. As early as 1337 the legate, Bernard of Albi, had been working with Jean de Vienne, the French ambassador, to bring to a peaceful end the hostilities which had broken out between Alfonso XI and his Portuguese neighbour Alfonso IV. Later, plans for a marriage between an English princess and the heir presumptive to the Castilian throne caused considerable anxiety to Clement VI, who wished to bring about an alliance between France and Castile. His activities were so successful that, in 1345, the youthful Pedro was betrothed to Blanche of Navarre. But English diplomacy undismayed pursued its intrigues, and despite the angry protests of Clement VI, Alfonso XI abandoned his earlier plan and in 1346 decided to marry his son to Joanna, daughter of Edward III. But in 1348 when the princess was crossing the Bordelais on her way to Castile she died of a sudden sickness.

Immediately Clement VI set to work to arrange a French marriage. First he offered to Pedro the daughter of Philip of Évreux and then the daughter of Philip of Valois. Finally, on 3 June 1353 at Valladolid, the young prince was married to Blanche of Bourbon.

Pedro was a man of a revengeful and passionate nature who was completely dominated by his mistress, Doña Maria de Padilla. He took a violent dislike to his wife and subjected her to many indignities. The bishops of Salamanca and Avila, on some trifling pretext, declared the marriage to be null, and even dared to bless their sovereign's new union with an attractive widow, Doña Juana de Castro.

Innocent VI, a rigorous disciplinarian, could not condone such flouting of morality and justice. Bertrand, bishop of Senez, was ordered to annul the marriage authorised by the bishops of Salamanca and Avila, to begin proceedings against the two prelates and to summon the king of Castile to appear before the court at Avignon.

[1] A. Lecoy de la Marche, *Les Relations politiques de la France et du royaume de Majorque*, Paris 1892, VOL. II.

As if in support of this action of the pope, Alfonso XI's bastard sons, Don Enrico and Don Tello, helped by Don Juan Alfonso Albuquerque, revolted against their brother and besieged him in the town of Toro. The legate was in no hurry to reach Castile. He feared the reception he would get from the king, who was notorious for his cruelty, and Innocent VI had to quicken his zeal. When at last Bertrand ventured to appear in Pedro's presence, he heard all his demands rejected. In accordance with the terms of his mandate, he bided his time for a while and fixed a date before which the king was to recall Blanche of Bourbon; but, when the date has passed, he laid the kingdom under an interdict, and declared Pedro excommunicate (1354).

The league formed by Don Enrico and Don Tello could not profit by its advantages. Thanks to disagreements which he skilfully fomented, Pedro overcame his enemies, recaptured Toledo in May 1355 and imprisoned Blanche of Bourbon at Sigüenza.

Innocent VI, hearing of the fate that had befallen the wretched queen, decided to send to Castile a new legate, Cardinal Guillaume de la Jugie. Pedro knew that the pope sympathised with his enemies and he feared lest the papal envoy should thwart his plans, and lend support to the insurgents, who were still in arms. Resorting to artifice, Pedro ceased to consort openly with Maria de Padilla, made a series of overtures to the court at Avignon, announced his reconciliation with his legitimate wife, and, in consequence, asked for the lifting of the interdict from his kingdom, and did his best to show that there was no point in sending a legate. But the pope was not deceived. On 24 November 1355, Guillaume de la Jugie arrived before the walls of Toro where, in their turn, Don Enrico and Don Tello were then being besieged, and tried to persuade both sides to lay down their arms. But the king was not to be moved. He would neither agree to make peace with his opponents, nor to take back Blanche of Bourbon.

Discouraged by his lack of success, which was made complete by the capture of Toro on 5 January 1356, Cardinal de la Jugie fell ill and asked to be recalled. His request was granted on condition that he tried to end the war that had begun on 26 September between Castile and Aragon. Bertrand de Cosnac came to help him in this arduous task; but all the efforts to mediate made by the two nuncios were of no avail.

On 10 March 1357, the truce of Tudela was signed. For some time Pedro's envoy, Juan Fernandez de Henestrosa, a past-master in double-dealing, had succeeded in deceiving Innocent VI, but the pope soon saw the error into which he had fallen, and in August told

Guillaume de la Jugie that he was definitely recalled. The legate obeyed, but not without first excommunicating the king.

In April 1359, the papal court resumed relations with Castile. Cardinal Guy de Boulogne left Avignon and persuaded the king of Aragon to sign a peace treaty with Pedro in May 1361. But his efforts to bring the king of Castile and Blanche of Bourbon together were uncompromisingly rejected, and the princess, forsaken by France, died of grief at Jerez in 1361.

The succession of Henry of Trastamara to the throne of Castile must have caused rejoicing at the court of Avignon, for this king was a faithful ally of France, and there was every prospect that relations with him would be cordial. And so, when the king of Portugal threatened to seize Castile in 1371, the Holy See hastened to avert the danger and, through the intermediacy of the papal legates, restored peace between the two countries.[1]

---

[1] G. Daumet, *Étude sur l'alliance de la France et de la Castille au XIVe et au XVe siècle,* Paris 1898; *Innocent VI et Blanche de Bourbon. Lettres du pape publiées d'après les registres du Vatican,* Paris 1899.

For the relations of the papacy at Avignon with the Scandinavian states, see: J. Moltesen, *De Avignonske Pavers forhold til Danmark,* Copenhagen 1896; Brilioth, *Den pafliga bes Kattningen of Sverige intill den Stora Schisma,* Upsala 1915.

Book Three: Papal Institutions

CHAPTER I

Avignon and the Papal Court

1

Avignon

NOBODY who has ever read it can have forgotten Daudet's charming story in which he describes the papal city in the time of Benedict XII and still less the poem of Mistral in which in rapturous tones he sings of 'Avignon! Avignon on her mighty rock! Avignon, the joyful ringer of bells, whose stone-carved belfries, side by side, point heavenwards; St Peter's god-child, Avignon, who saw the saint's bark ride at anchor in her haven and who bears his keys at her battlemented girdle; Avignon, that lovely city, tumbled and dishevelled by the mistral. . . .'[1]

And yet the picture of Avignon that is usually foremost in our minds is the sombre one drawn by Petrarch in his characteristically figurative style of that city in his own day: 'Unholy Babylon, thou Hell on earth, thou sink of iniquity, thou cess-pool of the world! There is neither faith, nor charity, nor religion, nor fear of God, no shame, no truth, no holiness, albeit the residence within its walls of the supreme pontiff should have made of it a shrine and the very stronghold of religion. . . . Of all cities that I know, its stench is the worst. . . . What dishonour to see it suddenly become the capital of the world, when it should be but the least of all cities!'[2]

For St Bridget the court of Avignon was 'like a field full of tares, that must first be rooted out with a sharp steel, then purified with fire, and finally levelled with the plough.' These tares she boldly enumerated: pride, avarice, luxury and simony.[3]

Like most towns in the south of France in the fourteenth century, Avignon was not at all attractive inside the city walls. Its narrow muddy streets, from which the filth was not cleared, gave off foetid smells which so incommoded an ambassador from Aragon as to make

---

[1] A. Hallays, *Avignon et le Comtat-Venaissin*, Paris 1909, p. 2.
[2] De Sade, *Mémoires pour la vie de François Pétrarque*, Amsterdam 1764–7, VOL. I, pp. 25–7.
[3] St Bridget of Sweden, *Revelationes*, Bk IV, ch. lvii; Bk V, ch. cxlii.

him ill.[1] Few of the houses were two stories high. The dwellings were usually low, and were badly arranged, ill-ventilated and ill-lit. Rents were comparatively high: a small lodging consisting of three rooms, a store-room, a kitchen, a loft and a privy, cost one florin per month; a single room with use of kitchen, five *sous* of Vienne; a two-storied house with stabling for four horses, a courtyard, three bedrooms, a hall, a kitchen and a paddock, was four florins.[2]

It was not easy to find lodgings. In 1316, the ambassadors from Aragon had to go outside Avignon to find somewhere to stay. From the time of Benedict XII, when it seemed that the return to Rome was indefinitely postponed, the cardinals built themselves palaces on the right bank of the Rhône, at Villeneuve on French soil. 'In every direction the papal city overflows the confines of the ancient city.' Outside the thirteenth-century ramparts, now mostly derelict, new quarters and suburbs were being rapidly constructed. The old town was changing too. On the Rocher des Doms rose the immense towers of the papal palace, while the cardinals took delight in adding new beauties to monasteries and ancient churches, or in building such monuments as the clock-tower, the little palace, St Didier, St Martial's college and the church and cloister, now no longer in existence, of the Dominican friars. The fourteenth-century visitor, however, had great difficulty in seeing these wonders of Avignon, for he had no space to step back and admire them at leisure: there was scarcely an alley's width between the papal palace and the neighbouring houses.

In 1366 the appearance of the city changed again. Gone were the happy days of Clement VI. The incursions of the Great Companies into the Comtat-Venaissin caused general terror, and the inhabitants of Avignon, with the help of papal subsidies, hastened to enclose both the old and the new town within a common circle of massive ramparts, from whose shelter they could defy the attacks of the mercenaries.[3] Once Avignon had become the centre of the Catholic world, an extraordinary crowd of foreigners gathered within its walls. There were enough Germans to form a confraternity. Italian banking-houses, famed for their credit, opened branches there: in 1327–8 there were known to be forty-three money-changers (*campsores Camerae*). Tuscan painters rubbed shoulders with French architects. Lawyers of every sort—attorneys, advocates and notaries—went

[1] Finke, *Acta Aragonensia*, VOL. I, p. 225.
[2] K. H. Schäfer, 'Deutsche in Avignon und ihre Wohnungen zur Zeit Johanns XXII,' *Römische Quartalschrift*, VOL. XX, 1906, pp. 162–4.
[3] R. Michel, 'La Construction des remparts d'Avignon au XIVe siècle,' *Congrès archéologique de France*, session LXXIII, VOL. II, Paris 1910, pp. 341–60.

about their business. In another part of the city, all kinds of merchants and craftsmen had their shops—embroiderers, furriers, illuminators, bookbinders and booksellers, goldsmiths, bakers, butchers and a host of others.

All these people, who had some kind of link with the papal court, if only that of supplying goods, were generically termed courtiers (*cortesani*) and citizens of the Roman court (*cives Romanae curiae*). After Gregory XI had left for Rome, 2,359 courtiers and 1,1471 citizens of the Roman court were counted in the parishes of St Pierre, St Symphorien, St Didier, St Agricol, St Étienne, St Geniès, and Notre-Dame-la-Principale. It must be remembered, however, that this count included children, women and domestic servants.[1]

The language spoken in Avignon was not French, but Provençal. Latin was used for the administration of Church affairs.

As the papal palace was much too small to accommodate all the administrative departments of the Curia, the Apostolic Camera hired premises in the town for the Almonry (known as *la Pignotte*), for the headquarters of the marshal, for the cook and the cellarer, and for the office of the *bullatores*, as well as for lodgings for the pope's servants and for the cardinals and their retinue, known as their liveried retainers (*librata*). It was the duty of commissioners (*taxatores domorum*) approved by the Curia and the civic magistrates, to decide the amount of rent to be paid by members of the Curia, to give each one the dwelling that was his due, and to settle the differences between landlords and tenants.[2]

Like all cosmopolitan towns, Avignon became the haunt of adventurers of every kind—professional thieves, usurers and prostitutes. For that reason, the marshal of the Curia,[3] whose duties included the supervision of the police and the prison, was a very busy man. Under him he had a judge for civil and criminal cases, a captain in command of thirty or forty sergeants at arms, and a treasurer. Crimes and offences were severely punished. Men-at-arms convicted of complicity in the attempt made on 13 April 1340 on the person of the ambassador to England, Nicolino Fieschi, were hanged on gibbets from the windows of Fieschi's lodging. In the time of Innocent VI, a gang of robbers, who worked only at night, were cast into the Rhône.[4]

---

[1] H. Denifle, 'Liber divisionis Cortesianorum et civium Romanae Curiae et civitatis Avinionis,' *Archiv*, VOL. I, 1885, pp. 627–30.
[2] P. M. Baumgarten, *Aus Kanzlei und Kammer*, Freiburg 1907, pp. 47–78.
[3] E. Göller, 'Zur Entstehung der Supplikenregister,' *Römische Quartalschrift*, VOL. XIX, 1905, pp. 190–3.
[4] Baluze, *Vitae*, VOL. I, col. 353.

2

The Papal Court

Foremost among those surrounding the supreme pontiff were his kinsmen: brothers, nephews, cousins and more distant relatives. His sisters, sisters-in-law and nieces assumed the title of 'Ladies of the pope's family'; like the wives and daughters of the marshal of the Curia and of the provost, like the baronesses and great ladies of Avignon, they enjoyed the exclusive privilege of wearing ermine or miniver, and 'things made of gold, silver or silk.'[1]

In attendance on the pope were knights and squires from noble families. In 1320 there were one hundred and eight squires.

At the pope's own door, first-class or master-porters (*hostarii* or *porterii majores*) were on guard, to announce and introduce visitors. Second-class porters (*hostarii minores*) stood at lesser doorways, and prepared the necessary carpets and chairs when the supreme pontiff appeared in Consistory or in the *aula*. Those who opened and closed the outside doors were known as *hostarii exteriores*.

The sergeants-at-arms (*servientes armorum*), whose number varied during the fourteenth century from twenty-three to seventy-two, guarded the inside of the apostolic palace. At night, they lodged in barracks, in three guard-rooms lit by oil-lamps. They had to hold themselves in constant readiness to ride out in search of delinquent clergy, to arrest them and bring them to the Curia. They also had the duty of guarding the papal prison.

Thirty chaplains officiated in the pope's private chapel. Every night the resident chaplains (*capellani commensales*) were roused by a bell to sing matins. At daybreak they celebrated mass and recited vespers. If the Holy Father took part in a procession or rode on horseback, they bore the cross before him. A priest handed the psalter to the pope for the reciting of vespers. A sub-deacon read to him at mealtimes. Those chaplains more especially concerned with the offices of the Church were called *capellani capellae*, *capellani capellae intrinsecae* or *capellani intrinseci*, though their duties were very similar to those of the *capellani commensales*. Indeed, the chief difference between them was that the *capellani commensales* had a salary of 200 florins, whereas the others had only 100.[2]

[1] De Sade, *Mémoires pour la vie de François Pétrarque*, VOL. II, p. 91.
[2] K. H. Schäfer, 'Päpstliche Ehrenkapläne aus deutschen Diözesen im vierzehnten Jahrhundert,' *Römische Quartalschrift*, VOL. XXI, 1907, pp. 97–113.

Chamberlains (*cubicularii, camerarii,* or *cambrerii*) were those servants who vested the pope in his mantle, placed the stole about his neck and the mitre on his head when he went to Consistory or to a solemn ceremony, or when he received distinguished visitors. The chamberlains had duties to perform also at ordinary receptions: they uncovered the papal slipper that the visitor was to kiss, and stood in rows on either side of their master. On solemn occasions they carried the *flabelli.*

Inside the palace teaching was done by a master of theology chosen from the Dominican Order. In Clement VI's day his pulpit stood in a rectangular room, in the easternmost alcove of the Audience Chamber. In the time of John XXII a master of languages taught oriental tongues.

There were many grades in the kitchen staff. An official, known as the *emptor coquinae* or *administrator expensarum coquinae,* bought meat, game, and fish and the wood required for the fires. The chief cooks (*supracoci* or *magistri coquinae*) arranged the bills of fare and provided the members of the pope's household with their commons. They served the pope after they had tasted the dishes. Scribes or notaries (*scriptores* or *notarii coquinae*) kept a note of all purchases and of the distribution of the food. There were two kitchens, a large and a small, where cooks, assisted by scullions (*brodarii*) exercised their culinary arts.

Two masters of the buttery bought corn or bread, salt, cheese, certain fruits, tables and table-knives, gave every member of the household the helping he was entitled to, arranged the seats and tables at mealtimes, and offered the pope the napkins with which he wiped his hands before dinner and luncheon.

The butlers (*buticularii*) tasted the wine before pouring it into the supreme pontiff's cup. Two, three or four of them saw that the cellars, of which they had charge, were filled with wines from Burgundy, Bédarrides, Lunel and Carpentras, and distributed an allowance to those who lived in the palace. One of them, the 'fruiterer', supplied the papal table with apples, pears, grapes, nuts, figs and oranges.

Two or three masters of the stable (*magistri marescalle, marescalli*) were concerned with the fodder for the horses and mules, and with the care of the harness, carriages and carts. They had a staff of grooms, stable-boys, mule-drivers and carters.

A furrier (*furrerius*) distributed summer and winter garments to court officials and saw to the furnishings of the palace.

The papal prison was supervised by a gaoler, the *soldanus,* with sergeants under him. He himself was subordinate to a prison governor (*custos* or *magister carceris*).

Couriers,[1] either on foot (*cursores pedestres*) or on horseback (*cursores equitatores*), carried the pope's commands within Avignon and to distant parts. No distinction was made between them until after 1378. A master-courier (*magister cursorum*)—this title is occasionally used for the first time in 1362—acted as intermediary between the couriers and the Apostolic Camera, organised the despatch of messages and collected the wages of those who were away. In the course of their journeys the couriers had the right to demand a lodging for themselves and their horses, whersoever they went; but they were expressly forbidden to ask for or to accept gratuities. Their task was to carry the pope's letters to their destination, to affix proclamations made by the Holy See to church doors, to call and summon all persons cited to appear at the Court, and to give to the auditors powers to enquire into cases under litigation. Sometimes they carried out police duties, seeking out culprits, arresting them and bringing them back under safe escort to appear before the Court tribunals. The Apostolic Camera also commissioned them to buy commodities of all kinds, and to bring back any available funds from the tax-collectors.

The list of the pope's household also included a certain number of other officials whose titles are sufficient indication of the kind of work they did; among these were the keeper of the plate, the keeper of the arms, the keeper of the wax, the keeper of the deer, of the camel and of the other animals; sweepers, water-bearers, bell-ringers, launderers and washerwomen, the barber, the physicians, the master of works and many others. From the time of Benedict XII there was also the private almoner.[2]

In all, the papal court included from three to four hundred persons, and perhaps more.

All these people, of course, had their clothing and board and lodging provided, and received a fairly high salary. Members of the Curia also frequently received presents. They also received part of the *servitia minuta*.[3] Those who were clerks became incumbents and received the income from their benefices. The available documents make it possible to calculate that, in the year 1329–30, John XXII

[1] Y. Renouard, 'Comment les papes d'Avignon expédiaient leur courrier,' *Revue historique*, VOL. CLXXX, 1937, pp. 1–29. (The delivery of papal letters was sometimes entrusted to the messengers of those corresponding with the Curia, or to casual visitors or to employees of Merchant Companies.) See also Baumgarten, *op. cit.* pp. 223–47.
[2] J. Haller, 'Zwei Aufzeichnungen über die Beamte der Kürie im 13. und 14. Jahrhundert,' *Quellen*, VOL. I, 1898, pp. 1–38. K. H. Schäffer, *Die Ausgaben der apostolischen Kammer unter den Päpsten Urban V. und Gregor XI.*, Paderborn 1937 (VOL. VI, Görres-Gesellschaft). [3] See below, pp. 319–20.

spent almost three million gold francs on the maintenance and payment of members of his staff.[1]

3

The Central Administration of the Roman Church

During the Avignon papacy, the central administration of the Roman Church was divided between four chief institutions: the Apostolic Camera, the Chancery, the administration of justice and the Penitentiary.

A. *The Apostolic Camera*

The various departments dealing with the financial business of the Holy See were collectively known as the Apostolic Camera (*Camera apostolica*). Two high officials were in charge of these departments: the Camerarius and the Treasurer (*thesaurarius*).

The camerarius was in effect the minister of finances and he was chosen by the pope. Always a bishop or an archbishop, he generally received a cardinal's hat at the end of his period of office as a reward for his services.

The camerarius supervised all officials under his administration, whether or not they were resident at the Curia. He appointed the Collectors and also the commissioners charged with carrying out temporary missions; he supervised their activities and had authority to suspend or recall them. Every regulation, report and order had to be scrutinised by him and authenticated by his seal, mark or signature. The camerarius gave receipts to the collectors for the money coming into the Camera, and signed acknowledgment of sums paid into the Treasury through the banks. His most important duty was to check the accounts of receipts and expenditure submitted by the various departments of the Curia, and in particular to supervise the accounts periodically submitted by the collectors. A clerk of the Camera had the task of compiling a report on these accounts, but the camerarius usually presided at the meetings when they were examined.

Through the day-to-day practice of this exacting discipline, the camerarius acquired a profound knowledge of the rights of the

[1] In the same year, the household expenses of the king of France, the queen, the duke of Normandy and the duke of Orleans together amounted to 265,873 livres, 5 sous, 3 deniers *parisis*. J. Viard ('L'Hôtel de Philippe VI de Valois,' *B.E.C.* VOL. LV, pp. 465–87, 598–626) gives a list of the officers of the king's household.

Roman church. Consequently he became the pope's most intimate and most heeded adviser, consulted by him not only on financial matters, but also on political affairs affecting the Holy See. It was he who sometimes drew up the instructions for the nuncios, and conveyed his master's intentions direct to the various sovereigns. Under his direction, scribes—known from 1341 as secretaries—dealt with political correspondence and secret letters.[1]

As a result of these manifold duties, the camerarius was the most important personage at the papal court. Almost all the palace officials had to take an oath of loyalty and obedience to him.

Subject to his authority the treasurer, appointed by the pope, administered the treasure and funds of the Roman church. He was usually a bishop, more rarely an abbot. Although he was subordinate to the camerarius, he also approved accounts, issued receipts and acknowledgments and gave orders to the collectors. But he had, nevertheless, to be careful to mention the approval of his superior in the hierarchy.

In the offices of the Camera there were two distinct grades of staff: some, of a very inferior status, were no more than copyists (*scriptores*) and couriers (*cursores*); others, known as clerks of the Camera, were really lawyers who drew up contracts and acts in due form, made out inventories, checked the books, audited the accounts and wrote the letters called *litterae camerales* because they emanated from the camerarius. These clerks were sometimes sent on a special mission to supervise on the spot the activities of the collectors. They lived at Avignon and, together with the camerarius and the treasurer, formed the Upper Council of the Camera. About the middle of the fourteenth century they were given the title of Counsellors. There were seven of them in the days of Clement V, but only three or four from the time of John XXII.

Financial transactions often gave rise to litigation: if a dispute occurred between the tax-payers and the collectors, or an incumbent refused to pay his due, or a collector became over-zealous or guilty of embezzlement or extortion, the judicial court of the Camera had to settle these affairs. The auditor and vice-auditor were judges in the first instance, both in civil and criminal cases. A procurator fiscal represented in his official capacity the temporal interests of the Holy See, and led the prosecution; advocates fiscal pleaded in his name and gave legal opinions to the camerarius on request; there was a keeper of the auditors' seal; and notaries enrolled the proceedings

---

[1] E. Göller, 'Zur Geschichte des päpstlichen Sekretariats,' *Quellen*, VOL. XI, 1909, pp. 360–4; *Mitteilungen und Untersuchungen*, Rome 1904, pp. 42–60.

and despatched the various documents required for the case and for the judicial sentence.

Appeal could be made from this first court to that of the camerarius, who either pronounced judgment in person or through proxies. His sentences were final and without appeal. He was, moreover, entitled to demand that financial suits should be brought directly to his court, and to make a summary decision from which there was no appeal, *summarie, simpliciter et de plano, sine strepitu et forma judicii.*[1]

The court of the Camera had its own prison, where the sentences it imposed were served. Various penalties, including confiscation of property, were imposed on those found guilty.

The camerarius was in charge of the mint, which until 1354 was set up in the papal castle at Sorgues, and was subsequently transferred to Avignon after that town had been given to the Holy See.

There were five chief officers of the papal mint: the master of the mint, the warden, the provost, the cuneator and the assayer. Under them were moneyers and workmen.

All these officials, except the provost, made an oath of fealty to the camerarius or the treasurer within a month of their appointment; then, and not till then, they were given permission to bear the titles corresponding to the nature of their office. All these employees, including the master of the mint, were justiciable to the provost, who received his authority from the pope himself, or from the camerarius or treasurer.

Their appointments carried with them certain hereditary privileges: exemption from various taxes (1 July 1342); exemption from all judicial authority, except that of the provost, their normal judge, or of ordinary judges whom the Holy See had entrusted with cases in which they were involved (1 July 1352).

Those who enjoyed these privileges had to fulfil certain obligations. They must never have made any attempt to falsify the weight or the standard of monies entrusted to them, or to have forged money, or been guilty of murder, arson, rape or treason. This last crime had reference to the persons of the pope, the cardinals, the camerarius, the treasurer and the clerks of the Apostolic Camera. Finally, they must have made an oath of loyalty. There was a special clause affecting the moneyers and workmen, who were obliged, after taking their oath, to write their surnames and Christian names in two registers, one of which remained in the possession of the treasurer or

[1] C. Samaran—G. Mollat, *La Fiscalité pontificale en France au XIV* siècle. Période d'Avignon et Grand Schisme d'Occident,* Paris 1905, pp. 1–10, 132–41.

camerarius, while the other was given to the provost. This regulation has enabled us to know exactly how many people of the inferior grades were employed at the mint at Sorgues in July 1352. At that time the moneyers included five clerks and twenty-eight citizens of Avignon.

When the pope decreed that a certain coinage should be issued, he entered into an agreement with those who were to make it and who were accordingly known as 'Masters of this coinage';[1] he then notified the warden by Bull of the value and denomination of the specie that were to be made. More Bulls were sent appointing by name persons skilled in the manufacture of the tools needed to strike the coinage, at the same time warning them not to start work without previous instruction from the warden acting during the pontificate of John XXII in conjunction with the masters of the coinage to be struck, and from the warden alone in the time of Clement VI. They were also forbidden to engrave certain letters except in the presence of the camerarius or the treasurer. A deed, drawn up by a notary, laid down, moreover, the various conditions to be observed in the manufacture of the tools. When these were ready, they had to be given to the warden and the masters of the coinage to be issued, in the presence of the camerarius and the treasurer. Finally, by means of still more Bulls, the pope appointed assayers, usually Italian merchants, whom he put in charge of assaying the specie delivered by the said masters of the coinage.

Then the master of the papal mint and the provost summoned the moneyers and the workmen to come and strike the coinage in whatever place had been appointed: if they refused after being offered a good wage, the master and the provost were entitled to punish them by imposing a fine proportionate to the wages they would have been paid if they had carried out the required work. If they refused three times, the case having been submitted to the camerarius and the treasurer, and their defiance duly noted, these subordinate employees forfeited the privileges attached to their duties.[2]

B. *The Chancery*

The chancery consisted of the various departments dealing with the despatch of papal letters, and had at its head the Vice-Chancellor. At the time of his appointment he might be an abbot, a bishop or an

[1] The duties of these officers, as distinct from those of the master of the papal mint, were temporary and lasted only for the time required to strike the particular coinage which the pope had entrusted to them.

[2] G. Mollat, *Les Papes d'Avignon et leur hôtel des monnaies à Sorgues (Comtat-Venaissin)*, Paris 1908.

auditor of apostolic causes, but he was usually made a cardinal, a status which was compatible with his duties.

He could act only upon a special mandate from the pope and did not enjoy the freedom of action of the camerarius. He was not even allowed to appoint his own staff; or at least there is no document granting him this privilege. His very title of vice-chancellor indicates in itself how subordinate the pope considered him to be.

He took an oath not to commit, directly or indirectly, any injustice or fraud in the despatch of papal letters, to accept no gratuity, and to confer no benefice upon himself, his subordinates or any other person without the consent of the supreme pontiff.[1]

If he were absent from the Curia, he was provided with a deputy, known as his vice-regent, or 'lieutenant.'

From the time of Clement V, with certain exceptions, the chancellor was by right the examiner resident at the court for all candidates for the office of apostolic notary. He it was who issued them with certificates of proficiency and received their oath.[2]

When there was doubt about the despatch of a papal document, he presided over the committee which discussed and elucidated the matter.

Seven departments were under the control of the vice-chancellor: the office of petitions, the office of examinations, the abbreviators' office, the engrossers' office, the corrector's office, the office of the *bullatores* and the registry.

1. *The Office of Petitions*. To obtain a letter of pardon or redress, it was always necessary first to present a petition to the pope, drawn up in correct chancery style, according to formulae that had been in use since the beginning of the thirteenth century.

The cardinals, the camerarius or the notaries delivered the petitions of the supplicants to the pope, who would make a note of his reply on the original itself, thus: *Fiat, fiat ut petitur, fiat si ita est.* This was followed by a conventional initial, used without variation throughout the pontificate. Experts in diplomatic have been unable to discover the significance of these initials: John XXII signed 'B', as did Benedict XII; Clement VI used 'R', Innocent VI 'G', Urban V 'B' and Gregory XI 'R'.

A verbal consent might be given, in which case the vice-chancellor was authorised to write on the petition the word *Concessum*. No doubt he was responsible for the mandates beginning with the formula: *De mandato domini nostri papae*.

---

[1] Tangl, *Die päpstlichen Kanzleiordnungen (1200–1500)*, Innsbruck 1894, p. 34. See also P. M. Baumgarten, *Von der apostolischen Kanzlei*, Cologne 1908, p. 147.
[2] Baumgarten, *op. cit.* pp. 9–68.

At the bottom of the petitions, an official—the *datarius*—added the date of the pope's decision. On 22 June 1371, for example, he would write, *Datum apud Villamnovam, Avinionensis dyocesis, decimo kalendas julii, anno primo.*

When they had been dated, the petitions were sent to the office of petitions, where a note was made in a book called the *Liber de vacantibus* of the name of petitioner, the date on which his request had reached the Curia, and the order in which it was filed, probably by being strung up on a cord by means of a metal tag. When the person concerned or his representative arrived to claim his petition, in order to have it registered, he would look first in the *Liber de vacantibus* to see if the petition had been signed, and on what date, and in which division of the file it had been placed. He would then make the request to a clerk specially delegated for this task, in the following terms: 'Please look for the petition for X, on such and such a date, first division.' Then the clerk would look for it in the file, take it from the string and write the name of the person concerned in the *Liber distributionum*. After this, the registration of the document was carried out. A capital R, on the reverse side, indicated that this had been done. The register into which the originals had been transcribed was called the *Registrum supplicationum*.[1]

A sworn clerk then put the petition into a bag which he sealed and took to the Chancery.

2. *The Office of Examinations.* Unless he were a doctor, or a bachelor or master of arts, every beneficed clerk was obliged to have his competency tested by examination. A porter would show him into the examiners' office, where he would be examined in reading, singing and rhetorical style. The result was given in marks of *bene*, *competenter* or *male*, and was put down in a register by a notary. In the time of Benedict XII the examiners endorsed the petition itself with their signature, but under his successors they issued certificates which had to be presented at the Chancery.[2]

3. *The Abbreviators' Office.* The vice-chancellor provided the ab-

---

[1] In order to elucidate the highly controversial question of the origin of the registers of petitions, distinction should be made between (a) the actual registration of the petitions, and (b) the systematisation of this registration as it appears in the registers available to us. There is no basis for the supposition that Benedict XII introduced the actual registration of petitions, and every reason to believe that it was in use before his reign (see J. Schwalm, *Das Formelbuch des Heinrich Bucglant*, Hamburg 1910, pp. xxxiv–xxxviii). The only innovation that can be attributed to Benedict XII is the transcription of the petitions in their entirety, as has been suggested by one of his biographers (see Baluze, *Vitae*, VOL. I, p. 228). Nevertheless, as no register of the time of Benedict XII is in existence, it must be supposed that the reform promulgated before the end of his pontificate was not implemented until the reign of his successor (see *Bulletin Critique*, ser. 2, VOL. XII, 1906, pp. 381–3).

[2] U. Berlière, *Épaves d'archives pontificales au XIVe siècle*, Bruges 1908, p. 50.

breviators (*abbreviatores*) with the work which they had to do, namely changing petitions from the form of requests to rescripts. On each document he would write the name of the clerk responsible for the work, thus: '*R[ecipe]* *G[uillelme]* *Baronis*—Take this, Guillaume Baron'—and would sign it '*P[etrus]* *Pampil[onensis]*—Pierre de Pampelune.'[1]

Then, basing their work upon the content of the signed petition, the abbreviators would summarise in a few lines the substance of the Bull to be issued. This summary was called a minute (*minuta* or *nota*).

After being checked by the corrector, the minute was handed on to the engrossers' office.

4. *The Engrossers' Office.* The engrossment (*grossa, littera grossata,* or *littera redacta in grossam*) was merely the writing out on parchment of the final version of the Bull, complete with all the formulae and legal phraseology in full.

The office where this work was done was open every day, except on feast-days that were holidays, from nones until suppertime. The scribes (*scriptores litterarum apostolicarum*, or *grossatores*) who worked there in the time of Clement V numbered at first one hundred and ten then, from 27 October 1310, ninety. Under John XXII there were seventy and one hundred and one under Urban V. A distributor of minutes to be engrossed (*distributor notarum grossandarum*) shared out amongst these scribes the work which had to be completed within six days.[2]

5. *The Corrector's Office.* From the engrossing office, the papal rescript was passed to that of the corrector (*correctorius*).

He was a very important official, receiving a salary of as much as 200 florins a year, who revised the engrossed version, examined the privileges and the legal documents produced by those begging indulgences, and made sure that the letters of execution agreed with the favour actually granted. The *auscultator* checked the engrossed version against the minute. The *rescribendarius* handed it back to the engrossers, with a rebuke if necessary, if for any reason a new version had to be prepared. If a scribe had made a mistake so that a second version had to be made, he was deprived of his wages.

When the work of revising the letters of grace and justice was completed, the corrector divided them according to the content of the document, the rank of the person for whom it was intended, and the

[1] *Deutsche Literaturzeitung*, 1908, no. 19, cols. 1209–11.
[2] J. M. Vidal, *Benoît XII (1334–1342). Lettres communes* etc., VOL. III, Paris 1911, pp. viii–ix; Tangl, *op. cit.* pp. 115–17.

circumstances in which it was issued into two categories, namely the *litterae legendae*, which before being given to the parties concerned, were read to the pope, and the *litterae communes* or *simplices*, which were read to the *auditores litterarum contradictarum*.[1]

6. *The Office of the Bullatores*. Two officials called *bullatores* or *fratres de bulla* (or, occasionally, between 1338 and 1342, three) were responsible for affixing the seals to the original copies of Bulls.

They were lay brothers from the Cistercian abbey at Fontfroide in the diocese of Narbonne, and before taking up their duties had, for the most part, held responsible posts in the papal court, such as master of the stable, butler or head gardener.

Unlike the other papal officials, they were not appointed either by the camerarius or by the treasurer; they did not take an oath to them nor were they invested by either of them. The pope was directly responsible for their appointment.

They were appointed for life, and if they were prevented by sickness or old age from carrying out their duties, they supervised their deputies, and received an allowance. If they proved incapable or unworthy, they were retired with a small pension. If they had committed serious misdemeanours, they lost their right to a pension or retirement, and had to return to the monastery from which they came.

The *bullatores* who were deliberately chosen from lay-brethren who could neither read nor write nor speak Latin, employed lettered clerks as scribes, as well as a considerable staff, including a cook, squires whose task was to fetch the lead from the merchants, office boys and personal servants.

Three times a week, one of the *bullatores* went to the chancery after his own office had closed, collected the documents to be sealed, and put them into a bag which a servant, under his supervision, carried back to the office of the *bulla*. This office was outside the papal palace at Avignon, in the parish of St Symphorien; after Urban V and Gregory XI had gone back to Rome, it was set up in the Lateran.

When the Bulls reached the office of the *bulla*, they were locked up in a chest, and taken out to be sealed only as the occasion arose. The manner of their ensealing varied according as to whether they were letters close, patent or of grace. So that the illiterate sealers could tell which had to be sealed on silken strings and which on hempen, the scribes of the chancery filled in with red or left unilluminated the initial letter of the reigning pope's name. The leaden seal, or *bulla*, which gave its name to certain documents issued by

[1] W. von Hofman, in *Römische Quartalschrift*, VOL. XX, 1906, pp. 91–6; Tangl, *op. cit.* p. 36.

the Holy See, was attached to the rescript. A pair of pincers, both sides of which bore a matrix, was used to imprint on one side of the seal the name of the reigning pope, and the other the heads of the apostles Peter and Paul.[1]

7. *The Registry*. The registering of ordinary letters or of those emanating from the Curia does not appear to have been, in principle, compulsory. Nevertheless, incumbents of benefices preferred to incur this expense, so that they might have a double authentication of documents emanating from the chancery, to provide documentary proof if any doubt arose. The Holy See set the example, for the pope was careful to keep up to date the copying of his diplomatic correspondence.

The employees, called registrars (*registratores*) entrusted the writing to scribes (*scriptores registri*), who copied the documents in the order in which they were handed over to them into paper registers, which are known today as the Avignon Registers. The long super scription of the original bull (*N. episcopus, servus servorum Dei, dilecto filio N.*) was there reduced to the shorter formula *Dilecto filio*. The words *Pontificatus nostri* were almost always omitted from the *Datum*. The text of the Bull itself appeared in full in the register.

Underneath this there appeared the formula *In eundem modum*, followed by the names and styles of the executors, and then the summary, where necessary, of a so-called letter of execution, which was in fact sent in triplicate.

In the early part of the fourteenth century, no attempt was made at methodical classification in the registering of Bulls. An experimental method, started under John XXII and continued under Benedict XII, seems to have proved satisfactory to the chancery. From the time of Clement VI, however, the documents were arranged under headings showing their subject-matter. In this way Bulls making appointments to episcopal sees were put together in a section called *De provisionibus praelatorum*, and indulgences for those at the point of death in one entitled *De absolutione in articulo mortis*, and so forth.

A corrector made sure that the transcript was true to the original. The *auscultator* checked the original against the copy. Both of these have left evidence of their activity in the alterations, erasures, words written in, and marginal additions which are to be found in such profusion in the Avignon Registers.

Rubricatores made very brief summaries of the registered documents. These summaries appear at the beginning of the registers,

---

[1] Baumgarten, *op. cit.* pp. 1–154, 247–78.

and serve as a table of contents. Thus, summarising a mandate addressed to the bishop-elect of Ravenna, they would write: *Francisco electo Ravennatensi mandatur ut infra duorum mensium spatium apostolico conspectui se presentet.*

In the spaces separating one document from another was written the number given to the Bull and the amount paid for its registration in Roman figures placed vertically. The sign $\overline{\overline{\overline{X}}}$ indicated that the sum to be paid was fourteen sous *tournois*; $\underset{\underline{\underline{\vee}}}{X}$ that it was seventeen sous *tournois*.

During the Avignon papacy, the chancery had the Bulls that were entered in the paper registers recopied for its own use and in a different order into luxurious parchment ones. These parchment registers were transferred to the Vatican in the time of Eugenius IV and, to differentiate them from the paper registers, which remained at Avignon until 1784, were known as the Vatican Registers.[1]

C. *The Administration of Justice*

During the fourteenth century, the number of cases submitted to the Holy See, either in the first instance or on appeal, rose to such proportions that it became essential to subdivide the power of the judiciary. Until that time, the judges delegated by the pope had had only restricted prerogatives. Their duties consisted simply in pursuing enquiries and hearing pleas. With a few exceptions, the supreme pontiff reserved to himself the right to pronounce judgment. But in the time of Clement V, John XXII and Benedict XII, real courts of justice were set up, such as the Court of the Apostolic Palace, which gave sentence without the possibility of appeal.

Nevertheless, there still existed, as there had done in the past, three other kinds of tribunal at the papal court: the Consistory, the Cardinals' tribunals and the *Audientia Litterarum Contradictarum*.

1. *The Consistory.* The pope and his cardinals, assembled in Consistory, received 'every complaint, denunciation, accusation and other cases of litigation' (*querele, denuntiatio, accusatio et alie jurgantium cause*).[2]

The consistorial advocates, duly registered at the chancery, put forward their clients' requests. Behind them stood the principal parties concerned, and the attorneys and solicitors, ready, if need arose, to refresh their memory, or to ask them to insist upon some particular point of law. While the advocates were speaking, the op-

---

[1] Vidal, *op. cit.* VOL. III, pp. lvii ff.   [2] Tangl, *op. cit.* p. 197.

posing party was obliged to listen to them in silence without noisy interruptions.[1]

With the pope's permission, the chief party concerned could himself present his plea or his defence. When, in 1348, Queen Joanna of Naples was accused of having plotted the death of her first husband, Andrew of Hungary, she defended herself in tones of such sincerity that Clement VI and the Sacred College then and there declared themselves convinced of her innocence.

The procedure in cases submitted to the judgment of the Consistory differed according as to whether the case was heard in the papal see itself, or in the place where the dispute had arisen.

When the dispute was not very important, the Holy See issued Bulls authorising local judges—usually three in number—to take cognizance of the affair (*vocatis qui fuerint evocandi*), hear what the two parties had to say (*auditis hinc inde propositis*) and make a just decision, against which no appeal could be made (*quod justum fuerit, appellatione remota, decernatis*). In order to obtain accurate depositions and make sure that their judgments were carried out, the commissiaries were authorised to employ ecclesiastical censure (*facientes quod decreveritis per censuram ecclesiasticam firmiter observari: testes autem, qui fuerint nominati, si se gratia, odio vel timore subtraxerint censura simili, appellatione cessante, cogatis veritati testimonium perhibere*).[2]

In criminal cases, the procedure was more complicated. In 1339, Benedict XII, being informed that four monks of the abbey of Boulbonne had secretly practised sorcery and alchemy, requested the abbot, Durand, to set up a secret enquiry, to seize the books, papers and effects of the accused, and to prevent their escape. He declared, moreover, that anyone impeding the action of the apostolic commissiary would be liable to ecclesiastical censure, and stated in advance that any appeal would be null. The records of the enquiry carried out by Abbot Durand convinced the pope that the monks were guilty. The abbot of Boulbonne, together with the abbot of Berdoues, was instructed to pronounce sentence on the guilty with the pope's authority, and without possibility of appeal.[3]

When a case was tried in Avignon, apostolic commissiaries carried out an enquiry on the spot in the first instance. If this enquiry made it clear that the complaint was well-founded, the pope either issued Bulls summoning the offending party to appear at his court within a

[1] *Ibid.* pp. 118–24, Constitution *Decens et necessarium*, 27 October 1340.
[2] J. Berthelé, *Plaquettes montpelliéraines et languedociennes*, VOL. V, 1909, pp. 203–08.
[3] J. M. Vidal, 'Moines alchimistes à l'abbaye de Boulbonne (1399),' *Bulletin périodique de la Société ariégeoise des sciences, lettres et arts*, VOL. IX, 1903, pp. 133–40.

stated time on pain of censure, or else he gave to specially appointed magistrates the task of bringing the summons to the notice of the person concerned. In that case, if the magistrates feared reprisals, they would make clear their authority for issuing the summons by affixing the letters patent in which it was given, to the doors of the churches in the dioceses in which the persons summoned possessed lands or had their chief domicile.

If the summons were not heeded, other commissiaries, also appointed by Bull, carried out a summary enquiry and then declared the contumacious party excommunicate and placed his lands under an interdict. If he proved recalcitrant and persisted in his defiance, he was first punished by the *aggrave*, which deprived him of spiritual benefits and excluded him from public life, and then by the *reaggrave*, which isolated him still further by forbidding him either to eat or drink with his fellow-men.

Excommunication, in the fourteenth century, brought with it as its civil consequences loss of all legal existence and, after a year and a day, confiscation of property and seizure of the person. Through lack of co-operation of the part of public authorities, however, the law was seldom rigorously applied in the civil courts. But this was not so in the ecclesiastical tribunals. There the excommunicate lost many rights; he could neither administer nor receive the sacraments, nor even be present at the divine office; he could not be buried according to the rites of the Church, neither elect nor be elected to any benefice or office, nor exercise any temporal jurisdiction. Moreover, if a prelate celebrated the divine office in defiance of the excommunication, he was *ipso facto* guilty of irregularity. So it was that the contumacious rarely persisted in their defiance. They would generally mend their ways in a very short time, and appear in Consistory either in person or by proxy, as soon as the pope admitted the validity of their excuses.

If the parties agreed to sign a compromise, the supreme pontiff confirmed it by Bull, freed the contumacious person from the sentence of excommunication he had incurred and his lands from the interdict and, lastly, appointed local commissiaries to carry out the final award.[1] But only when one of the litigants had a very weak case indeed would he agree to a friendly arrangement. Men of the Middle Ages were fond of litigation, and were in no way daunted by the loss of time and money that a trial involved. For this reason, law-suits would go on from the Consistory to the cardinals' tribunals, or to the Court of the Apostolic Palace.

[1] G. Mollat, *Études et documents sur l'histoire de Bretagne*, pp. 3-21, 157-67.

2. *The Cardinals' Tribunals*. The number of people employed in
the cardinals' tribunals was limited. They consisted of an auditor, a
duly sworn doorkeeper, one or more notaries and a keeper of the
seals.

The auditor took the place of the cardinal, carried out the duties
of an examining magistrate, summoned the litigants to appear before
him, and listened to the pleading. There his activities ended. Judge-
ment was given by the cardinal for whom he deputised.

The notary or clerk of the court drew up the summonses and the
documents of the trial. It was he who placed on the final sentence the
seal of the cardinal who had pronounced it.

The sworn doorkeeper gave notice of summonses, and saw to the
execution of the awards of which he was informed by the notary.

The carrying out of sentences was surrounded by more or less
symbolic formalities. A curious document, dated 28 January 1378,
describes in minute detail those that took place after Cardinal Jean de
Blandiac had pronounced judgment in favour of the bishop of
Avignon, who had been dispossessed of a garden as a result of an
illicit grant made by Gregory XI. The bishop had to be repossessed
of his property. In the presence of the cardinal's sworn doorkeeper,
the bishop's proxy turned the key in the lock, opened the door
into the garden and, having closed it behind him, prodded the earth
with his stick and walked up and down within the walls. Then, in
the name of Jean de Blandiac, the doorkeeper forbade Jeannette de
Bourgogne, the caretaker, and all persons present and absent, to
deliver to anyone but the bishop of Avignon the fruits and the rent
of the garden.[1]

The function of the cardinals' tribunals was not so much to deliver
final judgments, as to institute summary legal proceedings and refer
them to the pope, who pronounced judgment.

The summary procedure, which was introduced by Clement V,
seems to have been highly esteemed at the court of Avignon because
it dealt rapidly with litigation. 'It did not open,' says Paul Fournier,
'with the delivery of the *libellus* (a written document in which the
suppliant briefly set forth his plea) but with an oral account of the
case. This account was summarised by the notary in the *acta causae*,
so that the judge and the defendant could know the nature and purpose of the plea. The defendant was as usual called to appear before
the judge by a summons. The judge disregarded all delaying demur-
rers, and all frivolous appeals inspired by a spirit of chicanery with

[1] P. Pansier, *L'Œuvre des repenties à Avignon du XIIIe au XVIIIe siècle*, Paris
1910, pp. 229–31, 233.

the sole object of impeding the progress of the case. The formality of the *litis contestatio* [1] was not required, but, on the other hand, the oaths *de calumnia* and *de veritate dicenda* were insisted upon, since they provided a guarantee that there would be no dissimulation of the truth. The opposing parties developed their proofs and discussed them freely; the judge was careful only to prevent the advocates and attorneys from being too long-winded and to cut short the depositions where the witnesses appeared too numerous and irrelevant. He interrogated the parties if necessary in order to form his own opinion; he then gave the verdict which had to be written down and which took into consideration every point raised in the plea.' [2]

Unlike the auditors of cases heard in the Apostolic Palace, the cardinals had to receive from the pope a specific delegation of authority detailing their powers every time they examined a case. Their tribunals were accordingly nothing more than tribunals of demurrer.

While recourse to their court had the advantage of speeding the outcome of litigation, it also involved some rather serious inconvenience. The sudden departure of a cardinal on a mission might interrupt the progress of the suit; in this case the litigants had to make a formal request to the pope for their case to be heard by another magistrate. Even if the cardinal did not leave the papal court, proceedings often suffered unexpected delays. Just as the cardinal was about to hear the plaintiffs' case, a messenger might summon him to the pope's palace, or a visitor of note knock at his door. Then the hearing would be put off until a later date, which the judge, because of his manifold duties, was unable to specify exactly.

To win the cardinal's favour, the attorneys, in the name of their clients, would bring presents—chickens, capons, partridges, rabbits, calves, oxen and other gifts of food. They were lavish, too, in giving tips to the door-keeper, so that they might come in out of their turn, and to the chamberlains and chaplains who might show them into their masters' presence. [3] Henry Bucglant, the representative of the burghers of Hamburg at the court of Avignon, complained in 1338 that the chamberlain of the cardinal of Autun was favouring his opponents. On their instigation the chamberlain had him driven out of his house by the cardinal's squires, on the pretext that this dwelling

---

[1] The *litis contestatio* was a formality whereby the defendant, having taken cognizance of the *libellus*, met the plea with a formal contradiction in the presence of the judge and the plaintiff (P. Fournier, *Les Officialités au moyen âge*, Paris 1880, pp. 170–4).
[2] P. Fournier, *op. cit.* pp. 231–2.
[3] *Inventaire des archives de la ville de Bruges*, VOL. I, pp. 206–18. See also Th. Schrader, *Die Rechnungsbücher*, pp. 93 ff.

belonged to those wearing the cardinal's livery. Bucglant had to bring an action before the camerarius, before he could return to his lodging.[1]

3. *The Court of the Apostolic Palace*. The Court of the Apostolic Palace became known as the tribunal of the Rota, a name which was in common use from 1330, but which does not appear in papal documents. The *rota* was the name given to a circular bench on which the judges sat and which was padded in 1352. The shape of this bench caused the tribunal itself to be called the Rota. The oldest document in which it is mentioned is dated 10 April 1274. At that time the auditor could not make an award except on the pope's orders and after consultation with his colleagues. In documents of a later date, specific delegation of power is no longer mentioned.[2] On the other hand, we know that on 18 January 1307, Bernard Rouiard received general authority to take cognizance of all cases relating to benefices and to deliver final judgments upon them.[3] On 16 November 1331, the Constitution *Ratio juris*[4] drew up the definitive regulations for the working of the court.

Every day, about the hour of terce, after the bell had rung from Notre-Dame-des-Doms, the auditors of apostolic causes took their seats in their respective lodgings, or in the convent of the Dominican friars, or, later, in a room on the south side of the palace fitted out for them by John XXII. This building was badly constructed and disappeared in the time of Clement VI who placed at the judges' disposal the magnificent hall known as the *Audienzia*, which is still to be seen. On feast days the judges did not sit except on special instruction from the pope.

No limits were placed on the competency of the auditors of apostolic causes. They examined all cases referred to them by the pope and the vice-camerarius. Nevertheless, suits arising from the collation of benefices as a result of papal reservation were their principal concern.

They were forbidden, on pain of one month's suspension, to accept any 'consideration' either directly or indirectly, or to reveal to the interested parties anything concerning the proceedings before they were over. On a second offence, they were permanently deprived of office. If by chance they gave advice to one of the parties summoned before them, the case went to other auditors.

Before any affair could be dealt with at the Roman Curia, the

---

[1] Schrader, *op. cit.* p. 67.
[2] F. E. Schneider, 'Zur Entstehungsgeschichte der römischen Rota als Kollegialgericht,' *Kirchengeschichtliche Festgabe A. de Waal*, Freiburg 1913, pp. 20–36.
[3] *Regestum Clementis Papae V*, no. 2262.   [4] Tangl, *op. cit.* pp. 63–91.

admissibility of the case at issue had to be established. The plaintiff's attorney sent in an application stating the nature of the dispute, and asking for the appointment of an auditor to examine and settle it. On this original document the pope or the vice-camerarius wrote their reply.

The judge thus appointed issued a summons to the absent party. This summons was made in public session of the *audientia litterarum contradictarum*, and the document effecting it carried the seal of the *audientia* on the dorso.

After the issuing of the usual summonses, the representatives of the opposing parties appeared before the appointed auditor, and each received an injunction to present a written declaration (*libellus*) within a stated time. This done, they took the oaths *de calumnia et veritate dicenda* and were invited to produce, on a specific date, their depositions (*positiones*), counts of indictment and pleas of exception, together with all deeds, letters, instruments, rights and proofs, except when the rules of legal procedure permitted a postponement.

After the representatives had made their concluding statements, the auditors declared the discussion closed, and gave a date to the opposing parties to come and hear the final verdict.[1]

When they had set out their conclusions in detail, the auditors signed the document and appended on silken cords the seal of red wax. After 1331 they were obliged to communicate their findings to their colleagues of the same status, and from about 1341, to those on the same roster. These colleagues had to give their opinion within twelve days.[2]

They wrote it in their own hand, in terms such as these: *supradictam conclusionem veram esse credo et meum sigillum appono, idem credo et sigillo prefatam conclusionem tam ex pretactis quam aliis rationibus credo esse veram et de jure procedere in quorum robur manu propria subscripsi et sigillum meum appendi*, etc.

Each auditor had in his service not more than four clerks or notaries who entered the verdicts in a register and sent copies to the parties concerned. These copies were sent free if the supplicant could prove poverty.

The office of auditor could only be administered by jurisconsults of some reputation, who were graded according to their seniority and referred to as of the first, second or third class. This classification, legalised by the Constitution *Ratio juris* in 1331, was already in exist-

[1] G. Mollat, 'Contribution à l'histoire de l'administration judiciaire de l'Église romaine au XIVe siècle,' *R.H.E.* VOL. XXXII, 1936, pp. 877–96.
[2] Ottenthal, *Die päpstlichen Kanzleiregeln*, Innsbruck 1888, p. 36, no. 60.

ence in 1317–18 but presumably fell into disuse in the time of Clement VI.

The auditors, whose exact number is not known,[1] were obliged to wear cope and rochet out of doors in the place where the Curia was residing.

They could not be excommunicated, suspended or interdicted, except by the camerarius.[2] No-one could appeal from a decision made by the auditors; but while a trial was in progress, the parties concerned could use every delaying tactic that the spirit of chicanery could devise to impede its smooth running. In 1355, the nuns of Coyroux, near Obasine in the diocese of Limoges, complained to Innocent VI that their suit had been dragging on for eighteen months. Hugues de Guiscard was disputing their right to the parish church of Cornac in the diocese of Cahors, and for this purpose was making use of quibbles which the nuns were pleased to enumerate.

The case was being heard by the auditor Jean Aubert, and had reached the stage of the *litis contestatio*, when the attorney of Hugues de Guiscard lodged an appeal. The magistrate, Simon Subuca, made certain orders, against which the sisters of Coyroux appealed in their turn, alleging *gravamina*. A third auditor, Guillaume de Gimel, brought the case to its final stages, the award excepted. At this precise moment, the abbot and monks of Figeac asked for an injunction against the principal party, and laid before the first auditor, Jean Aubert, *libelli* against both Hugues de Guiscard and the nuns of Coyroux; hence the interruption of the hearing before Guillaume de Gimel.

Meanwhile, at the request of Hugues, Jean Aubert was discharged and Pierre d'Ylhan entrusted with the action brought by the abbot of Figeac, although this had already reached the stage of *litis contestatio*.

At the demand of Hugues de Guiscard again, both affairs were submitted to Pierre d'Ylhan. But an interlocutory decision by this judge failed to satisfy and notice of appeal was given. Guillaume de Gimel was put in charge of the appeal, but as he was away from the Curia, the litigants had to take their case to a fourth auditor, Oldrad de Maynières.

Weary of their opponents' frivolous appeals and quibblings, destined only to delay the matter, the nuns of Coyroux, as a last resort, implored Innocent VI to hand over their case to a cardinal

---

[1] Sixtus IV, on 14 May 1472, fixed the number of auditors at twelve. In 1323, there were eight. See Tangl, 'Eine Rota-Verhandlung vom Jahre 1323,' *Mitteilungen*, additional VOL. VI, 1901, pp. 320–32. [2] Ottenthal, *op. cit.* p. 33, no. 52.

who, despite any appeals that might be made, would examine it quickly and bring it to an end; this request was granted.[1]

This one example, chosen from thousands, shows how inventive could be the spirit of chicanery and how long a law-suit could last. That of the sisters of Coyroux had dragged on for eighteen months; but this was nothing compared with the suit brought by the canons of Hamburg against the burgesses of that town, which began at the court of Avignon in 1337 and only ended—and then in a compromise—in 1353.

4. *The Audientia Litterarum Contradictarum.* Before a suit had reached the stage of *litis contestatio*,[2] the defendant was entitled to challenge the person of the plaintiff or the magistrate, or to refuse to attend at the place where the court of justice was set up. He might, for example, object on the grounds that the plaintiff was excommunicate and therefore debarred from bringing a legal action; plead that the attorneys had insufficient authority, or none at all; accuse the judge of partiality; or point out that his life would be endangered if he had to appear in a certain locality. In the same way, he was allowed to object to the despatch of a papal rescript committing a case to a deputy, or to question the authenticity of documents submitted by his opponent. The examination of expedients invented by the spirit of chicanery to delay the progress of an action took place in a special office called, from the thirteenth century, the 'Court of Objections,' *audientia litterarum contradictarum*, or more simply, the 'Public Audience,' *audientia publica*.

The auditor who was in charge of this court acted as a judge. He decided the validity of dilatory objections. When the parties could not agree on the choice of the examining magistrate, he appointed one by virtue of his office. He took cognizance of all disputes provoked by documents produced for the trial, verified the authenticity of such documents and ordered copies to be made of them, or declared them invalid. It was part of his duty to make sure that the letters of award sent by the pope or by the vice-chancellor or the corrector of apostolic letters were read in public audience to allow the persons concerned to object if they so wished.

The auditor employed two sworn readers who, starting early in the morning, read aloud in a clear voice, omitting nothing and adding nothing of their own.

When this reading was completed, the attorneys for the parties concerned rose to their feet and stated their objections. It appears

---

[1] E. Albe, *Titres et documents concernant le Quercy et le Limousin*, Brive 1905, pp. 18–19.   [2] See above, p. 298.

from the Constitution *Qui exacti temporis*, dated 16 November 1331,[1] which lays down the rules of procedure for the *audientia litterarum contradictarum*, that incidents often occurred during the reading sessions. The attorneys did not wait for the correct moment to protest. They tried to drown the readers' voices, and prevent them from continuing their reading by raucous shouts, whistles and all kinds of uproar. John XXII punished the first breaking of silence by a fine of one sou *tournois*, and the third by a further fine of three sous *tournois* and suspension from office for a year. The pope took every precaution to prevent frauds from being committed by the attorneys. The auditors followed his example, and in the fourteenth century issued a large number of regulations intended to check fraudulent practices. The fact that these attempts were so often renewed shows the futility of the measures.

Sworn notaries drew up the text of summonses, monitory letters, authentications and in general all documents issued by the auditor.[2]

D. *The Apostolic Penitentiary*

It was the function of the Apostolic Penitentiary to remove ecclesiastical censures (excommunication, suspension or interdict), to lift sentences of irregularity (that is the canonical prohibition from exercising sacerdotal duties), and to grant marriage dispensations and absolution in certain special cases.

The person in charge of this administration was called the Grand Penitentiary; he was always a cardinal-priest or a cardinal-bishop, and was directly responsible to the pope to whom he took oath. His duties continued during a vacancy of the Holy See, unless he took part in the Conclave. If he happened to die during this period, the cardinals had the right to appoint his successor. The symbol of his office was the *ferula* or wand that he bore on solemn feast-days. The staff who carried out his orders were under his supervision.

A confidential official (*persona sufficiens*) accepted and examined the pleas from the petitioners or their attorneys. When the proposal was not ambiguous, he ordered a mandate to be issued. When it presented some difficulty, he submitted it to a doctor of canon law who in his turn, if he were at a loss, passed it on to the Grand Penitentiary. In the last resort, the pope was consulted, but only with the consent of the Grand Penitentiary.

The doctor of canon law also read those letters called 'declaratory

---

[1] Tangl, *op. cit.* pp. 111–15.
[2] J. Teige, *Beiträge zur Geschichte der Audientia litterarum contradictarum*, Prague 1897, pp. 5–92.

or deliberative', written by scribes of the Penitentiary, examined them and gave them, either in person or through an accredited courier, to the Sealer.

The Distributor accepted petitions, divided the work amongst the scribes, taxed the letters, accepted the sums of money paid out by the petitioners, and each month divided this money among the scribes.

There were twelve scribes (*scriptores*) of the Penitentiary, under Clement V, and eighteen under Clement VI. They were obliged, on pain of a fine, to despatch the letters they had been entrusted to write within twenty-four hours of the receipt of the petitions and not to refuse to write out the graces where these had been granted free of charge.

At the hour of prime, or at whatever time had been arranged, the Correctors (*correctores*) looked over the letters written by the scribes, and then took them to the Sealer, who affixed the seal of the Grand Penitentiary. After this a Distributor or some trustworthy person handed over the documents to the parties concerned.

The lesser penitentiaries (*penitentarii minores*), who varied from twelve to eighteen in number during the course of the fourteenth century, belonged to the mendicant orders. Very occasionally they were chosen from the secular clergy, or from the Benedictines or the Cluniacs. Whatever their origin, they were subjected to a very searching examination before taking up office. Their duties consisted in hearing confessions, from prime until terce, in the cathedral or principal church of the place where the pope was residing. Their powers were strictly limited to the persons whose confessions they heard, and were not transferable. If a penitent's case presented difficulties or was outside their scope, they referred it to the Grand Penitentiary or to the supreme pontiff, in the form of a petition. Otherwise they granted either dispensation or absolution. If an authenticated document were required, the distributor ordered the scribes present to write a letter immediately; this was then revised and the seal of one of the penitentiaries affixed if that of the confessor of the party concerned were not available.

Such was the staff of the Apostolic Penitentiary as listed in the Bull *In agro Dominico* which, on 8 April 1338, laid down regulations for the running of this department.[1] Various contemporary documents reveal the existence of other officials: the lieutenant (*locumtenens*) of the Penitentiary who acted for the Grand Penitentiary during his absence; the auditor of the Penitentiary (*auditor Penitentiariae*) whose duties were similar to those of the doctor of canon law and

---

[1] Cocquelines, *Bullarum*, VOL. III, pt 2, pp. 259–64.

who, in addition, tried forgers of penitentiary letters and offenders coming within the jurisdiction of the Grand Penitentiary, and sentenced the guilty to imprisonment or signed discharges. Lastly, there was the auditor's notary.[1]

As will now be readily understood, the organisation of the various parts of the machinery of the central administration of the Roman Church in the fourteenth century was extremely complicated. The detailed nature of papal prescriptions indicates the constant anxiety of the popes who framed them to prevent fraud and forestall corrupt practice. This is the characteristic feature of the work of the popes at Avignon, particularly of John XXII and Benedict XII. It bears the stamp of French genius and was to last and to serve as a basis for the innovations in points of detail that popes in future ages were to deem necessary.

4

The Cardinals

In the formal language of the Chancery, the cardinals are 'the pillars of the Church,' and their importance in the fourteenth century does not belie this description.

The oligarchic tendencies which had produced the systematic reduction in the number of the cardinals in the Sacred College from the twelfth century onwards, were even more apparent in the fourteenth.[2] This tendency was particularly noticeable in the Conclave of Innocent VI, when the elected pope signed an agreement[3] which he hastened to revoke as soon as he was crowned.

The cardinals took a very large share in the general administration of the Roman Church. The pope often summoned them to meet in open or secret Consistory. He acted only after consulting them. Before making any promotion to the cardinalate, he sounded them on the opportuneness of such a promotion, and on the number and character of possible candidates. In grave matters such as, for instance, the question of the crusade or the definition of a dogma, his 'brothers,' the cardinals, supplied him with written memoranda (*vota*) and gave reasons for their views.[4]

---

[1] E. Göller, *Die päpstliche Poenitentiarie*, VOL. I, pt I, Rome 1907.
[2] In the various conclaves to elect the Avignon popes, the lowest number of cardinals was eighteen, and the highest twenty-six.
[3] See above, p. 44–5. See also J. Lulvès, 'Päpstliche Wahlkapitulationen,' *Quellen*, VOL. XII, 1909, pp. 189–211.
[4] Coulon, VOL. II, cols. 281–318. See also F. Tocco, *La quistione della povertà nel secolo XIV*, 1910.

Such was their influence in politics that governments contended for their favour. The highly informative correspondence of the Aragonese ambassadors at the courts of Clement V and John XXII shows by what intrigues the cardinals were surrounded. Kings and princes carried on uninterrupted correspondence with the cardinals, and did not disdain to call them their 'friends.' They even granted them pensions. The needy Emperor Charles IV allowed Pietro Corsini an annual income of 1,000 florins from the revenues of Florence.[1] In 1354, in return for an annual payment of 300 florins, the Florentines succeeded in persuading Pierre Bertrand, Rinaldo Orsini and Bertrand de Déaulx to further their interests, and greeted them with the significant title of 'Protectors.'[2] The Visconti were unsparing with their gold in Avignon in their efforts to thwart the Italian policy of Albornoz.

The cardinals did, in fact, have their own political opinions, or at least represented, in general, that of their native land. Moreover, some of them did not fear to cross the pope, as did Napoleone Orsini, who openly made common cause with Louis of Bavaria and the rebel Franciscans against the Holy See, or Pierre de Colombiers and Guy de Boulogne who, unknown to Innocent VI, conspired to work out a plan to dismember the kingdom of France and allowed meetings to take place in their own residences between the duke of Lancaster and the king of Navarre.[3]

It would, indeed, have been difficult for these prelates not to act like politicians, since there were usually political reasons for their elevation to the purple. It was very much in the interests of the kings of France to have champions at the court of Avignon, especially while they were at war with England. They were always urgently requesting the pope to consider as candidates men who had often been their clerks, counsellors, vice-chancellors or members of their household. Moreover, the preponderance of French cardinals in the Sacred College is one of the characteristics of the Avignon Papacy. Of the one hundred and thirty-four cardinals created by Clement V, John XXII, Benedict XII, Clement VI, Innocent VI, Urban V and Gregory XI, thirteen were Italian, five Spanish, two English, one Genoan and one hundred and thirteen French. It should be noted, however, that the exclusion of Germans from the Sacred College dates back to Gregory IX, and was to continue until the time of the Great Schism, when Urban VI, repudiated by France, sought sup-

[1] H. Otto, 'Ungedruckte Aktenstücke aus der Zeit Karls IV.,' *Quellen*, VOL. IX, 1906, pp. 72–83.
[2] *Archivio storico italiano*, ser. 5, VOL. XXXVII, 1906, p. 29.
[3] G. Mollat, *R.H.E.* VOL. X, 1909, p. 742.

port from the Emperor, and in an effort to please him, nominated one of his subjects as cardinal.

Although the cardinals were chiefly chosen on political grounds, they were personages of some importance in the fourteenth century, and worthy servants of the Church. Most of them were still young and actively employed as legates and nuncios; on occasion they did not even hesitate to visit battlefields, to compel the belligerents to accept their mediation. Gaucelme de Jean, Napoleone Orsini, Guy de Boulogne, and Simon Langham were skilful diplomats. Bertrand du Poujet and Albornoz had genuine talents both as warriors and as statesmen. Legal experts of repute were worthily represented by Guillaume de Mandagout, Bérenger Frédol, Bertrand de Montfavès, Gozzo di Rimini, Bertrand de Déaulx, Pierre Flandrin and Pierre Bertrand.

The dignity of cardinal demanded a glittering retinue. His household consisted of a chamberlain, an auditor, a sworn porter, one or more clerks, an attorney, scribes and footmen, a doctor, an apothecary, chaplains, resident clergy, a master of the horse, grooms and many other servants.[1] In 1316, John XXII forbade his cardinals to have more than ten squires in their retinue, and reduced the splendour of their train.[2] In addition to their staff they had a following, almost as numerous, of clerks and laymen, scholars and artists, poets and humanists, who came to seek fame, fortune and honours at Avignon. Petrarch excelled himself in his attacks on the cardinals: 'Instead of the Apostles who went barefoot,' he wrote, 'we now see satraps mounted on horses decked with gold and champing golden bits, and whose very hoofs will soon be shod with gold if God do not restrain their arrogant display of wealth. They could be taken for kings of the Persians or of the Parthians, who demand to be worshipped and into whose presence must no man come empty-handed.'[3] But Petrarch as much as anybody else was eager to gain their favour.

To house his little court, a cardinal needed extensive premises. In 1316, the establishment of Arnaud d'Aux occupied thirty-one houses or parts of houses; in 1321, that of Bernard de Garves needed fifty-one.[4] When Urban V returned to Italy, Pierre de Banhac had so many horses that he had to rent ten stables for them in Rome. Five of these stables held thirty-nine horses.[5]

[1] F. Duchesne, *Histoire de tous les cardinaux françois*, VOL. II, Paris 1666, p. 433.
[2] H. Finke, *Acta Aragonensia*, VOL. I, p. 225.
[3] De Sade, *Mémoires pour la vie de François Pétrarque*, VOL. II, p. 95. Petrarch, *Seniles*, Bk XV.
[4] S. Fantoni Castrucci, *Istoria della città d'Avignone*, Bk II, VOL. I, Venice 1678, pp. 164-5.
[5] P. M. Baumgarten, *Aus Kanzlei und Kammer*, Freiburg 1907, p. 63.

We may gain some idea of the splendour and state in which these cardinals lived from their wills and the inventories of their furniture made after death. When Hugues Roger, the son of a country squire from near Limoges, died in 1364, he left 150,000 gold florins in his coffers, not counting about 20,000 seized by his executors, and 6,000 later paid by a debtor; in other words, more than ten million francs in gold.[1] The wills of other members of the Sacred College specify vast sums to be given to charity or for pious foundations. It is typical of their extreme wealth that even popes borrowed from them. Thus in 1350, Clement VI acknowledged that he owed the Sacred College 16,000 gold florins; and in 1358 Innocent VI made a similar acknowledgement for 7,000.[2]

The wealth of the cardinals came from various sources. In the first place, they received gifts from the pope at the time of his election: John XXII and Benedict XII bestowed 100,000 florins on those who had elected them; Clement VI gave them 108,000, Innocent VI 75,000 and Urban V 40,000.[3] At each anniversary of the coronation of the reigning pontiff and at the great religious feasts, the members of the Sacred College received generous gifts of food, jewels or cash. The cardinals were allowed to accumulate benefices, and took full advantage of this apostolic dispensation. Even obscure benefices were sought after if they brought in a substantial income, as we may see from this short note written by Armand de Villemur and doubtless addressed to one of his colleagues: 'My most reverend lord, I have just learned through a friend that the bishop-elect of Constance, who has just been promoted today, is at present the incumbent of an excellent church or living at Veine. If His Holiness saw fit to grant it to me, he would be performing a work of piety.'[4]

In addition to these extraordinary sources of income, the cardinals had also regular ones. Since the assignment made to them by Nicholas IV, 18 July 1289, the cardinals had the right to half the regular income of the Church, that is to say, to half of the taxes both great and small paid by monasteries, churches, feudatories and castellans, to half of the taxes owed by kingdoms subject to the Holy See, to half of Peter's Pence, and to half the net amounts received from the Comtat-Venaissin and the Papal States in Italy.[5] In addition to those benefits already granted, on 23 December 1334,

[1] Baluze, *Vitae*, VOL. IV, p. 127.
[2] P. M. Baumgarten, *Untersuchungen und Urkunden*, Leipzig 1898, pp. 192, 245.
[3] P. M. Baumgarten, 'Wahlgeschenke der Päpste an das heilige Kollegium,' *Römische Quartalschrift*, VOL. XXII, 1908, pp. 36–47.
[4] U. Berlière, *Suppliques de Clément VI*, Paris 1906, p. xvii.
[5] Potthast, *Regesta Pontif. roman.*, no. 23010.

Benedict XII allowed them to receive for the term of his life the visitation tax (*visitationes ad limina apostolorum*).[1] As for the ordinary services not mentioned either by him or by Nicholas IV, numerous documents prove that the Sacred College had had a share in them from the twelfth century onwards, but not a half share.[2]

The finances of the Sacred College were administered by a special department, the Chamber (*Camera*) of the College of Cardinals (*Camera Collegii reverendissimorum in Christo patrum dominorum Sanctae Romanae Ecclesiae cardinalium*), directed by a cardinal appointed jointly by the pope and the cardinals, and known as the Cardinal-Camerarius of the Sacred College.

The charge of the cardinal-camerarius was twofold: he had to supervise the incoming of the revenues of the Sacred College and effect their division among those entitled to receive them.

The Common Services provided at once the most substantial and the most regular source of income for the Sacred College. Consequently the cardinal-camerarius was present, either in person or by proxy, in the Apostolic Camera whenever prelates newly elected to bishoprics or abbeys solemnly swore to pay, within an agreed period, the tax fixed by custom. He remained, moreover, in constant relation with the camerarius of the Apostolic Camera. Together they granted remission of debts or deferment of payment, issued quittances, lifted sentences of irregularity and of excommunication incurred as the result of delays in payment. The tax-payers, however, did not make direct payment in the cardinal-camerarius, but to the Apostolic Camera, which then paid the cardinals their share.

A very strict check was kept on the administration of the cardinals' revenues and the way they were divided among members of the Sacred College. Cardinals were not entitled to draw on the budget until after the ceremony of their enthronement. This consisted of three rites: the *aperitio oris*, when the pope granted them the right to be present at Consistories and take part in discussions there; the assignment to them of a titular church; and the receiving of the ring, the symbol of their relationship with the Roman Church.[3]

Cardinals absent from the Curia for any reason, other than sickness or a regular dispensation, received no share of the revenues of the Sacred College, even if they were absent on a legation. This did

---

[1] E. Göller, *Die Einnahmen der apostolischen Kammer unter Benedikt XII* (Görres-Gesellschaft, VOL. IV, Paderborn 1910–37), p. 2.
[2] E. Göller, *Die Einnahmen der apostolischen Kammer unter Johann XXII* (Görres-Gesellschaft, VOL. I), pp. 20*–52*.
[3] The ceremonial of the nomination and enthronement of the cardinals, as used in the time of Benedict XII, is set out in Rinaldi, *ad annum* 1338, §83–7.

not, however, involve the legates in any loss, for the supreme pontiff compensated them in other ways, notably by granting them the right to claim lodging wherever they might be.

To help him carry out his duties, the cardinal-camerarius had a staff directly responsible to him. Until the death of Clement V, he had one clerk called the *procurator et officialis Sacri Collegii*, and from then on two clerks, known until 1332 as *distributores et receptores pecuniarum Collegii* and later as clerks of the Sacred College (*clerici Collegii*). These clerks kept the registers and had charge of the distribution of the cardinals' monies. They had *servitores* and scribes to help them.[1]

5

Extravagant Living at the Court of Avignon; Feasts and Expenditure

The papal court outshone all the other courts of Europe by the extravagance of its living and the splendour of its feasts.

The furnishings inside the Palais des Doms 'showed a strange mixture of sumptuousness and simplicity.' The stone floors of the bedrooms were covered with matting which, until the time of Clement VI, was made of straw and rushes. The windows in the palace, except those in the chapel and the Consistory, contained not glass, but waxed linen. The rooms were decorated with great display of luxury. Carpets ornamented the halls and rooms of state. Rich materials hid the furniture which in itself was simple enough. When the walls were not covered with paintings, they were hung with finely woven tapestries made in the workshops of Spain and Flanders, or with hangings of silk, taffeta, or green or red serge.

The gold and silver plate included utensils of every kind: trays, drinking-vessels, goblets with lids, ewers, sauce-boats, bowls, jugs for wine and water, basins, silver-gilt flagons elaborately wrought, knives and forks with handles of ivory or jasper. The plate of Clement V weighed seven hundred marks, or about 159 kilograms; that of Clement VI in 1348 weighed eight hundred and sixty-two marks, or nearly 196 kilograms.[2]

Clothes were expensive. A length of scarlet cloth for the pope cost from 70 to 150 florins; a piece of gold brocade imported from Venice,

---

[1] P. M. Baumgarten, *Untersuchungen und Urkunden*, pp. xxxiv–clxxvii.
[2] One mark at the papal court was equivalent to 226·623 grammes. See P. Guilhiermoz, 'Note sur les poids du moyen âge,' *B.E.C.* VOL. LXVII, 1906, pp. 413–14.

30 florins, the sable lining for a cloak, 75 to 100 florins. In 1347 Clement VI bought forty cloths of gold diversely coloured and woven at Damascus in Syria at a cost of 1,278 florins. Silk came from Tuscany, serge from Tournai, white woollen cloth from Carcassonne, and broad-cloth from Brussels, Malines, Louvain, Arras, Anduze, Alais, St Gilles in Gard, Narbonne in Aude, Béziers, Clermont, Montpellier, Pézenas, St Thibéry in Hérault and Toulouse. Fine linen was exported from Rheims, Paris or Flanders.

During John XXII's reign the cost of clothing the papal household amounted on an average to 7,842 florins a year. Clothes for the summer were distributed in the spring and clothes for the winter in the autumn. The winter clothing of a sergeant was worth five florins, a penitentiary's eight and a master of theology's twelve.

Fur being considered a luxury article, its use was restricted to knights, pages, squires, gentlemen of the bedchamber and ladies of the court. It was used on an enormous scale. Clement VI used up to 1,080 ermine pelts for the following purposes: 68 for a hood, 430 for a cape, 310 for a mantle, 150 for two hoods, 64 for another hood, 30 for a hat, 80 for a large hood, 88 for nine birettas.[1] John XXII even had his pillow trimmed with fur.

The normal bill of fare for the pope's table gives little evidence of refined taste. The caterer for the kitchens used to buy whalemeat by the hundredweight, and lay in a large stock of salt meat. But if the pope's guests were no gourmets, they had healthy appetites as we can see from the account of the food served on 22 November 1324 at the dinner given by John XXII to celebrate the marriage of his great-niece, Jeanne de Trian, with the young Guichard de Poitiers. On that occasion they ate 4,012 loaves of bread, $8\frac{3}{4}$ oxen, $55\frac{1}{4}$ sheep, 8 pigs, 4 boars, a large quantity of different kinds of fish, 200 capons, 690 chickens, 580 partridges, 270 rabbits, 40 plovers, 37 ducks, 50 pigeons, 4 cranes, 2 pheasants, 2 peacocks, 292 small birds, 3 cwt. 2 lbs. of cheese, 3,000 eggs, a mere 2,000 apples, pears and other fruits; they drank 11 barrels of wine.[2] In 1323, at the wedding-feast of Bernarde de Via, the great-niece of John XXII, and in 1324 at that of the pope's brother Pierre, more than 931 and 720 florins respectively were spent, that is about 70,000 and 54,000 francs in gold coin.[3]

To provision the court necessitated extensive commercial dealings. It was easy for the Apostolic Camera to find corn, wine, oil and fruits from the fertile valleys of the Saône and the Rhône or the

---

[1] E. Müntz, 'L'Argent et le luxe à la cour pontificale d'Avignon,' *R.Q.H.* VOL. LXVI, 1899, p. 388.   [2] *Introitus et exitus*, 65 fol. 39ᵛ.
[3] Schäfer, *Die Ausgaben*, pp. 76–8, 82–6.

surrounding countryside; wood it procured from the Genevan region, tunny-fish from Marseilles and Montpellier, whalemeat from La Rochelle and herring from Bordeaux. In the time of Gregory XI, instead of getting supplies from the Mediterranean ports near to Avignon, the Apostolic Camera brought salt fish from the north and west of France. At Quimper, the collector for the ecclesiastical province of Tours, transformed for the moment into a travelling merchant, bought stockfish and *toilljs* costing, in 1372, 2 sous and 11 deniers and, in 1373, 2 sous apiece; at Dieppe and Boulogne-sur-Mer he bought herrings at 8 francs 5 sous the thousand; at Orleans he bought them for 4 francs 10 sous the five hundred, and at Tours he bought salmon at the rate of 26 sous 8 deniers each. The purchase price included the cost of transport to Avignon by land and water, and of providing board and lodging for those who accompanied the convoy, but not their wages. Moreover, toll dues were payable in kind, and varied considerably. Of the 3,010 stockfish that left Quimper in 1372, 40 were taken in two tolls (representing a cash value of 5 francs, 16 sous and 8 deniers); of 19,370 herrings, only 1,370 (about 10 francs) were seized; and of the 3,283 stockfish despatched from Quimper in 1372, only 33 (worth 3 francs 5 sous) were taken. To sum up, in 1372 and 1373, the purchases made by the collector Guy de La Roche in Brittany and elsewhere amounted to 954 francs, 12 sous and 2 deniers.[1]

Religious festivals were celebrated with great ceremony. In Holy Week and at certain solemn feasts, the people of Avignon came thronging to the courtyard of the papal palace. A great bay-window opposite Clement VI's chapel, opened above the passage-way leading to the audience chambers and the grand staircase. There the pope would appear and give the crowd his pontifical blessing.[2]

At Notre-Dame-des-Doms the supreme pontiff himself would very often officiate, and would preach to his court. The sermons delivered by John XXII and Clement VI are famous.

On the fourth Sunday in Lent took place the ceremony of presenting the golden rose. This precious jewel, of which an example may still be seen at the Musée de Cluny in Paris, was worth more than 100 florins, or 6,000–7,500 gold francs. In the fourteenth century it was made like the branch of a rose-tree. A sapphire shone at the centre of a rose whose petals were wide open. The buds were adorned with pearls and garnets. In 1368, despite the protests of his

[1] G. Mollat, *Études et documents sur l'histoire de Bretagne*, pp. 168–71.
[2] Colombe, 'Au palais des papes; la grande fenêtre,' *Revue du Midi*, VOL. XLII, 1909, pp. 791–5; 'La Fenêtre de l'indulgence au palais des papes d'Avignon,' *Mémoires de l'académie de Vaucluse*, ser. 2, VOL. X, 1910, pp. 33–40.

cardinals, Urban V gave the rose to Queen Joanna of Naples although, according to the rules of protocol, this honour should really have gone to the king of Cyprus who was at the court at the time.[1]

Once a year, on Christmas Day, the pope presented a belt of silver, a sword, and a hat or cap ornamented with fine pearls, to a lord who had distinguished himself by some outstanding act in the service of Christendom, or had shown unusual ability in some important negotiation. The recipient was present at matins and read one of the lessons. This papal gift had considerable value: in 1365 it cost 324 florins, that is about 20,000 gold francs.[2]

The obsequies of popes were marked by the abundant distribution of alms and by the giving of gratuities to court officials. When Clement VI died, the Apostolic Camera spent 440 Avignonese pounds in bread given to the poor, 700 florins divided amongst the houses of the mendicant orders in Avignon, and 425 florins given to charitable institutions and the hospitals of the town. For nine successive days, fifty priests said masses for the repose of the pope's soul. Knights and high officials of the court were given black robes of sendal (a fine, smooth silk) and fine wool. The decoration of the mortuary chapel was very simple in comparison with its elaborate lighting which cost as much as 1,104 florins. Around the catafalque, which was hung with black sendal, were candelabra draped in black, and funerary urns; on the bier a pall of black sendal carried the pope's arms embroidered in gold on a background of red silk; at each corner of the catafalque stood an escutcheon of arms.

The actual obsequies consisted of three ceremonies. The first took place in the great chapel of the Palace, where a cardinal pronounced a funeral oration in praise of the deceased; the second was held in Notre-Dame-des-Doms and went on for nine days; the last and by far the most onerous ceremony was the bearing of the body with great pomp to its final burial-place.[3]

More accounts of civil feasts than of religious banquets have been preserved: we have seen the splendid scale on which the nuptials of relatives of the pope were celebrated. There is nothing, however, to equal the reception given to Clement VI by Cardinal Annibale di Ceccano in 1343, in the outskirts of Avignon. An Italian has left us the following eye-witness account:

'The pope was led into a room hung from floor to ceiling with tapestries of great richness. The ground was covered with a velvet

[1] *Revue de l'art chrétien*, VOL. XLIV, 1901, pp. 1–11.
[2] *Ibid.* VOL. XXXII, 1889, pp. 408–11.
[3] E. Déprez, 'Les Funérailles de Clément VI et d'Innocent VI,' *Mélanges*, VOL. XX, 1900, pp. 235–50.

carpet. The state bed was hung with the finest crimson velvet, lined with white ermine, and covered with cloths of gold and of silk. Four knights and twelve squires of the pope's household waited at table; the knights received from the host a rich belt of silver and a purse worth 25 gold florins; and the squires, a belt and a purse to the value of 12 florins. Fifty squires from Cardinal Annibale's suite assisted the papal knights and squires. The meal consisted of nine courses (*vivande*) each having three dishes, that is a total of twenty-seven dishes. We saw brought in, among other things, a sort of castle containing a huge stag, a boar, kids, hares and rabbits. At the end of the fourth course, the cardinal presented the pope with a white charger, worth 400 florins, and two rings, valued at 150 florins, one set with an enormous sapphire and the other with an equally enormous topaz; and last of all, a *nappo* worth 100 florins. Each of the sixteen cardinals received a ring set with fine stones, and so did the twenty prelates and the noble laymen. The twelve young clerks of the papal household were each given a belt and a purse worth 25 gold florins; and the twenty-four sergeants-at-arms, a belt worth 3 florins. After the fifth course, they brought in a fountain surmounted by a tree and a pillar, flowing with five kinds of wine. The margins of the fountain were decked with peacocks, pheasants, partridges, cranes and other birds. In the interval between the seventh and eighth courses there was a tournament, which took place in the banqueting hall itself. A concert brought the main part of the feast to a close. At dessert, two trees were brought in; one seemed made of silver, and bore apples, pears, figs, peaches and grapes of gold; the other was green as laurel, and was decorated with crystallised fruits of many colours.

'The wines came from Provence, La Rochelle, Beaune, St Pourçain and the Rhine. After dessert the master cook danced, together with his thirty assistants. When the pope had retired to his apartments, wines and spices were set before us.'

The day was brought to an end with singing, tournaments, dancing and, as a climax, a farce which the pope and cardinals found highly diverting. Over the Sorgue a dummy bridge had been built looking as though it led to the scene of the festivities; many unsuspecting and inquisitive folk, clerks, monks and lay, innocently ventured on to this bridge; when the crowd on it was thick, the bridge gave way and the artless sight-seers all tumbled headlong into the river.[1]

Must we believe that the banquets at the papal court sometimes degenerated into orgies? Petrarch has described some of them with a

[1] E. Müntz, in *R.Q.H.* VOL. LXVI, 1899, pp. 403–04. See also E. Casanova, 'Visità di un papa avignonese,' *A.S.R.S.P.* VOL. XXII, 1899, pp. 371–81.

wealth of truly scabrous detail. But the Italian poet had a very lively imagination. Moreover, his undisguised hatred of the Avignon popes gives the historian good reason to view his descriptions with extreme reserve. We have no means of checking the point at which straight-forward description ends and satire begins.

Ambassadors from every nation were constantly to be seen passing to and fro in Avignon. In 1338, the khan of Tartary sent sixteen personages to pay his respects to Benedict XII. In 1342, eighteen Romans, chosen to represent the three classes of citizens, came to beg Clement VI to accept the office of Senator, and to return to their city and grant them the indulgence of his Jubilee.[1] Undoubtedly the most magnificent of all the embassies was that which, on the morrow of the battle of Tarifa, came from Castile to bring to Benedict XII his share of the booty. A long caravan wended its way from Spain: a hundred Moorish slaves held the bridles of a hundred horses from whose harness hung scimitars and shields taken from the enemy. Citizens of Castile led the war-horse of King Alfonso XI, and bore the twenty-four standards picked up on the banks of the river Salado. In order to perpetuate the memory of the victory of the Christian army, Benedict XII ordered the spoils of battle to be hung from the roof of his chapel, by the side of Alfonso's standard.[2]

Sovereigns were not content with merely sending embassies to the popes. They came to Avignon in person, and during the reign of Urban V, three monarchs were to be found there at the same time: John II ('the Good'), Peter of Lusignan, king of Cyprus, and Waldemar IV, king of Denmark. In 1365, the Emperor Charles IV in his turn entered the papal city. The sojourn of kings and princes occasioned magnificent festivities, including banquets of inordinate length after the fashion of the day. The duke of Lancaster kept open table for six weeks in the year 1354–5, and the citizens of Avignon, who had seen a hundred barrels of wine brought to the cellars of his lodging, were full of admiration for such a man, and freely said of him that 'he had no equal in all the world.'[3]

Ever since the reign of Pope Clement II in the middle of the eleventh century, the political authority of the popes had been con-stantly increasing. Their pre-eminence had become apparent during the conflict between the Papacy and the Empire. It was believed in Christendom during the twelfth and thirteenth centuries that neither king nor emperor was the equal of the supreme pontiff: he surpassed

[1] C. Gipolla, 'Note Petrarchesche desunte dall' Archivio Vaticano,' *Atti e memorie della R. Accademia della scienze di Torino*, VOL. LIX, 1909, pp. 1–32.
[2] L. Duhamel, *Une Ambassade à la cour pontificale. Épisode de l'histoire du palais des papes*, Avignon 1883.   [3] G. Mollat, in *R.H.E.* VOL. X, 1909, p. 740.

them all. As general prosperity increased, he became by the thirteenth century, and more especially in the fourteenth, the centre of a glittering society. The Avignon popes lived like princes and sustained this character magnificently. But the maintenance of themselves and their court consumed only a small part of their wealth.[1] The war which they were obliged to wage in Italy throughout the fourteenth century in order to keep their hold on the Papal States, swallowed up vast sums of money. Whereas John XXII's total expenditure amounted to about 4,200,000 florins, the maintenance of the papal forces in Italy between 1321 and 1331 cost 2,390,433 florins. Karl Heinrich Schäfer, who has set himself the task of balancing the pope's accounts, estimates that the cost of the war in Italy amounted to 63·7 per cent of the whole expenses of the reign.[2] The conquest of the Papal States during the reigns of Clement VI, Innocent VI, Urban V and Gregory XI involved equally heavy sacrifices. The Apostolic Camera was always in debt, and to remedy this the popes were compelled to raise large loans and extort money from ecclesiastical benefices.

Despite their financial worries, the Avignon popes never forgot that they were 'Fathers of the poor.' John XXII had scarcely settled in the city when he determined to organise his almsgiving as he had already organised his other expenditure. He set up a kind of office of good works, the *Pignotte*,[3] which gave its name to the square where it stood: this square still exists today.

In charge of the *Pignotte* was an administrator who was assisted by two auxiliaries chosen from the Cistercians, and referred to in the documents as almoners. The duty of the three almoners was to administer the monies paid out to them by the camerarius and the treasurer who demanded formal receipts. They kept account-books in which they made a note of their day-to-day purchases and, after making a fair copy, presented these accounts at the end of every financial transaction to the clerks of the Camera who audited them. They also had ten full-time servants, whose task was to cook, to give help to the poor and to see that the stores were well supplied.

The *Pignotte* dealt, as the need arose, with a large number of tradesmen—bankers, dressmakers, tailors, washerwomen, cobblers and victuallers of all kinds. It provided the needy with clothing, medicines, wine and food. The fare provided was somewhat monotonous, but

---

[1] See J. Guiraud, *L'Église romaine*, pp. 23–87: chapters dealing with humanism and the arts at the courts of both Avignon and Rome during the fourteenth century.

[2] *Die Ausgaben*, p. 37*.

[3] According to Du Cange, the name is supposed to come from the Italian *pagnotta*, a small loaf of about 60 grammes which was distributed to the poor. According to Cottier and de Loye it derives from the shape of the loaves distributed, which were made like pine seeds or pine cones.

very substantial: it included soup, meat and eggs, fish during Lent and, more rarely, beans, salt and oil. On an average 67,500 loaves of bread were distributed each week during John XXII's reign. In 1344 the number of the poor receiving assistance was so great that the buildings of the *Pignotte* had to be enlarged. A neighbouring house was taken over from the monastery of St Véran at an annual rent of 40 florins and 5 sous *viennois*. In 1348, Clement VI gave to the *Pignotte* a garden near Notre-Dame-des-Miracles, which supplied them with vegetables and fruit.[1]

The brethren and sisters of the mendicant orders in Avignon derived especial benefit from the pope's generosity. On feast days, when the poor were dining under the open porticos of the *Pignotte*, the convents received an extra allowance of food, referred to in the accounts as a pittance (*pitancia*); and there were many of these days in the course of the year. In certain serious situations, the Apostolic Camera gave them rich presents. There is an entry showing a gift of 800 florins, together with an invitation to sing a *Te Deum* of thanksgiving and to pray for divine mercy. Often, too, the popes would supply the brethren with gifts of vestments, chalices, priestly ornaments, missals, altar-linen, or financial help in the building and maintenance of their houses and churches.[2] Outside Avignon the Carthusians at Bonpas, Cahors, and Val-de-Bénédiction at Villeneuve-lès-Avignon and the monasteries of Chaise-Dieu, St Victor at Marseilles and Montpellier received exceedingly generous benefactions from John XXII, Innocent VI, Clement VI and Urban V.

The churches of the secular clergy had no less a share in the generosity of the supreme pontiffs. After he was elected, the pope was not unmindful of his native village, or the district where he had carried out his episcopal duties. The churches in these areas were especially privileged. They received great quantities of rich silks, cloth of gold, ornaments, reliquaries, altar furnishings and sacred vessels. John XXII did not hesitate to convert his gold and silver plate into chalices, and to send them to the East.[3] He was fond of presenting bells, no doubt in order to encourage the saying of the Angelus, a devotion which he had popularised by the granting of indulgences.[4]

It has been alleged that the Avignon popes were indifferent to the fate of the churches in Rome. The books of the Apostolic Camera give the lie to this accusation.[5] In 1320, a Roman banker sent Pietro

[1] P. Pansier, *L'Œuvre des repenties à Avignon*, Paris 1910, pp. 47–9.
[2] G. Mollat, 'Jean XXII fut-il un avare?,' *R.H.E.* VOL. VI, 1906, pp. 34–45.
[3] Schäfer, *Die Ausgaben*, pp. 803–14.
[4] G. Mollat, in *R,H.E.* VOL. VI, 1906, p. 44.
[5] J. Guiraud, *L'Église romaine*, pp. 79–87.

Capocci 5,000 florins for the repair of St John Lateran, and a little later 3,000 florins were allocated to the fabric of St Peter's.[1] In the vaults of the Vatican inscriptions commemorate Benedict XII's generosity to the basilica. The gifts of Urban V deserve especial mention. Not content with erecting the graceful ciborium of St John Lateran, the pope ordered the Siennese sculptor Giovanni Bartolo to make two busts of the apostles Peter and Paul, each weighing 1,700 marks. The bust of St Paul was silver-gilt. Sapphires and emeralds formed the borders of his tunic and mantle. In one hand the saint brandished a silver sword; in the other he held a book decorated with enamels. A royal crown set with rare pearls was on his brow. The tiara of St Peter shone with precious stones. The heads of the apostles were laid with great ceremony in the new reliquaries, and they were then placed beneath the ciborium. Urban V spent on this occasion 30,000 florins, and the queens of France, Navarre and Naples shared in the expense.[2]

This does not end the list of papal charities. We need only mention, in addition, the care of the sick in the hospitals at Avignon, grants to students to allow them to buy books, dowries given to girls of small fortune, gifts to prisoners and the huge sums of money spent on missions and the Crusade.

Above all, the generosity of the Avignon popes is proved by their accounts. Each year John XXII spent in almsgiving on an average more than 16,000 florins, that is from 172,000 to 320,000 gold francs. In the general picture of the accounts of his reign, his gifts come third in order, and represent 7·16 per cent of his total expenditure.[3] Louis Sanctus of Beeringen, a friend of Petrarch, tells us that in the reign of Clement VI, the *Pignotte* distributed daily 64 *salmatae* of corn. As he is careful to tell us that each *salmata* provided enough to make 500 loaves, the total number of loaves given to the poor every day amounted to no less than 32,000.[4]

[1] G. Mollat, *loc. cit.*
[2] M. Chaillan, *Le Bienheureux Urbain V*, pp. 174–6. See also Baluze, *Vitae*, VOL. I, col. 390.
[3] Schäfer, *Die Ausgaben*, pp. 35*–37*.
[4] De Smet, *Recueil des chroniques de Flandre*, VOL. III, Brussels 1856, p. 17.

CHAPTER II

Papal Finances

IN order to maintain their court, and to meet the expenses arising out of their political or religious activities, the popes had to find considerable sources of income. These were chiefly found in the creation of taxes on ecclesiastical benefices. Such taxes may be divided into two kinds: those paid directly to the Curia and those levied on the spot by agents of the papal treasury.

1

Taxes Paid Directly to the Curia

1. *The Common Services* (*servitia communia*). This was the name given to the dues paid to the Apostolic Camera by bishops and abbots immediately on their nomination, on the confirmation of their election, on their consecration, and on their translation to another see or another abbey by the supreme pontiff.

Originally a free gift and purely optional, the common services became before the middle of the thirteenth century a compulsory tax which, from the time of Boniface VIII amounted to one-third of the gross annual income derived by the papacy from its taxes on the revenues of bishops and abbots. The rate of the tax was subject to variations in the second half of the fourteenth century and the scales adopted by different popes were entered in the *Liber taxarum Camerae Apostolicae*.[1]

The only prelates and abbots obliged to pay this tax were those whose incomes from their sees and abbeys exceeded 100 gold florins and had been made subject to special or general reservations. In practice, very few escaped, owing to the way in which the Avignon popes extended the use of their rights of reservation.

2. *Petty Services* (*servitia minuta*). In addition to the common

---

[1] M. H. Hoberg, *Taxae episcopatuum et abbatiarum pro communibus servitiis solvendis, ex libris Obligationum ab anno 1295 ad annum 1455 confectis*, Vatican City 1947. See also E. Göller, *Der 'Liber taxarum' der päpstlichen Kammer*, Rome 1905.

services, newly-appointed bishops and abbots were obliged to pay the 'petty services,' that is, gifts or gratuities to the staff of the Curia or to members of the cardinals' households. By the fourteenth century there were five of these petty services. Each one was equivalent to the share of the common services received by each cardinal at the Curia; consequently the rate for these became higher as the number of cardinals present at the Curia decreased.

3. *The Sacra, the Subdiaconum and the Quittance Fees.* At the time of their consecration or their benediction at the papal court, bishops and abbots paid the following dues: the *sacra*, or gift made at the consecration, amounting to one-twentieth of the total paid in common services, and shared by the camerarius, the clerks of the Camera and the sergeants at arms; the *subdiaconum*, the perquisite of the papal subdeacons, and amounting to one-third of the *sacra*; and the quittance fees, proportional to the diverse sums of money paid both to the Apostolic Camera and to the cardinals' Camera.

4. *Chancery fees* were exacted for the despatching of letters of grace and justice, for their sealing (*emollumentum bullae*) and their registration. The scale for the payment of fees to scribes, abbreviators and registrars, first drawn up by John XXII in the Constitutions *Cum ad sacrosanctae* and *Pater familias*, dated 10 December 1316 and 16 November 1331 respectively, and later modified by subsequent popes, was eventually incorporated in the *Liber taxarum Cancellariae*, the manual in common use at the Chancery.[1]

5. *Visitationes ad limina apostolorum.* The term *visitationes ad limina apostolorum* was given not only to pilgrimages made to the tombs of the apostles Peter and Paul in Rome, but also to the dues originally payable on this occasion.

These dues were strictly payable at the time of the visits which certain bishops and abbots were compelled to make to the Curia at regular and specified intervals. If, however, special permission were obtained, the dues could be sent to the papal court by proxy.

6. *Pallium dues* were 'small sums paid for the despatch of the Bulls whereby the pope conferred the *pallium*.'

7. *The cense from kingdoms subject to the Roman Church.* The kingdom of Naples paid 8,000 ounces of gold a year, Sicily (Trinacria) 3,000 ounces of gold, Aragon 2,000 silver marks sterling for Corsica and Sardinia, and the king of England 700 silver marks sterling for England and 300 for Ireland.

8. Legacies and unsolicited gifts to the popes, and the reversion of the goods of those who died intestate at the papal court.

[1] See above, pp. 288–94.

9. Fines imposed by papal tribunals on clergy and laymen for various offences; sums of money paid by way of commutation of vows and penances imposed by the penitentiaries; coinage fees; revenues from the see of Avignon held *in commendam* by the popes; and other small sums.

2

Taxes Levied in the Taxpayer's Own Country by the Agents of the Curia

More important, more numerous and more oppressive were the taxes levied on the spot in the taxpayer's own country, first by extraordinary envoys and later by special officials called collectors (*collectores*). These taxes fell into seven different categories: tenths, annates, procurations, rights of spoil, caritative subsidies, cense and vacancies.

1. *Tenths* (*decimae*). A tenth was an extraordinary aid exacted by the Avignon popes from holders of ecclesiastical benefices, sometimes to organise a crusade, sometimes to enable the popes to meet the heavy demands on their finances made chiefly by the conquest of the Papal States in Italy and the war against the Visconti.

To ensure the equitable distribution of this tax, the approximate value of the clergy's property had to be ascertained. For this purpose the Apostolic Camera sent special agents all over Christendom to draw up a complete list of ecclesiastical benefices, to indicate as accurately as possible the size of the income of each one, the charges on that income and the extent of the contribution with which it could be assessed. This assessment was called the *taxatio*, and it was commonly said of a benefice that it was assessed for tenths (*taxatus ad decimam*) or more simply, assessed (*taxatus*).

The term tenth should not mislead us as to the amount of the tax. The incumbent did not have to pay the tenth part of his gross income, but only the tenth part of the assessment, that is, that part of the income which remained after all expenses had been deducted and whose figure had been settled in the thirteenth century by the agents of the papal treasury.

In certain dioceses and certain ecclesiastical provinces in France that had suffered particularly from plague, war and famine, Urban V in 1363 and Gregory XI in 1372, 1373 and 1374 reduced the assessment for the tenth by half. This reduced assessment was denoted in the official records by the term *nova taxatio*, as opposed to *antiqua taxatio.* The tenth underwent the same vicissitudes as the assessment and remained in the same proportion to it of one to ten. Thus the assessment of the priory of Odars in the diocese of Toulouse amounting in 1357 to 140 livres *tournois,* was reduced to 70 livres in 1374, and consequently its tenth was then only 7 livres.[1]

A moderate subsidy (*subsidium loco decime*) was deducted from unassessed benefices. It was left to the collectors to estimate this sum, in proportion to the resources of the benefice and its incumbent.

In principle, no one was exempt from tenths: patriarchs, archbishops and bishops were subject to them just as much as other clergy. Only cardinals and members of the Order of St John of Jerusalem were formally exempt. In certain circumstances, the knights of the Teutonic Order shared this unusual privilege.

2. *Annates (annatae, fructus primi anni, annualia, annalia).* In the fourteenth century annates were the revenues derived from a benefice during the first year's tenure of a new incumbent and reserved to the Apostolic Camera.

Although John XXII has for long been considered 'the inventor, author and father of annates,' in fact Clement V, in 1306, was the first pope to claim them from England for the benefit of the papal treasury.

Apart from France, which only became subject to them from 20 February 1326,[2] all the other Christian kingdoms paid annates in the time of the Avignon popes, from John XXII till Gregory XI. Only Benedict XII, having abandoned the Crusade which had been the pretext for levying them, refrained from exacting them, and contented himself with making sure that the sums of money that the clergy had been unable to pay during his predecessor's lifetime were duly collected.

This tax had originally fallen only on those benefices that were vacant *apud Sedem apostolicam*; but from 12 January 1334 it affected all those disposed of or conferred by the Holy See by virtue of general or particular reservations. As, from the time of Clement VI onwards, the pope retained the right of collation of an ever-increasing number of benefices, and caused a greater proportion of them to fall vacant *in Curia*, it followed that a very large number of prelates— almost all of them by 1376—had to pay annates.

The payment of annates was calculated in two ways. Sometimes the Apostolic Camera would seize the portion of the revenue that the

[1] J.-M. Vidal, *Documents pour servir à dresser le pouillé de la province ecclésiastique de Toulouse au XIVe siècle,* pp. 23, 24, 54, 58, 62, 63.
[2] *Regesta Vaticana 113,* fol. 295ᵛ.

incumbent nominally drew each year, in other words the assessed value, and leave him what remained (the *residuum*) to provide for the carrying out of his duties. On other occasions, however, if it were to the Camera's advantage, it would take this *residuum*, and leave the other part of the income to meet the expenses of the benefice. The collectors could choose which of these two methods they preferred.

If the benefice were not assessed, the Camera and the incumbent shared the gross income before deduction of charges, which had to be met by the incumbent only. If the benefice fell vacant several times in one year, the annates were nevertheless only collected once.

Sometimes the incumbent handed over the entire income to the collectors; when this happened, they received all the profits and paid all the charges, and appointed some intermediary to conduct the services and administer the sacraments, in short, to carry out all the duties of a cure of souls.

3. *Procurations.* 'An ancient feudal custom, known as the *droit de gîte*, had changed in time to a tax known to the clergy as procuration.' When the bishop or lesser prelates such as abbots, archdeacons, archpriests or deans, visited benefices under their jurisdiction, they and their retinue were entitled to receive hospitality.

Originally a simple subsidy in kind, a procuration soon became a tax in money whose maximum rate was finally fixed by the Constitution *Vas electionis*, promulgated by Benedict XII on 18 December 1336.[1]

Because of the wars that devastated Europe during the fourteenth century, and also for reasons of generosity, the popes allowed the prelates to levy the procuration without personally making the visitation. These dispensations could be bought at the court of Avignon for half the value of the procuration or even for two-thirds of its assessed value. Urban V was the first to publish, on 1 June 1369, a general reservation forbidding the bishops to levy subsidies on their diocesans by way of compensation. This fiscal measure had highly regrettable consequences: as soon as the emoluments attached to the pastoral visitation disappeared, the bishops seem to have felt this to be a duty they were no longer bound in conscience to undertake. There was, however, some excuse for this attitude. The state of poverty into which France had sunk as a result of the Hundred Years' War made it difficult or even impossible to undertake lengthy journeys without some form of compensation.

4. *Rights of Spoil (spolia).* The right of spoil was originally the right to seize the house and goods of any deceased bishop. Bishops

---

[1] *Corpus juris canonici, Extravagantes communes*, Bk III, tit. x, ch. 1.

and abbots in their turn seized the spoils of deceased incumbents who were their subordinates. The Holy See, by putting itself in the place of the legitimate collators of benefices was able, whenever a vacancy occurred, to appropriate the advantages which had hitherto been enjoyed by abbots and bishops. John XXII made a general extension of the right of spoil, and under his successors this right became more and more frequently and extensively applied, as the number of benefices reserved to papal collation increased.

On 11 December 1362,[1] Urban V claimed the right, during his lifetime, to inherit the property of any ecclesiastic regular or secular, dying anywhere in Christendom. This fiscal measure was, however, not applied to French and English churches. In these countries, whenever an incumbent died, a reservation was made, which the pope might or might not claim, according to the circumstances. A Bull dated 9 July 1371 [2] reserved henceforth for the Holy See the property of all clerks dying in the dioceses of Auch and Bordeaux, and in Spain.

The first legislative document to regulate the application of the right of spoil (*jus spolii*) dates from 16 May 1345.[3] From then on, the collectors were required to settle the debts contracted by the deceased on behalf of his church or his benefice, to defray the expenses of a suitable funeral, and to pay the wages of his servants and any fines that might be due. The legitimate heirs, if there were any, received the books and other items belonging to the patrimony of the deceased prelate or acquired by his own efforts. Similarly reservation did not extend to the ornaments of the church or to the vessels used in the offices, unless they had been bought with the sole object of evading the law. In the same way bed-linen, casks of wine, arms and the tools necessary for the care and maintenance of church property, the cattle and the agricultural implements were all exempt from spoil.

The application of the right of spoil provided the papacy in the fourteenth century with one of its most substantial sources of income. The sale of the furniture of deceased prelates produced enormous sums of money. The popes, however, put the most precious ornaments and jewels into their own treasury and the rare books into their library. In this way the library of the palace at Avignon acquired, between 1343 and 1350, more than twelve hundred valuable works.[4]

5. *Caritative subsidies* (*subsidia caritativa*). In imitation of bishops

[1] G. Mollat, *La Fiscalité pontificale*, p. 233.
[2] Vatican Archives: *Collectoria 358*, fol. 2ʳ⁻ᵛ.
[3] Vatican Archives: *Instrumenta miscellanea ad annum 1345*.
[4] F. Ehrle, *Historia bibliothecae pontificum Romanorum*, Rome 1890, VOL. I, p. 246.

and abbots who, from the twelfth century onwards, had been wont in times of financial stress to beg free gifts from their subordinates, the popes, in the fourteenth century, appealed to the generosity of the clergy in time of need. As its name suggests, the contribution may well have been, at the outset, a token of love and affection, but by the fourteenth century it had lost much of its pristine significance. A voluntary subsidy was the equivalent of a subsidy whose amount was not fixed, and to obtain which it was necessary to appeal to the goodwill of the clergy. The pope made his request in courteous terms, and entrusted his own fiscal agents with the task of collecting it. This subsidy was in fact the opposite of 'charitable,' since any incumbent who proved backward in paying his quota risked excommunication.

6. *The Cense.*[1] This was of two kinds: the *greater*, paid as a rent for the effective enjoyment of lands belonging to the Holy See; and the *lesser*, paid in order to obtain or to keep papal protection.

Payments were very irregular, and provided only a slender source of income to the papal treasury. Payment was usually made in coin, but occasionally in kind.

7. *Vacancies (fructus medii temporis, fructus intercalares, fructus vacantes).* The term 'vacancies' was given to the revenue of benefices in the pope's conferment and which, for that reason, were said to be *vacantes in Curia.* The pope reserved the right to collect these revenues until a new incumbent had been appointed. Except during the reign of Clement VI, this tax was compulsory from the time of John XXII until that of Gregory XI.

Among vacancies are included the *fructus indebite* or *male percepti,* that is, revenues of a benefice improperly collected by a clerk, either because he had not been canonically provided to that benefice, or because he held it concurrently with other benefices in defiance of the Constitution *Execrabilis*, or because he had not asked for a dispensation on account of his age, or because he had not received Holy Orders within the time prescribed by canon law. In all these cases, the Holy See considered the benefice to be vacant and claimed the income improperly drawn by the incumbent. In these instances there was usually a 'composition,' that is an arrangement between the incumbent and the papacy.

8. *Revenues from the Papal States in Italy, from the Comtat-Venaissin and from Avignon* after that town had been ceded to the Papacy. Among these revenues should be included the cense paid by

---

[1] C. Daux, 'Le Cens pontifical dans l'Église de France,' *R.Q.H.* VOL. LXXV, 1904, pp. 5–73.

the great vassals of the Roman Church: the Marchesi d' Este (10,000 florins), the commune of Bologna (8,000 florins), the della Scala for the vicariate of Verona, Parma and Vicenza (5,000 florins) and the Visconti for that of Piacenza and other places (10,000 florins). Other revenues came from tolls, customs' duties, the salt-tax, the poll-tax, tithes, confiscation of property, fines imposed by the courts, legacies and inheritances, etc.[1]

9. *Peter's Pence*. This direct tax was levied in England, Denmark, Sweden, Norway, Poland, Bohemia, Croatia, Dalmatia, in the lands lying between the Baltic sea and the kingdom of Poland, conquered by the knights of the Teutonic Order, and in Aragon and Portugal.

3

The Methods of Collecting Taxes

The machinery for the payment of the common services is known to us in the most minute detail. First of all, the staff of the Camera and the prelates concerned, or their representatives, agreed upon the assessment of the revenues of benefices. Sometimes the papal collectors or special commissioners held an enquiry. The tax amounted to one-third of the gross income. When the assessment had been settled, the prelate took an oath, either at the Curia or very occasionally elsewhere, to pay the tax within two terms; at least this was so from the end of John XXII's reign. If the term expired without payment having been made, the pope, after consulting the cardinals in Consistory, granted delays. If, after being warned, the defaulter still did not pay his tax, ecclesiastical censures were imposed upon him and only removed when he had paid his debt in full.[2]

There is nothing particularly remarkable or unexpected about the bureaucratic formalities which arose in the payment of other taxes direct to the Curia. The collection of taxes on the spot, however, is more interesting. It necessitated the employment of a large number of treasury agents.

Chief among these agents were the collectors (*collectores*) who were put in charge of financial districts known as collectorates (*collectoriae*).[3]

The financial districts seldom corresponded to ecclesiastical

---

[1] K. H. Schäfer, *Deutsche Ritter*, Paderborn 1909, VOL. I, pp. 16–44.
[2] A. Clergeac, *La Curie et les bénéfices consistoriaux*, Paris 1911, pp. 80–156.
[3] G. Mollat, *op. cit.* includes two maps showing French collectorates.

provinces. A single collectorate sometimes included two or three ecclesiastical provinces; on the other hand, a single ecclesiastical province might be large enough to constitute two or three collectorates. In France the number of collectorates varied greatly and fluctuated between twelve and seventeen; but it was always equal to, if not greater than, the total number of collectorates for all the other countries in the world.

The office of collector is older than the name, and goes back to the beginning of the thirteenth century. The collector was at first simply a special envoy charged with levying taxes for the Crusade. From an itinerant official, as he was in the days of Clement V and John XXII, he became an official with a permanent headquarters when, in the time of Clement VI, taxes on the revenues of the Church became customary.

The collectors were nominated for an indefinite period by the pope, or, more frequently, by the camerarius. Their duties could only be terminated by their resignation, recall or transfer to another charge. Chosen from all ranks of the ecclesiastical hierarchy, and usually graduates, they enjoyed extensive powers, superior in some respects to those of the bishops whom they had the authority to excommunicate. The freedom of action which was left to collectors in places far removed from the immediate control of the Camera made their office by no means a sinecure, for their duties were often difficult and always heavy; but the position was much sought after, and inspired respect and fear in the taxpayers.

After taking an oath of loyalty to the camerarius and receiving their Bulls of appointment and letters of safe conduct, the newly-appointed collectors hired horses or hackneys and escorted by notaries and servants, left Avignon for their districts.

On arrival at their destination, they notified their presence to the ecclesiastical authorities and the taxpayers by publishing their letters of appointment. Their chief preoccupation was to collect around them a number of subordinates upon whom they unloaded almost all the practical work. They themselves were usually content to direct and supervise their staff, and more particularly, to look after the cash-box.

The most important members of their staff were the sub-collectors to whom they deputed the task of raising the taxes in the various dioceses attached to their collectorate. In general there was one to each diocese.

The sub-collectors had strictly to obey the orders of their superiors. At certain times of the year, and at very irregular intervals, they sent them the account-books together with the money collected and in exchange got a sealed receipt. In the more extensive collectorates, they were headed by a general sub-collector, who was directly responsible to the collector.

Under the sub-collectors there were a certain number of sworn subordinates, such as notaries, servants and members of the household.

The collectors also employed money-changers, so that the taxes, which were necessarily collected in the currency of the country concerned, could be converted into French gold coin, money of Tours or, most frequently, florins, which were accepted currency in Avignon. This operation, already difficult enough because of the constant fluctuations in currency values in the fourteenth century, was made even more complicated by the fact that in the thirteenth century the agreed assessment for the levying of tenths, and later used as a basis for assessing annates, had been calculated in livres, sous and deniers, that is in money of account. The collector had therefore to be able to tell what actual specie corresponded to this notional money.

When the conversion had been made, the collector still had to send the money to Avignon, or dispose of it in accordance with the orders of the Camera. The most frequent method of avoiding the transport of coin, always long, costly and dangerous, was to assign it to some third person to whom the Holy See acknowledged itself a creditor. If the money were assigned direct to the Camera, the collector, one of the sub-collectors or some other trusted person, escorted to the papal court the sum derived from the taxes. On other occasions, special delegates from the Holy See received the money and encouraged the collectors. Lastly, among intermediaries often used must be included, except in France, Italian and French banking houses.

Accounts were rendered to the court at Avignon at somewhat irregular intervals. In principle this took place every two years, at least at the end of the fourteenth century. As a general rule, the Apostolic Camera would order its collectors to come to Avignon to render their accounts, and would use various forms of compulsion to enforce this order, if they did not obey or made frivolous excuses. If necessary, a sub-collector could take the place of the collector for the rendering of accounts.

The accounts themselves were drawn up in a kind of register, of which at least two copies were made. One remained in the keeping of the collector, while the other, after checking, was placed in the archives of the Camera. There was no fixed plan for the way in which accounts were drawn up: some were detailed, others very brief; some were arranged under the dioceses of the financial district, and others under the different kinds of tax.

At the Camera a clerk was appointed by the camerarius to check the accounts carefully and make a report. His task was usually facilitated by the collector who summarised the very diffuse information contained in his large books into a few pages of figures which formed a note-book (the *compotus abbreviatus* or *compotus brevis*) attached to his register. The auditor informed his superior when his task was complete and then read his report on a certain day in the office of the treasury, in the presence of the camerarius, the treasurer and the other clerks of the Camera; then the *quitus* was granted as required, and the collector rewarded for his trouble.

In case of a dispute between incumbents and collectors, or of malversations on the part of the collectors, a secret enquiry was held. When the informers had proved the alleged facts, a public enquiry was held, presided over by a clerk of the Apostolic Camera or a special commissioner. Collectors who were found guilty usually had their property confiscated and were imprisoned. In the fourteenth century some of them abused their authority to use the 'spiritual weapons'—excommunication, interdict, *aggrave* and *reaggrave*—and employed them to extort money for their own profit. But in general they carried out their duties conscientiously, faithfully and honestly. This is clear from a study of their books, and explains the favours and rewards that the pope granted to so many of them.[1]

4

The Effects and Results of the Financial Policy of the Avignon Popes

We must now try to assess the amount of money obtained by the Avignon popes by means of their fiscal measures, and as the consequences of their financial policy.

In 1313 Clement V possessed 1,040,000 gold florins, but the grandiose provisions of his will emptied the treasury. In August 1316 the cardinals and John XXII had only 70,000 florins to share between them.

In these financial straits the new pope created taxes inspired by ideas taken from his predecessors. This extraordinary move, which

[1] G. Mollat, *La Fiscalité pontificale*. See also E. Göller, *Die Einnahmen*.

in the long run had disastrous moral consequences and necessitated the immediate reorganisation of a complex financial system, at first produced very fine material results. The money collected reached an average of 228,000 florins a year, or a total of 4,100,000 for the whole pontificate. Expenditure, however, chiefly occasioned by the Italian wars, amounted to 4,191,446 florins. The Apostolic Camera would have been entirely bankrupt if John XXII had not paid out 440,000 florins from his own private resources, and if a lawsuit after the death of Clement V had not turned out well and supplied his successor with 150,000 florins.

The reserve fund that John XXII left—about 750,000 florins—was quite sufficient for Benedict XII, who discontinued certain taxes. Receipts went down by 62,000 florins a year. In spite of this, thanks to his wise economy, Benedict left at his death 1,117,000 florins.

This very favourable financial situation was rapidly altered after the accession of Clement VI. Although the money received annually by the pope reached an average of 188,500 florins, the amount in the papal coffers at his death fell to 311,115 florins, and this sum had only been obtained by means of loans.

Innocent VI had an annual income of 253,600 florins. The Italian war swallowed up more than all this, and the Camera fell into debt. Urban V and Gregory XI lived from hand to mouth. They borrowed wherever they could, and at the same time oppressed incumbents with taxes.

It was, therefore, chiefly the Italian wars which ruined the Avignon popes, and caused them to extort money from the clergy.[1]

However justified they may have been, the fiscal measures of the Avignon popes roused very lively discontent. Contemporary accounts reflect public feeling and leave us in no doubt as to its nature. Even if we leave aside Dante's[2] or Petrarch's[3] over-prejudiced diatribes stigmatising the rapacity of the princes of the Church; even if we pay no attention to the ill-natured tales of Italian, English and German chroniclers, who were all blinded by their national hatred of the French popes, there are still eye-witness accounts which show the same characteristics. For instance, one can listen to the strong

[1] K. H. Schäfer, *Die Ausgaben*, pp. 13*–19*, 8–44.
[2]   In vesta di pastor' lupi rapaci
       Si veggion di quassù per tutti i paschi,
       O difesa di Dio, perchè pur giaci?

       Del sangue nostro Caorsini e Guaschi
       S' apparecchian di bere. O buon principio
       A che vil fin convien che tu caschi!
                                    (*Paradiso*, XXVII, 55–60)
[3] See in particular Petrarch's sonnets.

words of one chronicler telling how Charles the Fair, having opposed
the levy of a tenth, hastily authorised it as soon as the pope had
allowed him to raise one for himself: 'And so, when Holy Church has
been shorn by one, another flays her alive.'[1] A little later, in his *De
planctu ecclesiae*,[2] Alvarez Pelayo, a firm supporter of papal omnipotence, lashes out vigorously at the greed of the Curia, the source,
according to him, of all the ills from which the Church was suffering.
St Catherine of Siena and St Bridget of Sweden also reproach the
pontiffs bitterly for the spirit of worldly gain that, they say, is para-
mount in Avignon.

The state of mind of the clergy is shown even more clearly in the
documents in the papal archives, and even in the collectors' account
books. As we have already seen, Parliaments in England protested
bitterly against papal exactions.[3] In France the incumbents expressed
their opposition by hindering the collectors in the carrying out of
their duties. From the reign of Philip VI, the pope's agents more and
more frequently ran up against the king's officers who defended the
interests of the taxpayers. A canon of Cahors, for example, had
accepted the custody of the hereditament of the bishop of Tulle,
which had been seized in accordance with the right of spoil. King's
officers, on the demand of the disappointed heirs, entered his house,
searched it from top to bottom, found his strong room, forced open
the coffer where the hereditament was kept, and carried off the contents.[4] In the diocese of Nîmes, the sub-collector's delegate was
about to sequester the goods of a church when a young man leapt
upon him, stabbed him and left him on the spot for dead. Then,
turning to the delegate's companion, a notary now petrified with fear,
he cried, brandishing his sword, 'Ha! villain, you too shall die!' But
at this the scrivener, screwing up his courage, leapt on to his horse
and fled.[5]

Such scenes of violence were not confined to France. In Germany,
collectors were so frequently being seized and cast into unsavoury
prisons that, in 1347, one of them had great difficulty in recruiting any
assistants. Of two of his couriers, one had had his hand cut off, the
other had been strangled.[6] Moreover, the clergy's opposition to the
payment of papal taxes was greater in Germany than in any other
country. Thus the collection of the sexennial tenth, decreed by the

---

[1] *Grandes Chroniques de France*, ed. Paris, VOL. V, p. 300.
[2] Venice 1560, pp. 28 f, 48.   [3] See above, p. 163.
[4] Vatican Archives: *Collectoria* 91. G. Mollat, *op. cit.* p. 104.
[5] *Ibid.* pp. 95–6.
[6] J. P. Kirsch, *Die päpstlichen Kollektorien*, Paderborn 1894, pp. 119, 137 f, 150,
162 f, 178, 184, 189, 195.

Council of Vienne in 1312, was still not complete in the diocese of Breslau in 1335.[1] Collectors had recourse to violent measures, such as excommunication and interdict, which were for the most part quite ineffective. In 1357 the Holy See was driven to agree to a compromise, and even then had to send a nuncio, Philippe de Cabassole, to see that it was carried out. His exhortations had little result, for in 1371 the collectors were still doing their best to see that the tax was paid.[2] The resistance of the German clergy is perhaps best shown by the curious agreement signed in 1372 by the ecclesiastics of the dioceses of Cologne, Bonn, Xanten, Söst and Mainz: the contracting parties undertook upon oath not to pay any part of the tenth demanded by Gregory XI, and to give each other mutual support if the Holy See should institute proceedings against any one of them; any incumbent who did not stand by these promises was to be deprived of his benefices and declared unfit to hold any others. But despite these protestations, the German clergy gave way before the proceedings brought against them by the papacy.[3] It is true that the princes and the Emperor supported the pope's action, and not in an entirely disinterested spirit, for their zeal had its reward: they were authorised to make good their depleted finances with the aid of ecclesiastical property, in accordance with the policy that the pontiffs had followed since the time of Clement V.

It is easy to understand the grievances of the clergy. When they brought forward, as their reasons for asking for a relief from taxation, the misfortunes of the times, the disasters of war, the high price of food, the scarcity of money, the ravages of famine and pestilence, they were telling the truth. Throughout nearly all Christendom, most benefices were ruined, laid waste and destroyed by the Great Companies and other soldiers, and bringing in practically no revenue. Consequently papal taxes inevitably reduced the incumbents to direst poverty. What more eloquent in their brevity than the notes written in the collectors' account books against the name of some church: 'Destructa est; deserta est.' Some time ago, Father Denifle drew up a harrowing list of the disasters, ruins, fires and 'desolations' that befell France during the Hundred Years' War.[4]

Various other circumstances, too, made the taxes heavy to bear: their number and variety in the first place, and then their nature and the means employed to collect them.

Lapse of time never wiped out the debts incurred by the tax-

[1] E. Hennig, *Die päpstlichen Zehnten*, Halle 1909, pp. 14–23.
[2] *Ibid.* pp. 27–35.   [3] *Ibid.* pp. 36–41.
[4] Denifle, *La Désolation des églises, monastères et hôpitaux en France pendant la guerre de Cent Ans*, Paris 1899.

payers. Personal and real alike, the debts remained the responsibility of the benefice whose revenues were burdened by all the obligations that had been contracted and not honoured, however far back they might date. Each incumbent was responsible for his predecessors; this provided the papal treasury with unquestionable security, but was a heavy and sometimes intolerable burden on the incumbents. Thus in 1342, the arrears of common services owed by Nicolino Canali, who had recently been provided to the archbishopric of Ravenna, amounted to 14,700 gold florins, without counting the corresponding petty services. From 11 March 1361 to 13 November 1366 there were five successive occupants of the archbishopric of Palermo. The last of them, Matteo da Cumae, found himself under the obligation to pay the services owed by his four deceased predecessors who had died without having rendered them.[1]

It is true that incumbents had some means of redress against those whose debts they paid, or, where they had died, against their heirs. The Apostolic Camera usually made no difficulties about yielding the conduct of the action against the debtors to the incumbent, provided that it did not prefer to act itself in this matter. It usually did so when there was some security for the debt owed, or when it was too heavy for one person, and sometimes, in the latter case, the collector assumed responsibility for the recovery of a part only of the debt, and left the incumbent to take care of the rest. It is evident that this system guaranteed the imprescriptibility of papal finances: the benefice and its holder were always responsible for them. Is it surprising that, by the end of the fourteenth century, so many benefices were without priests to serve them?[2]

The methods of compulsion used to break down opposition and ensure that the taxes were gathered also played their part in making the papal treasury an object of hatred. Financial theory was not very advanced in the Middle Ages: its sole object was to supply authorities with rough-and-ready expedients, rather like the means employed by conquerors in times of war. Harsh methods prevailed both outside and inside the Church at this period. Because appeals to the secular arm were almost a complete mockery and public authorities sometimes obstructed the sequestration of goods, attempts were made to enforce all the consequences of excommunication. On 5 July 1328, in the *audientia litterarum contradictarum,* no fewer than one patriarch, five archbishops, thirty bishops and forty-six abbots were excommunicated because they had not paid their common services

---

[1] A. Clergeac, *La Curie et les bénéfices consistoriaux,* p. 99.
[2] G. Mollat, *op. cit.* pp. 63–5.

at the proper time. We may judge from this one example what a deplorable effect it must have made upon Christian communities when at High Mass on Sundays or feast-days, they heard sentences of excommunication against their own pastors solemnly read out.[1] The effect of these sanctions was occasionally both uncivilised and absurd: the coffin of Bishop Gonsalvo of Mondonnedo had to remain outside the graveyard until his heirs had undertaken to pay their kinsfolks' debts.[2]

Although the papal treasury did grant delays, respites and post-ponements, it was generally uncompromising in its insistence on the principle that payment must be made. The structure of taxation was such that it was virtually impossible for the taxpayers to escape from its stranglehold.

[1] E. Göller, *Die Einnahmen*, pp. 45*–46*.   [2] Vidal, no. 6351.

CHAPTER III

The Centralisation of the Church during
the Avignon Papacy

FROM the time of Gregory VII, the government of the Church had become increasingly centralised under the personal control of the Roman pontiff. In many respects this movement reached its climax in the fourteenth century.

Appeals to the court of Avignon became extremely frequent. The popes awarded university degrees directly, having exempted the recipients from keeping the terms required in the faculties of law and theology. They intervened still more in the affairs of the religious orders, reformed them whether they would or no, and made appointments to offices and dignities within the order. In the time of Gregory XI the Dominicans had for the first time a cardinal 'Protector' at the papal court.[1] During the whole of the 'Babylonian exile' only one œcumenical council met, at Vienne in 1311–12. There Clement V clearly stated his supreme authority. When some of the Fathers refused to support the plan to unite the property of the Templars with that of the knights of St John, he replied, 'If you agree to the assignment of the property to the Hospital, I shall decree it in your names and mine with pleasure; but if not, I shall still do it whether you like it or not.'[2] As this plain speaking did not silence the opposition, Clement ignored it. Contemporaries were in no doubt as to the real implication of the pope's attitude. An English chronicler declared—with some little exaggeration—that the Council of Vienne 'did not deserve the name of Council, for the Lord Pope did everything on his own authority.'[3]

The progressive centralisation of the Church, however, is nowhere more clearly shown than in the manner in which the Avignon popes laid claim to an ever-increasing share in the collation of benefices. To attain their ends the popes exercised their right of reservation, that is, the right claimed by the Roman pontiff, in virtue of the primacy

[1] Mortier, *Histoire des maîtres généraux de l'ordre des Frères Prêcheurs*, VOL. III, p. 399.
[2] Lizerand, *Clément V et Philippe le Bel*, p. 270.
[3] Walter of Hemingburgh, ed. Hamilton, London 1848, VOL. II, p. 293.

of his jurisdiction, to confer a benefice vacant or about to become vacant, without reference to the ordinary collators.

There were two kinds of reservation: general and special. General reservations affected, either in perpetuity or temporarily, all benefices of a certain category, vacant or due to fall vacant, either in the whole Church or in some specified province, diocese or kingdom. Special reservations were concerned with one benefice only, by reason either of its location, or its status, or its persons, and lasted either for a specified time or for ever.[1]

The use of general reservation dates back to Clement IV. The Decretal *Licet ecclesiarum*, dated 27 August 1265, gave the pope full authority to dispose of benefices of persons dying at the Curia. Boniface VIII extended this measure to include those whose holders died in the neighbourhood of the papal court, within a radius of two days' march (*dietae*).[2] Clement V, not satisfied with providing to these ecclesiastical charges whose vacancies literally occurred at the Curia, used all kinds of pretexts to extend his powers of reservation. Then John XXII codified the usage introduced by his predecessors, with a few additions, and promulgated the Constitution *Ex debito*.[3] Reservation was thenceforward extended to affect all benefices which lost their incumbent by deposition or deprivation, by disallowance of an election, by refusal to allow a request to elect, by disclaimer into the hands of the reigning pontiff, by provision or translation to another benefice by the same authority. To these were also added the benefices of abbots and bishops blessed or consecrated by Clement V or John XXII, those possessed by cardinals at the time of their death, whether or not this took place at the Curia, those of papal officials, vice-chancellors, chamberlains, notaries, *auditores litterarum contradictarum*, correctors, scribes and abbreviators of apostolic letters, penitentiaries and resident chaplains of the Holy See, and indeed of all persons attached to the Curia, whether or not they died while on legation or special missions.

It would be tedious to give a detailed account of the many emendations and additions made to the Constitution *Ex debito* by the successors of John XXII. Suffice it to say that special and general reservations were constantly being increased and widened in scope. The last stage in their development occurred when Gregory XI retained during his lifetime the right to appoint to all patriarchal, archiepiscopal and episcopal churches, as well as to all houses of

[1] Lux, *Constitutionum apostolicarum de generali beneficiorum reservatione collectio et interpretatio*, Breslau 1904, pp. 4–8.
[2] *Corpus juris canonici*, Bk III, tit. IV, chaps, 2, 34 *in VI°*.
[3] Lux, *op. cit.* pp. 51–4.

monks and friars, regardless of their revenue, wherever and however they fell vacant.[1] Thus, under the last of the Avignon popes, the decay of the elective principle reached its nadir, and the conferment of benefices not subject to election was in almost all cases taken out of the hands of the rightful collators. Possibly at no other period of history, has the Roman pontiff exercised his powers of jurisdiction to such an extent.

To the question what had led the Avignon popes to take over the collation of charges and ecclesiastical offices, the Bulls suggest various answers: the primacy of the Apostolic See; the neglect of the ordinary collators to provide incumbents to vacant benefices, and the infringements of the law that they made in their choice of candidates; the prolonged vacancies in episcopal sees, to the detriment of the spiritual welfare of the faithful and of the proper distribution of the mensal revenues of the see; and especially the disputes arising out of abbatial and episcopal elections.

Although the electoral system had been very well organised in the thirteenth century, it did in fact leave the way open for intrigues within cathedral and conventual chapters; for fierce rivalries; for compromises dishonourable and not without a taint of simony on the part of those elected; for long and disastrous schisms where the electors could not agree and for endless lawsuits.

The detailed formalities laid down to ensure the choice of the right persons gave rise to incessant disputes. To be duly elected bishop, for example, a priest must not only have received a majority vote; this majority had also to be recognised as the wiser party (*sanior*).[2] To make sure that this condition had been fulfilled, the intentions guiding the choice of the electors had to be scrutinised, and the merits of the successful candidate carefully considered. Consequently, if the minority considered itself the wiser party, its vote might prevail. If the majority persisted in supporting its original candidate, a double election took place; there followed a period of irritating discussions, quarrels, litigation, long lawsuits before the competent authority, and sometimes even brawls and bloodshed. Thus direct appointments by the Holy See could, from certain points of view, be of benefit to the Church, and at the least a real remedy for the evils arising from elections.

At Constance, for instance, where the episcopal see fell vacant six times between 1306 and 1356, there were four occasions on which the canons formed two opposing camps, each one electing its own

---

[1] *Ibid.* pp. 21–46.
[2] P. Viollet, in *Histoire littéraire de la France*, VOL. XXXIV, pp. 35–41.

bishop.[1] In other places, where the members of chapters were deeply divided amongst themselves, they were not dismayed at the prospect of the harm their schism might do to the Church. In Gascony, the canons' repeated appeals to the Curia had drawn the attention of the papacy to the pitiful plight of churches left without pastors, sometimes for five or six years.[2] In a word, if the Holy See seized the right to appoint bishops and thus deprived the chapters, the chapters were nevertheless the agents of their own downfall for discord was endemic in their midst, diverse abuses all too frequently vitiated their elections, and the authority of metropolitan bishops no longer provided a remedy prompt enough or sufficiently effective to deal with the misfortunes of the churches.

Another important reason behind the papal reservations was a political one. In Italy, where the Avignon popes were constantly waging war, it was vitally important for them to feel that they could be assured of an episcopate completely devoted to their material interests. In the same way, in Germany, the Holy See wished to make sure that no partisan, open or secret, of Louis of Bavaria was holding episcopal office. In the rest of Christendom there was a kind of tacit agreement between the papacy and public authorities or ordinary collators, which was advantageous to both sides. Instead of using uncanonical methods to force their candidates on to the chapters, the kings preferred to have recourse to the Holy See, to ask the pope to reserve such and such a church to himself, and then to recommend their candidates to the pope. Doubtless their wishes were not always granted; nevertheless, they received satisfaction often enough to give them no cause for complaint. In 1307, the canons of Constance had simultaneously elected Rodolfus von Hewen and Ludwig von Strasbourg. The two rivals had recourse to the Holy See, which rejected them both. Clement V appointed as bishop a Frenchman, Gérard, archdeacon of Autun, under pressure from Philip the Fair, who coveted the Empire and wanted to have some supporters there. French influence also carried the day in 1306, when Peter von Aichspalt and Otto de Grandson were appointed as archbishop of Mainz and bishop of Basle.[3] In 1318 the Count de la Marche requested that the see of Rouen should be given to his chancellor, Guillaume de Flavacourt. But he was politely ignored, because John XXII was well aware of the prince's intrigues against Philip V, the Tall.[4] By 1322, the Count de la Marche had become king of France

[1] Rieder, *Römische Quellen zur Konstanzer Bistumsgeschichte*, Innsbruck 1908, pp. 40*–68*.
[2] A. Clergeac, in *Revue de Gascogne*, 1906, p. 57.
[3] Rieder, *op. cit.* p. 40.　　　　　　　　　　　[4] Coulon, no. 773.

and wished to put his favourite in the important see of Auch. Although the canons of the cathedral had voted unanimously in favour of Roger d'Armagnac, the pope supported the king's candidate.[1] After the death of the bishop of Mantua, Ruffino di Lodi, the court at Avignon had decided that a certain Filippino should succeed him. To satisfy the Gonzaga family, Urban V quashed this provision and, on 16 August 1367, nominated Guido di Arezzo.[2] In England it rarely happened that the popes did not accept the bishops suggested by the kings.[3] On the other hand, in the Iberian peninsula and in Sicily, the Holy See usually set aside the royal candidates, because the political interests of the papacy were diametrically opposed to those of the house of Aragon.[4]

The Holy See had also a financial object in increasing the number of reservations. The pope assured himself of a source of income by compelling prelates, who owed their appointments to him, to pay chancery dues and petty and common services. We may judge how profitable such a course proved, by noting that from 7 August 1316 until 16 April 1334, the cardinals and John XXII divided between them the vast sum of 1,097,957 gold florins, received as common services. According to Göller, the common services constituted the chief source of income of the Holy See.[5]

Reservation also had the advantage of allowing the popes to abrogate to themselves the right of regale, that is to draw the mensal revenues of episcopal sees when they were vacant. A curious example which can be quoted is that of the succession of Amanieu d'Armagnac, archbishop of Auch, who died in 1318. Out of the possible mensal revenues, John XXII gave 25,000 gold florins to the duke of Bourbon and devoted the rest to the Crusade, except for 10,000 florins, which he graciously left for Guillaume de Flavacourt, who was provided to the see on 26 August 1323.[6]

It was equally to the pope's advantage to claim the right to confer non-elective benefices. In this instance, reservation allowed him to levy annates and *vacantes*.

Lastly, the Holy See retained the right to dispose of benefices, elective or otherwise, in order to provide cardinals and officials of the papal court. This was an ingenious means whereby the pope could give stipends to his staff, without paying for them. In this he

[1] Guérard, *Documents pontificaux sur la Gascogne*, VOL. II, Paris 1903, nos. 193, 252, 297.　　　　[2] F. Novati, *Niccolò Spinelli.*
[3] Haller, *Papsttum und Kirchenreform*, pp. 115–21.
[4] Finke, *Acta Aragonensia*, VOL. I, nos. 135, 140, 142–4, 147–9; VOL. II, nos. 739, 784 f, 796.　　　　[5] Göller, *Die Einnahmen*, p. 46*.
[6] G. Mollat, *La Fiscalité pontificale*, p. 63.

followed the example of the kings of France, who gave their courtiers gifts in money or kind, generally lands which they had obtained through confiscation.[1] This strange conception had tiresome results. The more important the post at court, the more was the income required for it, and consequently the more numerous the benefices needed. Thus, in the course of the one year 1317, Cardinal Gaucelme de Jean was possessed of the office of cantor, endowed with a canonry and prebend in the church of Saintes; of the office of treasurer, endowed with a canonry and a prebend in the cathedral of Lichfield; of a canonry in the cathedral chapter of Cahors; of various expectative graces, soon to become actual benefices, in the dioceses of Canterbury, York, Rheims and Rouen; of the parish churches of Hollingbourne and Hackney, in the dioceses of Canterbury and London; of the priory of Ribenhac in the diocese of Saintes; and of a canonry in the cathedral of Lincoln, with all the rights held by the late Thomas de Grandson in the archdeaconry of Northampton. The generosity of the Holy See did not limit itself to these many favours: John XXII and Benedict XII heaped still more benefices upon the cardinal.[2]

Papal reservations deprived chapters of their electoral rights, and ordinary collators of their privilege to nominate to non-elective charges. The resistance offered by these aggrieved persons varied in intensity and effectiveness in different countries.

At first, the reservations decreed by John XXII were favourably received in England. The clergy felt that they were now freed from the bondage in which they had been held by the king's power. They thought that kings would no longer allow themselves to confer ecclesiastical offices on their courtiers, on unworthy recipients or on laymen. They praised the wise measures of the Constitution *Execrabilis* which forbade the accumulation of benefices, and which gave to the Holy See the right to collate to those that fell vacant on this count. But the clergy soon lost their illusions when they saw how the pope gave more benefices than ever to foreigners, and allowed tenure of pluralities to members of the Curia and especially to cardinals. Enthusiasm gave way to cries of rage. We have already told how the opposition made itself felt in England.[3] As a rule it was so vigorous that ecclesiastics were prevented from taking possession of the non-elective benefices granted them by the Holy See; but the English clergy had no power to prevent the encroachment of the pope's authority in another direction—that of reserving bishoprics as he thought fit, and

[1] J. Viard, *Documents parisiens du règne de Philippe VI de Valois*, VOL. I, Paris 1899, pp. viii–ix.
[2] E. Albe, *Autour de Jean XXII*, Rome 1903–6, VOL. I, pp. 117–24.
[3] See above, p. 263. See also Haller, *op. cit.* VOL. I, pp. 99–101, 107–21.

conferring them, with very few exceptions, on the king's candidates.

In Germany, the papacy met with almost complete failure in the provinces subject to Louis of Bavaria. In vain did the pope declare chapter elections null and void, appoint new bishops and pronounce an anathema against those who had been first elected; his candidates did not succeed in making their authority recognised in the dioceses entrusted to them. The accession of Charles IV to the imperial throne brought little change in the situation. Most of the time elections took place in spite of, and in defiance of, papal reservations. All the popes could do to uphold the principle of their sovereign right was to quash chapter elections, and then to elevate to the episcopate precisely those persons whom the chapters had elected. They could not always be sure even of this purely formal triumph. Ludwig von Wetten, for instance, whom Gregory XI had appointed archbishop of Mainz on 28 April 1374 on the Emperor's request, was never able to take possession of his see. The canons supported their own candidate, Adolf von Nassau, by force of arms and enthroned him.[1]

Direct collation of non-elective benefices by the Holy See was opposed with equal violence. At Würzburg, to cite a typical example, the bishop and the chapter had threatened with capital punishment 'whomsoever shall carry, publish or execute apostolic letters' in the whole of the diocese. Innocent VI having conferred on a Frenchman, Jean Guilabert, the archdeaconry of Künzelsau, together with a canonry and a prebend in the cathedral, three clerks came to Würzburg and made it their duty to carry out the papal mandate. When they were reading out the Bulls of collation in the church, the canons' servants set upon them, snatched the Bulls from their hands, and bore them off to prison. That very evening, the unfortunate clerks were cast into the Main.[2]

In France, the bishops of Mende and Angers, Guillaume Durant and Guillaume le Maire, had denounced the abuses inherent in papal reservations to the Fathers at the Council of Vienne. Guillaume le Maire deplored the influx of unworthy clerks to the Roman court, where their unedifying way of life was ignored. The number of expectative graces granted to them had reached such proportions that, he declared, 'today prelates cannot supply the benefices with good men, or good men with benefices.'[3] Guillaume Durant called for the suppression of papal provisions; otherwise, he said, 'order in the Church will be set at nought.'[4] At the beginning of his pontificate,

[1] F. Vigener, 'Karl IV und der Mainzer Bistumsstreit,' *Westdeutsche Zeitschrift*, Ergänzungsheft XII, 1908.
[2] Kirsch, 'Ein Prozess,' *Römische Quartalschrift*, VOL. XXI, 1907, pp. 67–96.
[3] C. Port, in *Mélanges historiques*, VOL. II, p. 481.   [4] *De modo*, pt 3, tit. xxvii.

John XXII seemed to wish to limit his powers of reservation. When the king of France begged him to make extensive use of it, he replied that to suppress elections caused men to murmur against him. He declared: 'Experience has proved to me, and does still, that prelates promoted by the Holy See have not shown and do not show themselves to be grateful and devoted sons of the Church, but rather degenerate offspring, who do all in their power to stir up trouble in the Church.'[1] But the pope's scruples were short-lived, and he began with characteristic tenacity to pursue a domineering policy. If the canons, acting in ignorance of a papal reservation, made an election, John XXII would first quash it and then bestow canonical approval on the person they had elected. If their ignorance was not genuine, he either deposed or confirmed their candidate, according to the circumstances, having first annulled the election. Thus, on 19 January 1327, John XXII refused to recognise Raymond Arnaud de Poylohaut, who had been elected by the chapter, as bishop of Dax, and appointed instead Bernard de Liposse, one of his chaplains.[2] When his chosen candidate did not succeed in taking possession of his see, the pope provided him with another, caused a fresh election to take place, and confirmed in office the person whom he had not been able to evict. The pope had another crafty but sure method of overcoming resistance: he would transfer prelates from one see to another that had fallen vacant, and give churches a new bishop on the very day that he had taken the former one from them. Thus it became quite impossible to hold elections.[3]

In Spain, Italy, the Low Countries and the Scandinavian and Slav states, John XXII used the same tactics as in France. His successors, realising the advantages of such methods, zealously adopted them. Thus the downfall of the chapters was confirmed and the triumph of papal omnipotence assured, as is abundantly shown by Eubel's *Hierarchia Catholica Medii Aevi*, compiled from the Vatican archives. The bishops themselves showed how dependent they were upon the Roman pontiff, by their growing habit in the fourteenth century of styling themselves 'Bishop by the Grace of God and of the Apostolic See,'—*Dei et Sedis Apostolicae gratia episcopus N.*

The Vatican registers provide the clearest proof of the frequency of direct collation of non-elective benefices by the Holy See. Sicily was almost the only place where, as a result of their disagreements with the kings, the popes were unable to exercise their authority.

---

[1] Coulon, no. 667 (Bull dated 30 July 1318).
[2] Degert, *Histore des évêques de Dax*, pp. 161–3.
[3] Clergeac, in the article quoted, pp. 147 f.

Conclusion

IT was for long customary to judge the Avignon popes only in the
light of the malevolent accounts of contemporary chroniclers, and the
tendentious writings of Petrarch, St Catherine of Siena and St
Bridget of Sweden. All these used to be accepted quite uncritically
and without question.

Since, however, documents from the archives were published,
though only in an abridged form some seventy or eighty years ago, it
has become possible to modify the judgment of history which had
hitherto remained uniformly unfavourable to the Avignon papacy.

In the first place, the Avignon popes have frequently been
criticised for being too humble in their attitude towards France, and
too willing to modify their general policy to suit the particular con-
venience of the French royal house. In certain instances, such as the
trial of the Templars, and in the case of certain popes, such as
Clement V and Benedict XII, this criticism still seems justified. But
to take a more general view, the diplomatic activities of the Avignon
popes were carried on with a real independence both in the East and
in the West, and in their foreign policy they unremittingly pursued
a threefold aim: to bring peace to Europe, to conquer the Holy Land
and to recapture the Papal States.

It must be admitted that the Avignon popes failed to realise their
plans for a Crusade. It is difficult to decide how Utopian such plans
were, in view of the political situation in fourteenth-century Europe.
The popes may well have thought that their influence over the
princes of Christendom was still sufficient to justify a hope of success
in the noble enterprise. Indeed, throughout the century, their arbitration and intervention were constantly requested, or at least accepted,
except in the case of the imperial election, which was now beyond the
Roman pontiff's sphere of influence.

The most commonly held grievance against the Avignon popes is
that they continued to stay on the bank of the Rhône, far from the
Eternal City, which seemed abandoned 'without hope of return.' On
this particular point, the results of our historical investigations are
quite unambiguous. Italy was plunged into political anarchy and
could not guarantee safe shelter to the papacy. Throughout the
fourteenth century the popes tried, with varying success, to restore

343

peace in the peninsula and to take their place once more among the small states that were in process of formation. The victories of Cardinal Albornoz and his skilful policy, which was carried on by Gregory XI, eventually made Rome once more a fitting habitation for the pope.

The Italian policy of the Avignon popes provides at least an explanation and to a certain extent an excuse for their financial system, which was in many ways a new one, and which was eventually to cause serious harm to Christian countries. This discontent was to come into the full light of day at the time of the Great Schism of the West.

The financial policy of the Avignon popes was closely linked with the increasing tendency to centralise the administration of the Roman Church. This tendency received a lively impetus from, and was very similar to, the corresponding centralisation which was going on in the various European states during the fourteenth and fifteenth centuries as a result of the constitution of national monarchies. It was to give rise to the dangerous forces of reaction which almost carried the day at the Council of Basle.

In conclusion, the religious activities of the Avignon popes stand out in the zeal with which they put down heresy, reformed the religious orders and brought the knowledge of the Gospel to distant lands.

Index

357